THE OFFICIAL
Formula 1™
SEASON REVIEW 2010
FOREWORD BY BERNIE ECCLESTONE

Published in November 2010

A catalogue record for this book is available from the British Library

ISBN 978 0 85733 001 7

Library of Congress control no. 2010927386

Editor Bruce Jones
Managing Editor Steve Rendle

Design Richard Parsons, Lee Parsons, Dominic Stickland

Contributors Adam Cooper (race reports, driver interviews and season overview), Tony Dodgins (round table, teams' technical review and race report panels)

Photographs All by LAT (Steven Tee, Lorenzo Bellanca, Charles Coates, Alberto Crippa, Glenn Dunbar, Steve Etherington, Andrew Ferraro, Peter Van Egmond)
Group Operations Manager LAT Tim Wright
Digital Technicians LAT Steve Carpenter, Tim Clarke, Will Taylor-Medhurst, Chris Singleton, John Tingle

Illustrations Alan Eldridge

Publishing Manager Sam Jempson
Publisher Rob Aherne
Publishing Directors Peter Higham, Mark Hughes

**Published by Haynes Publishing
in association with Haymarket Consumer Media**

Haynes Publishing, Sparkford, Yeovil,
Somerset BA22 7JJ, UK
Tel: +44 (0) 1963 442030
Fax: +44 (0) 1963 440001
E-mail: sales@haynes.co.uk
Website: www.haynes.co.uk

Haymarket Consumer Media, Teddington Studios,
Broom Road, Teddington, Middlesex TW11 9BE, UK
Tel: +44 (0) 208 267 5000
Fax: +44 (0) 208 267 5022
E-mail: F1Review@haymarket.com
Website: www.haymarket.com

Printed and bound in the UK by JF Print Ltd

CONTENTS

FOREWORD   5

This was the most exciting World Championship battle for a generation, with four drivers all in with a shot at the title until the end of the season, as three new teams attempted to find their feet at the back of the grid

THE SEASON   6

Red Bull Racing's failure to convert all their opportunities into victories gave McLaren and Ferrari a chance to keep the title battle going right to the final race. Korea was the lastest nation to join the World Championship and survived heavy rain to produce an enthralling race

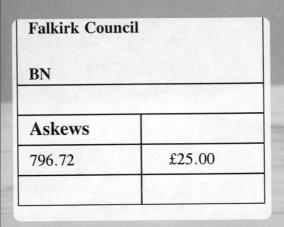

ROUND TABLE 14
Each World Championship in recent years seems to surpass the previous one in terms of action, intrigue, politics and technical developments. Our expert panel of paddock insiders discuss the matters that kept them busy from Bahrain to Abu Dhabi, and pick their winners and losers of 2010

THE DRIVERS 22
Each of the 27 drivers who took to the circuits to race in anger during the 2010 Formula One World Championship season reveals to us his own perspective on the challenges, highs and lows of his campaign

THE TEAMS 38
HRT, Lotus and Virgin joined the World Championship and found the going extremely tough. Their technical chiefs and those of the nine established teams explain precisely how they sought to make their cars go ever faster through the course of the season

THE RACES 70
Every one of the year's 19 grands prix was packed with excitement and colour, and our race reports bring you the best of the action supported by insight from the drivers and team personnel on what really went on out there on the track and in the pits

THE RESULTS 262
The 2010 World Championship table, showing who finished where on a race-by-race basis

FOREWORD

It's been a wonderful season, and nobody could ever predict that it would finish as it did, with four guys involved, especially as the first race was a disaster. Bahrain was the worst race of the year, then it just turned around on its own. We didn't do anything.

It would be difficult to single out any one of the four title challengers. If you put any one of them in a quick car, they'd win.

Vettel was always going to be World Champion one day wasn't he, if not this year, then next? He's very good. Had Webber been in a good car five years ago, maybe he would have been World Champion five years ago. I think he's a Ferrari driver, as he's got the sort of character that the Old Man would have liked. It was good to see Lewis in contention, and I was pleased to see Jenson up there as well.

Alonso is probably not the most popular driver in F1, it would appear, although I get on very well with him, but he's extremely talented, and competitive. Early on, the car wasn't up together and he was sort of outdriving it.

Wherever you go, and whoever you talk to, people talk about Michael Schumacher. You'd have to look at it and ask did Michael need to come back? What was the purpose? He wanted to come back because he knows he can win, but unfortunately the car didn't allow that to happen. I'd love to see him winning. Put him in one of the Red Bulls, and then see what happens. But then we don't know how good Rosberg is. Maybe Rosberg in a Red Bull would beat all of them...

As for the new teams, their problems weren't their fault in all fairness. It was really Max Mosley's fault, telling them they could come in and be contenders for the championship for £30 million. But they're here now and, provided they don't walk around with begging bowls, it's good to have them.

Korea worked out well, as they did a first-class job. It's the same as some of the teams, as when new people come on board they don't quite appreciate what they've got to come up with… We've got a race in India in 2011, and that will be good.

Jean Todt is a completely different animal to Max. I had dinner with him the other night and we were talking about it: he's visited 51 countries this year, so he's been on the road a bit. In fairness, he's left F1 to get on with it, which is good.

Overall, I was very happy with the way the year went in the end, although I've been a bit busy…

BERNIE ECCLESTONE

REFLECTING ON THE 2010
FORMULA ONE SEASON
AN INTENSE YEAR OF RACING

FOUR-WAY SHOOT-OUT

New rules can improve the breed, but no
one could have predicted how the shuffling
of the pack would produce a classic season,
with the title in doubt until the final round

Was 2010 the best Formula One season ever? It's an impossible call to make, of course. You need only two competitors to have a race, and we've seen some fabulous head-to-head duels in the past, but never have we had a year when five men battled to the penultimate race, and four were still in the hunt at the finale.

Furthermore, it really did go down to the last lap of the last race. Not only did Sebastian Vettel have to bring his Red Bull home safely in front, but he had to wait for the five cars in between himself and Fernando Alonso to cross the finish line before his title was assured.

Such a scenario certainly could not have been predicted some eight months earlier in Bahrain, the opening race of the season and the first since 1994 not to feature refuelling stops. It immediately became clear that this rule change had made strategy options rather limited, and F1 fans the world over watched a dull race, as everyone came into and out of the pits in pretty much the same order, and the lack of fuel-weight variation offered drivers no chance to use strategy to pass.

For a few days F1 seemed to be in crisis, but then we went to Australia, and rain at the start of the race mixed things up to produce an entertaining show. More rain during qualifying in Malaysia produced a

topsy-turvy grid, and then yet more precipitation in the race in China generated action aplenty there. So the procession in the Bahrain GP was soon forgotten...

You can't rely on the weather spicing up the show every fortnight, though, and after China the entertainment came from the brilliant show that the teams and drivers were producing. Red Bull Racing may have been dominant in qualifying, but the team didn't always get things right on Sundays, and both McLaren and Ferrari were there to keep the pressure on and take advantage of any errors.

There wasn't always a great deal of overtaking, but the intensity of the battle was the thing. In Turkey, Webber, Vettel, Hamilton and Button ran virtually nose-to-tail for lap after lap, and even without the drama that followed when Vettel made his ill-judged move and collected team-mate Webber, it would have been a thrilling and memorable contest.

The tension that subsequently emerged in the Red Bull Racing camp was great theatre, and added an edge to proceedings for the rest of the season. Then there was the German GP, and the controversy that followed the use of team orders, as a reluctant Felipe Massa handed the lead to Alonso. Given the stage of the season, with eight grands prix still to be run, it was a clumsy move by the team, and one that did the sport no good at all. Ultimately, the FIA ducked out when the matter came to judgement, admitting that the rule lacked clarity. There was an ongoing debate about the potential validity of the title should Alonso win it by fewer than the seven points he gained that day, but in the end thankfully that became irrelevant.

The German GP was the only major controversy of the first year of Jean Todt's presidency of the FIA and, while the Frenchman occasionally turned up for Grands Prix, he seemed determined to keep a low profile. There was plenty for the race stewards to discuss, but few decisions raised any eyebrows.

The addition of a driver to the panel – the likes of former World Champions Mansell, Prost and Fittipaldi took turns during the year – seemed to be a successful move. On the wider front, the sport remained mercifully free of major political controversies, and the teams appeared to be working in harmony with the FIA and F1 supremo Bernie Ecclestone.

Fortunately, that allowed everyone to concentrate fully on the action on the track. Nobody could remember a time when we had so many truly great drivers in so many quick cars. That's why we got such a good show, and indeed why the returning Michael Schumacher found life tougher than expected.

Red Bull Racing had proved to be the team to beat at the end of the 2009 season, and that form continued into 2010. Apart from a few tracks that didn't play to the car's strengths, Vettel and Webber were on pole position at almost every circuit the championship visited. Converting that speed into race wins wasn't always easy, though, and there were a few glitches. The collision between the team-mates in Turkey was a low point, and at times the team management struggled to convince the world that the drivers were getting equal treatment, especially after the front-wing controversy at the British GP.

Vettel made some mistakes, but there was no doubting his ultimate talent, and especially his ability to bring a car home once he'd got safely in front, something that he demonstrated superbly in the final few races. All of the frontrunners suffered misfortunes, but had his late-race Korean GP engine failure cost Vettel the title, it would have been cruel indeed. He will be a major star for years to come.

Webber was a revelation, pushing hard in qualifying and races, and seemingly taking every chance that came his way to log vital points. However, over the final few races he seemed to lose a little spark, as Vettel seemed to find an extra gear, and in Abu Dhabi it just slipped away from him. Webber had a huge dose of good fortune when he escaped from his massive crash in Valencia, but in the end it was his shunt in Korea – where he could have inherited the win from Vettel – that ultimately ended his chances.

McLaren bounced back in style this year after a disappointing 2009 campaign, and the addition of World Champion Jenson Button to the ranks proved to be a huge positive for the team. Hamilton had learned a great deal from the previous year's struggles, and he put that to good use with some fine performances,

notably with his wins in Turkey, Canada and Belgium.

However, Hamilton's title challenge lost some momentum after his expensive retirements in Italy and Singapore, where he arguably pushed a little too hard and became involved in collisions, although many thought Webber was at fault in the latter.

Button used strategy and a delicate touch in the wet to score two great early-season wins in Australia and China, and subsequently adopted something of a stealth approach, remaining in the title fight thanks to finishing consistently in the points. Button showed when he battled into the lead in Italy that he can be aggressive when he has to, although ultimately he lost out to Alonso in the pit stops.

The arrival of Alonso at Ferrari was expected to give the team a boost, and the determined Spaniard quickly established himself as the dominant force in the camp. Back after last year's injury, Massa struggled to fight his corner as Alonso made his presence felt on and off the track. Being forced to move aside in Germany was a bitter blow, and it was easy to forget that in 2008 the Brazilian challenged for the World Championship all the way to the final lap of the final race.

Alonso's season got off to a great start when he

OPPOSITE TOP A midfield mix-up as Buemi heads Heidfeld, Massa, Rosberg, Petrov and Barrichello behind the safety car in Brazil

OPPOSITE BOTTOM Fans weren't happy at Alonso's and Massa's finishing order being reversed in the German GP

TOP Nico Rosberg had his most impressive year yet, for Mercedes

ABOVE LEFT Bernie Ecclestone makes a point to Korean GP promoter Yung Cho Chung and FIA President Jean Todt

ABOVE RIGHT McLaren's form was up and down, but Hamilton and Button claimed second and third in the season finale at Abu Dhabi

RULE CHANGES FOR 2010

The shape of Formula One races changed dramatically in 2010, thanks to a ban on refuelling, which had been a key feature of the sport from 1994 until 2009.

One simple line in the rule book meant that teams had to design their 2010 cars with a tank capacity that would safely get them to the end of high-consumption races such as Valencia and Montréal, but new team Virgin got its sums wrong and had to redesign the chassis.

Drivers had to get used to starting races with an ultra-heavy car and dealing with changes in handling as the fuel load reduced. Inevitably, fastest laps were set close to the end of the race, even if tyres were past their best.

The lack of refuelling also put a new emphasis on fuel saving during the grands prix, and drivers were frequently asked to 'turn down' their engines in the later stages of races after being free to race hard early on.

Drivers were still obliged to make at least one pit stop, as they still had to use both the prime and option tyres at some stage. However, one stop was usually the limit, and only in Montréal – where graining was a major issue – did drivers routinely stop twice. Strategy was much more clear-cut than in the past, and places changes frustratingly rare. However, we often saw those who made a late switch to new tyres, by accident or design, carving through the field.

Pit stops were much faster than in the past. Previously, once the tyre swap was complete, the car stayed put, since it was the time taken to put the fuel in that determined the length of the stop. As a consequence, teams worked harder than ever to speed up their tyre changes. By coincidence, a ban on the unpopular wheel covers, or fairings, made access to the tyres slightly easier.

Qualifying strategy was impacted by a rule that required drivers who made Q3 to start the race on exactly the same set of tyres on which they qualified, although that only applied to dry conditions. Invariably, everyone went for options in qualifying.

Two other elements ensured that tyres were a key factor. Firstly, the fronts were narrowed by 20mm, reducing grip and making life difficult for those who found their driving styles compromised. Secondly, the huge fuel weight with which the cars started the race put greater stress on tyres.

Restarts after safety-car periods were more spectacular, because the field was now released at the safety-car line – usually adjacent to the pit entry – rather than at the start/finish line. Overtaking was allowed as soon as cars passed the safety-car line. This caused some confusion at Monaco, where Michael Schumacher was penalised for passing on the last lap, as the FIA decreed that in such a situation cars still had to maintain position.

Finally, the points allocation was stretched to cover the top 10, with points awarded on the basis of 25–18–15–12–10–8–6–4–3–2–1.

won the opening race in Bahrain, and even some mistakes in the early races didn't seem to faze him. The package got stronger in the middle of the season and Alonso was genuinely unlucky to lose out to the safety car in the European GP on the Valencia street circuit.

It was Alonso's controversial win in Germany that really gave his title campaign some momentum. That was quickly followed by a run of wins and strong podium finishes, and he seemed to be surging inexorably towards the title. Then his luck ran out in Abu Dhabi, when the team made a bad strategy call.

Everyone expected that the combination of Brawn GP, backing from Mercedes and Michael Schumacher would create a winning package, but the rebadged Mercedes GP had to settle for being fourth best. It was a tough year for Schumacher, who paid the price for being out of action for three whole years, and more importantly has had to contend with a talented young team-mate in Nico Rosberg.

Many were quick to criticise Schumacher, and it didn't take long for people to suggest that he wouldn't continue into the 2011 season, but the man himself remained convinced that with tyres that were more suited to his style he would be back on the pace. The bottom line was Michael was having fun, so why stop ahead of his three-year schedule?

OPPOSITE City life continues as F1 goes racing in the spectacular setting of Singapore

ABOVE F1's fast five: Webber, Vettel, Hamilton, Alonso and Button

BELOW LEFT Ross Brawn and Michael Schumacher together again

BELOW RIGHT Rubens Barrichello enters Korea's pitlane – a whole new backdrop for F1's racers

Rosberg had a superb season, finishing in the points with astonishing regularity and getting onto the podium in Malaysia, China and Britain. The bottom line is that the car wasn't competitive enough, and the team's focus inevitably turned to 2011.

Renault's morale hit rock bottom in 2009, but the arrival of new owners and a lead driver in the form of Robert Kubica transformed the team's fortunes. Indeed, for much of the year, the Pole was one of the few guys who could mix it with the title contenders, at least at tracks that favoured the yellow car. He finished second in Australia and third in both Monaco and Belgium, and would have had another podium in Japan, but for a lost wheel. The season ended on a high in Abu Dhabi, when both Kubica and erratic team-mate Vitaly Petrov played a big part in frustrating Alonso's title hopes.

After a shaky start, Williams made steady progress over the course of 2010. Rubens Barrichello finished his 2009 season with Brawn on a high, and continued to show that he is as competitive and motivated as ever. He finished fourth in Valencia and fifth at Silverstone and, given the strength of the top teams, that was about as good as it could get. Nico Hulkenberg enjoyed a steady if unspectacular rookie season, until his amazing pole in

Brazil earned him 15 minutes of fame. He occasionally beat his veteran team-mate, but given his impressive CV, you could argue that more was expected of him.

Force India finished the 2009 championship well, and the cars were regular scorers in the first part of this season. However, the team's form faded somewhat in the last part of the year as others progressed. It was a good season for Adrian Sutil, though, who made few mistakes and put himself high on the 'most wanted' list of other teams. Team-mate Vitantonio Liuzzi had most of the bad luck going, and always seemed to be involved in incidents that weren't always his fault.

Sauber got off to a shaky start, as the team suffered with a car that wasn't fast enough on the straights and had a string of reliability problems, but things improved in the second half of the year and Kamui Kobayashi proved to be something of a star, regularly hauling himself into the points and producing stunning overtaking moves. He outshone Pedro de la Rosa, who was dropped after 14 rounds, allowing Nick Heidfeld to return to the team for Singapore. He was quickly up to speed, scoring on his second appearance in Suzuka.

Scuderia Toro Rosso had to design and build its own car this year, so the gap to sister team Red Bull Racing

BELOW LEFT Tony Fernandes and Heikki Kovalainen enjoyed life as the Team Lotus name returned to F1

BELOW RIGHT Renault worked hard and was finding its feet again by the end of the season

BOTTOM Sakon Yamamoto was one of the four drivers who raced for F1 newcomers HRT, with Glock racing well for fellow rookies Virgin

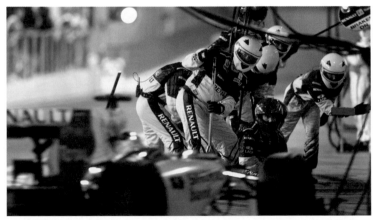

inevitably grew. The blue cars usually qualified towards the back of Q2 in and around 16–17th places, and sometimes the drivers had to battle hard to make their way out of Q1. Sebastien Buemi was a little more experienced and generally had the upper hand, and he was particularly impressive in Canada, where he finished eighth. Jaime Alguersuari got better as the year went on, and showed that he's not afraid to fight with anybody.

Inevitably, it was a year of learning for the three new teams, which were put together in a hurry. Lotus was generally ahead of main rivals Virgin on pure pace, and Heikki Kovalainen, on balance, had the edge on veteran team-mate Jarno Trulli. The team switched its focus early to developing its Renault-powered 2011 package, so there has been little chance to close the gap to those ahead, while a debate over the use of the Lotus name took some shine off the season.

Reliability problems hampered progress early on at Virgin, but for much of the season the cars were battling with Lotus for the role of top new team. There have been weekends where the team has done a good job in wet or mixed qualifying sessions, and Timo Glock has on occasion sneaked into Q2.

At one stage, it looked as though HRT wouldn't make the start of the season, but against the odds the team battled through and performed respectably as the year progressed. Chopping and changing drivers didn't help, but the real problem was an almost total lack of development after a split with Dallara, who built the Spanish-run car.

So now attention turns to 2011. There will be some interesting changes to the rules, with KERS (voluntarily abandoned by the teams for 2010) back on the agenda, while the switch from Bridgestone to Pirelli tyres will add something to the mix. The Italian company says it's willing to help spice up the show with tyres that need more careful management, although it's likely to take a cautious approach in its first year back.

There's no reason to suppose that any of the top-three teams will lose performance, while there's a good chance that Mercedes will make a step forward and find the sort of form that won it the 2009 title under the Brawn GP name.

A new race in India in October adds interest, and stretches the calendar to a tiring 20 races. Will the title still be in doubt when we get to the finale in Brazil at the end of November? Let's hope so...

ABOVE The T-shirts are new as Helmut Marko, Adrian Newey and Christian Horner join 2010 World Champion Sebastian Vettel in celebration in Abu Dhabi

THE PANEL

MARTIN BRUNDLE
TV COMMENTATOR, *BBC*

CHRISTIAN HORNER
TEAM PRINCIPAL, RED BULL RACING

MARK HUGHES
JOURNALIST, *AUTOSPORT*

MARTIN WHITMARSH
TEAM PRINCIPAL, McLAREN

CHAIRED BY
TONY DODGINS
JOURNALIST, *AUTOSPORT*

ROUND TABLE

After the best racing season in memory, the leading players found a lot to be happy about as Formula 1 stretched its legs and kept politics to a minimum in 2010

Every year, there's something new for the Formula 1 teams to embrace. This year, it was more than simply the addition of another new circuit, in South Korea, as there was also the banning of refuelling for the teams to get their heads around. As ever, there were technical breakthroughs, this year with F-ducts and exhaust-blown floors, and the teams displayed their capacity for reacting almost instantaneously as any successful new concept was adopted within a few races.

For the first time in years, there was also the arrival of three new teams, and their trials and tribulations were like those of the nine established teams, only magnified as they faced all the problems that were new to them without the advantage-of-old that was in-season testing.

Under the benign and pleasingly low-profile leadership of new FIA President Jean Todt, there were operational improvements too, with the introduction of former F1 drivers to the ranks of race stewards. Best of all, politics were kept to the minimum, to the extent that Ferrari's team orders furore at the German Grand Prix was the worst storm in the teacup.

So, after a season during which F1 fans were entertained by intra-team as well as inter-team battles, F1 can feel very pleased with itself.

TD: *Thinking back to the tedious race in Bahrain and the clamour for change afterwards, with hindsight was it just the circuit?*

CH: My memories of Bahrain aren't particularly happy. It was the first race without refuelling and there was a lot of discussion about what effect it was going to have, and from our point of view we handed Fernando his first Ferrari win with a spark-plug failure. I think there was concern coming out of that race that it was going to be a fairly static season.

MW: There was a lot of worry coming out of it, and you have to say now, when you talk about strategy, and we have a strategy team, that if you're in the top 10 generally you're going to qualify on the option, start on the option and stop when the gap in the traffic allows you, which is quite prescriptive. And yet, if you hadn't had this remarkable season and you'd said that's what's going to happen, I think we'd have predicted a terrible season. Bahrain aside though, every race has been fantastic, or at least pretty good.

MB: The only mistake they made was that the long track didn't work. It was just complete circumstance. I commentated on all of Michael's dominant years when we looked forward to advertising breaks for a bit of respite, and I think it was a huge over-reaction, as they can't all be last-minute thrillers. Bahrain just didn't work out, just like we've had some pretty tedious Silverstones from time to time.

TD: *How much were some of the things we're getting for 2011, like movable rear wings, a response to that Bahrain race? Is that fair?*

CH: An element of it is, yes. Next year, we've taken away the double diffuser, which is a significant change, reintroduced KERS and that, combined with a movable rear wing that looks like it can only be used when you are in the proximity of another car, is going to be very interesting.

MB: I'm concerned that there will be so much going on with the technical side. Goodness knows how the teams are going to choose a seventh gear when they've got effectively 160bhp extra on-tap with the rear-wing-slot gap and KERS. I think it's essential now that the cars have some sort of light on the back, for example, and another light on the front so that the viewers and the fans at the track understand. It's a safety thing as well: if someone's coming at you in the slipstream and then all of a sudden he can change his rear wing and hit the KERS button, you're going to have contact at the worst place on the track, the end of the high-speed straight, because you can't judge – you're looking in your mirrors, you're doing 200mph and it's quite a judgement call as to how quickly the guy is coming at you. Ask Michael and Rubens about that in Hungary, although Michael actually seemed to have that quite well under control, didn't he... I think there has to be a red light front and rear which says he's used his wing option, and a flashing red light that says he's used his wing and his KERS. Whatever they do needs to be very transparent, because rule number one is, don't confuse your audience.

TD: *We went on from Bahrain to have a fantastic championship. Can anyone recall a better one?*

MW: We've probably all had our championships that have been absorbing as we've been involved, but I think if you look at this one – mathematically, five drivers in it with two races to go – it's the best. We've seen very often Red Bull with the fastest car and Ferrari stage a fantastic comeback from where they were mid-season, and us winning a few races as well. All of the drivers have made mistakes, which added to the drama of it all. Most of them can say, "If I hadn't done that, I'd have been leading the championship quite comfortably." Have there been this many World Champions fighting it out in this many good cars? It's been a cracking championship.

MH: The fact that there were five contenders so late in the season just made the permutations difficult and impossible to predict. You've had intense championships in the past where you've had a duel, in effect, but nothing like this.

CH: I think it's been a great year for the sport. Interest in F1 is probably as high as it has ever been. Red Bull has done its bit to try and contribute to some of the drama, but overall it's been a terrific year.

MW: People often read about what's happening on the paddock side of the garages and all the dramas there, which is a shame for our sport, but that has been relatively low-key in the past 12 months and people have been able to concentrate on what they should be, which is what's happening on the track.

MB: It's been a classic because the quality and depth of the drivers is as good as it's been since the mid-1980s. They redid that well-known picture from 1986 (Mansell, Piquet, Prost and Senna) with this year's five contenders, yet you have drivers like Kubica and Rosberg not even in that picture. You've had three teams, and the only interchangeable parts between the Red Bull, Ferrari and McLaren are the Bridgestone tyres, and they go about their racing in completely different ways. The cars have different strengths and have ended up doing roughly the same times in the race, which has been fantastic. I don't see why it should change next year either.

MW: One of the things you mention that's interesting, Martin, is the number of times you look at the split times and you'll see Red Bull absolutely dominant in one and then Ferrari or ourselves in another, to a much greater extent. When you've had dominant performance before, it's often been purple, purple, purple on the timing screens. I haven't done the analysis, but I sense that's more prevalent as a phenomenon this year.

CH: I'd agree with that. Take the race in Korea. The time that Kubica did in P3, we thought, okay, we can't do that. Then in qualifying things turned around and he wasn't quite as competitive as he'd been. There have even been changes in how the cars have performed on the soft tyre and the hard tyre.

MB: Something must also be controlling the performance of the cars as well, because you've got three different engines and somehow the envelope is keeping it close. I don't know if it's the tyres, the cost restrictions, the engine freeze.

Martin Brundle shows that TV commentators can listen as well as talk

Chairman Tony Dodgins lines up the questions as Christian Horner fires in a reply

MW: Ultimately, what controls the performance of the cars is the load you can generate on four contact patches and the tarmac. The other thing this year is that I've been more aware of sensing that the car will be, in the course of a lap, overheating its tyres. So you get to a stage where the first sector is quick and the next three corners you've probably put too much heat in the tyres and you suffer through the next three corners. I sense that more than we've had in the past as well.

TD: *There was a huge public reaction to the Ferrari team orders at Hockenheim. Why so big compared to, say, Brazil 2007 where Felipe clearly ceded to Kimi [Räikkönen] and it decided the championship?*

MW: It was early in the championship, there were a lot of contenders and we still have a rule which says that there are no team orders. People believed that they saw a team order and were told 'no it wasn't', and I think that amplified it, but I think it was mainly how early in the season it was. Maybe they had a premonition of their resurgence, but at that time Alonso didn't look such a frontrunner anyway.

MB: I remember on the *BBC* we said at the end of the first lap, the wrong Ferrari is in front and how are they going to fix that?

CH: Well they tried to do it at the pit stop didn't they...

MB: Yeah, exactly. Instinctively, I accept and expect team orders because if I was running a team that's exactly what I would do. Teams are here a long time, drivers come and go. You operate as a team, but it's a highly emotive issue and there's no right and wrong answer. However, quite clearly, back in July I think everybody agrees that, a) the way they did it and, b) when they did it, was unacceptable.

MH: It was heavy-handed as well, the way they did it, and the circumstances behind that. I think it probably goes back to it not having been talked through beforehand.

TD: *Was it unprofessional for Ferrari not to have pre-planned that situation?*

CH: It was extremely embarrassing for the sport to find itself in a situation where you've got guys very uncomfortable doing their best to say that exactly what the entire world had just seen happen, didn't really happen at all. And I think the most important thing in this matter is clarity. It's still not totally clear to me whether team orders are allowed or disallowed. And I think the one thing you must never underestimate is the public. As Martin says, it's wrong to underestimate their intelligence and you shouldn't try to deceive them either. As a sport, that's something we need to learn from.

TD: *There were whispers also that they did something in Korea, when Alonso was delayed in the pits. How do you regard that?*

CH: There will always be strategic preference you can give to one driver or the other. In that race at Hockenheim, it made no sense to give Fernando the undercut opportunity, which they elected to do. Unfortunately, Felipe was too quick and Fernando wasn't able to use that undercut, so not having been able to do it through strategy, the only option for them was to do it on track.

Martin Whitmarsh
holds court, as Horner,
Mark Hughes, Brundle
and Dodgins listen in

MW: I don't think we should overshadow this year. Whatever happened, it's been an absolutely fantastic season. It's been full of human drama. You could sense within Red Bull Racing the human drama there, and really with all of them. It was clear at the Brazilian GP that Jenson didn't want to cede position to Lewis but, if at the end of the season Lewis lost the championship by one point I, as team principal, would be vilified. What didn't come out of Hockenheim was the clarity. What is a team order? If you ask a driver not to hit his team-mate at the first corner, is that a team order? If you ask them to look after their tyres, conserve fuel, look after the car, take it easy in slippery conditions, is that team orders? If consciously, or by mistake or strategic decision, you stop a driver two or three laps before the other, and as a consequence he is advantaged, in retrospect was that a team order?

MB: That's the real story isn't it? It's rewriting that unworkable rule this winter. That's the clever bit, because nobody came out of Hockenheim well.

MW: I don't think any of the things I've just described are team orders. But a blatant request to cede the position you have on the track to your team-mate, however coded, is a team order.

CH: It's all about transparency. For example, if Jenson Button had said in Brazil, I'm not in a position to win this championship and I'm going to let my team-mate through, that's clear, everybody knows, the press knows it going into the event and that's okay.

TD: *The major players all made some fairly high-profile errors during the year. Is that purely a function of how hard they were pushing each other?*

CH: It's a function of the best drivers in the world going at it absolutely hammer and tongs and inevitably they'll drop the ball now and again.

MW: The drivers winning the races have been absolutely flat-out for every single lap. It's that tight. Even if one of the cars turned out to be dominant, you still had to beat your team-mate.

MH: That's the other fascinating thing about the

strategy: it contains two sets of team-mates. We've had battles in the past between team-mates, but not between two sets of team-mates.

TD: *And, in the case of Red Bull and McLaren, two sets of number-one drivers taking on Ferrari, who put all their eggs in one basket. What are the difficulties and pros and cons of that?*

MW: First, there is what the regulations say, and we all agree that we need some clarity and transparency. We never need a situation where the public are absolutely clear that they've seen something, and leading figures in F1 have to lie to camera, which is pretty shocking. However, put that aside and with regard to the rules, then as a team you decide how you want to run things. I don't have a problem if a team, and there have been plenty of examples of it in the past, decide that the most effective way of running their team is to put all their eggs in one basket and make the other driver subservient. Schumacher enjoyed that for most of his career. We've taken a different view, and in 2007 that different view cost us the World Championship. Had we marginally favoured one or other of our

situation in which potentially you lose a Drivers' World Championship as a consequence.

TD: *Martin, you've had Stefan Bellof, Mika Häkkinen, Michael Schumacher as team-mates. What kind of mindset do you need to compete against drivers like that in the same team?*

MB: I also observed David Coulthard closely when he had tough team-mates in Häkkinen and Räikkönen. You do emotionally over-react to some things. I think you're hyper-sensitive to every little movement of Adrian Newey across the garage or something like that. The drivers are necessarily massively selfish, and that's how they've got to be F1 drivers. They want everything focused on them, they want the success. Two heads are better than one and so you want to work together, but at the same time I can bet that with Sebastian Vettel, the last person he wanted to be World Champion if he wasn't, was Mark Webber. It just doubles your pain if you fail to win in the car and your team-mate does. He's had the opportunity and performance that you had and he made it and you didn't, so there's this element of: 'if I can't win, I don't want him to'. It's hardly team spirit but, if we go back to Australia, Massa should never have held Alonso up. Alonso would have won that race. It's lunacy for team-mates to hold each other up at any point because you're employees. When you're told to do things, it's not a request, it's an instruction. You have to somehow manage your individual goals with the team goals. Some do it better than others. What happens is that Michael and Ayrton and people like that have got their elbows out and had everything focused on them. It's a complex thing and the team principals know better than I do that it's about different personalities. Some need an arm around the shoulder, some a kick up the backside or the riot act read. It's just like life itself. I'll

never forget Michael Schumacher, about three years after we were team-mates, he asked me to have dinner when we were testing at Estoril. He said, "I just want to say, I'm really sorry I held you up. How stupid was that?" He used to run me off the road rather than let me through. When he was then held up by some team-mates later on, he realised that it was lunacy to compromise your own team.

CH: Our situation this year has arguably been a tougher situation, as the drivers have been so evenly matched. The team has done its utmost to support each of those guys and give them equal opportunity. Nobody has a crystal ball. The hindsight specialists come out at the end of the year, but when you've got two competitive cars, inevitably they will push and, as Martin says, the last person they want to be beaten by is their team-mate. They'll use whatever weapons are in their armoury, as we've seen very clearly with our guys, to try to fulfil their ultimate goal, because there's so much at stake with that Drivers' World Championship.

TD: *We've had F-ducts, exhaust-blown floors, Ferrari with its tilted engine and gearbox. It's been fascinating but, in years gone by, would teams with money have been able to develop everything? Have you had to be selective?*

MW: The resource-restriction agreement has had an impact on the bigger teams, and certainly it has arrested concerns of the mass arms race we had previously. It's been an interesting year and the blown diffuser, for which Adrian Newey was the prime mover, left us playing catch-up there. We've seen F-duct, and we reached a point where it's quite interesting. The fact is, next year's Red Bull is in the wind tunnel, our car is and you can't help wondering if someone will come out of the box next year, just before Bahrain,

drivers during that year, we'd have won the World Championship. And that's hard to take.

MB: And been $100 million better off, possibly…

MW: That was also hard to take! I think the fact is, as an example, we have a fantastic driver like Lewis Hamilton and it has been a pleasure to have known him, develop him and win a World Championship with him a couple of years ago. However, it's been fantastic to have Jenson in our team, and the only way that Jenson joined our team was in the belief that he would be given a fair crack at beating Lewis and trying to retain his world title. He had a fantastic option to stay where he was – at Mercedes GP – he knew the team, had just won the title with them [as Brawn GP] and was very comfortable with Mercedes investing in them. So Jenson had all sorts of good reasons to stay, but in the end the challenge of coming to McLaren appealed to him. If over the past 20 years we'd shown that we favoured one driver to the detriment of the other driver, he wouldn't have joined us. There are tangible benefits of that policy, but every now and again you're going to find yourself in a

Martin Brundle knows of what he talks when it comes to having a rapid team-mate

Christian Horner is rightfully proud of the pace of development at Red Bull in 2010

safe, people are going to be run into the ground and so on, but we've all saved ourselves 15 or 20 tickets and hotel rooms per weekend and, actually, it could have been 40 people.

MH: It's also fascinating that, despite greater control of the resources, two fundamental new technologies emerged with the blown diffuser and F-duct. It just illustrates the creativity.

MW: Again, with F-duct, the guy who came up with it is a real boffin and at first you think; 'my God, is this for real?' However, the nice thing is that the little teams were doing it as well. It was a case of make up some carbon ducts, put a slot in the wing and away you go.

CH: I think the challenge with the F-duct, and it was a very creative innovation that McLaren introduced, was that in the first year with a homologated chassis we were unable to modify the chassis to accommodate that duct. Basically, we had a hole where a wiring loom went through to manipulate the air through, and it was incredibly creative engineering to accommodate that, particularly within a car into which it wasn't originally incorporated.

MB: Did you know you had a slam-dunk with that system, Martin?

MW: We thought so. In fairness though, we had blown slots from Monaco the previous year. It came up with the basking-shark rear wing and people didn't really pay too much attention to it. We were testing on airfields and trying to disguise it.

TD: *Bernie was quoted recently in the* Financial Times *on F1's new teams: "They do nothing for us, they're an embarrassment, we need to get rid of some of those cripples." Discuss...*

MW: A classic example of Bernie bringing positive press and media upon our sport...

MB: Well, today, I think he said, "They're gonna be alright, I've got a new sponsor I'm taking them..." or something. From a media point of view, I think they've added something. These guys might not agree because their two cars ended up colliding in Singapore because one of the slower cars got in their way on the restart, but you need 24 cars on the grid. You certainly need more than 18 to make it a proper show.

MW: In Q1, I don't know what it looks like from the commentary box, but it's a scary old process. You've got all the cars out there...

CH: And you're looking for a seven-second gap...

MW: And sometimes it's impossible.

MB: That's why our qualifying audience has doubled...

CH: Absolutely. But all teams have to start somewhere,

with something that's going to make us all go 'oh rats!' The championship development has been really interesting, where every fortnight you get a snapshot of where the enemy is, and then they all go off the radar for a month or two and you just haven't got a clue. You get really enthusiastic about the car, as the engineers and people around it are, but you never know what's going to happen. Doing a blown diffuser and not setting the thing on fire was challenging, but it's not high-cost. F-duct was basically some carbon-fibre ducts.

MB: That's the essence of F1 for me.

CH: Absolutely. If you look at the development this year, it's been as aggressive as any year in F1. Between the start and end of the season, we've put close to two seconds [per lap] of performance on our car and there were still upgrades by the leading contenders right to the end. You go to a circuit, have a strong performance and think, 'okay, we've got a bit of a buffer to our opponents', then you go to the next circuit and they're right back there. Some of it can be circuit-specific, but the pace of development among

the major teams, within the restrictions, without pounding around mile after mile on a test track, has been phenomenal.

MW: It's been interesting the way the process in F1 teams is now focused much more on efficiency. It always should have been, but there was a sense of there being lots of resource. Now though, the finite number of wind-tunnel hours is a good example. Most of the top teams are doing less time blowing wind in a wind tunnel, which consumes a lot of energy, but they're probably testing more variants. Everyone knows they can only run 'x' hours of wind, so they set out to make every hour count. They've all got kill buttons now, so that in the control room, if a test isn't going well you stop it, as you don't want to use up all your hours. We've got limits on our teraflops of computing. Historically, you'd just have the aero boys coming to you and saying; 'I need another 10 teraflops please, another million quid'. Now, because they can't, they're squeezing their heads over the code and how they use it to get the best out of that finite resource. At first too, we had a great drama over a 45-people limit at the circuit, with people saying it wasn't going to be all three are still here and there was a lot of scepticism about whether they would be. Lotus appears to have been the most serious in its intent, but that's not taking anything away from the other two teams. Designing and building your own F1 car and then operating it at 19 venues during a year is a massive undertaking, and hopefully they'll all be there next year, developing from what they started this year.

MW: The 45 people from those teams will work just as hard or harder than our 45. As Christian said, you sense that Lotus is developing infrastructure and is here to stay and is healthy. The others, what they have done is a miracle really with the lack of infrastructure that they appear to have.

MB: I was a bit surprised that they hadn't caught the pack but, now I hear Christian saying that they've improved their car by two seconds, you realise why. You'd have thought there would have been some low-hanging fruit for them to ramp up, but I guess they've been busy getting to races.

MW: Well, I'm sure they've improved and they've got lower-hanging fruit, but they've also got less experience and capability to exploit it.

MH: Lotus is still at about 104% from the front, which is where they were at the start of the year, so they've improved as well.

TD: What's your impression of Jean Todt's first year as FIA President? He seems to have adopted a lower profile. And, has it been better having drivers in the stewards' room instead of Alan Donnelly?

MW: I think you've got to give credit to Jean on lots of fronts. He's quietly trying to change a recalcitrant organisation and I think that's a big challenge. He hasn't tried to use F1 as a personal platform for his ego, which is always a very tempting thing. If you're a commander of FIA, mobility section and all, and they talk about millions of members, it doesn't actually give you the profile that F1 gives you, and I think he's been very controlled and disciplined there. I think he's sought not to create controversy, and the stewarding, in my opinion, has changed dramatically. It can still get better, but having a driver in there, arguably such an easy thing to do although we hadn't done it before, has made such a difference. I think we were starting to get to the point where with a normal racing incident – and you want some of them – you'd be thinking, 'oh God, we're at the stewards now'…

MB: Yeah. Get the flight booked to Paris…

MH: Everything was politicised, every little move.

MW: Christian's been there, I've been there, we've been in stewards' rooms in the past and you're thinking, a) are they listening? b) do they understand? and, c) do they care? It's been deeply frustrating.

MB: Just to put a real couple of incidents on that, when Alonso nailed Massa into the pitlane in China and where we've seen cars going out of the pitlane together and on the safety-car line at China at the restart, all those things you wouldn't have seen a year or two ago because drivers wouldn't have dared try.

CH: It's worked very well.

MB: It's right up there with F-duct and blown diffuser as the success of the year.

CH: I agree. We had an incident in Malaysia where Sebastian was leading, well ahead of the opposition with Mark behind him, and they came up to lap Jarno Trulli on the last lap, who'd lost six of his seven gears and was going round at a snail's pace. He waved Sebastian through in a yellow area. A couple of the stewards were fairly keen to penalise him, but Johnny Herbert said; "Hang on, he couldn't have gone any slower" and just applied some common sense. That's been massively useful. It would have been fun to be a fly on the wall in the Damon Hill/Michael Schumacher Monaco meeting though!

MB: I think fans and drivers alike, while they might not always agree with the decision, are more ready to accept it now that they know it isn't being used as a political device but is a rational process instead.

MW: I do believe the drivers being present has made a big difference, but I also think we all sense that the stewards' room doesn't have as many incoming calls… I still think, though, that permanent stewards and one driver would be even better.

MB: You wouldn't want to change the guy who starts the race or the guy who drives the safety car, so why change the stewards every weekend?

CH: Coming back to the original question about Jean, I think he's had a very solid first year. There's been less controversy in the sport than for some time.

TD: *Are you confident that when it's time to agree a new Concorde Agreement for 2013, we'll have common sense and not squabbling?*

MW: I don't think the teams and the FIA will have any difficulty when we get to the Concorde Agreement…

It's unusual to find F1 insiders in such agreement, but it's been a rare season

voda f
Mercedes-Benz
vodafone
afone
vodafone
JOHNNIE WALKER
BOSS
Red Bull
Mobil 1
vodafone

THE DRIVERS

It was a season of intense competition and oft changing form as teams ebbed and flowed. All 27 drivers who took part share their thoughts on how it went for them

"I ACCEPTED THAT SOMETIMES THINGS DON'T GO YOUR WAY, BUT IN THE LONG TERM THERE'S SOMETHING CALLED JUSTICE"

"We have seen incredible fights and a tight season. I don't know how many times we had a different leader in the championship. Some people got written off from this championship very early, then they came back, like Fernando with Ferrari, whereas in the beginning you thought 'OK, Ferrari is dropping back'.

They fought back very hard. McLaren came back. Lewis was leading the championship. All of us can write a book about races where we should have finished in higher positions. Lewis had a retirement in Hungary, myself in Australia and Korea.

We all had to go through ups and downs. It has been an extremely intense season, mentally especially, to always be there and sometimes just be able to ignore what people are saying and try to get your own thing done. Now it all worked and I am very, very proud.

With the way things went and how the races developed, it wasn't always easy to come back. After Spa, I got a lot of bad press. It wasn't easy at that time, with a lot of people saying bad things and trying to knock us down, but that's when you realise who your friends are, who belongs to you and who is supporting you.

In the end, the whole paddock is a group full of people, and it was important to invest my energy into them, in order to get it back until I took the title in Abu Dhabi. At some points, I accepted the fact that sometimes things don't go your way but, in the long term, there's something called justice and, at least in my calculation, it turned out to be right. Sometimes it goes that way, sometimes it goes the other way.

I think the atmosphere in the whole team was great. Even though we had a moment when people tried to knock us down and give us a hard time, we still had the ability to focus on what matters, not getting distracted by all sorts of talk and so on which was going on.

I kept believing in myself, in the team, and I got a lot of positive energy from the people around me, tapping on my shoulder, and I could see that they were believing in me as well, so obviously then it's a bit easier.

You have things like the Korean GP, when you know it is three races to go and obviously what has happened you can't change any more. But you can still change what will happen in the future. We were in a good position and then boom, the engine went, so of course that's disappointing, but straight back then I said the positive is the most important thing. It wasn't impossible, indeed it was very difficult to go to Brazil, but on the other hand I think there was a bit of pressure taken away after Korea, and we could just focus on what we usually do.

Sometimes it's important to keep your head cool, and we knew what we had to do in the race at Abu Dhabi and that's what we wanted to do. We achieved the title and the bit of luck that meant other people

didn't finish as high up in this race helped us to be in the position we are now, as World Champions.

I think the car this year was phenomenal. In a way, it was a masterpiece. I think there are areas that we need to work, on because in hindsight we had races where we could have finished better. On the other hand, sometimes it was an extremely fine line between being successful and not.

For instance, at Silverstone, Lewis tried to get close into Copse on lap 1. It seemed that he touched my rear tyre and I got a puncture. That wasn't his intention, but that's how it goes sometimes, and instead of finishing first or second, we finished further back. All in all, it's always a very special thing if you have a car under you where you know you can fight the guys at the top and fight for pole positions and race wins."

NATIONALITY German
DATE OF BIRTH 3/7/87
PLACE OF BIRTH Heppenheim, Germany
GRANDS PRIX 62
WINS 10
POLES 15
FASTEST LAPS 6
POINTS 381
HONOURS F1 World Champion 2010, German Formula BMW Champion 2004, European Junior Kart Champion 2001

2 FERNANDO ALONSO

FERRARI

NATIONALITY Spanish
DATE OF BIRTH 29/7/81
PLACE OF BIRTH Oviedo, Spain
GRANDS PRIX 159
WINS 26
POLES 20
FASTEST LAPS 18
POINTS 829
HONOURS F1 World Champion 2005 & 2006, Formula Nissan Champion 1999, Italian & Spanish Kart Champion 1997, World Kart Champion 1996

"I WILL REMEMBER 2010 VERY WELL, DESPITE THE FINAL RESULT, AS I FOUGHT UNTIL THE LAST RACE WITH MAYBE THE THIRD-QUICKEST CAR"

"In Abu Dhabi, we felt there were maybe three championship contenders, as for Hamilton it was maybe more difficult. Between the three of us, we knew that between the two Red Bulls, Vettel was the more dangerous, because he was the quicker normally. So if they were first and second in terms of where they normally were, it was a risk to have Vettel in front. Because of that, we needed a fourth place on the grid. The McLarens were quick, though, so we found ourselves behind fourth place.

The race didn't go as we wanted. We really hoped that the McLarens would overtake Vettel at the start, that would clear things a little bit. But this time, Button started very well, not Hamilton.

It's always easy to see the strategy after the race. Obviously there was a safety car, so Rosberg and Petrov decided to stop, and that was a little bit unexpected. And then Webber stopped very early as well. Then we had to protect either from Webber or Rosberg.

We decided to cover Webber, to be sure to exit the pits in front of him, and that in the end was not the right thing maybe. There's nothing we can do or we can change. Someone did a better job than us because they have more points than us at the end of the championship, so we congratulate them and next year we try again.

It was an interesting season, with some ups and downs for everybody. For us, it was a very good year, the first year of the relationship with Ferrari. I'd been fighting to be in Q3 for the last two years, and now I'm finally fighting for the World Championship once more, so I'm really happy for this.

For sure, there were some good moments in the year, some bad moments. Maybe the best was Monza, maybe the worst was Monaco, without being able to get a run in qualifying. I will remember 2010 very well, despite the final result. I think we fought until the last race, with maybe the third-quickest car, because we are third in the Constructors' Championship.

So I'm very proud of this, with the job, with the team and how we approached the last part of the year. We had engine problems in the first part, so we were limited with engines from race four onwards, and we managed to fight for the championship until the last lap of the last race. Overall, we did our best.

I think we don't have the cornering speed of Red Bull and maybe do not have the straightline speed of McLaren. We are not the best in a straight line, we are not the best in the corners, but in general overall we are always quite competitive. We can adapt to any circuit in a good way.

I'll definitely be much stronger next year. This year there was not much time to test or do anything. I tested for seven days before Bahrain, and I arrived in Bahrain not knowing completely the buttons on the steering wheel, not knowing the names of the mechanics or the engineers, and it wasn't until race five or race six that I felt more comfortable. Now, at the end of the year, I feel very comfortable with the support from all the team.

I'll be starting next year with much more confidence. I think also we started the year after a not super good season for Ferrari in 2009. So it was a huge comeback for the team, fighting for the championship. Therefore, I think we start next year from a more normal position. I think if we can fight for the championship until the last race with, as I said, maybe the third-quickest car, I have no doubts that we'll fight for the championship in the near future."

"I'M REMINDED OF THAT ADAGE 'WHAT DOESN'T KILL YOU MAKES YOU STRONGER'. I'M STILL ALIVE AND HOPE TO BOUNCE BACK A BETTER DRIVER"

"When you aim high and miss the target, the arrow's got a long way to fall. I'm very disappointed by what happened on Sunday evening, as I aimed for the biggest target in motor sport, and it didn't work out.

There are still lots of positives to take out of the 2010 season, though. I've taken five pole positions, four victories, and I'm even proud of some of my second places, because they were well-executed race weekends. In due course, I'll probably look back and think that this season wasn't a bad effort.

I'm reminded of that great adage 'what doesn't kill you makes you stronger'. Well, I'm still alive and I hope to bounce back from this season a better driver.

It's been an absolutely incredibly rewarding season, just lots of races and special situations that have really been unique, I suppose. As my old man says to me, they can never take those away from you. You've got them, and they were fair and square. That's the most important thing for me, and always has been, that if I got to win at this level I wanted to make sure it was fair and square.

Obviously, I was never supposed to survive against Sebastian, and that's worked out pretty well. Yes there have been a few incidents, which are never to be desired. I wouldn't say it was inevitable but, when you're at the front, with two drivers always close together, as a team, incidents can happen.

Clear highlights were obviously the victories, especially Monaco. It would have been beautiful to win there by over 25s, instead of under the safety car, but that's being greedy obviously. It was just a unique day to tame that circuit. I always say it's not a track where you race against other people. It's you and the track, you race against the track. That was a very, very special day to join the other winners there.

I mustn't forget the team's home race and my other home race, the British GP, as it was beautiful to win at Silverstone as well. Budapest was a different type of win, a unique strategy, and that required something very different from me again, and that was very rewarding. The Spanish GP was a pretty straightforward race.

Other ones that stand out? I think when you look at it, Belgium was a very, very easy grand prix to screw up for all of us. I was seventh after lap 1, after a shocking start. OK, there was a bit of attrition with Jenson and Seb, but I had to keep the pressure on Robert at the second pit stop, and he made a mistake there, and Lewis made a mistake. It was a tricky race for all of us, and you'd expect nothing different from that track.

That was a testing race, and then I think Singapore was probably the most rewarding grand prix for third place that I've ever had, in terms of rolling the dice with the strategy, clearing the backmarkers when I had Lewis

3 MARK WEBBER
RED BULL RACING

behind me on fresh prime tyres when mine had done 25 laps, so there were some key parts to that race. Team communication was awesome.

I knew how important qualifying was with these new regulations, but it hit you between the eyes after you'd done a few races. It was everything, so I know I need to get my finger out. It's not like I was cruising in qualifying before, but now you can't do anything in a race if you don't qualify well. There's a huge amount of energy and focus that goes into Saturday afternoon.

I've got to take my hat off to Sebastian, as he's done a good job this year. We've had our ups and downs, but we've pushed each other and it's always rewarding to get out of bed to do that. It's amazing to think that the only time he led the championship was after the last race, but that's the only time it matters. Well done him."

NATIONALITY Australian
DATE OF BIRTH 27/8/76
PLACE OF BIRTH Queanbeyan, Australia
GRANDS PRIX 158
WINS 6
POLES 6
FASTEST LAPS 6
POINTS 411.5
HONOURS Formula Ford Festival winner 1996

4 LEWIS HAMILTON
McLAREN

will be better, and we can fight from the first race on.

I've only been at the top of the championship once this year. In 2007, I was the points leader quite often. Then, in 2008, I was at the top quite often. This year, though, it's been a lot harder to stay right at the top with consistency and performance.

The Turkish GP was a great weekend, with obviously a little bit of confusion in the final laps of the race. Looking back, it was a great battle with Jenson. He came past me, then I went past him. We finished 1–2 and it was a great weekend for the team. My missus [Nicole] was there, so that was the icing on the cake. She had just won *Dancing with the Stars*, so I had to kind of step up my game to match her!

Then we went to the next race, Montréal. It seems to be a good race for me. It's one that I've won in the past and I generally have been close to winning in Montréal every year. This win was more straightforward. Actually, it's qualifying that I remember. I had my first pole position there, and it was the same feeling this time.

The Italian GP was a race where I went for a gap that I didn't really have to go for. I could have bided my time. After all, the race isn't always won in the first lap. I knew the trackrod had snapped after contact, and I knew my race was over, but I kept it flat in the hope that the car would turn, but it didn't and I went straight off... I was quite gutted, for the team especially. I feel like I let them down a little bit there. You learn from those things, but you can't turn back time.

At the end of the day I'm sitting here at 25 years old, I've got the best job in the world, I race for Vodafone McLaren Mercedes, I've won a World Championship, missed out on one in my first year and was still in this championship at the last race. I'm so blessed and privileged. There are only 24 of us that do it, and I'm at the top of those 24. I can't complain. Of course, I'd love to have a little bit more fortune in some of the races and not have the failures, but that's the name of the sport.

May I offer my congratulations to Sebastian Vettel, as I think that he did a fantastic job throughout the season. Really, he took the lead in his team, and did a phenomenal job. He was very, very quick all year, kept his head, kept his cool, so he's a deserving champion.

Red Bull Racing had the fastest car clearly, and they won the Constructors' Championship, and to top it off they won the Drivers' Championship too. So it was a great job by them. At the end of the day, the quickest team won, and we've got to try and do a better job next year. We'll push extremely hard to have the car to do that from the beginning.

We want to get both championships next year. It's going to be tough, but we really want to turn the tables on Red Bull, that's for sure."

NATIONALITY British
DATE OF BIRTH 7/1/85
PLACE OF BIRTH Stevenage, England
GRANDS PRIX 71
WINS 14
POLES 18
FASTEST LAPS 8
POINTS 496
HONOURS F1 World Champion 2008, GP2 Champion 2006, European F3 Champion 2005, British Formula Renault Champion 2003, World Kart Champion 2000

"It's definitely not been our best year as a team. In terms of atmosphere in the team and balance and happiness and effort, it's been fantastic. Jenson's done a great job, he's brought a great feeling into the team. The team has worked endlessly and pushed as hard as they possibly could, but it's just unfortunate that the other guys have been just a little bit faster than us during the year.

Our reliability probably hasn't been where we would have hoped it to be. Yet, as a driver, I think my reliability hasn't been as good as I'd hoped it would be, and I'd prefer to have finished every race. We'll take what we've learned from this year, though, and move forward.

I'd have liked to have had a better year, and I'd have liked to have had the fastest car all year long, but the team never gave up. I'm very, very proud of them. I'm really looking forward to 2011 and hoping that the car

"IT WAS IMPORTANT TO POSITION MYSELF IN THE TEAM, MAKE SURE I HAD PEOPLE AROUND ME WHO SUPPORTED ME AND WANTED ME TO ACHIEVE"

"For me, joining McLaren was easy, because everyone was great and really good to work with. They didn't judge me at all, they waited for me to get the results. The great thing is, I gave as much feedback as I could over the winter, so I could find some direction with the car, and I could give my input.

Even though the car was designed before I arrived at the team, and I didn't get to drive or have any input until January, I still felt that over the 10 weeks before the first race I could have some input that made a difference, and made it a better car for both Lewis and myself.

In this way, the team realises you're dedicated and that it's not just about driving fast. It's about being good with your team-mates, and being dedicated to try and make the car quicker, not just driving it.

I'm happy with the season. The most important thing for me was to get used to working with new people. After seven years of working with the same engineers, and working in the same factory, it's a big change to move to another team. I felt I got to grips with the team very quickly, and that was because the team really welcomed me in, which was great.

A few of the qualifying sessions haven't been great. It's something that I've really worked on, and it's been getting a lot better, finding a balance that really suits me in qualifying and on low fuel. It's improved quite a bit.

I think it was important to position myself in the team, make sure that I had people around me who supported me and wanted me to achieve. I definitely have that here. It's a great team, and they're very supportive towards their drivers. It's something that I didn't quite expect. They really listen to what the driver has to say, and that's massively important.

Lewis is super fast, and it's always tough to be quicker than Lewis in a car with which he's comfortable. But that's what's exciting, that's what's a challenge, and that's why I wanted to be here in the first place.

The wins were in tricky conditions, and I really enjoyed that situation of making the right call at the right time. You can't always make the right call, but I did over those two weekends. Some people might have said I was lucky in Australia, but three weeks later I did the same thing in China and you can't be that lucky!

Making the right call at the right time isn't just down to you, it's also down to the team. You win and lose as a team, but it's important to have an opinion in that situation, and that will make the difference.

It was frustrating that we didn't win at Monza. I thought I could come away with that victory but, for whatever reason, it didn't happen. We were very close, though, and it would have been interesting trying to get out of the paddock if I had beaten both Ferraris! It was a good weekend and we had good pace there.

5 JENSON BUTTON
McLAREN

Silverstone was another great race, I really enjoyed that in front of the home crowd. I didn't get on the podium, but to come from 14th to fourth on a circuit where it's difficult to overtake, I really enjoyed that. We didn't win, and I would have liked to have been on the podium, but it was a fun race for me, I really enjoyed it. It was definitely a British GP that I'll remember.

Barcelona was possibly the most frustrating race. Qualifying wasn't great, and I got stuck behind Michael, which completely destroyed my race. That was the most frustrating race for me. I was in fifth and I should have been so much higher up, as my pace was very good.

Spa was very frustrating, as we didn't make a mistake in any way. It was made by a competitor. It wasn't even an overtaking attempt that wiped us out of the race, and he was able to carry on... That cost a lot of points."

NATIONALITY British
DATE OF BIRTH 19/1/80
PLACE OF BIRTH Frome, England
GRANDS PRIX 190
WINS 9
POLES 7
FASTEST LAPS 3
POINTS 541
HONOURS F1 World Champion 2009, Formula Ford Festival winner 1998, European Super A Kart Champion 1997

6 FELIPE MASSA
FERRARI

"I was happy to be back on the track this year, but after the first test, the first race, you don't think any more about that, because you're already back on the job. You don't think every day you go in the car 'I'm happy to be here'. You just think about the job.

I don't think the year was so great for me. In many races I couldn't finish when I was heading to score points, and for sure this took me out of the title fight.

I had a lot of issues, especially in preparing the tyres for qualifying. That was the main issue I had this season, and it's something that really was a problem.

Strangely, I never had a problem preparing the tyres for the first lap before. In previous years, the tyre was much softer than it is now, and this year I was struggling. Many times in the race the pace was OK, but qualifying was always more difficult.

After finishing second in the first race, we thought the car was going to be a very, very strong car for the whole season, but then we saw after the first race that the others did a really good job on development, and I think we missed a little bit of time from Australia to Turkey in terms of development.

From Turkey to the end of the season, I think we were the team who did the best job, compared to the others. For sure we missed quite a bit between these early races where we were less strong than we expected.

Third place in Malaysia was good. Unfortunately, the qualifying in the wet was a disaster, but the race was good, and we were quite strong. Scoring no points in Canada, Valencia and Britain, I think that was the worst thing. The amount of points I lost wasn't a small number, it was quite a bit. Canada was a good race, and Valencia was a great race, then there was Silverstone, where we had a problem on the opening lap. Without the safety car, we could have had a podium in Valencia, so it was a very tough race for us. For sure, Germany was a good race. I was leading, so the performance was OK. Then Hungary, Belgium and Italy were all good, I scored some good points."

NATIONALITY Brazilian
DATE OF BIRTH 25/4/81
PLACE OF BIRTH São Paulo, Brazil
GRANDS PRIX 134
WINS 11
POLES 14
FASTEST LAPS 13
POINTS 464
HONOURS Euro F3000 Champion 2001, European Formula Renault Champion 2000

7 NICO ROSBERG
MERCEDES GP

"There are two sides to this season. One is the comparison to my team-mate, and from that side I'm pleased with how it went, because it was definitely better than I expected.

And then there's the other side obviously, just general results, where I'm below what I expected. I guess in the end, though, that's the one that's important, because I want to win races. That's definitely not been possible this year, because as a team we haven't done a good enough job in general.

It was a surprise that we were where we were. There was a likelihood that we wouldn't be winning the championship this year, looking at last year and how it kind of tailed off towards the end. But where we ended up, fourth in the constructors' and holding off Renault, that was a surprise, I didn't see that coming. I didn't think it would be that bad...

I've made so much progress as a driver, though, because of the change of team. You start to question things again, which maybe you stopped questioning. It's not so much on the driving, because I don't think you improve a lot as a driver, but it's the capacity to use your mind to set up and to help yourself driving on the track with the things that you are doing.

I was happy with Michael, because it's important to have a strong team-mate. I like the challenge of beating a strong team-mate too. In the past two years, I didn't have that. Michael coming to the team brings a lot to the team, and it's helped me too, because he's an asset for everything. I'm technically quite strong now, but there are always things he adds that maybe I missed.

I'm confident we can improve things in 2011, especially having Ross there. He's working hard and making a lot of changes at the moment and you can really see his work in progress, and I believe he can turn things around. Of course, there's everybody involved, but he has a very important role, and I think we'll be on the right track for sure.

We'll make a big step for next year. If it's enough, who knows. We will see, but I look forward to hopefully being able to challenge at least for race wins next year."

NATIONALITY German
DATE OF BIRTH 27/6/85
PLACE OF BIRTH Wiesbaden, Germany
GRANDS PRIX 89
WINS 0
POLES 0
FASTEST LAPS 2
POINTS 217.5
HONOURS GP2 Champion 2005, German Formula BMW Champion 2002

8 ROBERT KUBICA
RENAULT

"Am I happy with three podiums? I think from where we were starting at the beginning of my collaboration with Renault, I would say I would sign straight away.

You have to look at the situation realistically. Somehow of course expectations are welcome, but you have to always be cool in your mind and expect real things. I think it was obvious we weren't expecting to win races. I think it was obvious we have a lot to do to improve, and a long way to go to be in a position where we can win. So I would say I would sign straight away.

Of course, once we got a podium like we got in the second race in Australia, we wanted more. It was the same after Monaco. But you have to remember we aren't the only ones working here, we aren't the only ones pushing here, as there are really tough competitors in F1. So it's not as easy as it might look. It's not enough, your desire, you have to change this desire into the competitiveness of the package, of the team and of the driver.

I think I found in Renault some very good stuff, and some areas where we have to improve.

Definitely I found a good team, a team in which I found an atmosphere which permits you to have a bit more fun away from driving. So I have to say I'm happy in Renault, and feeling good.

I think the Australian GP was really good. It was a tricky race, so we really did everything nearly perfectly. The only gamble was, if we had stopped one lap earlier for slick tyres, then maybe we had a chance to win. I was happy with third in Monaco, but if you think starting second there you might still be second in the first corner, you are a dreamer...

The Belgian GP was a mistake from my side in the pitlane, and I was for sure unhappy about it. I lost a second place, but we still got third. In Malaysia, I finished fourth, but only because some strong cars were completely behind.

There was no really weak weekend from our side, and there was never a period where we were clearly off the pace or lacking performance. We had a couple of races, at Silverstone and the Hungaroring, which were not ideal, where unfortunately we had one technical failure and an incident in the pitlane."

NATIONALITY Polish
DATE OF BIRTH 7/12/84
PLACE OF BIRTH Krakow, Poland
GRANDS PRIX 76
WINS 1
POLES 1
FASTEST LAPS 1
POINTS 273
HONOURS World Series by Renault Champion 2005, German & Italian Junior Kart Champion 2000, Polish Junior Kart Champion 1997

9 MICHAEL SCHUMACHER
MERCEDES GP

"Everybody expected success, including myself, particularly if you think of where the team was in 2009, Mercedes joining, me joining. But then me being away for three years and Brawn joining a new partnership meant there were a lot of new components.

Never forget, we're a young team. We're a small team in a way, that already has the size of a team that you have to have in the future. So to get all the infrastructure working in the most efficient way is something we're focusing on and developing race by race.

I'm getting more and more into all the little items that are important in our business. Although I have a lot of experience, I've been out three years, and things change and develop. With time I pick up more of the little puzzle that is important for the final picture.

I think the weight of expectation was off the team pretty early in the season. Even in winter testing there was good reason not to be that optimistic. It's natural, you have a certain tool in your hands, and you know what the possibilities are with it. That's why

I was very keen on stopping this project early and focusing for next year, to be prepared and have a slight edge on the other guys.

In hindsight, the last races were pretty much OK, and I'm certainly more happy than I was about the mid-season races. We sorted the car in a good and reasonable way for those races. It was basically since Suzuka that the car was on a level that we could compete on a better playing field, and that suited me. Naturally, getting into the rhythm more and more made it look a bit better for me as well. The car is the car, and we're really desperate for next year's car!

We're all pretty encouraged and can't wait for next year's car. The guys are putting a lot of effort into the development of our car for 2011, and Mercedes will have a lot more input, although you can't expect miracles.

From where we are, to build up the strengths that Brawn had last year is a ladder that you have to climb, and you can't jump two steps at the same time, you really have to go through the process."

NATIONALITY German
DATE OF BIRTH 3/1/69
PLACE OF BIRTH Kerpen, Germany
GRANDS PRIX 269
WINS 91
POLES 68
FASTEST LAPS 75
POINTS 1441
HONOURS F1 World Champion 1994, 1995, 2000, 2001, 2002, 2003, 2004; German F3 Champion 1990, German Formula Konig Champion 1988

10 RUBENS BARRICHELLO
WILLIAMS

NATIONALITY Brazilian DATE OF BIRTH 23/5/72 PLACE OF BIRTH São Paulo, Brazil GRANDS PRIX 306 WINS 11 POLES 14 FASTEST LAPS 17 POINTS 654 HONOURS British F3 Champion 1991, European Formula Opel Champion 1990

"When we first drove the car, we thought we were a little bit more competitive than we actually were. Saying that, I've been very proud of the work achieved. The best example was that halfway through the season they said Singapore would be the last race for an improvement, to allow us to focus on 2011. The new car was advanced, but we still brought something new after that. For a sort of a smallish team, it's really good.

At Sepang, the engine was down on power. In Spain, I came from 17th to ninth, and in Monaco I was sixth when I hit the wall. Turkey was the worst race ever, there was no performance, and we had to have a step backwards in some of the things that we'd done there. It never worked.

It's been one of the best times of my career. Teams that have employed me have used me well enough, but not as well as Williams have used me. They hear me fully, and they act. They may sense that 'this is bullshit, but let's try it anyway.' And then they try and see some benefit. There's been some fantastic work.

Canada was a great race, but I touched Alguersuari, who put me in the wall. Valencia and Silverstone were great, fourth and fifth. In Germany, everyone was too competitive. Belgium was my 300th, it should have been different, but I was on the hard tyre and I touched that water and went into Alonso. Italy I didn't have a great qualifying, but I finished OK, and sixth in Singapore was a good one, and Korea was good too."

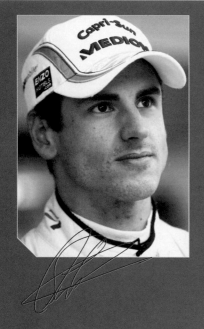

11 ADRIAN SUTIL
FORCE INDIA

NATIONALITY German DATE OF BIRTH 11/1/83 PLACE OF BIRTH Graefeling, Germany GRANDS PRIX 71 WINS 0 POLES 0 FASTEST LAPS 1 POINTS 53 HONOURS Swiss Formula Ford Champion 2002

"It's been a good season, with very strong races. The only race where I made a mistake was Korea. We had some mechanical problems at the beginning and in Suzuka, but nothing else, so the team did a good job.

Compared to 2009, maybe we lost a little bit, but it's just more competitive in the top 10. It's a shame we couldn't continue our early-season form, when we were a top-10 contender in qualifying. Later we were more around P13/14. Sauber and Williams struggled at the beginning and then got stronger. But we still had a strong race pace, and we were close to them.

We were losing out in the corners, downforce-wise. We couldn't put any more grip on the car, as we didn't have it. That was the only problem. The straightline speed was still good, and the balance very nice.

The only race that was really disappointing was Korea, and then in Suzuka I had an engine failure. I was very happy with fifth in Malaysia, we got qualifying right in the rain and held Lewis up. And he had a great car, but was just unlucky in qualifying. P6 in Valencia was also nice, as I started 13th and you never expect such a big jump, but with the safety-car period we got everything right. I had P5 in Belgium. Singapore was another one. The car wasn't very fast, but we managed to be eighth, holding a lot of cars up for around two hours. It was hard work, but fun."

12 KAMUI KOBAYASHI
BMW SAUBER

NATIONALITY Japanese DATE OF BIRTH 13/9/86 PLACE OF BIRTH Hyogo, Japan GRANDS PRIX 21 WINS 0 POLES 0 FASTEST LAPS 0 POINTS 35 HONOURS European & Italian Formula Renault Champion 2005, Japanese Kart Champion 2001, Suzuka Kart Champion 2000, Japanese Cadet Kart Champion 1997

"At first, we had poor performance and reliability problems. We were surprised, as we expected better.

I was learning a lot in a short period, but I wasn't happy that I couldn't race. In the first four races, I did just 19 laps. Bahrain was hydraulics. In Australia, the front wing collapsed. In Malaysia, it was engine failure. Then Liuzzi hit me in China.

In Barcelona, we had a good chance to score points, but at the start I had an accident with Robert [Kubica], and lost my position. At that point, I got quite good confidence. In Monaco, I was running in the points as well, then in Turkey I scored a point. In Canada, I crashed on the first lap, which was bad! Then I scored points at Valencia. So, if you look at that, I was quite

constantly in the points, so I was quite confident that if I could finish races with no accident then I would always be fighting for championship points.

The best race was at Silverstone. Qualifying was quite OK, and in the race I finished sixth. Pace-wise, it wasn't too bad, and the strategy was OK as well.

Japan was a very special day because we had qualifying in the morning and the race in the afternoon, so we didn't have time to think like usual about strategy. But I was quite confident to start with the prime, and also the team said we have to do something different because I'm 14th. We had to do some different strategy. After seven years away, I felt really good going back to race in Japan."

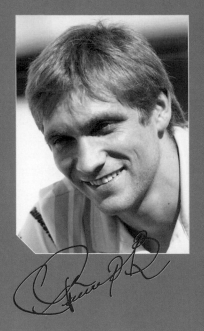

13 VITALY PETROV
RENAULT

NATIONALITY Russian DATE OF BIRTH 8/9/84 PLACE OF BIRTH Vyborg, Russia GRANDS PRIX 19 WINS 0 POLES 0 FASTEST LAPS 1 POINTS 27 HONOURS Formula 1600 Russia Champion 2005, Lada Revolution Champion 2005, Lada Cup Champion 2002

"The season wasn't easy for anyone, but from my side it was that much harder, as it was my first time in an F1 car, and also my first time in an F1 car at every circuit at which I arrived.

At some circuits it was good, some circuits not so good. But it's always hard to manage the right speed and the right set-up altogether. Sometimes you have a feeling that everything is fine, in the right moment and the right place, and sometimes it's not like this.

I did just one or two days dry testing, and then it was completely wet. It was a pity for me, and of course I needed to do more kilometres with an F1 car to understand how it was working.

The first time I drove, I realised it was incredible. F1 is another life, another story. Each time I arrived at the circuit the guys were making something new for the car, and it changed the driving style. So it was hard.

Robert and I liked different things. I don't like it when a car has too much oversteer. I worked my way with my engineers, he worked his way with his, and sometimes we just compared what was better to do.

Fifth place in Hungary was the highlight of my season. I know the track, it's a technical track and it's about driving style. Everything was right, as I was very happy with the car and how they gave it to me. It was very easy to drive there without any problem, and then I just pushed, pushed, pushed all the time to keep my speed up. It was a great weekend for us."

14 NICO HULKENBERG
WILLIAMS

NATIONALITY German DATE OF BIRTH 19/8/87 PLACE OF BIRTH Emmerich, Germany GRANDS PRIX 19 WINS 0 POLES 1 FASTEST LAPS 0 POINTS 22 HONOURS GP2 Champion 2009, European F3 Champion 2008, A1GP Champion 2006/2007, German Formula BMW Champion 2005, German Kart Champion 2003

"I think I could have achieved more, but it was very tough for me, starting the season having only seven test days before Bahrain and with a car that we thought would be better than it was. So, to deliver the job in qualifying and the race, with that little experience, and the car as it was, was difficult.

Clearly, I wasn't able to do it in the beginning, compared to Rubens. Since mid-season, I got better, and I feel a lot more comfortable and can deliver these performances consistently, which I have to if I want to stay in F1. It's good to see the progress I've made.

Winning is great, and then you come to F1 and find yourself in P16, P17, P18. You have to re-set your measures. You also have to consider that you're in F1 now, and winning is not an everyday thing. You realise that quickly. As I said, it's tough, especially if your team colleague outperforms you consistently. At that moment, you need to take into account that you're new and that he's done 17 or 18 years in F1, and if somebody is that long in the sport, he must have done something right.

Rubens is good at what he does. I saw there were several practices and qualifying where I could have been there, but because of little mistakes, or uncertain things where I didn't choose the right set-up, I couldn't be close to him. I knew that if I get everything together eventually, and I feel better, then I can be right there. Now I've just a lot more confidence."

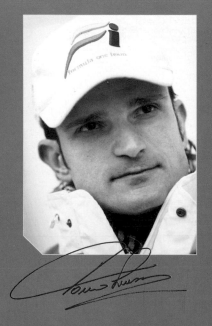

15 VITANTONIO LIUZZI
FORCE INDIA

NATIONALITY Italian DATE OF BIRTH 6/8/81 PLACE OF BIRTH Locorotondo, Italy GRANDS PRIX 63 WINS 0 POLES 0 FASTEST LAPS 0 POINTS 26 HONOURS Formula 3000 Champion 2004, World Kart Champion 2001, Italian Kart Champion 1996

"We had a lot of ups and downs this year. We started really strongly, and it's a shame that we lost a few good points in the middle of the season when the car was at its best. We had quite a few issues with the F-duct and the chassis as well, a few issues that stopped us getting points in the best part of the season.

From the middle to the end of the season we lost a little bit of pace. Maybe everybody was expecting us to fly again like last year in races at Spa and Monza, but we were obviously aware that the other teams didn't sleep. We were in a similar condition to all the other circuits, and I think the F-duct didn't help us, because everybody now is fast on the straight, so we lost a bit of the advantage that we had in 2009. It's a balance in the end. We became much more competitive in every race, but we lost the peak that we had last year.

We didn't get the results that we wanted to achieve, because we were highly motivated and targeting really high. But, in the end, I had a really strong season, and I'm proud of it for sure. I knew that we couldn't get podiums this year – nobody was expecting podiums from Force India last year.

Also, nobody expected that we could be fighting for sixth in the Constructors' Championship. People forget that we are a team with 280 people, and at the beginning we were fighting with Renault and Mercedes. In a way, I think it's kind of normal that compared to them our pace would kind of drift away."

16 SEBASTIEN BUEMI
TORO ROSSO

NATIONALITY Swiss DATE OF BIRTH 13/10/88
PLACE OF BIRTH Aigle, Switzerland GRANDS PRIX
36 WINS 0 POLES 0 FASTEST LAPS 0 POINTS 14
HONOURS Italian Kart Champion 2003, European &
Swiss Junior Kart Champion 2002, Swiss Super Mini
Kart Champion 2000

"I was expecting more from this year – when it's your second season you expect to be more competitive and to have a better year. However, it's been pretty much the same, or a little bit worse. My car was less good, but I think I was definitely more competitive, but I wasn't able to get the same results, or better results.

We had to make the car completely on our own, and we knew it would be difficult. This is F1, and you need to accept sometime that you might be a little bit less competitive.

We started pretty well. I think I would have been able to finish in the points in the first four races, as we were quick, but I had so much bad luck in the beginning of the season, it was unbelievable.

We had a good, competitive car, and the others were not very good. But then they got better. We got better, but slowly, and this was the problem. We had to work with own CFD, which we didn't have last year, with the wind tunnel, and put a lot of guys together to make it work properly. And this is definitely not easy.

We were missing downforce. We were quick on the straights because we had a really low wing, but in general the problem was that we didn't have downforce, and we didn't have an F-duct. This was a big problem. We had the blown diffuser for the Italian GP. I think we could have worked more on that, but we did it as fast as we could. It's better late than never, but next year will be good, I think."

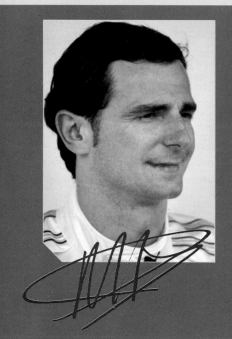

17 PEDRO DE LA ROSA
BMW SAUBER

NATIONALITY Spanish DATE OF BIRTH 24/2/71
PLACE OF BIRTH Barcelona, Spain GRANDS PRIX
84 WINS 0 POLES 0 FASTEST LAPS 1 POINTS
35 HONOURS Formula Nippon Champion 1997,
Japanese GT Champion 1997, Japanese F3 Champion
1995, British & European Formula Renault Champion
1992, Spanish Formula Ford Champion 1990

"At the last test before the first race, we saw signs that we weren't quick enough. We had too much drag, so were slow on the straights. It was obviously a wake-up call, and our worries were then confirmed in Bahrain.

We were unreliable initially, as we had several engine failures. We also had hydraulic problems.

It rained in China and we decided to stay out with slicks. There was a point when I got up to fourth. It was a good call to stay out, but the engine failed.

Also, in Monaco our race pace was extremely competitive, we had a very good strategy, but I had a hydraulic problem. Then, in Barcelona we were competitive until I was hit by a Toro Rosso at the start.

To qualify ninth twice was my highlight, without forgetting the points in Hungary for 7th, again on a track with no straights. We were mostly competitive in high-speed corners, and that's why we were strong at Silverstone, and our weak point was mainly our high drag levels, thus affecting us at Montréal and Monza.

I had no indication that they would replace me. It was a sad decision from the team, from Peter basically. The car had been a lot better in the last two or three races before then and we knew that we could do it.

Everyone looks at the points table. You have to score the goals when you have the chance. If you look into it on detail, though, Kamui and I qualified 7–7."

18 NICK HEIDFELD
BMW SAUBER

NATIONALITY German DATE OF BIRTH 10/5/77
PLACE OF BIRTH Mönchengladbach, Germany
GRANDS PRIX 174 WINS 0 POLES 1 FASTEST
LAPS 2 POINTS 225 HONOURS Formula 3000
Champion 1999, German F3 Champion 1997

"I first spoke to Mercedes about a race drive for 2010, not a test drive, and I think I was in a good position. But I knew, and they were pretty open also, that there was a chance that Michael was coming back. But it was by far the best option I had at the time.

That didn't work out, and from what was left, in my eyes it was the best opportunity to go there as a test driver. But I only ever drove last year's car, in a demo in Malaysia and then up the hill at Goodwood...

There were only positives with the Pirelli deal. I could be in a car again driving, and I could help develop the tyres for next year, which would make me more interesting for teams, of course. I did three tests for them, at Paul Ricard, Jerez and Mugello.

I was in talks with Sauber for a while – I'm totally convinced I would have signed without doing any laps in an F1 car this year. It was difficult knowing last winter that with Peter the reason I wasn't there wasn't my driving, he just wanted to do something completely new. Maybe it was not the right reason, but I have to accept it. I'm glad that he took me back on board.

Knowing the team helped me focus on getting to know the car and tyres. That made it easier. However, especially in qualifying in Singapore in hindsight, it was clear that it was difficult to just jump in and show a great performance. That said, it was great to score points in the next two races, as Suzuka is my favourite circuit, so it was great fun."

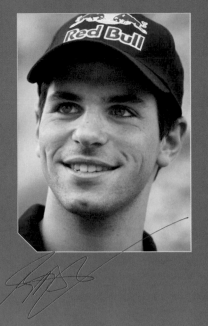

19 JAIME ALGUERSUARI
TORO ROSSO

NATIONALITY Spanish DATE OF BIRTH 23/3/90 PLACE OF BIRTH Barcelona, Spain GRANDS PRIX 27 WINS 0 POLES 0 FASTEST LAPS 0 POINTS 5 HONOURS British F3 Champion 2008, Italian Formula Renault Winter Series Champion 2006

"I think always in life you can achieve more in your work, or your job, or whatever you do. But I'm happy with the season, compared with 2009. I can't compare myself with other drivers, there are no tools to compare.

Regarding last year, which is the only comparison for me, I'm much happier, and the development is coming. It's always related to the team performance and the car performance, but on my side I can finish a race with no problem, can deal with a car on the limit much more easily, and I'm starting to understand much better the tyres and to be fast in qualifying.

I'm much closer to my team-mate. Sometimes I'm faster, sometimes he's a bit faster. And this is what I was aiming for. I'm quite satisfied with how everything went. I'm sure I could have had more points without some mistakes, but I know where the team is.

I started prepared this year and now have a little experience of F1. I know all the tracks, I have a good feeling for the car, and I have much more self control.

The car was a good car, the balance was quite good, but obviously the other teams were faster, and that was the difficult thing. It was difficult for us to be at the same level as Renault and Williams and Force India, because they have much more experience and they've been developing their cars longer than us.

This was the first year for Scuderia Toro Rosso since it was Minardi, as before we were always helped by Red Bull Technology."

20 HEIKKI KOVALAINEN
LOTUS RACING

NATIONALITY Finnish DATE OF BIRTH 19/10/81 PLACE OF BIRTH Suomussalmi, Finland GRANDS PRIX 71 WINS 1 POLES 1 FASTEST LAPS 2 POINTS 105 HONOURS World Series by Nissan Champion 2004

"People were expecting more from us initially. But when I went to see Lotus for the first time before Christmas, I knew that this would be a tough call: four people at the factory, and no sign of a car or anything!

I thought we would probably struggle to make the first race, and that the winter testing would be tough. But talking to Tony Fernandes and Mike Gascoyne, they convinced me that it would work out eventually. I thought it was the best option for me at that time, so I thought, 'let's go for it and see where we get to'.

We made the first race and a few tests in the winter too. Reliability was poor, but we got the thing moving. We were hitting the schedule, which for me initially looked optimistic. We knew from the testing that we'd be far away from the established guys, and that we could only battle with the other new teams.

That's been pretty much the story all season. The car was not optimised in any area. It was too heavy to start with, and we had to release a lot of weight to actually get to the minimum weight initially.

At a few circuits – Monaco, Montréal, these special types of circuits – we've been a bit closer. But then, when you really need the performance in the car, like at Silverstone, Spa and Suzuka, the gap is big.

That was a secondary problem, the most important thing for the team was to make 2011's car quicker, and I'm looking forward to that. We already look professional, now we just need to have a good car."

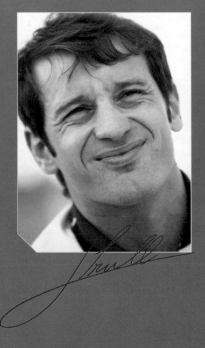

21 JARNO TRULLI
LOTUS RACING

NATIONALITY Italian DATE OF BIRTH 13/7/74 PLACE OF BIRTH Pescara, Italy GRANDS PRIX 238 WINS 1 POLES 4 FASTEST LAPS 1 POINTS 246.5 HONOURS German F3 Champion 1996, World Kart Champion 1995, European Kart Champion 1994

"I knew it would be a very hard season, but I expected a bit more reliability and for other things to be better. And I didn't expect such a big gap to the others!

It didn't change the target of the season itself, as we knew we had no chance compared to the rest of the people. The only thing is, that before the season my guess was that we'd be closer, not 4–5 seconds away. We found out that it was going to be a tough job.

Apart from that, reliability has been really poor for me. Never mind, better this year than next year, because we will probably fight for points. I know what we can achieve with this team next year, given the tools that Mike and Tony are putting together.

It was hard for everyone that we had so little testing, and there were a lot of questionmarks over reliability. All in all, the team has hit all the targets, and we've achieved great things. Especially, I would say, for the first half of the season, this is motivating you, because obviously you want as much as possible.

However, from halfway through the season, all we were doing was trying to beat our main rival, which was Virgin. The only thing was to hope to finish the race without a problem, and then you could probably beat Virgin. This was what we could do.

I knew that this was a transition season, so I had to be patient, and I had to be working for the team, in order to prepare for next year. Things are moving in the right direction, so I'm really happy."

22 KARUN CHANDHOK
HISPANIA RACING TEAM

NATIONALITY Indian DATE OF BIRTH 19/1/84 PLACE OF BIRTH Chennai, India GRANDS PRIX 10 WINS 0 POLES 0 FASTEST LAPS 0 POINTS 0 HONOURS FV6 Asia Champion 2006, Formula 2000 Asia Champion 2001, Formula Maruti Champion 2000

"I think I looked pretty good against both of the team-mates that I raced against. I think I did a good job and made no real mistakes. I was pretty consistent and I finished a lot of races. Given the situation, I made the most of it. I'm not quite sure what more I could have done with what we had...

The start in Bahrain wasn't ideal. The light went green to start qualifying, I saw Vettel going out of the pitlane and they were still putting the floor on my car, with me having not driven it at that point. But I think I did a respectable job and didn't disgrace myself.

That's the main thing. When you are a small team in a situation like ours, at the back of the grid, the only thing you can do is establish yourself as a respectable

F1 driver. We were never in a position to score points, so you just have to go out there and be sensible and not be stupid, and show that you deserve to be in F1 in the long term. I think that's what I've achieved.

I'd never been lapped in a race until this year, so in learning the art of not losing time when making way for the leaders and racing in traffic and not getting in people's way, but at the same time not compromising yourself, I've learned a lot about F1 this year.

We had some good races relative to the other new teams. In Monaco, I was ahead of them after we jumped Jarno Trulli and the Virgins at the pit stops. I had good pace in between in free air, and we used the strategy to jump them."

23 BRUNO SENNA
HISPANIA RACING TEAM

NATIONALITY Brazilian DATE OF BIRTH 15/10/83 PLACE OF BIRTH São Paulo, Brazil GRANDS PRIX 18 WINS 0 POLES 0 FASTEST LAPS 0 POINTS 0 HONOURS None

"The pre-season was quite thrilling, not in a good way unfortunately... We had times when I didn't believe it was going to happen, though late, it came together.

We knew so little about the car and the tyres, so initially the objective was purely to get some miles on the car and some miles on myself. From the first race on, we were just learning, learning, learning. We came to a point where we knew everything that could be done to the car to make it better, we knew what the problems were in terms of reliability, and we usually took almost 100% out of the car on each weekend.

We started in a difficult way by not testing and coming very late into the championship, and it's been

a really big learning curve for me and the team.

It's been a big opportunity to learn and develop. You learn all sorts of things like the technical things, but also how to handle the pressure, to handle how to work in a bigger team, and just being in the F1 paddock and getting to know the people.

We had some really good races, and we had some bad races as well. Some fun times, some frustrating times. It's been a season where I've had all types of experiences. Sometimes it's been better than expected, sometimes worse than expected. Fortunately, I've been able to take all these experiences in a good way, as keeping motivated is very important."

24 LUCAS DI GRASSI
VIRGIN RACING

NATIONALITY Brazilian DATE OF BIRTH 11/8/84 PLACE OF BIRTH São Paulo, Brazil GRANDS PRIX 18 WINS 0 POLES 0 FASTEST LAPS 0 POINTS 0 HONOURS Macau F3 GP winner 2005

"I think most people don't really understand how difficult F1 is, the level that it is at, and how difficult it is to build an F1 car and how difficult it is to drive one.

I've been participating on this since the beginning, and I have to say that everyone in the team did a good job in building the car that was straight away something like 1.5–2s from the midfield. People tend to see us finishing every race 15th or 16th as something bad, but actually to be in F1, to be able to improve and close the gap to these teams, is I think a massive accomplishment for the team.

I did the best that I could. I had a very experienced team-mate, and I tried to learn from him. Sometimes I didn't have the same equipment: for two races I had a

different car, with the fuel tank story and so on.

It was my rookie year, and I had to learn a lot, like the circuits I didn't know, using the correct type of tyre, the many different settings that you change on the car. I had to try to understand that and how it affected the car on a circuit that I didn't know. There are many more engineers to work with too, and also it's a much busier time, because you have all the PR work to do. Life in F1 is so much more complex.

I've been trying my best, I've been trying really hard, been pushing on the physical preparation, mental preparation, trying to approach everything as best as I could so that I can look back and say I did everything I could to achieve the best results."

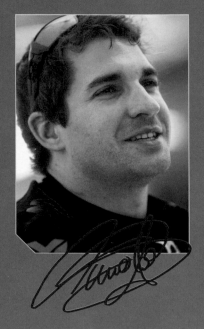

25 TIMO GLOCK
VIRGIN RACING

NATIONALITY German DATE OF BIRTH 13/3/82 PLACE OF BIRTH Lindenfels, Germany GRANDS PRIX 54 WINS 0 POLES 0 FASTEST LAPS 1 POINTS 51 HONOURS GP2 Champion 2007, German Formula BMW Champion 2001, German Formula BMW Junior Champion 2000

"The year was quite a lot harder than I expected. I didn't expect that we would have so many technical problems in the team, and so many ups and downs. Especially from the beginning of the year, we made quite a positive step in the right direction in terms of reliability and all that stuff, but in general I'm quite disappointed about the speed we've had.

It improved, but I didn't expect that we'd be that far off. We just made our life quite difficult with all the problems we had in the beginning, with the fuel tank and all that stuff, which was not good and not how it should be. So it wasn't a very good year for us... In the end, though, it was definitely a good experience for me to build a team up. It was good fun.

I expected bigger steps and more steps, like the one we did in Silverstone, because to work only in CFD is a chance to develop quickly, but we didn't achieve what some people tried to do at the beginning of the year. To close the gap, or make the car 3–4s quicker was Nick Wirth's target, but we have to be really straight and say that it didn't work out. But at least we got enough experience to sort the stuff out for next year.

The potential is still there. We have some good guys, and that's what keeps me still positive. But in some areas we have to rethink and restructure a little bit. Overall, the possibilities are there. You need the budget to make a really big step, and that's what the team is working on for the future."

26 SAKON YAMAMOTO
HISPANIA RACING TEAM

NATIONALITY Japanese DATE OF BIRTH 9/7/82 PLACE OF BIRTH Toyohashi City, Japan GRANDS PRIX 28 WINS 0 POLES 0 FASTEST LAPS 0 POINTS 0 HONOURS Japanese Kart Champion 1999

"This year I joined HRT as test driver to start with, but for the British GP I got the chance to do a race. I did a good job for the team there, and they decided to use me in the following races as well. I hadn't driven in a Grand Prix for two-and-a-half years, but it was really a good experience to be back again.

I did seven races with them, I finished six of them, and most of the time I was in front of Bruno Senna. I think my best races were Suzuka and Korea. In Japan, I had a really good race with Timo Glock and the Lotus of Jarno Trulli, so the team was very happy that I could battle with them. I was in front of my home crowd as well, and everyone told me they were quite impressed with what we did.

Korea was an interesting race for everyone and we didn't know what to expect. Also, we had the race in rain conditions, and no one knew about that. The pace was quite good, and also my qualifying lap was good, because we were so close to the other new teams. That was one of the best qualifying sessions for me.

We had very small updates through the season, not like the other competitors. But still the team worked very hard, and we had very good reliability on my car. Therefore, we could finish nearly all the races, and that was a very important point for us.

It's obvious that performance-wise we needed to improve. We all understood that the situation was very limited, but still we tried to do our best."

27 CHRISTIAN KLIEN
HISPANIA RACING TEAM

NATIONALITY Austrian DATE OF BIRTH 7/2/83 PLACE OF BIRTH Hohenems, Austria GRANDS PRIX 51 WINS 0 POLES 0 FASTEST LAPS 0 POINTS 14 HONOURS Marlboro Masters winner 2003, German Formula Renault Champion 2002

"It was a four-year wait, since the 2006 Italian Grand Prix with Red Bull Racing, to get a full race weekend again in Singapore.

We got in contact with Colin Kolles in Bahrain for the first time, when HRT started. The plan was that there would be some development on the car. As the team's other drivers had no F1 experience, he brought me to the team to do the Friday tests. Yet there were only two Fridays when I was in the car.

It was good to get time in the car, but one-and-a-half hours is a bit short… It was about 20 laps in Barcelona. Then I had a problem with the car in Valencia, so it was only 13 laps there.

When the chance came in Singapore, I just went step-by-step from free practice. I adjusted the seat, pedals and everything, so by Saturday I was comfortable and the lap times came together.

Qualifying was fine. All I could do with the HRT was be in front of my team-mate [Senna], as the gap to Virgin and Lotus was quite big, and performance-wise there wasn't much chance to do anything else.

Singapore is great, a night race, which is easy if you've done Le Mans... I quite liked the circuit, so being on the grid after four years was exciting.

After racing twice more, I want to thank the team for the extraordinary job they did over the season and for giving me the opportunity to compete in the Singapore, Brazil and Abu Dhabi races."

THE TEAMS

Three teams joined the World Championship, and were shown how high they must aim as Red Bull Racing, McLaren and Ferrari put on a masterclass while adapting to the new rules

RED BULL

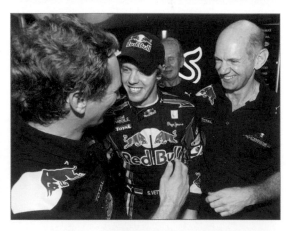

McLAREN

MERCEDES GP

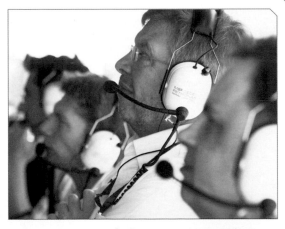

RENAULT

WILLIAMS

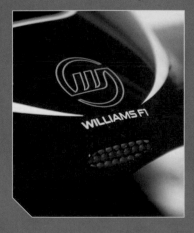

FORCE INDIA

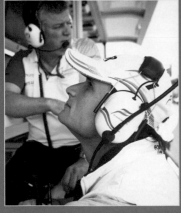

BMW SAUBER

TORO ROSSO

LOTUS

RED BULL

THE TEAM

PERSONNEL

CHAIRMAN Dietrich Mateschitz
TEAM PRINCIPAL Christian Horner
CHIEF TECHNICAL OFFICER Adrian Newey (above)
HEAD OF AERODYNAMICS Peter Prodromou
CHIEF DESIGNER Rob Marshall
HEAD OF CAR ENGINEERING Paul Monaghan
HEAD OF RACE ENGINEERING Ian Morgan
CHIEF ENGINEER, VEHICLE DYNAMICS Mark Ellis
TECHNICAL DIRECTOR, RENAULT ENGINES Rob White
TEAM MANAGER Jonathan Wheatley
CHIEF ENGINEER, RENAULT ENGINES Fabrice Lom
DRIVERS Sebastian Vettel, Mark Webber
RACE ENGINEER (Vettel) Guillaume Rocquelin
RACE ENGINEER (Webber) Ciaron Pilbeam
SUPPORT TEAM MANAGER Tony Burrows
TEST/THIRD DRIVER Daniel Ricciardo
CHIEF MECHANIC Kenny Handkammer
TOTAL NUMBER OF EMPLOYEES 550
NUMBER IN RACE TEAM 85
TEAM BASE Milton Keynes, England
TELEPHONE +44 (0)1908 279700
WEBSITE www.redbullracing.com

TEAM STATS

IN F1 SINCE 1997 as Stewart Grand Prix then Jaguar Racing
FIRST GRAND PRIX Australia 1997 **STARTS** 244
WINS 15 **POLE POSITIONS** 21 **FASTEST LAPS** 12
PODIUMS 33 **POINTS** 842.5 **CONSTRUCTORS' TITLES** 1
DRIVERS' TITLES 1

SPONSORS

Red Bull, Red Bull Cola, Red Bull Mobile, Total, Rauch, Pepe Jeans, LG Electronics, FXDD, Casio, Singha Beer, Logwin, Hangar-7, Bridgestone

 5 SEBASTIAN VETTEL   **6 MARK WEBBER**

LEADING THE WAY WITH ITS FRONT WING

**By Adrian Newey
(Chief Technical Officer)**

"The main difference with RB6 was starting with a clean sheet of paper to suit a double diffuser. We changed the main gearbox casing, which we decided we didn't have the resource to do with RB5. The step-up feature was something you only introduce for a double diffuser, as structurally it's slightly more compromised.

We debated a conventional rear suspension, and if double diffusers had been understood from the start of 2009, we'd probably have done a pushrod in the first place, but we preferred to evolve the pullrod rather than start again.

We went a bit longer with the chassis to maximise the length available for the diffuser slot. The rest of it was really a mix of a few new bits – the side-blown exhausts – then refining RB5, allied to changes to suit no refuelling.

In the 1980s and 1990s, blown floors developed up to the point that diffusers were chopped off post-1994 San Marino GP and became so short that there wasn't really enough length to act on.

MAKING THE BLOWN FLOOR WORK

Then, in terms of the old way of doing blown floors, where the exhaust outlet was physically in the diffuser on the underside of the car, it became illegal, as the exhaust came to be considered part of the bodywork and there can't be any holes in the diffuser apart from the starter-shaft hole. So, in that sense, today's blown floors are different, as the exhaust outlet itself is still on the top side of the car, but then blows at a slot inside the rear wheel. So the gas exits the exhaust on the top side but ends up underneath the car, through the slot.

F-ducts were another feature of the season. If I'd known I was designing the car to suit that, I might have been able to make it easier to get the porting in and out of the chassis, but our F-duct wasn't too badly compromised.

The principle is very simple and was established in the Cold War [in the 1950s and early 1960s] when the Americans were worried that the Russians would be able to jam the electronics on their fighter aircraft, so they wanted a pneumatic or hydraulic-fluid logic that would replace electronics. Effectively, an F-duct is a pneumatic amplifier, and all credit to the McLaren team for applying it in that way.

RB6 seemed to have its biggest advantage at tracks with the longest-duration corners and the shortest straights… I was particularly impressed by it going through Barcelona Turn 9 flat. We just about managed to get Copse flat at Silverstone in 2009 and went one better at Barcelona Turn 9.

FALLING SHORT ON HORSEPOWER

Our car had good downforce, but the engine has fallen behind Mercedes and Ferrari, particularly Mercedes. At circuits where power is a lesser factor, like Monaco and Hungary, we had a good benefit but, get to somewhere like Spa-Francorchamps or Monza, where power is more important, and we started to fall behind.

McLaren blocked us from having a Mercedes engine and it really came down to staying with Renault. That sounds as if it was by default, but I've always said that Renault as a partner treats us extremely well. We've had parity, we could have frank discussions in terms of what we'd like for the chassis side out of the engine, but there's no doubt that they froze the engine much earlier in 2006 and they didn't keep working on it like others and haven't done so since the freeze came in.

Our analysis suggests that we are at least 4% behind a Mercedes which, at most circuits, is getting on for half-a-second a lap. Mercedes has blocked all conversations with regard to Renault being able to retune or redress the balance. They've systematically gone through FOTA and blocked all that. It was just a very frustrating position to be in, because some people argued that if they gave us an engine-performance upgrade, then we should have given them our front wing, for instance. That has been one of the conversations with a senior person at Mercedes. That's all very well and good, but we aren't stopping Mercedes or McLaren from developing a front wing that's the same as ours, whereas they are stopping Renault from developing an engine to match the Mercedes.

FRONT-WING DEFLECTION WAS LEGAL

The front wings did seem to generate a bit of controversy that, as I understand it, was prompted by an article in a French magazine,

TECHNICAL SPECIFICATIONS

ENGINE
MAKE/MODEL Renault RS27-2010
CONFIGURATION 2400cc V8
(90 degree)
SPARK PLUGS NGK
ECU FIA standard issue
KERS n/a
FUEL Total
OIL Total
BATTERY Not disclosed

TRANSMISSION
GEARBOX Red Bull Racing
FORWARD GEARS Seven
CLUTCH AP Racing

CHASSIS
CHASSIS MODEL Red Bull RB6
FRONT SUSPENSION LAYOUT
Double wishbones and pushrod
REAR SUSPENSION LAYOUT
Double wishbones and pullrod

DAMPERS Multimatic
TYRES Bridgestone
WHEELS OZ Racing
BRAKE DISCS Brembo
BRAKE PADS Brembo
BRAKE CALIPERS Brembo
FUEL TANK ATL
INSTRUMENTS MESL

DIMENSIONS
LENGTH Not disclosed
WIDTH 1800mm
HEIGHT 950mm
WHEELBASE >3000mm
TRACK front 1800mm
rear 1800mm
WEIGHT 620kg (including driver and camera)

after which various teams jumped on the bandwagon. The irony is that the regulations quite clearly state that with a 50kg load you are allowed 10mm of deflection. Prior to 2009, it was a 50kg load and 5mm of deflection but, because the wing span went up for 2009, McLaren asked in the Technical Working Group that the deflection should be increased to 10mm. So it was rather ironic that they were the ones getting so excited about it… I suppose we should take it as a form of flattery that two of our competitors in particular spent most of their time looking at our car rather than their own.

We didn't have to make any modifications at all to pass the changed front-wing test introduced at the Belgian GP. For the front floor tea-tray test introduced at Monza, where the load is offset from the car centreline, we had to run slightly higher front ride height in common with everyone else in the pitlane.

THAT BRITISH GP FRONT WING
As for our own little front-wing controversy at Silverstone, with no testing I frankly wanted to see the wing raced to find out more about it. Dare I say, the media managed to make a frenzy over it, in which perhaps one or two of our team members acquiesced… Which car it went on, to be perfectly honest, I wasn't bothered. We went with championship position, but it could just as easily have been on a coin toss. I don't think we ever actually proved a lap-time benefit. It was a detail change and it was circuit specific; I felt we would need it for Hungary, but at Spa and Monza we didn't run it.

GREATER DRIVER PARITY IN QUALIFYING
The drivers were more even in qualifying this year, although there was no obvious explanation for this. I guess the car was a bit less nervous on corner entry and that's primarily down to the front tyre, so possibly that helped Mark's side more than Sebastian's. But Mark had his cycling accident prior to 2009 and through the first half of that season, I think, must have been putting on a very brave face.

There are pluses and minuses to having such even drivers. If the downside was Turkey [when they clashed], the upside is always that they're capable of pushing each other and do exactly that. The drivers are able to learn and develop off each other. People tried to big their rivalry up everywhere, but the lads are pretty professional."

McLAREN

THE TEAM

PERSONNEL

TEAM PRINCIPAL, VODAFONE MCLAREN MERCEDES Martin Whitmarsh
MANAGING DIRECTOR Jonathan Neale
ENGINEERING DIRECTOR Paddy Lowe
DESIGN & DEVELOPMENT DIRECTOR Neil Oatley
HEAD OF VEHICLE DESIGN Andrew Bailey
HEAD OF AERODYNAMICS John Iley
HEAD OF RACE OPERATIONS Simon Roberts
HEAD OF VEHICLE ENGINEERING Mark Williams
CHIEF ENGINEER MP4-25 Tim Goss (above)
TEAM MANAGER David Redding
DRIVERS Jenson Button, Lewis Hamilton
CHIEF ENGINEER Philip Prew
RACE ENGINEER (Button) Jakob Andreasen
RACE ENGINEER (Hamilton) Andy Latham
TEST TEAM MANAGER Indy Lall
TEST/THIRD DRIVER Gary Paffett
CHIEF MECHANIC Pete Vale
TOTAL NUMBER OF EMPLOYEES 550 (McLaren Racing)
TEAM BASE Woking, England
TELEPHONE +44 (0)1483 261000
WEBSITE www.mclaren.com

TEAM STATS

IN F1 SINCE 1966 **FIRST GRAND PRIX** Monaco 1966
STARTS 684 **WINS** 168 **POLE POSITIONS** 145
FASTEST LAPS 142 **PODIUMS** 448 **POINTS** 3816.5
CONSTRUCTORS' TITLES 8 **DRIVERS' TITLES** 12

SPONSORS

Vodafone, Santander, Mobil 1, Johnnie Walker, Aigo, Boss, xtb, SAP, AON, TAG Heuer Hilton, Bridgestone

1 JENSON BUTTON   **2** LEWIS HAMILTON

F-FLAPS WERE GOOD, BUT BUMPS WEREN'T WELCOME

By Tim Goss
(Chief Engineer MP4-25)

"The car philosophy was to get the absolute maximum out of the diffusers, and legalisation was a complex process to get the biggest, widest, longest diffuser.

MP4-25 had a particularly long gearbox and rear wheelbase so, despite the fact that the fuel tank was longer for the additional capacity, we still stretched the gearbox. That was to push the engine as far forward and get the rear wishbone forward leg as far forward as possible, which to some extent dictates the start of the duct, the inlet.

We had a wide, long-ducted diffuser that linked into the rear main plane, so the gearbox had to be quite long to control the expansion rate. The sidepods necked down quickly and you got a good clean flow to the rear of the car, which drove the ducted diffuser, which then drove the floor hard. That's how MP4-25 ended up being a long car.

Our rear suspension was back to front to make room for the main duct geometry. Traditionally, you put the main toe link at the back, whereas we flipped it the other way around and the toe link sits at the front end of the upright, in order to clear everything out of the way so that the duct runs up underneath the suspension and there's only one leg that runs through the duct.

USING LOUVRES WAS A GOOD TRICK

Where we think we stole a bit of an advantage is that if you look down the back of our car into the duct, you see louvres. That's a complex way of getting around the floor regulations. We did that and effectively opened up the diffuser: instead of having a piece of floor, you end up with the louvres – it looks like floor from below, but it's open. To legalise that is structurally quite difficult, as the slots have to run forwards and back, so you end up with the louvres and the duct above it all cantilevered off the back end of the car.

We launched our car with that. Renault launched theirs shortly afterwards, without the louvres, as presumably they hadn't sorted out the structural solution or wanted to hide it. They followed us before the start of the season and subsequently probably 50% of the teams copied some sort of solution along that line.

It allowed us to open up the main duct and get more mass flow through it.

INTRODUCING THE F-FLAP

The F-flap was actually developed from the end of 2008. We considered running it in 2009, but figured we had more fundamental issues… We had an F-flap advantage early on, then improved it and so the original wing, RW80, was superseded by RW75, which is a more efficient version of F-flap, but the swing in performance up and down through the year was partly due to F-flap sensitivity.

Early on, circuits with high F-flap sensitivity, like Montréal, played into our hands, but subsequently there were other things. Around the time of the Turkish GP, we felt we'd closed the gap, but then had a run of races where we appeared to lose ground, for a variety of reasons, including issues we had with front wings, particularly our third iteration, FW3.

We were slow off the mark on the blown diffuser. We spotted it as soon as the Red Bull RB6 was launched, but were working on large aerodynamic projects at the time. A little bit later, we realised the value in it and dropped our other project. For that reason, we were a race after Ferrari and Renault in introducing it.

MP4-25 DIDN'T LIKE THE BUMPS

The car's unhappiness on bumps was pretty much down to the aerodynamic characteristics. To get the most out of it aerodynamically, we ran it at a given attitude and stiffness. Even though we played around with different set-ups, we kept coming back to the same one. We put a lot of effort in, from the first race in Bahrain where we were losing out to the Red Bulls in the bumpy corners. And we put a lot of effort in after Silverstone where we weren't handling the bumps particularly well.

We didn't need to change the stiffness for the blown floor, but the reason we've got more performance out of it is that we've learned more about how to rebalance the car. At Silverstone, it wasn't delivering to expectations, although it wasn't actually any worse than the old floor.

If you go back a few years, all the designers used to put the exhaust out through the diffuser, and we went away from it when Ferrari bucked the trend and went to high

TECHNICAL SPECIFICATIONS

ENGINE
MAKE/MODEL Mercedes-Benz FO 108X
CONFIGURATION 2400cc V8 (90 degree)
SPARK PLUGS NGK
ECU FIA standard issue
FUEL Mobil
OIL Mobil 1
BATTERY GS Yuasa

TRANSMISSION
GEARBOX McLaren
FORWARD GEARS Seven
CLUTCH AP Racing

CHASSIS
CHASSIS MODEL McLaren MP4-25
FRONT SUSPENSION LAYOUT Double wishbones and pushrod operating torsion bar and damper

REAR SUSPENSION LAYOUT
Double wishbone and pushrod operating torsion bar and damper
DAMPERS Koni
TYRES Bridgestone
WHEELS Enkei
BRAKE DISCS Carbone Industrie
BRAKE PADS Carbone Industrie
BRAKE CALIPERS Akebono
FUEL TANK ATL
INSTRUMENTS McLaren Electronic Systems

DIMENSIONS
LENGTH Not disclosed
WIDTH Not disclosed
HEIGHT Not disclosed
WHEELBASE Not disclosed
TRACK front Not disclosed
rear Not disclosed
WEIGHT Not disclosed

Team McLaren Mercedes

exhausts. The argument was primarily the instability you get from the on/off blowing of the floor, but now we're all a bit more intelligent in how we deal with that. One of the problems was that you'd get on the throttle, pick up rear downforce and the car understeered. It's great having a load of rear end mid-corner, but it doesn't necessarily make the car quicker if you're lacking front end. We learned more about the floor itself and the way to use it.

THE DRIVERS WORKED WELL TOGETHER
There wasn't much divergence between the drivers. In previous years, it's been quite problematic: Kimi and Montoya was a nightmare! We ended up going different routes on wings and even front suspension, but these two liked surprisingly similar set-ups. Lewis does use the brakes differently, as he brakes very hard and just prefers a different brake material.

Lewis and Jenson have different driving styles, but not so wildly different that we have to go in different directions. The biggest difference we saw was at Monza, where we had two packages developed in parallel, and it's a shame we didn't see which was the right choice!

The drivers have been good for each other. Lewis thought he was going to have an easy ride of it, then he was outqualified several times, Jenson picked up the wins where he didn't, and it made him raise his game. Every driver has a bad day and, if the guy on the other side of the garage is a good reference, then your performance is underwritten. If only one is strong and he's having a bad day, then you're in trouble.

EXXON MOBIL KEEPS PUSHING TO DEVELOP FUEL
There's no reason to say that the Mercedes engine had a significant advantage. The Ferrari certainly isn't a weak engine and the Renault can't be that bad, as you can't get pole at nearly every race without having a decent engine… It was unreasonable to complain that they've been hard done by with the engine freeze. Even now, there are plenty of parts of the engine inlet, let's say, that are free. Exxon Mobil put in a massive effort to develop our fuels, and somehow it's lumped in the pool and not recognised. Apparently that should be neutralised and I don't agree with that. Mercedes does do a fantastic job with the engine, though. It's certainly among the best and very reliable."

FERRARI

PIONEERING THE TILTED ENGINE AND GEARBOX

By Aldo Costa
(Technical Director)

"We had the opportunity to have a complete rethink of the back-end layout after the 2009 World Championship, and did various configurations of engine and gearbox positions. We ended up with a tilted position, about 3.5 degrees, with a very, very narrow gearbox at the bottom that allowed us a lot of scope for development of the double diffuser.

We had to have a performance gain reasonable enough to justify time loss for a rising centre of gravity, and it was a pretty deep analysis to establish the threshold. We had a much more extreme configuration in the wind tunnel and what we ended up with was something of a compromise.

There was also the different fuel regulation to consider, with the cancellation of refuelling. The tank area was massively different, so all packaging of that area was a lot more difficult. We had to have a reasonable wheelbase to optimise the packaging of radiators, and so on. It was an intense and difficult job.

It was good to see cars with unique solutions. We had the tilted engine/gearbox and the wheel rim design, Red Bull Racing had the blown exhaust, McLaren had the blown rear wing, so there was novelty in all the cars. At that time, we were already working on the blown diffuser, but we weren't ready to race it. We didn't think about the blown rear wing. Having seen these two solutions, there was an incentive to try to understand the blown exhaust more quickly and the blown wing from zero, plus our normal development. We knew that our double diffuser was just a first version and that there was a lot of development in it.

BLOWN DIFFUSER IS HARD TO MASTER
Our F-duct appeared first, because the blown diffuser was more difficult, not only as an aerodynamic concept, but for the car layout too. It was more intrusive, more demanding in terms of temperature generation, wishbone protection, floor protection, bodywork protection and with longer lead-time components.

An exhaust is a long-lead component, as running the dyno to verify and develop the exhaust is a bigger project. We saw the Red Bull RB6 at the end of February in Barcelona

with this solution, and our first one came at the European GP at Valencia in June. We and Renault were the first after Red Bull Racing, and it worked straight away. Instead of rushing it, we wanted to deeply understand and analyse the system and be sure that when we went on the track we had a positive result. You can't test, so it was very difficult. We were conservative with the first solution in some aspects of installation. By Suzuka, we were on the fourth iteration of exhaust system since Valencia.

THREE-PIECE FRONT WING WORKS WELL
The three-piece front wing for the British GP was a separate aero concept from the blown floor. It was pretty new for us, because we had a lot of experience with the two-plane wing. It was a development focused on the high-speed aero-balance types of circuit, and we found quite a good advantage there. We kept it for Singapore and other types of track where you need this kind of characteristic. At Monza and Spa-Francorchamps, we had a dedicated front wing specific to those tracks, which is slightly different to what other teams did.

We crash-tested a new gearbox in July. It was organised so that when we had a new-generation double diffuser available, both drivers had the possibility of running it. Fernando had tried this gearbox before, but without the new diffuser. There were several diffuser steps pre-planned, and we had to swap to a different gearbox main case at the correct time for the diffuser evolution. The gearbox was the same inside.

We had a bit of drop-off around the Turkish GP, and it was a combination of things. When you have a project like a blown exhaust, you dedicate a lot of resource to it and something suffers. Other teams maybe developed more traditional parts and waited longer for their blown floors and F-duct. We decided to do vice versa, and started both projects immediately. At Barcelona and Istanbul, we had the new blown wing, our first iteration, and probably didn't understand a couple of areas.

In my opinion, that wing was underperforming in those two races and, combined with not having any other developments at that time, it meant our performance wasn't that great. Once we understood it, we modified and improved it. From the Canadian GP, we

THE TEAM

PERSONNEL
PRESIDENT Luca di Montezemolo
CHIEF EXECUTIVE OFFICER Amedeo Felisa
TEAM PRINCIPAL Stefano Domenicali
TECHNICAL DIRECTOR Aldo Costa (above)
ASSISTANT TECHNICAL DIRECTOR Pat Fry
TEAM MANAGER Chris Dyer
ENGINE DIRECTOR Luca Marmorini
SPORTING DIRECTOR Massimo Rivola
CAR DESIGN & DEVELOPMENT CONSULTANT
Rory Byrne
CHIEF DESIGNER Nikolas Tombazis
CHIEF AERODYNAMICIST Marco de Luca
HEAD OF CAR PERFORMANCE Marco Fainello
HEAD OF STRUCTURES DEPARTMENT Davide Terletti
CHIEF TRACK ENGINEER Mattia Binotto
RACE ENGINE MANAGER Luigi Fraboni
DRIVERS Fernando Alonso, Felipe Massa
RACE ENGINEER (Massa) Rob Smedley
RACE ENGINEER (Alonso) Andrea Stella
TEST DRIVER Giancarlo Fisichella
PERFORMANCE DEVELOPMENT Luigi Mazzola
CHIEF MECHANIC (Massa) Filippo Milliani
CHIEF MECHANIC (Alonso) Giuseppe Rizzo
TOTAL NUMBER OF EMPLOYEES 900+
NUMBER IN RACE TEAM 90
TEAM BASE Maranello, Italy
TELEPHONE +39 0536 949450
WEBSITE www.ferrari.com

TEAM STATS
IN F1 SINCE 1950 **FIRST GRAND PRIX** Britain 1950
STARTS 812 **WINS** 215 **POLE POSITIONS** 205
FASTEST LAPS 223 **PODIUMS** 632 **POINTS** 4473.5
CONSTRUCTORS' TITLES 16 **DRIVERS' TITLES** 15

SPONSORS
FIAT, Marlboro, Shell, Santander, Etihad Airways, Bridgestone, AMD, Acer, Mubadala Abu Dhabi

7 FELIPE MASSA   **8** FERNANDO ALONSO

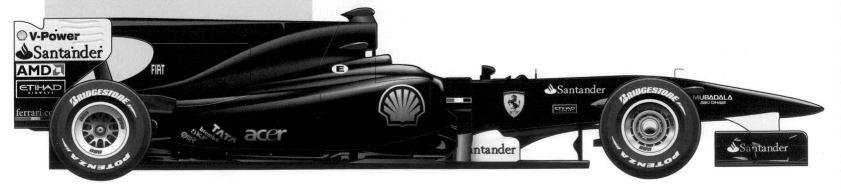

TECHNICAL SPECIFICATIONS

ENGINE
MAKE/MODEL Ferrari 056
CONFIGURATION 2398cc V8
(90 degree)
SPARK PLUGS Not disclosed
ECU FIA standard issue
FUEL Shell
OIL Shell
BATTERY Not disclosed

TRANSMISSION
GEARBOX Ferrari
FORWARD GEARS Seven
CLUTCH Not disclosed

CHASSIS
CHASSIS MODEL Ferrari F10
FRONT SUSPENSION LAYOUT
Independent pushrod-activated
torsion springs
REAR SUSPENSION LAYOUT
Independent pushrod-activated
torsion springs
DAMPERS Not disclosed
TYRES Bridgestone
WHEELS BBS
BRAKE DISCS Brembo
BRAKE PADS Not disclosed
BRAKE CALIPERS Not disclosed
FUEL TANK Not disclosed
INSTRUMENTS
Ferrari/Magneti Marelli

DIMENSIONS
LENGTH Not disclosed
WIDTH Not disclosed
HEIGHT Not disclosed
WHEELBASE Not disclosed
TRACK front Not disclosed
rear Not disclosed
WEIGHT 620kg (including
driver and camera)

started to have quite a big package of other developments at every race, because we'd done the wing and floor by then.

FAVOURING EITHER HARD OR SOFT
With the tyres, there were mixed messages depending on driver style and behaviour, in terms of how capable they were of warming up the tyre. There were drivers with fewer problems warming up the hard tyre than others, but then maybe they didn't like the soft tyre that much because of overheating reasons or moving sensation.

Conversely, other drivers preferred the higher grip of the soft tyre, and accepted this moving sensation, and didn't like the hard tyre because in damp or cold conditions at some circuits they were struggling with warm-up. For sure we have paid more attention in the past to saving the tyre, being gentle with it. It's not a secret that our car in the past was like this, and we saw it in Singapore, where we built a gap with the soft tyre, but it disappeared on the hard. Other cars were the opposite.

DIFFERENT DRIVING STYLES
We did quite a lot of development on brakes. At circuits that are hard on them – Montréal, Monza, Singapore – our car was very good. The brake system and performance in general was a strong point. We were struggling more on circuits like Barcelona, Istanbul and Budapest compared to our main rivals.

The arrival of Fernando [Alonso] in the team was very positive, as he is a two-time champion who'd driven with big teams. It took him very little time to settle in. It was like he'd been here 10 years. It was black and white, like a switch. As soon as we started working with him, there were no issues at all, and he was the most positive bloke in the team, always pushing, always optimistic. He was a real asset, both in the car and out of it.

In terms of driving style, Fernando and Felipe [Massa] are quite different. Yet, in terms of overall performance direction, like new components and development, they were in line. They require a slightly different mechanical set-up: Fernando is a bit more aggressive, Felipe smoother.

We had updates on the diffuser in Japan and Korea, then some other modifications for the last two races. It got harder and more difficult, because we had the 2011 car to think about. It's always difficult when you're fighting for the championship, as you need to be careful to make a well-balanced choice."

MERCEDES

THE TEAM

PERSONNEL

TEAM PRINCIPAL Ross Brawn (above)
CHIEF EXECUTIVE OFFICER Nick Fry
CHIEF OPERATING OFFICER Rob Thomas
VICE-PRESIDENT, MERCEDES-BENZ MOTORSPORT
Norbert Haug
MANAGING DIRECTOR, MERCEDES-BENZ
HIGH-PERFORMANCE ENGINES Thomas Fuhr
HEAD OF AERODYNAMICS Loic Bigois
HEAD OF VEHICLE ENGINEERING & DYNAMICS
Craig Wilson
CHIEF DESIGNER John Owen
SPORTING DIRECTOR Ron Meadows
CHIEF ENGINEER Russell Cooley
DRIVERS Nico Rosberg, Michael Schumacher
SPORTING DIRECTOR Ron Meadows
CHIEF RACE ENGINEER Simon Cole
SENIOR RACE ENGINEER (Schumacher) Andrew Shovlin
SENIOR RACE ENGINEER (Rosberg) Jock Clear
CHIEF MECHANIC Matthew Deane
TEST/THIRD DRIVER Nick Heidfeld
TOTAL NUMBER OF EMPLOYEES 450
NUMBER IN RACE TEAM 45
TEAM BASE Brackley, England
TELEPHONE +44 (0)1280 844000
WEBSITE www.mercedes-gp.com

TEAM STATS

IN F1 SINCE 1999, as BAR, then Honda Racing then Brawn GP
FIRST GRAND PRIX Australia 1999
STARTS 207 **WINS** 9 **POLE POSITIONS** 8
FASTEST LAPS 4 **PODIUMS** 33 **POINTS** 710
CONSTRUCTORS' TITLES 1 **DRIVERS' TITLES** 1

SPONSORS

Petronas, Autonomy, Syntium, Aabar, Bridgestone, MIG Bank,
Deutsche Post, Monster Energy, Henri Lloyd, Graham London

3 MICHAEL SCHUMACHER   **4 NICO ROSBERG**

MAKING UP FOR A SHORTFALL IN ENGINEERING

By Ross Brawn
(Team Principal)

"In the normal process of development, there is a core idea of what sort of car you want to create, and then the various departments of the team contribute towards achieving that vision. We got the 2009 vision very easily, but this time we didn't have enough clarity about what we wanted to do.

The 2010 car became a bit of a compromise in all sorts of areas. We changed the team quite a lot at the beginning of 2009, and I hadn't put in place a robust enough engineering strategy to give the clarity needed. The difference between an average car and a great one is half a second, and that's what we trailed by all year.

I think it was a combination of things. I chair various meetings that help firm up what we are doing, but with other issues I wasn't so active on that side. Also, [deputy technical director] Jorg Zander left at the beginning of 2009, which left a vacuum.

Because we didn't have the right engineering structure, we weren't adventurous enough. What I'm seeing now from our group is much more aggressive solutions, which are well engineered so there's no compromise in what we want to achieve. For next year, we've been pretty bold on what sort of car we want to create and we've got a good enough engineering structure now to support the ideas.

This time last year, we couldn't have done those ideas. We couldn't have done a pullrod suspension last year because the group was too fragmented. We basically carved 40% out of everything we had and it was as crude as that. It happened very quickly, and the only fair way was to say to every department that they had to lose 40% of their staff. And that takes a while to settle down. It's not an excuse, but starting a new car after that, you don't feel very confident about taking on anything too ambitious. We did some fairly ambitious things for 2009, and I think next year we'll have our confidence back.

SLOW TO ADOPT SEASON'S DESIGN TRICKS

The 2010 season started with a couple of interesting technologies that we didn't get

hold of quickly enough: the F-duct and the exhaust-energised diffuser, which is an area where we only later started to understand the nuances. Early in the season, we also lengthened the wheelbase to give a greater range on the weight distribution. We were too constrained by the original layout.

I think it's fair to say, too, that under the existing rules it's tougher to catch up than it used to be. We benefited from that in 2009, when we got ahead of most of our rivals with the double diffuser. Catching up during the season is very difficult, and all teams will be more limited with resources in the future, meaning that your approach and philosophy of how you design the car, develop the car and run the season have to reflect that.

IT'S NOW HARDER TO CHANGE MID-SEASON

A lot of stuff is homologated now as well, including the chassis and the crash structure, so if you don't quite get it right at the beginning of the year, there are limits on what you can do. You can change the gearbox in theory but, because you can't change the crash structure, you'd have to redo the crash tests with a different gearbox, so it's much more challenging and more difficult.

Our (foot-operated) F-duct worked differently to everyone else's, and we did wonder whether to take a step back to a conventional engine cover. What we had offered some benefits, obviously a more efficient flow to the rear wing, but that became rather redundant with the F-duct, and we tried to hang onto it and do the F-duct in a different way, which maybe we shouldn't have.

Also, the way things evolved, there were a couple of things that we would have done later on in the year with the floor that we couldn't do because it carries the channels for the F-duct. It's one of those things where conceptually you get a bit tied up. If we were doing it again for next year, we would do it very differently.

UNDERSTANDING THE BLOWN FLOOR

With the blown floor, we only got a reasonable understanding later on. I wouldn't say we didn't appreciate the exhaust complexities, but we certainly

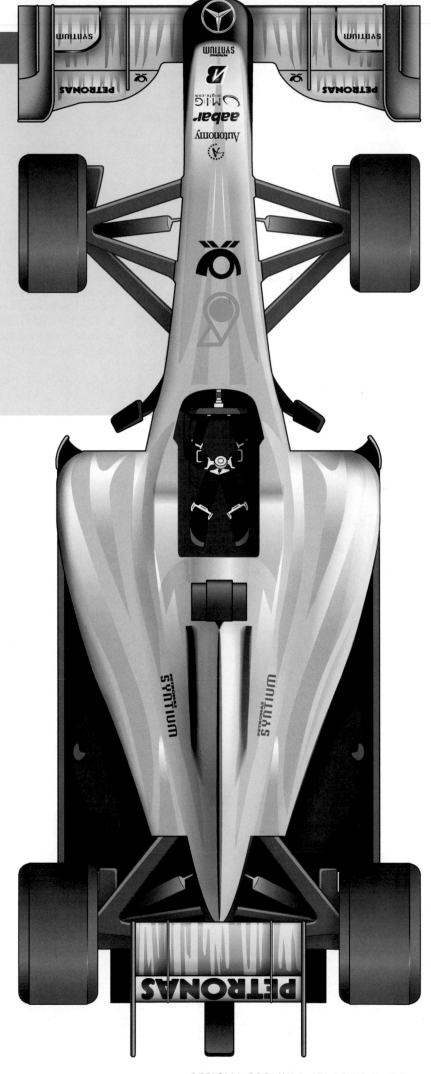

ENGINE
MAKE/MODEL Mercedes-Benz FO108X
CONFIGURATION 2400c V8 (90 degree)
SPARK PLUGS NGK
ECU FIA standard issue
FUEL Petronas
OIL Petronas
BATTERY Not disclosed

TRANSMISSION
GEARBOX Mercedes GP
FORWARD GEARS Seven
CLUTCH Not disclosed

CHASSIS
CHASSIS MODEL Mercedes MGP W01
FRONT SUSPENSION LAYOUT
Wishbones and pushrod-activated
torsion springs and rockers
REAR SUSPENSION LAYOUT
Wishbones and pushrod-activated
torsion springs and rockers
DAMPERS Sachs
TYRES Bridgestone

WHEELS BBS
BRAKE DISCS
Brembo
BRAKE PADS
Brembo
BRAKE CALIPERS
Brembo
FUEL TANK ATL
INSTRUMENTS
Not disclosed

DIMENSIONS
LENGTH 4800mm
WIDTH 1800mm
HEIGHT 950mm
WHEELBASE
Not disclosed
TRACK
front Not disclosed
rear Not disclosed
WEIGHT 620kg (including
driver and camera)

MERCEDES**GP**
PETRONAS
FORMULA ONE™ TEAM

didn't realise the subtleties of how the floor could work. We were also constrained by the gearbox, because we weren't adventurous enough with the layout. We toyed with having another go at the transmission case, but then decided that with the resources we had, we needed to deploy our efforts elsewhere.

At some tracks with certain combinations of corners, the car worked quite well. In Montréal for example, we had the F-duct working well, so that helped. It was pretty good on braking, and in slow/medium-speed stuff it wasn't bad. Generally, we got too much high-speed understeer, which is difficult to deal with, the balance of entry and exit. The car wasn't bad in Singapore. I'd say actually we got a reasonable balance most of the time. It's just that when we got to it we weren't quite fast enough.

MICHAEL FAILS TO HIT THE MARK
What we saw with Michael [Schumacher] was a little surprising. The first few races weren't a surprise, because Nico [Rosberg] is very strong, and Michael was gradually getting into that gap and at Barcelona was quicker. However, then it seemed to fall back, which was a surprise. I think Nico responded and did a fabulous job, setting a really good standard for Michael to try and match.

A lot of people talked about tyres. You can have one argument that drivers should cope with whatever they've got, and Michael went through a range of different situations at Ferrari, with different engineers and groups, and yet was always strong.

You could see the areas where Michael wasn't as quick as Nico, and it was mainly slow- and medium-speed stuff. At Monza, for instance, Nico was able to ride the kerbs with more confidence than Michael, so it's a slightly peculiar deficit. It wasn't high-speed stuff where bravery and reactions and car control are the factors. In those areas, they were well matched. I'm hopeful that with different tyres and different cars, plus a winter of reflecting and testing, we'll have two strong drivers next year.

Overall, the Mercedes MGP W01 evolved more than being a vision of what was needed. Since it became clear to me that we didn't have enough structure in the engineering department, the department has been reorganised for 2011. I can now feel that we've got a vision and an idea of what we want to do."

RENAULT

THE TEAM

PERSONNEL
CHAIRMAN Gerard Lopez
TEAM PRINCIPAL & MANAGING DIRECTOR
Eric Boullier
TECHNICAL DIRECTOR James Allison (above)
CHIEF OPERATING OFFICER Patrick Louis
CHIEF DESIGNER Tim Densham
DEPUTY TECHNICAL DIRECTOR Naoki Tokunaga
SPORTING DIRECTOR Steve Nielsen
CHIEF RACE ENGINEER Alan Permane
HEAD OF ENGINE TRACK OPERATIONS Remi Taffin
HEAD OF AERODYMANICS Dirk de Beer
CHIEF MECHANIC Gavin Hudson
DRIVERS Robert Kubica, Vitaly Petrov
RACE ENGINEER (Kubica) Simon Rennie
RACE ENGINEER (Petrov) Mark Slade
THIRD DRIVER Ho-Pin Tung
RESERVE DRIVERS Jan Charouz, Jerome d'Ambrosio
TOTAL NUMBER OF EMPLOYEES 740
NUMBER IN RACE TEAM 90
TEAM BASE Enstone, England
TELEPHONE +44 (0)1608 678000
WEBSITE www.renaultf1.com

TEAM STATS
IN F1 SINCE 1977–1985 then from 2002 **FIRST GRAND PRIX** Britain 1977, then Australia 2002 **STARTS** 282
WINS 35 **POLE POSITIONS** 50 **FASTEST LAPS** 31
PODIUMS 96 **POINTS** 1309 **CONSTRUCTORS' TITLES** 2 **DRIVERS' TITLES** 2

SPONSORS
Renault, Hewlett-Packard, Snoras Bank, Total, TW Steel, Bridgestone, Lada, Trina Solar, Vyborg Shipyard JSC, Flagman vodka, Japan Rags

 11 ROBERT KUBICA   **12** VITALY PETROV

A YEAR SPENT CATCHING THE TOP TEAMS

By James Allison
(Technical Director)

"There was considerable speculation about the team at the end of the 2009 season, but no-one at the coal face can influence that, so you just keep going. No-one ever said back off and, other than it being emotionally difficult, it didn't impact. The redundancies at the start of 2009 had a much bigger effect.

Last November, we shut the wind tunnel down for four weeks and put a new rolling road in, and just over 18 months ago we'd commissioned a considerably bigger CFD facility, three times what we had in terms of staffing. The bigger effect was the CFD, which produced a continuous stream of good, solid development work.

NEW ROLLING ROAD SPEEDS THINGS UP
The wind-tunnel investment was also extremely welcome. We had a canvas polyester belt before, and now, like pretty much everyone else, have a steel belt. The problem with the old canvas belts was that you have got to get the tyre the right shape on the belt, so you have to squash it into the belt in order to make it bulge to the correct shape. The canvas belts couldn't tolerate the amount of squash you needed, as it made them overheat and so wear out, and that was limiting.

The steel belt also speeds up and slows down much more quickly. Although it's only two or three minutes per run, when you do as many runs as we do, that's an awful lot of time, as throughput is so important. Our old rolling road used to take about 30s from one yaw angle to another, whereas this one does it in a couple of seconds. The productivity improvement is substantial, especially now that we have limited access to our tunnels through the resource-restriction agreement.

The basic car configuration, though, was all done prior to the implementation of the new rolling road, and shutting it down for four weeks probably cost us about 0.2s in car development terms. However, the subsequent rate of development – the gains around the front wing for example – more than justified that. Floors changed fast too. We were onto our mk7 floor by Singapore and, given the lead time, that's a high rate of change.

STICKING WITH THE BROAD NOSE
We stayed with the lower, broader nose. We tried other heights and widths endlessly but, at a certain point, you have to commit. You could say, 'Well, we believe a high, slender nose is going to allow the most high-energy air to make its way to the back of the car so we'll make it work', but it feels ever so pig-headed making something that you know is a little bit slower at that point than your other lower, fatter, less-fashionable nose. Actually, our nose was higher and slimmer than the 2009 nose, and as it bulges over the front wing it generates front downforce for you.

BLOWN FLOOR TRICKY TO IMPLEMENT
We had an inkling of the F-duct before it appeared. You hear noises from here and there and it was clear what was going on when McLaren launched their car. The blown floor was very clear the day Red Bull put it on their car at the final pre-season test. However, blown floors are quite tricky things to do, and it took us until Valencia. That was realising that it was going to be important and putting a lot of effort into it. Ferrari was the same.

A lot of teams did the F-duct much sooner than we did. That was down to a straightforward decision I took to push on with all our other developments. We were planning to introduce it at the British GP, but when we tried it in the tunnel we couldn't make it work reliably. I'd seen lots of other teams bring it out quickly and then struggle for a couple of race weekends, so we canned it and chose a different direction which pushed it back to Spa-Francorchamps, where it worked very well.

THROTTLE SENSITIVITY AFFECTS FLOOR
With the blown floor, throttle sensitivity was a big issue. It impacted on our set-up and was quite a change in the way that the car felt, one that initially wasn't at all popular… It's tricky to introduce something like that with no testing, and it's very hard to do back-to-back tests during a race weekend.

We ran it in Valencia and it was okay, but with corners that didn't really reveal some of the uglier sides of what it does. Then it wasn't quite so helpful and we resolved to settle the matter at the Hungaroring. We saw that we

ENGINE
MAKE/MODEL Renault RS27 2010
CONFIGURATION 2400cc V8 (90 degree)
SPARK PLUGS Not disclosed
ECU FIA standard issue
FUEL Total
OIL Elf
BATTERY Renault F1

TRANSMISSION
GEARBOX Renault
FORWARD GEARS Seven
CLUTCH AP Racing

CHASSIS
CHASSIS MODEL Renault R30
FRONT SUSPENSION LAYOUT
Carbon-fibre top and bottom wishbones operating an inboard rocker via a pushrod connected to a torsion bar and inboard dampers

REAR SUSPENSION LAYOUT
Carbon-fibre top and bottom wishbones with pushrod-operated torsion bars and transverse-mounted dampers
DAMPERS Penske
TYRES Bridgestone
WHEELS OZ Racing
BRAKE DISCS Hitco
BRAKE PADS Hitco
BRAKE CALIPERS AP Racing (up to Brtish GP) then Brembo
FUEL TANK ATL
INSTRUMENTS Renault F1

DIMENSIONS
LENGTH 5050mm
WIDTH 1800mm
HEIGHT 950mm
WHEELBASE Not disclosed
TRACK front 1450mm
rear 1400mm
WEIGHT 620kg (including driver and camera)

RENAULT F1 Team

were better with the blown floor than without, and the drivers could remind themselves what the old car felt like, which was far from a bed of roses.

We made progress relative to the leaders. We put about 1.7s on the car through 2010 but, in terms of relative movement, it was about 0.5s. There's only about 0.1s between grid positions where we are, so that 0.5s is four or five places.

There are issues associated with new drivers, and the two biggest areas where we lost a fair amount of development effort were power steering and brakes. Robert [Kubica] and Vitaly [Petrov] both like a much stiffer brake pedal than we've been used to, and it took us quite a while to get that to their taste. In the end, we had to commit to a stiffer caliper.

With the power steering, both drivers like a much lighter car than we've been used to providing in the past. It took a while to do. It's a fiddly bit of machining and a complex thing to get right. They were both saying, 'Look I'm going to be a lot better when you give me the brakes and steering I want!' At least they weren't dragging us down different routes with it, which was fortuitous.

KUBICA IS FAST BUT HE'S DEMANDING TOO
We're very fortunate to have Robert in the team. If we can give him a car that's even half capable of a championship, he'll get one. Not everyone in the pitlane can say that about their drivers. He expects a lot from everyone: he's positive, demanding and always pushing.

Vitaly ebbed and flowed. Some weekends he was absolutely first-rate, others he struggled. Many things are much to be admired: he's a brave and committed racer and he's not easily flustered in a race. He's also up against a fiercely good team-mate without much testing. It's a very tough point in F1 history to be a rookie, and particularly tough for him.

The rules change quite a lot for 2011: no double-deck diffusers, no F-duct, adjustable top rear wings, changed front-wing endplate rules, new tyres. Personally, I live in a state of perpetual fear that everything isn't going to be good enough. I find that it's better to feel that way, so long as you don't get ludicrous about it... We've got an absolutely top driver, the same engine as Red Bull Racing, and so you don't have to be a genius to work out why they're going quicker: they've got more downforce than us."

WILLIAMS

THE TEAM

PERSONNEL
TEAM PRINCIPAL Sir Frank Williams
DIRECTOR OF ENGINEERING Patrick Head
CHAIRMAN Adam Parr
TECHNICAL DIRECTOR Sam Michael (above)
CHIEF EXECUTIVE OFFICER Alex Burns
CHIEF DESIGNER Ed Wood
CHIEF OF AERODYNAMICS Jon Tomlinson
SENIOR SYSTEMS ENGINEER John Russell
TEAM MANAGER Tim Newton, then Dickie Stanford
DRIVERS Rubens Barrichello, Nico Hulkenberg
RACE ENGINEER (Barrichello) Tony Ross
RACE ENGINEER (Hulkenberg) Tom McCullough
TEST TEAM MANAGER Dickie Stanford
TEST/THIRD DRIVER Valtteri Bottas
CHIEF MECHANIC Carl Gaden
TOTAL NUMBER OF EMPLOYEES 520
NUMBER IN RACE TEAM 70
TEAM BASE Grove, England
TELEPHONE +44 (0)1235 777700
WEBSITE www.attwilliams.com

TEAM STATS
IN F1 SINCE 1973 **FIRST GRAND PRIX** Argentina 1973
STARTS 604 **WINS** 113 **POLE POSITIONS** 126
FASTEST LAPS 130 **PODIUMS** 296 **POINTS** 2675
CONSTRUCTORS' TITLES 9 **DRIVERS' TITLES** 7

SPONSORS
Philips, RBS, AT&T, Randstad, Accenture, Air Asia, Bridgestone, Hell Energy Drink, McGregor, Oris, Ridge, Thomson Reuters, Allianz, GAC, MAN, PPG, Rays, Sparco

9 RUBENS BARRICHELLO   **10** NICO HULKENBERG

HARNESSING A NEW ENGINE AND NEW THINKING

By Sam Michael
(Technical Director)
"The big change for us for the 2010 season was the arrival of the Cosworth engine. We certainly had a pretty busy time over the winter, packaging it and changing the gearbox and back of the chassis to suit.

Not having engine continuity going into a year with no refuelling made it difficult to size the fuel tank accurately. The amount of fuel that we had for the highest-consumption track was within 0.5kg of the tank capacity, so we got it bang on and a lot of effort went into that. We did our analysis through studying the Cosworth data we had from 2006, and looking at the brake-specific fuel consumption they had on their dyno, and comparing them.

OPTING FOR A LONGER CHASSIS
We put a lot of priority into chassis length, making it longer rather than wider. If you make it wider, you push the radiator out and make the undercut too small, losing downforce. We were shortish in terms of wheelbase between the back of the chassis and rear axle, but not short in terms of overall chassis length. It was just because the gearbox was short. It was very different from the transmission used with the Toyota engine in 2009, because the clutch moved from the engine to the gearbox. That changes all the clutch actuator and hydraulic system, and also changes the vibrations on the gearbox and engine.

We never thought of running an F-duct. The first time we saw one was at the tests in February and most teams brought them in at the same time. We certainly never considered that the driver wasn't part of the car. That's key to the interpretation, which could have been challenged, but no-one ever did.

CHANNELLING AIR THROUGH THE COCKPIT
We had a hole beneath the driver's leg and enough positive pressure inside the cockpit to stall the rear wing – we saw that from CFD. So the driver travels along with his left leg over the hole sealing the duct. Then, when he goes down the straight, he moves his leg off it and the air flows through the hole and through the chassis to the engine cover spine to the slot on the rear wing, which stalls. It was quite simple and we didn't need to take any feed ducts

from outside. The positive cockpit pressure was plenty. As soon as the driver pulls his leg off the hole, he can feel it trying to suck his leg back.

The downside to our system was that the driver had to keep it sealed all the time. For Rubens [Barrichello], it was easy because he's a right-foot braker. However, if Nico [Hulkenberg] had to brake really hard, his leg could come off the hole and unstall it. It took him a while to get used to it. We had to re-do his seat three or four times to accommodate his leg action.

The blown diffuser we did think of, and that was really annoying. We had it in our wind tunnel in October 2009 but, because we were changing engines, we didn't have an exhaust system and we had to release an exhaust system to the design team around November for the start of the season. Because we had a lot of loading on the design office due to the engine change, we postponed the blown diffuser project and put it on the back burner.

TAKING THE TOP-EXIT ROUTE
We said, 'right, let's get out a top-exit exhaust', because we didn't have enough confidence to just go with a blown diffuser. We had no idea whether the temperatures would be insane and whether we could cope with them. If you look at what Red Bull Racing did, that's exactly what we would have done. They did three tests with a top-exit exhaust and only then tried a blown diffuser, so they had a solid back-up. If, in that last test, they'd roasted the car, they could just have gone back to the top-exit exhaust.

The exhaust programme is completely integrated with the bodywork and aero programmes, so it gets quite complicated. We were onto it straight away after we saw them run it. That's why when we did bring it to the track it worked straight away – we knew immediately to blow straight into the diffuser. There were a couple of teams that even late into the season didn't blow into the spat.

On our car and the Red Bull, the closer you can get to the tyre, the more downforce you can get, but it's a matter of getting out there without burning the tyre. As soon as you have car speed it's fine, but the worst condition is when you're at a pit stop or on the grid. The plume is coming outboard, and if it starts to heat the side of the tyre you risk a tyre failure. We spent a lot of time fine-tuning that.

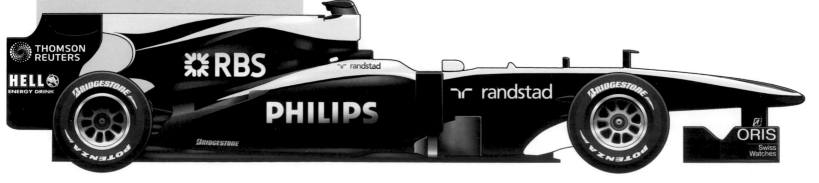

TECHNICAL SPECIFICATIONS

ENGINE
MAKE/MODEL Cosworth CA2010
CONFIGURATION 2400cc V8
SPARK PLUGS Not disclosed
ECU FIA standard issue
FUEL Not disclosed
OIL Not disclosed
BATTERY Not disclosed

TRANSMISSION
GEARBOX WilliamsF1
FORWARD GEARS Seven
CLUTCH AP Racing

CHASSIS
CHASSIS MODEL Williams FW32
FRONT SUSPENSION LAYOUT
Carbon-fibre double wishbones with
composite toelink and pushrod-activated
springs and anti-roll bar

REAR SUSPENSION LAYOUT
Double wishbones and
pushrod-activated springs
and anti-roll bar
DAMPERS WilliamsF1
TYRES Bridgestone
WHEELS RAYS
BRAKE DISCS Carbon Industrie
BRAKE PADS Carbon Industrie
BRAKE CALIPERS AP Racing
FUEL TANK Not disclosed
INSTRUMENTS WilliamsF1

DIMENSIONS
LENGTH 4900mm
WIDTH 1800mm
HEIGHT 950mm
WHEELBASE 3200mm
TRACK front Not disclosed
rear Not disclosed
WEIGHT 620kg (including
driver and camera)

HEAT PANELLING PROVES EXPENSIVE
Then there's the mechanical side of the floor. We use a
lot of what are called PyroSic panels on the floor for heat
resistance, and they're extremely expensive. The set of
panels for the first diffuser was 25,000 Euros per floor.
When we developed the plume and got confidence in
it, we got that down massively, to about a tenth of the
original cost. At first, we used PyroSic everywhere…

The downforce from the blown floor was 100%
consistent. We did a Kimball test pre-Valencia and, as
soon as the throttle is on, bang, it's there all the time.
That's why we didn't need to back-to-back test it at the
European GP.

ENGINE MAPPING WAS A BOON
Using the engine mapping to improve it makes a
difference. We didn't do that to start with, we did it
from the Belgian GP onwards. Once you start using it
in braking as well, it's better again, an even bigger step
than the initial floor. You get downforce everywhere
and there's no change between on- and off-throttle.
Cosworth spent a lot of time on the dyno doing that.
The job they did was impressive, because we went out at
Spa-Francorchamps, first lap in all those wet sessions, and
it worked straight away, and it's a massive difference in
engine control. Both drivers said, 'I'm racing it for sure.'

With development, around the time of the Spanish
GP the other teams took a bigger step than we did. Our
real turnaround was at the Canadian GP. The car was
more competitive. We changed the aero package very
significantly for there, and that changed our direction.
We changed how we developed the car, and in terms of
philosophy it was quite a big change to what we'd done
for the past couple of years.

BARRICHELLO'S EXPERIENCE HELPS A LOT
Rubens is very good at feeding back what the problems
with the car are. When you bring developments to the
track with a driver like Rubens and have him tell you
exactly and very quickly what it's doing, that's really very
important. He has been exceptional for the team from
that point of view."

FORCE INDIA

THE TEAM

PERSONNEL

CHAIRMAN & TEAM PRINCIPAL Vijay Mallya
CO-OWNER Michiel Mol
DEPUTY TEAM PRINCIPAL Bob Fernley
CHIEF TECHNICAL OFFICER Otmar Szafnauer
TECHNICAL DIRECTOR Mark Smith
PRODUCTION DIRECTOR Bob Halliwell
DESIGN PROJECT LEADER 2010 Akio Haga
DESIGN PROJECT LEADER 2011 Ian Hall
HEAD OF R&D Simon Gardner
TEAM MANAGER Andy Stevenson
DRIVERS Vitantonio Liuzzi, Adrian Sutil
CHIEF ENGINEER Dominic Harlow (above)
RACE ENGINEER (Sutil) Bradley Joyce
RACE ENGINEER (Liuzzi) Gianpiero Lambiase
TEST/THIRD DRIVER Paul di Resta
HEAD OF CAR BUILD Nick Burrows
ASSISTANT TEAM MANAGER Mark Gray
CHIEF MECHANIC Andy Deeming
TOTAL NUMBER OF EMPLOYEES 280
NUMBER IN RACE TEAM 45
TEAM BASE Silverstone, England
TELEPHONE +44 (0)1327 850800
WEBSITE www.forceindiaf1.com

TEAM STATS

IN F1 SINCE 1991, as Jordan then Midland then Spyker
until 2007 **FIRST GRAND PRIX** USA 1991 **STARTS** 339
WINS 4 **POLE POSITIONS** 3 **FASTEST LAPS** 3
PODIUMS 21 **POINTS** 369 **CONSTRUCTORS' TITLES** 0
DRIVERS' TITLES 0

SPONSORS

Kingfisher, Medion, Alpinestars, Bridgestone, Whyte &
Mackay, Royal Challenge, Doublemint, Medion Mobile,
EADS, Airbus, Fly Kingfisher, Signature, UB Group, Reebok

 14 ADRIAN SUTIL   **15** VITANTONIO LIUZZI

BUILDING THE TEAM BACK UP AGAIN

By Dominic Harlow
(Chief Engineer)

"The only thing that was carried over from 2009 was the engine and the fact that we had the same driveline. There was a lot of difference because of the new fuel regulations and some of the aero changes.

In the wheelbase league table, we were towards the upper quartile, driven by some of the things done with the gearbox architecture, which was long and narrow to get the best from the double diffuser. Weight distribution is the other thing led by that, and I think that we got a reasonable direction early on. We felt happier with that envelope on this year's car.

In 2009, we stood out on the higher-speed tracks. We made some changes to the way we developed our aero, and that flattened our performance across a lot of the tracks. There was still a tendency towards higher-efficiency circuits being better, but equally at lower-speed places we weren't really disadvantaged until later in the year when people started to really make their double diffusers work. You saw the top-end levels of downforce getting significantly higher at tracks like those in Hungary and Singapore.

INSTANT PROGRESS WITH ITS F-DUCT

We became aware of the F-duct early, took one to the Turkish GP, and opted to blow the main rear-wing plane rather than the flap. It made our system quite powerful and we gained quite a lot of top speed from it. We had some problems initially and I think everyone had a race or two of headaches with F-ducts.

There are pros and cons to blowing the main plane. The obvious pro is getting a bigger stall from main plane, and the cons are that it's slightly more difficult to implement.

You have a variety of different main-plane angles and if you're attaching something to that which is attached to the engine cover and the rest of the car, it can be quite painful to make that readily adjustable. Perhaps with the flap you have a bit more inherent stability in the system. Our main issues were more with the physical implementation of it: design, making it all work and not having hundreds and hundreds of parts for all the different scenarios.

It's fair to say that Adrian was more comfortable with it than Tonio, who had

difficulty with how it was activated. We did some development on that, but not as much as other teams. I think some people have changed where they block it almost as often as their trousers, and anything driver-fit related does tend to go through a vast number of different iterations. We were actually relatively stable.

Upgrade-wise we've had seven different floors and probably another two or three detail changes on top of that. We also had probably four or five wholesale iterations of the front wing. Really, it was a case of trying to bring something to every race and a larger package every other race.

HAVING TO STICK TO BUDGET

We've got plenty of head room both on personnel and budget. The Jordan model and history has always been to outsource a lot of supply, the theory being that from the market you get a quick reaction and a better price than if you do the job in-house.

Budget is never enough, but we set a target and stuck to it pretty rigidly and were able to bring all that aero development out of it. In terms of staff numbers, we're pretty close to the magic 280, but that includes the cleaners…

INTRODUCING A BLOWN FLOOR

We first ran a blown floor in practice for the Hungarian GP and then raced it at Spa-Francorchamps. The other Mercedes teams were able to give us some help with what we needed to be able to run it. It was quite an integrated project. It's a useful step, and perhaps with the rear wing we made a good call with the main-plane direction and fundamentals. With the floor though, we've probably started on the bottom of the curve, whereas Red Bull Racing is much nearer the top of what you can get out of it.

We didn't have any tremendous battles with rebalancing the car, how the driver uses the throttle or set-up, but maybe that was a measure of what we were getting out of it versus others. It helps under braking as well, with stability, which is sometimes easier for the driver to pick up than the on-throttle stuff, especially in some of the slower corners or where you've got a big stop.

We did a bit of brake development, as things changed with the tyre-grip distribution

TECHNICAL SPECIFICATIONS

ENGINE
MAKE/MODEL Mercedes-Benz FO 108X
CONFIGURATION 2400cc V8 (90 degree)
SPARK PLUGS NGK
ECU FIA standard issue
FUEL Mobil
OIL Mobil 1
BATTERY Not disclosed

TRANSMISSION
GEARBOX McLaren
FORWARD GEARS Seven
CLUTCH AP Racing

CHASSIS
CHASSIS MODEL Force India VJM03
FRONT SUSPENSION LAYOUT
Aluminium uprights with carbon-fibre composite wishbones, trackrod and pushrod. Inboard chassis-mounted torsion springs, dampers and anti-roll bar assembly

REAR SUSPENSION LAYOUT
Aluminium uprights with carbon-fibre composite wishbones, trackrod and pushrod. Inboard gearbox-mounted torsion springs, dampers and anti-roll bar assembly
DAMPERS Penske
TYRES Bridgestone
WHEELS BBS
BRAKE DISCS Carbone Industrie
BRAKE PADS Carbone Industrie
BRAKE CALIPERS Carbone Industrie
FUEL TANK Not disclosed
INSTRUMENTS Not disclosed

DIMENSIONS
LENGTH 4900mm
WIDTH Not disclosed
HEIGHT 950mm
WHEELBASE 3500mm
TRACK front 1480mm
rear 1420mm
WEIGHT 620kg (including driver and camera)

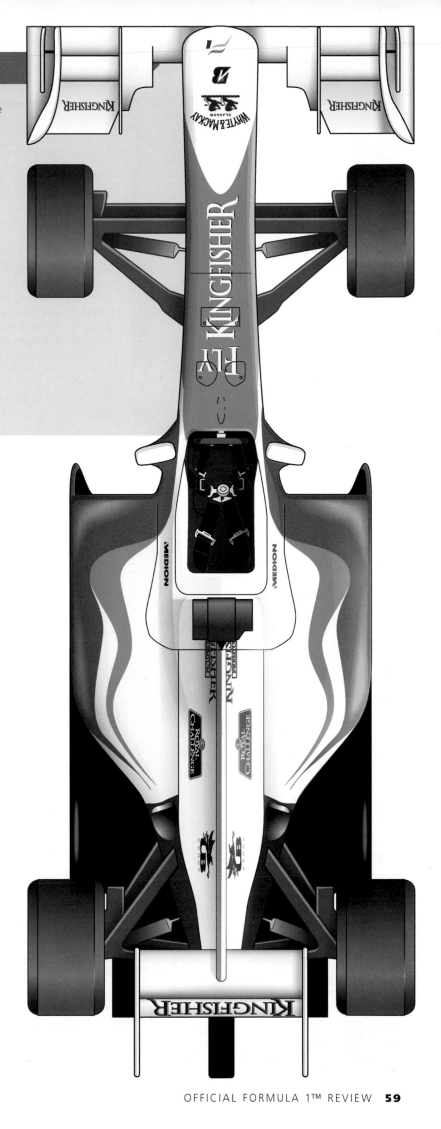

and fuel weights. We worked on cooling, with the expectation that the higher fuel weight would cause issues. However, it wasn't as bad as could have been expected. Maybe that was down to the way the drivers drove at the start of the race, or how the tyres behaved. It was quite a non-event actually. Our brake wear in Singapore was pretty much identical to the previous year.

SUTIL GAINS CONSISTENCY
It was good to have Tonio [Liuzzi] back in a race seat. He certainly impressed with the race driving. In Bahrain and Australia, I was expecting it to be a challenge for him to adapt to all that was different, but he did it very well. Adrian [Sutil] carried on his trajectory of improvement over the past few years and is still getting better and probably reaching maturity. He's pretty quick most of the time and can do it in races, whereas before the performance was more in and out at different tracks and in varying conditions.

It was a good experience running Paul [di Resta] in practice sessions. We had to back off a little towards the end of the year, as the points situation was tight and you've got to accept that missing a session with one of the race drivers doesn't come completely free. Paul's done quite a good job, but it's difficult to really assess how good because it's one set of tyres and just a snapshot. If you look at what he's done in terms of mileage, it's nothing compared to what used to be available, but it's better than nothing.

A STEADY JOB AS RIVALS STARTED BADLY
If we dropped off a little compared to Renault and Williams, it was probably down to relative team sizes and where they started relative to us. I think we had a good winter on the 2009 car, and then another year where we've had several whacking great innovations. You do need a lot of resource to get the best out of all those.

We did quite well with the rear wing, but the blown-diffuser starting point wasn't as good. The margin to Renault was 0.1s or 0.2s. Williams improved a bit more than us over the year, but they also started quite badly. Overall, I think we did a reasonably good job and had a better year than previous ones."

BMW SAUBER

THE TEAM

PERSONNEL

TEAM PRINCIPAL AND OWNER Peter Sauber
MANAGING DIRECTOR Monisha Kaltenborn
TECHNICAL DIRECTOR James Key (above)
DIRECTOR OF POWERTRAIN Markus Duesmann
CHIEF DESIGNER Christoph Zimmermann
HEAD OF AERODYNAMICS Seamus Mullarkey
TEAM MANAGER Beat Zehnder
HEAD OF TRACK ENGINEERING Giampaolo Dall'Ara
DRIVERS Pedro de la Rosa, Nick Heidfeld, Kamui Kobayashi
RACE ENGINEER (de la Rosa/Heidfeld) Paul Russell
RACE ENGINEER (Kobayashi) Francesco Nenci
CHIEF ENGINE ENGINEER Tomas Andor
CHIEF MECHANIC Urs Kuratle
TOTAL NUMBER OF EMPLOYEES 260
NUMBER IN RACE TEAM 59
TEAM BASE Hinwil, Switzerland
TELEPHONE +41 44 937 9000
WEBSITE www.sauber-motorsport.com

TEAM STATS

IN F1 SINCE 1993, as Sauber until 2005 **FIRST GRAND PRIX** South Africa 1993 **STARTS** 306 **WINS** 1 **POLE POSITIONS** 1 **FASTEST LAPS** 2 **PODIUMS** 22 **POINTS** 541 **CONSTRUCTORS' TITLES** 0 **DRIVERS' TITLES** 0

SPONSORS

Certina, Bridgestone, Emil Frey, Mad-Croc

22 PEDRO DE LA ROSA   **22** NICK HEIDFELD   **23** KAMUI KOBAYASHI

WORKING TO IMPROVE AN OVER-STIFF CHASSIS

By James Key
(Technical Director)

"The car had already done three grands prix by the time that I arrived. However, one of the things that attracted me to Sauber was the combination of an efficient small group of people, but with all the tools needed to do a good job. All the investment made over the years by BMW and Peter Sauber has put the team in a very good position.

On the aero side it's fantastic, absolutely top class. Some of that helps the team deal with the size it is, because you have the facilities to do more in a given time. But it means you have to make sure the shape of the team is right to make best use of the resources. That's a bit tricky when you have more facilities than you can use in some cases. It's certainly a different situation to what I've been used to… Things can happen so much more quickly when you have such manufacturing facilities.

A LACK OF RELIABILITY

The issue at the beginning of the season was that performance wasn't what everyone was hoping for and we had reliability problems. We needed to correct both of those very quickly in order to score points. Obviously the car was a bit white too, which plays on your mind. Not quite an emergency, but it was red alert!

There was a lot of work to do on the car, which everyone soaked up well. Part of that was helping the team adapt to its size by putting the right people in the right places, doing a bit of restructuring.

The car had been pretty quick and reliable in testing, so the problems caught everyone by surprise. I don't think they were running deliberately low fuel loads in order to set headline times, but it was just that the level chosen was perhaps less than that chosen by others. With no refuelling, there was suddenly a 4s difference between full and empty tanks, so it made it difficult to gauge.

TOO STIFF AND TOO MUCH DRAG

I got a bit of feedback from the drivers early on, and fairly quickly it seemed there were a couple of things not quite right. The straightline speed was an issue, and the drag number looked to me about 10% higher than I'd expect. The other thing was that the car was very stiff, spoiling a lot of mechanical grip and bringing with it instability.

We set a lot of priorities. Not just bread-and-butter development, but overcoming issues. We had to give more flexibility in how we set the car up. From the Spanish GP onwards, we experimented on Fridays with trying to get more out of it, taking us in new directions.

We went to China two days after I arrived, which was the first I saw of the car. There was a very good reaction from the team to get the F-duct on so quickly, at the second race in Australia, and it was a really good system too. It was clear though that it was a bit inconsistent, so we committed to getting a redesign on for the Spanish GP, which was a far more robust design for the same concept. That was why we made Q3 in Barcelona. The F-duct was a powerful thing at that stage of the season, later less so as everyone else got theirs.

I had numbers in my head different to where we were, and some of it was correlation in the wind tunnel as well as legacy stuff. A big mid-season update was aimed at making the car less sensitive, softening it off a little, getting the drag down and increasing downforce.

Removing drag and changing aero characteristics is a very difficult task, because it's built in over the previous six months of development. So that was the aim for the British GP.

A TRIO OF UPDATES

Development turned into three main updates, for Valencia, Silverstone and Hockenheim. There were mechanical upgrades too, working on the suspension to get better consistency of balance. One of the big issues was that low-speed performance was very poor. It was a big inconsistency because medium speed was okay and high-speed performance was very good. The stiffness caused some of the stability issues, particularly under braking, but it was also aero issues, as a combination. And, of course, there's more time to be lost in slow corners.

We took the decision not to do a blown floor. We were looking at it in CFD and the tunnel, but it took us a little while to realise

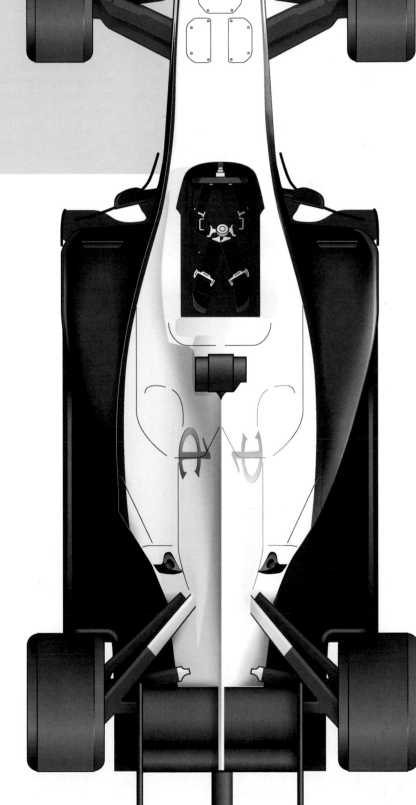

TECHNICAL SPECIFICATIONS

ENGINE
MAKE/MODEL Ferrari 056
CONFIGURATION 2398cc V8
(90 degree)
SPARK PLUGS Not disclosed
ECU FIA standard issue
FUEL Not disclosed
OIL Mobil 1
BATTERY Not disclosed

TRANSMISSION
GEARBOX Ferrari
FORWARD GEARS Seven
CLUTCH Not disclosed

CHASSIS
CHASSIS MODEL
Sauber C29
FRONT SUSPENSION LAYOUT
Upper and lower wishbones,
inboard springs and dampers
actuated by pushrods

REAR SUSPENSION LAYOUT
Upper and lower wishbones,
inboard springs and dampers
actuated by pushrods
DAMPERS Sachs
TYRES Bridgestone
WHEELS OZ Racing
BRAKE DISCS Carbone Industrie
BRAKE PADS Brembo
BRAKE CALIPERS Brembo
FUEL TANK ATL
INSTRUMENTS BMW Sauber F1

DIMENSIONS
LENGTH 4940mm
WIDTH 1800mm
HEIGHT 1000mm
WHEELBASE Not disclosed
TRACK front 1495mm
rear 1410mm
WEIGHT 620kg (including
driver and camera)

SAUBER Motorsport

just how potentially powerful it was. However, if we had committed to it at that point, we were almost upon the mid-season break with a load of refinement work to do to control the hot exhaust gases.

SAYING NO TO A BLOWN FLOOR
It was a major project and the earliest we could have got it on the car would have been Japan. So it was going to be a lot of aero time for a diffuser that was going to last four races. There was also the cost, looking at how else we could use that budget, given that we were actually following a fruitful direction on general aero work. It was a risk, but it didn't bite us too hard.

The engine reliability issues were a bit strange. It was one car that tended to get them: Pedro's [de la Rosa]. We looked at it intensively and got Ferrari to check the installation, but nothing was found to be particularly different. I think it was simply bad luck. As a precaution, we changed the procedure on how we chilled the fuel on Saturday morning, making it closer to what Ferrari was doing.

CONTINUITY WOULD HAVE HELPED
Having a new driver and a rookie was a challenge for the whole team, as there was no continuity. But the drivers were fine and gave good feedback, plus Kamui [Kobayashi] performed outstandingly for a rookie. As things settled down, the team got into a rhythm and it hasn't really hurt. The testing restrictions actually worked to our advantage in that we have a full-scale tunnel.

After the Chinese GP, we got the drivers in and they both identified the same weaknesses in the car. Nick Heidfeld's feedback was very similar. He rightly identified that the tyres were driving some of it, which is what Kamui learned at Valencia in the race…

Changing Pedro was a team decision. Both drivers were at a similar level, and without the continuity of previous years we were finding it difficult to understand where we were. Kamui had scored most of the points. Was he exceptional – and I think he is – or were we just missing something? It was a very difficult decision, but we felt we needed a reference.

The Telmex deal is great news for us. The Singapore package was the last one we did and we've been working on next year's car since June/July, so fingers crossed!"

TORO ROSSO

THE TEAM

PERSONNEL
TEAM OWNER Dietrich Mateschitz
TEAM PRINCIPAL Franz Tost
TECHNICAL DIRECTOR Giorgio Ascanelli (above)
TEAM MANAGER Gianfranco Fantuzzi
CHIEF DESIGNER Ben Butler
CHIEF ENGINEER Laurent Mekies
DRIVERS Jaime Alguersuari, Sebastien Buemi
TECHNICAL CO-ORDINATOR Sandro Parrini
LOGISTICS MANAGER Domenico Sangiorgi
RACE ENGINEER (Buemi) Riccardo Adami
RACE ENGINEER (Alguersuari) Andrea Landi
CHIEF MECHANIC Gerard Lecoq
ASSISTANT CHIEF MECHANIC Domiziano Facchinetti
NO 1 MECHANIC (Buemi) Gabriele Vergnana
NO 1 MECHANIC (Alguersuari) Alberto Gavarini
RELIABILITY MANAGER Gianvito Amico
SENIOR ENGINE ENGINEER Ernst Knoorst
RACE ENGINES MANAGER Mattia Binotto
TOTAL NUMBER OF EMPLOYEES 250
NUMBER IN RACE TEAM 50
TEAM BASE Faenza, Italy
TELEPHONE +39 (0)546 696111
WEBSITE www.scuderiatororosso.com

TEAM STATS
IN F1 SINCE 1985, as Minardi until 2005 **FIRST GRAND PRIX** Brazil 1985 **STARTS** 430 **WINS** 1 **POLE POSITIONS** 1 **FASTEST LAPS** 0 **PODIUMS** 1 **POINTS** 107 **CONSTRUCTORS' TITLES** 0 **DRIVERS' TITLES** 0

SPONSORS
Red Bull, Red Bull Cola, Red Bull Mobile, Money Service Group, Hangar-7, VW, Advanti, Bridgestone, USAG, Hexagon, Siemens, DALCO, Magneti Marelli

16 SEBASTIEN BUEMI   **17** JAIME ALGUERSUARI

EARLY START HELPS IN EARLY RACES

**By Giorgio Ascanelli
(Technical Director)**

"The patterns for 2011's pre-season test car were going through inspection in September, and the process for this year's STR5 was about the same in 2009. That's too early for the top teams, but we have to face our capacities. At that time, the tunnel wasn't working and we didn't know how to use the CFD...

Our story in the past year has been getting the people together and understanding the wind tunnel. There has to be a reason that Red Bull Racing ditched the tunnel in Bicester and went to one in Bedford. First of all, the rolling road starts being temperamental, then the chillers aren't working and then you've got inaccuracy in the repeatability of the measurement...

After 10 days being told tales, I pick up a plane, go to Bicester and say, 'Listen, I'm an old man, can you hang the model on the top of the scale and just let it alone and log it, with no wind running and no rolling road running?' The signal was drifting all over... You tell me? I still believe it's good enough, but it takes time. It's like a used car: temperamental. And, like babies, it didn't come with a user's manual!

UNDERSTANDING WHICH DATA TO BELIEVE
We used as much carry-over from the STR4 as we could and made an educated guess, let's say. Part of the car was wrong and it was conditioned by the choice made on the chassis, which was long and thin. We had to have rear wishbones shaped for the double-decker diffuser. We were suffering, as there was not enough diffuser inlet because our gearbox was very short. So it was the wrong choice of volumes in the end.

Overall though, we tried hard to do a positive job and the car wasn't bad. I think we understood this year's tyres earlier than most teams, and that explained why our performance improved after the first month's testing. We produced a couple of changes that were positive, but we were extremely slow in producing them, mainly because the CFD tells you something, the tunnel tells you something that may be the same or different, and then the circuit tells you something else. And the calibration of the model is just fundamental.

We had one development package at the Turkish GP and another for the Hungarian GP, which came out wrong. There was a little bit of a problem with the diffuser, something didn't quite go from aero to drawing office and unfortunately I didn't see it before leaving. I saw it on the circuit and said, 'that's not going to work.'

It happens. I tell you, it's terribly difficult to handle an operation with the wind tunnel in England and the drawing office in Italy.

BOOSTING THE AERO DEPARTMENT
Also, numerically, we are about one third of what the other aero departments are, so it becomes more difficult. We took on 30 staff in the wind tunnel, went up from 17 to 30 in the drawing office, and the structural department was invented as we didn't have one… Some of them have already left the team, so maybe I'm not easy to work with!

The blown floor was done completely in CFD. We could measure the effect and we were happy, it just took time. I wasn't sure that I had a good diffuser and, before doing an F-duct or a blown floor, I wanted to know what my diffuser did. The blown floor was probably more important than the F-duct, because that ended at the end of the year, whereas the exhausts will still be important next year.

We did a CFD study, had a few ideas and then struggled with how to measure and validate it. And then we had to be aware of how much we lost. We are a customer team and Ferrari was very good with us because we actually tested the change of performance caused by the exhaust. In the end, our step at the Italian GP was a good one and we went generally better. However, I don't think it was the exhaust, but the peculiarities of the circuit. We had the car with the lowest drag on the circuit. People still underestimate the effect of high speed at Monza and that's probably why we were a bit faster than normal.

F-DUCT IS A NIGHTMARE TO IMPLEMENT
The F-duct is a difficult exercise. It works with CFD, it works in the tunnel, it's just a nightmare in terms of implementation – accuracy of parts, leakages, unwanted flexibility changing the shape of the orifices. I think the best race for

ENGINE
MAKE/MODEL Ferrari 056
CONFIGURATION 2398cc V8
(90 degree)
SPARK PLUGS Not disclosed
ECU FIA standard issue
FUEL Not disclosed
OIL Not disclosed
BATTERY Not disclosed

TRANSMISSION
GEARBOX Not disclosed
FORWARD GEARS Seven
CLUTCH Sachs

CHASSIS
CHASSIS MODEL Toro Rosso STR5
FRONT SUSPENSION LAYOUT
Upper and lower carbon wishbones,
torsion-bar springs and anti-roll bars

REAR SUSPENSION LAYOUT
Upper and lower carbon wishbones,
torsion-bar springs and anti-roll bars
DAMPERS Sachs
TYRES Bridgestone
WHEELS Advanti Racing
BRAKE DISCS Brembo
BRAKE PADS Brembo
BRAKE CALIPERS Brembo
FUEL TANK ATL
INSTRUMENTS
Scuderia Toro Rosso

DIMENSIONS
LENGTH Not disclosed
WIDTH Not disclosed
HEIGHT Not disclosed
WHEELBASE
Not disclosed
TRACK front Not disclosed
rear Not disclosed
WEIGHT 620kg (including
driver and camera)

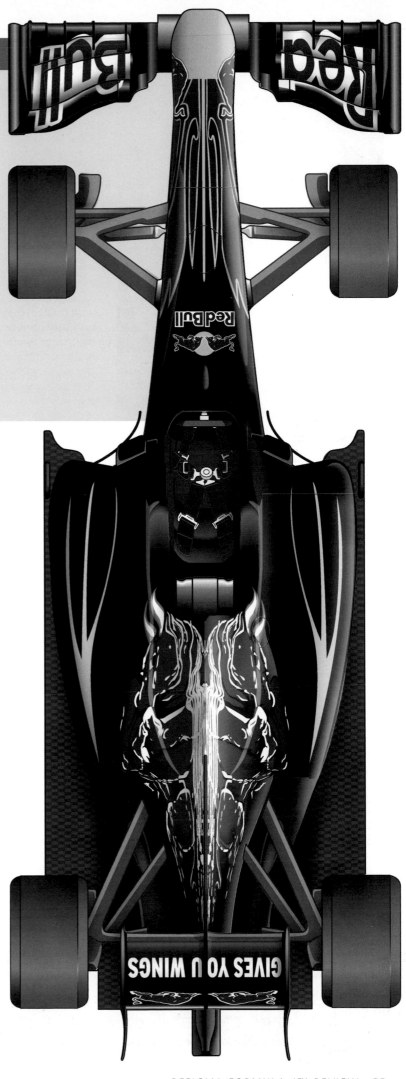

the F-duct would have been the Belgian GP, but we were not ready in time.

Jaime [Alguersuari] has progressed through 2010. More than anything he's fit. In 2009, he wasn't. He's now strong and a very good racing driver. He doesn't know how to brake yet – look at his legs! – but I think he knows that and is working on it. I don't think I can compare him to Schumacher, but he does what everyone else does.

Sebastien [Buemi] has been surprised by a team-mate who he expected to be far from him in terms of pace but instead isn't so far. I think he had a couple of races where he couldn't handle it, but has now got a grasp of it. Unfortunately, that period coincided with us running out of steam in terms of development.

Williams and Sauber messed up their Spanish GP package and went backwards instead of forwards, so we looked good, and then they got their acts together. Sebastien had his bit of drop-off at the moment when there was nothing coming up and the others were getting it together, and that hurt us a bit.

DRIVERS ARE TOO CONSERVATIVE
The general comment – which the drivers will probably get cheesed off about, but which they know – is that every time they have to choose whether to risk something to get something better or preserve what they have, they preserve. I think that's conditioned by the lack of testing, so that if they cause a stoppage of the car it's simply less miles, which they need, but thinking like that makes it hard to take a step forward.

Next year's car is going to be a bit different. I think we are a bit stronger than in 2009 and the big unknown is the tyre. Ross (Brawn) has gracefully fixed for us the weight distribution, so we can't get it wrong, which is a big help to everyone... I think it's a higher-risk road that we have taken, but if I don't take any risks it will be another year ranking ninth. My view is that if we're ranked ninth in the World Championship we've just done our job – not good, not bad. If we're 10th, we deserve to be shot and, if we're eighth, then it's extraordinary."

LOTUS

THE TEAM

PERSONNEL
TEAM PRINCIPAL Tony Fernandes
DEPUTY TEAM PRINCIPALS Kamarudin Meranun & SM Nasarudin
CHIEF EXECUTIVE OFFICER Riad Asmat
CHIEF TECHNICAL OFFICER Mike Gascoyne (above)
SPORTING DIRECTOR Dieter Gass
CHIEF OPERATING OFFICER (UK) Keith Saunt
HEAD OF OPERATIONS (ASIA) Mia Sharizman
HEAD OF VEHICLE TECHNOLOGY DESIGN Eliot Dason-Barber
CHIEF ENGINEER Jody Egginton
HEAD OF LOGISTICS Graham Smith
TEAM MANAGER Graham Watson
DRIVERS Heikki Kovalainen, Jarno Trulli
CHIEF RACE & TEST ENGINEER Dieter Gass
RACE ENGINEER (Trulli) Gianluca Pisanello
RACE ENGINEER (Kovalainen) Juann Pablo Ramirez
TEST/THIRD DRIVER Fairuz Fauzy
CHIEF MECHANICS Simon Beatson, Phil Spencer
TOTAL NUMBER OF EMPLOYEES Not disclosed
NUMBER IN RACE TEAM Not disclosed
TEAM BASE Hingham, England & Kuala Lumpur, Malaysia
TELEPHONE +49 (0)1953 851411
WEBSITE www.lotusracing.my

TEAM STATS
IN F1 SINCE 2010 **FIRST GRAND PRIX** Bahrain 2010
STARTS 19 **WINS** 0 **POLE POSITIONS** 0
FASTEST LAPS 0 **PODIUMS** 0 **POINTS** 0
CONSTRUCTORS' TITLES 0 **DRIVERS' TITLES** 0

SPONSORS
Air Asia, 1 Malaysia, Tune Group, Proton, Bridgestone, NAZA, Maxis, CNN, Hackett, LR8, PACT

18 JARNO TRULLI **19** HEIKKI KOVALAINEN

A GOOD START, BUT THERE'S MORE TO COME

By Mike Gascoyne
(Chief Technical Officer)

"I signed a contract on 12 May to do the initial entry, and when that failed on 12 June we were encouraged to keep going. There was the FOTA/Max [Mosley] war, and it was also predicted that other teams would drop out. Around that time, Tony Fernandes came on board. I met him at Silverstone and we arranged to see Tony Purnell and Mosley. Nino Judge had the idea of using the Lotus name, initially through Group Lotus which, when we met Mike Kimberley, was very supportive, but then [parent company] Proton said no. We then talked to David Hunt and put the initial entry in as Team Lotus. With Tony on board, he had the ability to talk at a high level in Malaysia to Proton and the government to pull together the agreement for Proton to let us go in with the Lotus name. But at that point peace broke out unexpectedly between FOTA and the FIA, so we really didn't know how we were going to get an entry.

Tony didn't want to spend a fortune if we didn't get a World Championship entry, so from the time of the British GP we made a 10-week plan to stay on target, but that was still £1million worth of work.

When BMW Sauber pulled out in 2009, we thought 'job done'. But they came back into the frame to be saved, so we really didn't know. In fact, we found out on Monday 11 September, before they announced it the next day. We'd been told that Max preferred Sauber, with us as reserve entry, which would have basically finished us, as we were at the point of no return, but obviously there was a suspicion that Toyota would pull out.

There were six people working at MGI (design company Mike Gascoyne International) in Cologne and the infamous four of us – Sylvie [Schaumloeffel, Mike's partner], myself, Paul Craig and Keith Saunt – who drove to Hingham to sit in this Marie Celeste of a building, look at each other and ask, 'What do we do?'

FROM A STANDING START
Through MGI, we had a load of contractors standing by on a day's notice, and within the next couple of weeks we shot up to 25 people on the design side. Jean-Claude Migeot and Aerolab started an aero programme when we got the entry, but we were still a month away from doing any wind-tunnel testing. The most pleasing thing was that on that first day at the factory, 14 September, we planned a fire-up day of 5 January and were just a day late. Considering what could have gone wrong, that was a hell of an effort.

We had no buying department, nothing. Keith – 20 years in the business, previously COO at Red Bull, head of production at Renault – had his notebook of suppliers. He was ringing up saying 'it's all coming!' Some things were done direct with suppliers we'd worked with at Toyota. Although they did a good job, they tended to be expensive, as the Toyota way of pricing isn't necessarily the rest of the world's…

MAKING A RELIABLE START
We were conservative with the cooling, and had to design maximum-size brake ducts because we had no data and were looking at full tanks and no refuelling. With the fuel tank, we had no data because they hadn't run the Cosworth engine at 18,000rpm. In the end, we had two cars classified in the opening race at Bahrain, the engines ran to temperature at a hot race and we didn't run out of brakes. We could have got two cars over the finish line, but we stopped one at the last corner so we could look in the gearbox. I don't think, with the cards we'd been dealt, that we could have done anything better. There were people with plenty more time and knowledge who didn't get it right.

KEEPING IT BEEFY FOR THE CRASH TEST
The other thing was, we were finalising the early things – like side-impact tubes and the nose box for the impact tests – and weren't going to get a chassis until mid-January. The thought of not passing the tests… That's it, you're dead. There would be no second go at it, no spare capacity, so with things like the radiator inlets it was a case of doing a generic Brawn-type intake with the sculpture so we could fit the crash tubes in. There was no case of, 'we'd like this slimmer or that moved up'.

We'd always planned to use MGI as a one-hit wonder to get us to race one and then take over and build a team in Hingham, but that

TECHNICAL SPECIFICATIONS

ENGINE
MAKE/MODEL Cosworth CA2010
CONFIGURATION 2400cc V8
SPARK PLUGS Champion
ECU FIA standard issue
FUEL Not disclosed
OIL Not disclosed
BATTERY Not disclosed

TRANSMISSION
GEARBOX Xtrac
FORWARD GEARS Seven
CLUTCH AP Racing

CHASSIS
CHASSIS MODEL Lotus T127
FRONT SUSPENSION LAYOUT
Carbon-fibre double wishbones with
carbon-fibre trackrod and pushrod
REAR SUSPENSION LAYOUT
Carbon-fibre double wishbones with
carbon-fibre trackrod and pushrod
DAMPERS Penske
TYRES Bridgestone
WHEELS BBS
BRAKE DISCS Hitco
BRAKE PADS Hitco
BRAKE CALIPERS AP Racing
FUEL TANK ATL
INSTRUMENTS McLaren
Electronic Systems

DIMENSIONS
LENGTH Not disclosed
WIDTH Not disclosed
HEIGHT Not disclosed
WHEELBASE Not disclosed
TRACK front Not disclosed
rear Not disclosed
WEIGHT Not disclosed

was going to take time because people were on six months notice. Toyota folding helped, as there were a lot of guys instantly available. Our race team, for instance, is all Toyota and practically all the aero team is Toyota.

We built the car to be reliable, and the bit that we built has been. Almost all our failures have been due to hydraulics. We had no inkling about that because between Xtrac and Cosworth you'd think they'd know how to do hydraulic systems and gearboxes.

We're going a different route in 2011 (with a Renault/Red Bull drivetrain) and when you have a split you end up saying nice things about each other for PR purposes. In Cosworth's case, though, it really isn't their fault. We're still not in a position to do our own gearbox and guarantee to be reliable. And we need a 2011 pullrod suspension spec and some of the things on offer aren't that, which meant we had to go and look for a turnkey solution.

UPDATES ONLY UNTIL THE BRITISH GP
Our big update came at Barcelona and the next two races, with quite a few lightweight bits, and we got the car 15–20kg under the limit so we could play with the weight distribution. Our Silverstone package was where it stopped. We were still 1–1.5s from the established teams, but we'd expected to be within half a second.

We didn't make the expected progress with the diffuser and I think that's because of the early compromises. We've got a single-diffuser car in the tunnel that already had more downforce by October, and you shouldn't be able to do that.

The T127 was a reasonably short car. We made the fuel cell quite wide, which compromised the radiators and meant that we couldn't cut things in more. Yet, at the end of the day, we were 10th, which is where we wanted to be. We were never going to finish ninth.

The drivers knew what they signed up for and took a longer view. It's a happy team, Heikki's relishing it, even though he's at the back. We're in a very good position."

HRT

THE TEAM

PERSONNEL

TEAM OWNER & CHAIRMAN Jose Ramon Carabante
TEAM PRINCIPAL & MANAGING DIRECTOR
Colin Kolles
TECHNICAL DIRECTOR Geoff Willis (above)
CHIEF RACE & TEST ENGINEER Antonio Cuquerella
TECHNICAL CO-ORDINATOR Jacky Eeckelaert
CHIEF DESIGNER (DALLARA) Luca Pinacca
TEAM MANAGER Boris Bernes
DRIVERS Karun Chandhok, Christian Klien, Bruno Senna, Sakon Yamamoto
RACE ENGINEER (Chandhok/Yamamoto/Klien)
Richard Connell
RACE ENGINEER (Senna/Yamamoto) Francisco Javier Pujolar
TEST/THIRD DRIVER Christian Klien
CHIEF MECHANIC Ernst Kopp
TOTAL NUMBER OF EMPLOYEES Not disclosed
NUMBER IN RACE TEAM Not disclosed
TEAM BASE Madrid, Spain & Greding, Germany
TELEPHONE +49 (0)8463 602679
WEBSITE www.hispaniaf1team.com

TEAM STATS

IN F1 SINCE 2010 **FIRST GRAND PRIX** Bahrain 2010
STARTS 19 **WINS** 0 **POLE POSITIONS** 0
FASTEST LAPS 0 **PODIUMS** 0 **POINTS** 0
CONSTRUCTORS' TITLES 0 **DRIVERS' TITLES** 0

SPONSORS

Banco Cruzeiro do Sul, Embratel, JAYPEE Group, murciaturistica.es, Bridgestone, Cosworth, OMP, Jim Rickey, RuRoC

20 KARUN CHANDHOK   **20*** SAKON YAMAMOTO   **20** CHRISTIAN KLIEN   **21** BRUNO SENNA

*Sakon Yamamoto ran as No 21 at the British Grand Prix

HAMPERED FOM THE VERY OUTSET

**By Geoff Willis
(Technical Director)**

"The car came together via a Dallara project that was quite stop-and-go towards the end of 2009. Colin Kolles brought it all together and I came in about two or three weeks before the opening race of the season.

Essentially, we had a part-finished project which Dallara had to very quickly complete. We had a car build/manufacturing fortnight down at Dallara and it was quite impressive that it all came together in time for the Bahrain GP.

PROBLEMS FROM THE OUTSET

We had a car with a very truncated aero development programme that was clearly going to be somewhat down on the aero targets. It was the first foray into F1 for Dallara since 1992 and – how can I put this diplomatically? – they underestimated just how refined and professional Formula One teams are today. Even the teams at the back of the grid are now at a level of refinement, packaging and quality of design undreamt of 10 years ago. Dallara just completely misjudged what was needed.

If you look at a current F1 car, everything has been packaged and thought about, from cooling, vibrations and tiny details where you've almost forgotten how you reached that level of refinement. The difference between a GP2 car and an F1 car is absolutely night and day. People thought the car would be a super-duper GP2 car, maybe 30% better, but it needed to be 10 times better.

Obviously there was the transmission from Xtrac, which has a lot of contemporary F1 technology experience, but not of doing the complete package. And particularly not of doing the casing and hydraulics, which was contracted elsewhere. That again missed the necessary level of refinement.

It wasn't just one thing. The reservoir that maintains constant low pressure and high pressure in the system, for example, is quite a complicated device. F1 hydraulics per se are not excessively complicated, as there is quite a lot of experience around, but the teams that have done it successfully year-in and year-out have learned the hard way. They have learned all the issues to do with surface coating, little failures

on connections, dirt getting in, being unable to bleed systems correctly, all of that. It's been learned and it's not a competitive advantage between teams any more but, for whatever reason, it was underestimated.

SUFFERING FROM A LACK OF EXPERIENCE

We had no performance development at all. Although we made numerous proposals, there was never any budget for us. There was a change to the hydraulics from Xtrac which arrived at the Spanish GP, and we then had an improved wiring loom and more sensors in time for the German GP.

We also completely changed the fuel system and fuel cells before the British GP, because we were having big problems with that. We were the only team not using ATL tanks, and we changed to them and saved ourselves about 10kg of fuel, and could then run the fuel load down to virtually empty. The problem had been picking up the last fuel in the tank. Again, that was down to using a supplier that didn't have F1 experience.

Operationally, it was a steep learning curve too. There were a few Campos Meta mechanics based in Spain, and Colin Kolles brought along a lot of his Kolles Racing people with DTM, LMP and F3 backgrounds, and we had a number of other people with F1 experience. For the first few races, everyone was new to each other, but quite rapidly it went from, if not quite comical, certainly disorganised – well-meaning but fraught – to starting to look quite slick in the garage by the end of the season.

We were running with minimal equipment and the key was to first of all make sure that all the cars were safely prepared, and secondly to try and do what we could with the reliability. I have to say 'well done' to all the guys involved, as they worked very hard to learn how to keep the car reliable. We still had problems, quite a few related to gearbox and hydraulics, which was the biggest single cause. Self-inflicted injuries we generally picked up on in free practice, because we had no pre-season testing.

A LACK OF DOWNFORCE

Wheelbase-wise, we were probably bang in the middle, but the car's level of aero performance compared with, say, Red Bull, was between

ENGINE
MAKE/MODEL Cosworth CA2010
CONFIGURATION 2400cc V8
SPARK PLUGS Champion
ECU FIA standard issue
FUEL BP
OIL BP
BATTERY GS Yuasa

TRANSMISSION
GEARBOX Xtrac
FORWARD GEARS Seven
CLUTCH Sachs

CHASSIS
CHASSIS MODEL HRT F110
FRONT SUSPENSION LAYOUT
Pushrod
REAR SUSPENSION LAYOUT
Pushrod

DAMPERS Sachs
TYRES Bridgestone
WHEELS OZ Racing
BRAKE DISCS Brembo
BRAKE PADS Brembo
BRAKE CALIPERS Brembo
FUEL TANK Premier
INSTRUMENTS McLaren
Electronic Systems

DIMENSIONS
LENGTH circa 4800mm
WIDTH 1790mm
HEIGHT 950mm
WHEELBASE circa 3200mm
TRACK front 1800mm
rear 1800mm
WEIGHT 620kg (including
driver and camera)

HISPANIA RACING
F1 team

130 and 150 points of downforce down. The F110 also had a fundamental understeer characteristic and we were never able to run the car with sufficiently forward-biased weight distribution to match the tyre characteristics because we couldn't balance it aerodynamically.

The car needed an aero fix. The top teams improve the aero performance by four or five points a week, and the number of weeks you don't test is the number of weeks you go backwards. It's as simple as that. We suffered much more at places where you need absolute levels of downforce and efficiency. Singapore hurt us quite a lot and we were 107.2% away in practice. Also, we didn't pick up as much time on low fuel loads on the softer tyres. I suspect we needed the additional energy you put into the tyres on high fuel loads, so we did relatively better in race trim than qualifying.

The drivers earned their keep. It was fairly impressive to have the car on high stands two or three minutes into the first qualifying session in Bahrain, and well done to everyone, Karun [Chandhok] included, for holding their nerve and getting on with it. Then, if you look at the first six or seven races, compared with the other new teams, we got closer rather than further away, then reached a plateau around the time of the British GP.

RELATIVE SPEED DICTATED RACE STRATEGY
Our approach to the races was that on pure performance we knew we were going to be last, so it was up to us to try to read any complicated situations better. Could we respond to a safety car a bit better than our rivals? We learned other things too, like how to deal with blue flags. What's the way you minimise lost lap time? So we didn't run our strategy according to optimal timing, we instead minimised our blue-flags losses, which for us gave a different optimum race strategy.

You might think, why pit early? Well, that's why. We let the first three runners through very quickly because they aren't fighting each other, then as soon as a gaggle comes, pit then and that's 12 blue flags we haven't suffered from. We were quite well organised from a race-engineering perspective. It was quite slick, we didn't make many strategic mistakes, and we became aware of how other teams could be doing better…

It took Bruno [Senna] a while to get back into the swing of single-seaters, but all the drivers have been very objective, understood the situation and worked hard to get the best out of it. I enjoyed working with all of them. It was a real battle for them."

VIRGIN

THE TEAM

PERSONNEL

CHIEF EXECUTIVE OFFICER Graeme Lowdon
TEAM PRINCIPAL John Booth (above)
TECHNICAL DIRECTOR Nick Wirth
HEAD OF PERFORMANCE & RACE ENGINEERING
Mark Herd
TEAM MANAGER Dave O'Neill
DRIVERS Lucas di Grassi, Timo Glock
CHIEF RACE & TEST ENGINEER Dieter Gass
RACE ENGINEER (Glock) Dave Greenwood
RACE ENGINEER (di Grassi) Mark Hutcheson
TEST/THIRD DRIVERS Luiz Razia, Jerome d'Ambrosio
CHIEF MECHANIC Richard Wrenn
NO 1 MECHANIC (Glock) Scott Walker
NO 1 MECHANIC (di Grassi) Rob Jones
TOTAL NUMBER OF EMPLOYEES Not disclosed
NUMBER IN RACE TEAM 45
TEAM BASE Dinnington, England
TELEPHONE +49 (0)1909 517250
WEBSITE www.virginracing.com

TEAM STATS

IN F1 SINCE 2010 **FIRST GRAND PRIX** Bahrain 2010
STARTS 19 **WINS** 0 **POLE POSITIONS** 0
FASTEST LAPS 0 **PODIUMS** 0 **POINTS** 0
CONSTRUCTORS' TITLES 0 **DRIVERS' TITLES** 0

SPONSORS

Virgin, Marussia, Full Tilt Poker.com, FXPro, UST Global, Carbon Green, Armin Racing Watches, Bridgestone, CSC, Kappa, LG Electronics

24 TIMO GLOCK   **25** LUCAS DI GRASSI

TAKING STEPS WITH SPEEDY CFD DEVELOPMENT

By John Booth
(Team Principal)

"We were introduced to Nick Wirth back in March 2009 when the budget cap concept was introduced. There was going to be £30m TV money, that was going to be the cost of the season and it all sounded a great idea.

We met the week after, then the week after that, and were all pumped up and going for it and started the application process. That was quite strict and luckily we had some racing infrastructure and could tick all the boxes. It was still a massive surprise when the announcement was made on 12 June... Kind of, what shall we do now? I think Nick had a few sketches on the back of a fag packet..

In hindsight, it wasn't exactly as we all expected. That started at Silverstone last year. We were signing with new sponsors, and they've got the radio on in the afternoon and the world blows up with walkouts and splits... It was a massive setback for us. Then, September time, the details came out, with no performance breaks and it was basically a different car. We had to think about whether we could continue.

Could we raise £90–100m and do it as other people do? That became a no-go for two reasons. First, it would have been impossible to ramp up the operation to utilise that amount of money, and secondly, I'm not sure it's out there at the moment. So we took the decision to continue, but within the financial framework we'd decided on for the old regulations We could only do that because of Nick's CFD capability. The Silverstone upgrade we made cost a sum of money, but if that had been developed in the conventional manner it would have cost six, eight times as much.

GETTING THE FUEL TANK WRONG

It was tough and we got it a bit wrong with the fuel tank. The fuel density wasn't quite what we thought, and there was no refuelling on the grid either. If we'd had an easier time in testing, we'd have had time to do something about it less publicly, but testing had so many problems.

The hydraulics and associated parts – we had a lot of problems with the differential – hampered testing, but I wasn't at all nervous about the concept of a car done entirely with

CFD. I always had faith in that. When you talk to guys in the pitlane who know what's happening it was a brave new world, but all the teams are relying more and more on CFD.

WHY CFD WILL BE ADOPTED BY ALL

My prediction is that wind tunnels will be a thing of the past and, by the time Malaysia1 get theirs built, they'll be redundant. When you look at the pace of development, particularly in the front-wing area, there's no way that can be done in a wind tunnel, there aren't enough hours in the day. People will start splitting the resource much more towards CFD.

The limitation of this car was reliability. That stopped us in our tracks. The upgrade we put on at Silverstone should have been on four races earlier, but we had to focus on the fuel tank and reliability. Some of the partners we thought were solid in that area turned out not to be, and we failed to identify some of the problems. They were maybe not of our making, but we should have identified them quicker.

HYDRAULIC PROBLEMS SLOW PROGRESS

With the hydraulics, because everything is such high pressure, the smallest impurity or crack or anything like that was a car stopper. And it controls four or five major components. Going forward, it's hard to be 100% confident, but it's 100 times better than it was, and next year we'll have another improved system.

I think we were also a bit harder on rear tyres than some of our competitors, particularly when we had the supersofts on. We tended to burn them up quite quickly, but it wasn't a big deal. The obvious limitation was downforce.

The longer car that we did, by about 135mm, was initially a bit slower. At the same time, we introduced an aero upgrade which masked it. The Silverstone upgrade was the first real performance upgrade and was a front wing, rear wing and floor. If things had gone to plan, it would have been on in Barcelona. Then it's been small refinements since and, in fact, the refinement we made for Hockenheim proved to be quite a big step. We introduced aero upgrades all the way up to Korea.

The drivers have both been superb. It would have been very easy for them, Timo particularly,

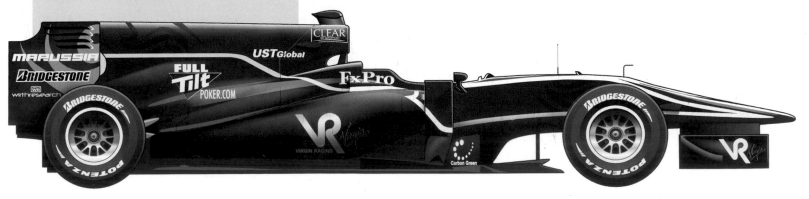

TECHNICAL SPECIFICATIONS

ENGINE
MAKE/MODEL Cosworth CA2010
CONFIGURATION 2400cc V8
(90 degree)
SPARK PLUGS Champion
ECU FIA standard issue
FUEL BP
OIL BP
BATTERY Braille

TRANSMISSION
GEARBOX Virgin Racing
FORWARD GEARS Seven
CLUTCH AP Racing

CHASSIS
CHASSIS MODEL Virgin VR-01
FRONT SUSPENSION LAYOUT
Double wishbone with pushrod-operated rockers connected to roll torsion bars, dampers and ARB
REAR SUSPENSION LAYOUT
Double wishbone with pushrod-operated rockers connected to roll torsion bars, dampers and ARB
DAMPERS Penske
TYRES Bridgestone
WHEELS BBS
BRAKE DISCS Hitco
BRAKE PADS Hitco
BRAKE CALIPERS AP Racing
FUEL TANK ATL
INSTRUMENTS Not disclosed

DIMENSIONS
LENGTH Not disclosed
WIDTH 1800mm (approx)
HEIGHT 950mm (approx)
WHEELBASE 3200mm (approx)
TRACK front 1800mm
rear 1755mm
WEIGHT 620kg (including driver and camera)

coming from Toyota, to get disillusioned, but they were very patient and supportive. Sure, we've had a few tough moments, but overall they've both been real team players. With Lucas, it was almost like taking two experienced drivers. He'd done so much testing with Renault and is an intelligent driver who understands engineering, so we got useful feedback from day one.

Team-wise we have about 60–65, with 50 travelling, then we've got 14 in the commercial department in London, while Wirth Research has about 85 dedicated to F1. We have about five travelling engineers from Wirth to make sure that what's going on at the track gets fed back to the design guys.

CONTROL ENGINEERS ARE VITAL
The most important people in that are the control engineers, who are Wirth Research employees. Mark Herd is head of performance engineering and then Gary Gannon is the reliability engineer who provides that link. They are vital for the operation to run smoothly.

Nick's a massive enthusiast, who finds the technology very stimulating, and he loves pushing CFD to the next level and is very big into simulators, so we've actually got two at Wirth Research which we use a lot. That's another area where we cost ourselves at the start of the year, because Nick's time was devoted to helping us get reliability, where really his strength and passion is making the thing go faster.

THE QUESTION OF BUDGETS
We heard about Bernie Ecclestone's comments on the three new teams, but he's led F1 successfully for so many years that we've got to trust his methods, even if we don't understand them. Bernie always comes down to the back of the grid and asks how we're doing...

We have to run within our budget framework and I think that it was most unfair to suggest that Richard Branson should put his hands deeper in his pockets. Richard was extremely brave joining a start-up operation which looked as though it might have all gone horribly wrong and he has been supportive throughout.

Actually, we got two new sponsors from Singapore through Richard. One was on the car at the Abu Dhabi GP and the other is for next year."

	2010 FORMULA 1 GULF AIR BAHRAIN GRAND PRIX **Sakhir**	**72**
	2010 FORMULA 1 QUANTAS AUSTRALIAN GRAND PRIX **Melbourne**	**82**
	2010 FORMULA 1 PETRONAS MALAYSIAN GRAND PRIX **Kuala Lumpur**	**92**
	2010 FORMULA 1 CHINESE GRAND PRIX **Shanghai**	**102**
	FORMULA 1 GRAN PREMIO DE ESPAÑA TELEFÓNICA 2010 **Catalunya**	**112**
	FORMULA 1 GRAND PRIX DE MONACO 2010 **Monte Carlo**	**122**
	2009 FORMULA 1 TURKISH GRAND PRIX **Istanbul**	**132**
	FORMULA 1 GRAND PRIX DU CANADA 2010 **Montreal**	**142**
	2010 FORMULA 1 TELEFÓNICA GRAND PRIX OF EUROPE **Valencia**	**152**
	2010 FORMULA 1 SANTANDER BRITISH GRAND PRIX **Silverstone**	**162**
	FORMULA 1 GROSSER PREIS SANTANDER VON DEUTSCHLAND 2010 **Hockenheim**	**172**
	FORMULA 1 ENI MAGYAR NAGYDÍJ 2010 **Budapest**	**182**
	2010 FORMULA 1 BELGIAN GRAND PRIX **Spa-Francorchamps**	**192**
	FORMULA 1 GRAN PREMIO SANTANDER D'ITALIA 2010 **Monza**	**202**
	2010 FORMULA 1 SINGTEL SINGAPORE GRAND PRIX **Singapore**	**212**
	2010 FORMULA 1 JAPANESE GRAND PRIX **Suzuka**	**222**
	2010 FORMULA 1 KOREAN GRAND PRIX **Yeongam**	**232**
	FORMULA 1 GRANDE PRÊMIO PETROBRAS DO BRASIL 2010 **São Paulo**	**242**
	2010 FORMULA 1 ETIHAD AIRWAYS ABU DHABI GRAND PRIX **Yas Marina Circuit**	**252**

THE RACES

The battle started at Bahrain in March and raged all the way through to Abu Dhabi in November, with the teams experiencing their first taste of Korea along the way

2010 FORMULA 1 GULF AIR BAHRAIN GRAND PRIX
SAKHIR

ALONSO LUCKS IN

Alonso had the best possible start to his Ferrari career by winning the season-opener, but he was helped into the lead by a mechanical problem hitting Sebastian Vettel's Red Bull

The 2010 season kicked off in Bahrain amid much anticipation, not just because of Michael Schumacher's comeback, but also because the top teams each had stellar line-ups.

In addition, this was the first race under the new rules, with no refuelling allowed and thus everyone starting on a full fuel load. No one knew quite what to expect in terms of strategy or how competitive the race would be.

As it turned out, Fernando Alonso won on his debut for Ferrari, repeating Kimi Räikkönen's feat in Melbourne in 2007. It was a spectacular result for the Spaniard but not, alas, a spectacular race for the fans. In fact, the afternoon proved to be something of a procession that did little to catch the attention of casual TV viewers encouraged to tune in by the publicity surrounding Schumacher's return.

As it happened, the main excitement was created by leader Sebastian Vettel hitting a technical problem and, without that mishap juggling the order a little, the show would have been even worse. Fortunately, this race was to prove to be something of an anomaly, and in the following weeks it was forgotten as a sensational World Championship battle began to take shape.

TOP **Mark Webber presents Kubica with a face full of smoke at Turn 2, as he mixes it with Rosberg, Schumacher and Button**

ABOVE **Sebastian Vettel leads away, followed by Alonso, Massa, Rosberg, Hamilton and Schumacher**

With so much shuffling around in the top teams over the winter, there was much to get used to in Bahrain. In addition, Brawn had become Mercedes GP, Sauber was an independent team once again and Renault had reinvented itself with new owners. There were also the three new teams – Lotus, Virgin and HRT – all of whom arrived in various degrees of preparedness.

However, the season began as the 2009 one had ended, with Vettel and Red Bull to the fore. The German popped up at the end of Q3 and outstripped the Ferraris to claim pole position and emphasise that Adrian Newey's RB6 was likely to be the car to beat.

In his comeback race after the head injuries he suffered in Hungary in 2009, Felipe Massa made a point by beating new team-mate Alonso in qualifying, thus winning round one of the many interesting intra-team battles. Boosted by its novel F-duct device, McLaren had been expected to set the pace, but Lewis Hamilton could not better fourth place, some way off the pace of those ahead.

Nico Rosberg made it four teams in the top five by claiming fifth on the grid for Mercedes and, like Massa, he made his mark by beating team-mate

Schumacher, who started seventh. The Mercedes were split by Vettel's Red Bull team-mate, Mark Webber.

All of the frontrunners used the option tyre for their final runs, and thus were committed to using the same tyres at the start of the race.

From the off, Vettel pulled away, while Alonso jumped up to second place after overtaking Massa at the start. Yet even he couldn't stay with the Red Bull, as Vettel made it look easy out front.

As expected, the single compulsory pit stops were triggered by the guys a little further back pitting first, thus causing everyone else ahead to defend their position by making their own stops straight away. Aside from Hamilton passing Rosberg for fourth, the stops did little to shake up the race and, with no second stops due, further changes looked unlikely.

Vettel stayed ahead, but through the second and final stint, on the harder tyre, he was gradually reeled in by Alonso. The double champion got within striking distance when he had a massive break after Vettel suffered a loss of power, due it turned out later to a spark plug issue. The German was unable to defend his lead, and ultimately he tumbled down to a frustrated fourth, as Massa then Hamilton got by.

INSIDE LINE
FERNANDO ALONSO
FERRARI DRIVER

"It's a very special day for me. Winning is always special, but I think it's even more special at Ferrari with all the history behind the team and all the expectations a driver has when he drives for Ferrari. There's no better way to start the relationship. I'm in the best team in the world.

We have been working very hard all winter, and the guys did a very good job in testing, so we arrived quite well prepared. This result is very positive and I'm very optimistic for the rest of the season.

I didn't know mid-race if I could have passed Vettel. I had some pace to spare, but I was concentrating on managing the tyres. We knew that we had to do 35 or 36 laps with the tyres. I was biding my time to attack, waiting for the last 10 or 12 laps, but suddenly he had a car problem and we had the chance to pass him earlier than expected. He was very quick, especially with soft tyres at the beginning, and I couldn't follow him. With the hard tyre, maybe we had a little bit more pace, but it's difficult to know.

It's great to win, but I always say that the first three or four races aren't crucial for anything. You just need to take some solid points, get used to the new regulations and understand the tyres a little bit better. It's hard to tell what the situation is during the winter tests with different fuel loads and everything, so it's good to confirm the car's performance. This win is thanks to a fantastic car.

You never know how a new championship will go with a big change in the regulations. For me also, changing teams, you never know, but at the moment everything has been perfect and this is a very good start. I think in equal conditions, as qualifying with low fuel these days shows the potential of the cars, having both Ferraris in the top three demonstrated we have a very good car. But it's a very long championship, 10 months of developing. It's very important to start scoring points from the first race. If not, you're always behind and needing to close the gap, and that's not ideal if you want to fight for a championship. That's what we're here for, and this is the first step, so let's see what happens."

Alonso duly cantered to a win that signalled a perfect start to his relationship with Ferrari. He said that there was no great mystery to the strategy and, as noted, all the top runners more or less followed each other into the pits.

"We knew that we had to do qualifying with the soft tyres, as they were quicker," he said. "I did a so-so lap in Q3, so I started third on the grid, and it wasn't a perfect position, but anyway it was good enough to be in the fight. Then we have been really open in terms of our strategy. Now there isn't a clear lap to stop. You have fuel enough to finish the race, so the engineers tell you when to stop.

"Then, after that, we switched to the prime tyre, but also to unknown territory as well. We didn't know how many laps the prime would do in good shape, but the car was so good that it managed the tyre very well and we finished the race with perfect conditions with the tyre."

Although he was helped by Vettel's problem, Alonso insisted that he still believed there was a chance to pass him on pure speed.

"I was thinking of winning at that time. I knew that it was a very difficult thing to do, overtaking Vettel,

BELOW Michael Schumacher was back, but not in a position to add to his record of 91 grand prix wins

TALKING POINT
A POOR START

With the return of Michael Schumacher after three years in retirement, and all the top drivers in top cars, expectation hung like never before. Yet, unfortunately, the opening race of the season at Sakhir turned out to be an insomniac's cure.

We were racing with full fuel loads for the first time since refuelling

returned 16 years earlier. Perhaps we should have seen it coming in the answers drivers gave when asked whether it was harder and more physically demanding to drive fuel-heavy cars.

To a man, their response was the same. "Oh no. It's less demanding. You can't really race them because you've got to look after the tyres. Flat-spot one early on and you'll have ruined your race..."

The early race pace was as much as seven or eight seconds slower than qualifying speed, and drivers talked about "fuel-heavy, unraceable boats that might as well have been from an entirely different formula than their qualifying spec".

Sebastian Vettel, pole man and likely winner before a rogue spark-plug problem, spelled out the situation

even more plainly. "It doesn't seem like there's been much overtaking apart from the lapped cars," said Red Bull Racing's German driver.

"It's pretty much what we expected from the simulations. You've lost the ability to attack every lap and really fight against your limits and the car's limits. Now it's much more about the challenge of controlling and pacing yourself through the race, and it was a one-stop race too."

Six months earlier, Red Bull's Christian Horner had voiced fears that this was the way it might turn out unless there were two mandatory tyre stops. Also, describing Mark Webber's race, he explained: "He didn't get the best out of his qualifying lap, then got boxed in at the first corner and dropped a position. With the format the way it was, he couldn't overtake.

He couldn't really pit, as you drop into traffic, and when he got fresh air he didn't have any tyres left.

"I pushed hard over the winter for two tyre stops," Horner went on, "but only a couple of people agreed with me. It would be a great shame for the fans if all the races were like this one and I do think that's a real danger.

"Everybody thought I wanted two stops because of problems with tyre degradation, but I think today we've proved that tyre degradation isn't a problem for Red Bull."

The Bahrain GP never produces the greatest of races, but this one was a major anti-climax. Everyone left Sakhir screaming for immediate action, even the possible reintroduction of refuelling. While, perhaps wisely, the powers-that-be warned against making any knee-jerk reaction.

but I was waiting for the opportunity. I knew that our car maybe manages the tyres in a very good way, as we saw that in the winter, so I was getting some relaxed laps behind me and then maybe waiting for the last 10 laps to attack. Then we were lucky with Vettel's problem to overtake a little bit earlier and win the race. We've been lucky, but in all victories you need some luck and this one was lucky as well."

Massa's run to second place was equally significant, as this was his comeback race, and it was clear that he was suffering no ill-effects.

However, of more importance perhaps was the way he was passed by Alonso at the start, the Spaniard laying down a marker as he made an aggressive move around the outside. Thereafter, Massa wasn't able to offer a consistent challenge, as his engine was running too hot in the slipstream of the other Ferrari. He was even told to pull out from behind Alonso, in order to cool his engine.

"It was a bit strange for me," said the Brazilian. "I didn't have a good start and I lost a position, an important position, to Fernando at the first corner. The race was just great for me as the car was perfect. I could manage to follow Fernando for the whole time

OPPOSITE Lotus made its return to F1, with Heikki Kovalainen finishing the race in 15th place, although Jarno Trulli narrowly failed to go the distance

BELOW Virgin Racing made its entrance. This is Lucas di Grassi, but his F1 debut proved to be brief

BOTTOM Alonso chased Vettel hard, and was rewarded when the Red Bull suffered a loss of power, allowing the Spaniard to dive by for victory on his first outing for Ferrari

local hero Mark Webber. Fernando Alonso qualified third, while Button already had the edge on Hamilton when he took fourth. Perhaps distracted by a much-publicised Friday night run-in with local police after a traffic offence, Hamilton had a scrappy Q2 session, and found himself stranded in 11th.

Rain had been forecast for Sunday and, with astonishing precision, it fell as the cars were waiting on the grid for the late 5pm start. There followed a mad scramble to fit intermediates.

Vettel got away well on the slick surface, while Felipe Massa charged up from fifth to second, getting ahead of Webber. Behind, Button nudged Alonso into a spin at Turn 1, and the Spaniard collected Michael Schumacher, dislodging the German's front wing.

The safety car then came out after a more serious shunt involving Kamui Kobayashi, Sebastien Buemi and Nico Hulkenberg further around the lap, allowing Alonso and Schumacher (who pitted for a new nose) to rejoin the pack.

At the restart, Webber soon relieved Massa of second. Meanwhile, the track was drying rapidly. Having lost a few places with the early contact, Button rolled the dice and charged into the pits for dries on lap 6. When he went out, he slithered around for a lap, even running onto the grass, and it looked like a disastrous call. But then he set fastest lap sectors, and the whole pitlane could see that he had got it right. Most of the field then came in on lap 8, while leader Vettel played it safe and came in on lap 9. RBR had to keep the unlucky Webber out for one more lap, as the team felt it couldn't service both cars on the same lap.

When the tyre changing was done, Vettel was still in front, but Button had leaped up to second. Having made a great start, Renault's Robert Kubica had passed Massa in the pits to move into third, while Webber had lost a few places.

On dry tyres, Vettel was able to consolidate his

advantage, pulling away from Button and looking set to make up for his Bahrain disappointment. Then, on lap 26 he felt a vibration, due it turned out to a front wheel working loose. He was heading for the pits when he spun off the track.

Button was handed the lead, and thereafter the World Champion drove a faultless race. It was far from easy, as he had to make his soft option tyres last for 52 of 58 laps, but his well-known capacity for smooth driving paid dividends.

"I made the call to pit early, as I thought if I don't pit early I am just going to keep going backwards," said Button. "I thought it was a terrible call initially, as the

OPPOSITE Lap 1, Turn 1, and Fernando Alonso spins across to strike Schumacher's Mercedes, as Massa and Webber escape towards Turn 2

ABOVE Felipe Massa holds off Kubica, Rosberg, Hamilton and Sutil into Turn 3, just before they all pitted for slick tyres as the track dried

BELOW Rubens Barrichello started and finished eighth for Williams

pitlane was so wet, and after my first lap out of the pits I thought it was a catastrophic mistake. But, after that, I could get into it. I found that I could push pretty hard on the dry parts and then really it was about picking people off as they came out onto the circuit.

"It was a nice feeling, as they were searching for the grip and I knew where it was and was able to overtake. I got up behind Sebastian and made a little mistake, ran wide, so I couldn't really have a go at him. He obviously had his own problems. From then on, though, I just had to conserve the tyres. I had a big issue on about lap 15 where the rears just started going away from me. I had a lot of graining from the rear and I thought 'that's it for me, they're just going to swallow me up.' I took a lot of front wing out, closed the diff and just hoped for the best really."

Kubica did an equally impressive job to secure a surprise second place for Renault, confirming that he was the strongest package outside the acknowledged 'big four' teams. The Pole qualified ninth, just as he had in Bahrain. In the opening race, he had been a victim of a first-corner tangle, but this time he benefited on the slippery track. When the dust settled, he was fourth, behind only Vettel, Massa and Webber.

As the track dried, and Button showed that slicks were the way to go, Massa and Kubica led the charge into the pits. Renault did a great job to get their car out ahead of the Ferrari. Renault's team leader lost a spot to Button, but gained another from late stopper Webber, and ended up third. Vettel's retirement promoted Kubica to second, and then he had his hands full keeping Hamilton at bay.

"He knew he was going to the end, so he was managing his tyres," said Renault engineering chief Alan Permane. "He wasn't pushing at all. He knew he couldn't get Button, and he had Hamilton behind him for quite a while, and he didn't get past."

Hamilton, Nico Rosberg and Webber had been behind the yellow car initially, but all three drivers dropped back when their teams decided that a fresh set of option tyres would get them to the flag more quickly. Kubica then had Massa in his mirrors.

"We'd never intended to make another pit stop when we started the race," added Permane. "It was always going to be a one-stop, whether we started on wets or didn't, although they had to do a bit more than we originally intended them to. I must admit, when I saw other cars coming in, I was very surprised.

TALKING POINT
SCHUEY'S STRUGGLE

Michael Schumacher came back to a Formula 1 very different from the one that he left at the end of the 2006 season when he'd finished the year as runner-up to Renault's Fernando Alonso.

Around 0.4s slower than his Mercedes team-mate Nico Rosberg on average, in low-fuel trim in both Bahrain and Melbourne, the seven-times champion knew that he had a struggle on his hands if he was to revisit former glories.

At 41, after three years out of the cockpit, he couldn't be expected to come back and dominate straight away. However, everyone felt that perhaps he expected more than he proved able to deliver in the first few races of his return.

The stopwatch in qualifying for the Australian GP said that Nico and Michael were separated by just 0.04s, but that flattered Michael as Nico had made an error on his best lap. Indeed, if you instead put their best lap sectors together, the gap was more like 0.4s, as before.

In Bahrain, Michael raced close to Nico's pace, but in Australia he could qualify only seventh and then found himself in a first-corner tangle that relegated him to the back of the field with car damage.

Out on the circuit, Michael didn't seem to be handling the car with the confidence of old. In his first stint in F1, Michael, who always liked a car with a very 'pointy' front end, was always at the forefront of Bridgestone tyre development. Towards the end of his first career, it was Bridgestone and Michael versus Michelin and Fernando. Always, therefore, he drove a bespoke tyre that suited his style.

Now though, with control rubber in F1, the tyres are less responsive, less 'edgy' and Michael doesn't seem able to access car performance in the way that he used to.

The understeering tendency of the Mercedes chassis certainly didn't help him, and very early in the season there was talk of a revised, longer-wheelbase chassis in order to try to improve the overall aerodynamic efficiency of the car.

Michael also faces a greater strength in depth than before. Whereas first time around he may always have had one particularly strong rival team and driver, nowadays he has to contend with three rival top-line teams, all with particularly strong driver line-ups.

While the extent of the challenge was probably unexpected, Michael still professed to be enjoying himself and fully up for it. It's just that he can't have expected teams with new cars, like Virgin Racing, to fight back as he fought his way through the field. Or to hear a radio message saying: "Push Michael. If you can get past Alguersuari, you might get a point..."

I was gobsmacked when I saw Hamilton pit, and then Rosberg. It didn't make any sense at all. Maybe they thought their tyre wear and degradation was going to be worse than ours, but we knew pretty much from our work on Friday that the tyres would do it durability- wise, no problem at all."

The last third of the race was fascinating, as the cars on new rubber lapped faster than those ahead and began to close the gap. Button, Kubica and Massa were safe in the top three positions, but Hamilton finally caught fourth-placed Alonso with around eight laps to go. However, the effort had put his own tyres over the edge and he didn't have

sufficient momentum to slip by the canny Spaniard. Hamilton's hopes ended when Webber ran into the McLaren, pitching both men off the road.

That left Massa and Alonso safe in third and fourth places, Alonso having come all the way from the back after his first-corner bump. It was a good drive too from the Brazilian.

"My tyres were suffering, I was trying to keep the tyres in the right condition, at the right temperature, especially at the beginning of the race," said Massa. "I was suffering from that yesterday as well, but then after 20 laps, let's say, they started to improve a lot. Maybe I picked up the pace with a bit of degradation and I started to do my race 20 laps after I changed my tyres. For sure, we had some fights and I lost some positions in the race. But the team did a great job with the strategy, not to stop."

Behind the Ferraris, Rosberg inherited fifth place after the Webber/Hamilton clash. He was running fourth when the team copied Webber and stopped for a new set of dries, only to lose a place to the RBR driver. Rosberg couldn't match the pace of either Webber or Hamilton on the new tyres initially, and looked set for seventh until they collided. He thus took a useful helping of points, and was the best-placed driver to have stopped twice.

Hamilton salvaged sixth, while Tonio Liuzzi and Rubens Barrichello also got by Webber, who had to be content with ninth place after stopping for a new nose. The final point went to Schumacher, who could never recover from his own lap 1 nose change. The man who traditionally shines in mixed conditions spent most of his race behind slower cars.

Jaime Alguersuari made some good progress in the first part of the race, and then the youngest man in the race spent most of his time holding off the oldest man... Schumacher finally got past in the closing laps, bumping the young Spaniard down to 11th.

SNAPSHOT FROM
AUSTRALIA

CLOCKWISE FROM RIGHT
The view of Melbourne from high above Turn 14; fans present their race programmes to Sebastian Vettel for signing; actor and F1 fan John Travolta was in town; multiple World Champions Michael Schumacher and Fernando Alonso compare notes; Jenson Button's number one and two supporters, Jessica Michibata and father John; neither Felipe Massa looked particularly happy...; F1 steering wheels have little space for any more technical features; two sexes, two different dress codes; the marshals signal their message of caution as the safety car is deployed

RACE RESULT
AUSTRALIA MELBOURNE

Official Results © [2010]
Formula One Administration Limited,
6 Princes Gate, London, SW7 1QJ.
No reproduction without permission.
All copyright and database rights reserved.

RACE DATE March 28th
CIRCUIT LENGTH 3.295 miles
NO. OF LAPS 58
RACE DISTANCE 191.110 miles
WEATHER Overcast, 26°C
TRACK TEMP 25°C
ATTENDANCE 305,000
LAP RECORD Michael Schumacher, 1m24.125s, 141.016mph, 2004

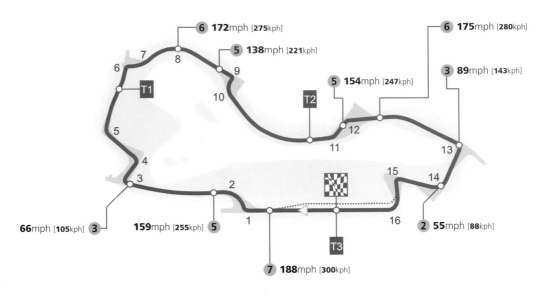

6 **172**mph [**275**kph]
6 **175**mph [**280**kph]
5 **138**mph [**221**kph]
3 **89**mph [**143**kph]
5 **154**mph [**247**kph]
66mph [105kph] 3
159mph [**255**kph] 5
2 **55**mph [**88**kph]
7 **188**mph [**300**kph]

	PRACTICE 1				PRACTICE 2				PRACTICE 3				QUALIFYING 1			QUALIFYING 2	
	Driver	Time	Laps		Driver	Time	Laps		Driver	Time	Laps		Driver	Time		Driver	Time
1	R Kubica	1m26.927s	22	1	L Hamilton	1m25.801s	13	1	M Webber	1m24.719s	16	1	S Vettel	1m24.774s	1	S Vettel	1m24.096s
2	N Rosberg	1m27.126s	18	2	J Button	1m26.076s	16	2	F Alonso	1m24.929s	19	2	N Rosberg	1m24.788s	2	M Webber	1m24.276s
3	J Button	1m27.482s	22	3	M Webber	1m26.248s	22	3	M Schumacher	1m24.963s	17	3	J Button	1m24.897s	3	F Alonso	1m24.335s
4	F Massa	1m27.511s	18	4	M Schumacher	1m26.511s	16	4	S Vettel	1m25.122s	19	4	L Hamilton	1m25.046s	4	J Button	1m24.531s
5	S Vettel	1m27.686s	23	5	V Petrov	1m26.732s	26	5	N Rosberg	1m25.366s	16	5	F Alonso	1m25.082s	5	N Rosberg	1m24.788s
6	F Alonso	1m27.747s	21	6	S Buemi	1m26.832s	29	6	J Button	1m25.399s	20	6	M Webber	1m25.286s	6	M Schumacher	1m24.871s
7	L Hamilton	1m27.793s	22	7	A Sutil	1m26.834s	22	7	L Hamilton	1m25.505s	14	7	M Schumacher	1m25.351s	7	F Massa	1m25.010s
8	S Buemi	1m28.014s	21	8	V Liuzzi	1m26.835s	17	8	A Sutil	1m25.525s	18	8	A Sutil	1m25.504s	8	A Sutil	1m25.046s
9	V Petrov	1m28.114s	25	9	R Barrichello	1m26.904s	25	9	F Massa	1m25.549s	20	9	F Massa	1m25.548s	9	R Barrichello	1m25.085s
10	V Liuzzi	1m28.192s	18	10	N Rosberg	1m26.956s	22	10	V Liuzzi	1m25.782s	19	10	R Kubica	1m25.588s	10	R Kubica	1m25.122s
11	P di Resta	1m28.537s	25	11	R Kubica	1m27.108s	28	11	R Barrichello	1m25.852s	17	11	R Barrichello	1m25.702s	11	L Hamilton	1m25.184s
12	M Schumacher	1m28.550s	19	12	P de la Rosa	1m27.108s	25	12	S Buemi	1m26.104s	21	12	N Hulkenberg	1m25.866s	12	S Buemi	1m25.638s
13	J Alguersuari	1m28.572s	21	13	K Kobayashi	1m27.455s	23	13	R Kubica	1m26.184s	21	13	S Buemi	1m26.061s	13	V Liuzzi	1m25.743s
14	M Webber	1m28.683s	22	14	N Hulkenberg	1m27.545s	25	14	K Kobayashi	1m26.275s	21	14	P de la Rosa	1m26.089s	14	P de la Rosa	1m25.747s
15	P de la Rosa	1m29.465s	13	15	F Alonso	1m29.025s	20	15	J Alguersuari	1m26.368s	17	15	J Alguersuari	1m26.095s	15	N Hulkenberg	1m25.748s
16	R Barrichello	1m29.712s	18	16	S Vettel	1m29.134s	19	16	V Petrov	1m26.661s	19	16	V Liuzzi	1m26.170s	16	K Kobayashi	1m25.777s
17	N Hulkenberg	1m30.249s	26	17	F Massa	1m29.591s	21	17	N Hulkenberg	1m26.804s	19	17	K Kobayashi	1m26.251s	17	J Alguersuari	1m26.089s
18	K Kobayashi	1m31.588s	5	18	H Kovalainen	1m29.860s	15	18	P de la Rosa	1m26.818s	18	18	V Petrov	1m26.471s			
19	J Trulli	1m31.652s	13	19	J Alguersuari	1m30.510s	43	19	H Kovalainen	1m29.539s	19	19	H Kovalainen	1m28.797s			
20	H Kovalainen	1m31.654s	28	20	J Trulli	1m30.695s	17	20	J Trulli	1m29.800s	16	20	J Trulli	1m29.111s			
21	L di Grassi	1m32.831s	25	21	T Glock	1m32.117s	9	21	L di Grassi	1m30.800s	18	21	T Glock	1m29.592s			
22	B Senna	1m33.401s	24	22	L di Grassi	No time	2	22	T Glock	1m31.114s	12	22	L di Grassi	1m30.185s			
23	K Chandhok	1m34.251s	19	23	K Chandhok	No time	1	23	K Chandhok	1m34.334s	11	23	B Senna	1m30.526s			
24	T Glock	1m34.925s	8	24	B Senna	No time	0	24	B Senna	1m36.649s	8	24	K Chandhok	1m30.613s			

Best sectors – Practice			Speed trap – Practice			Best sectors – Qualifying			Speed trap – Qualifying		
Sec 1	M Webber	28.311s	1	L Hamilton	193.495mph	Sec 1	M Webber	28.099s	1	L Hamilton	192.500mph
Sec 2	M Schumacher	22.770s	2	J Button	192.252mph	Sec 2	S Vettel	22.616s	2	J Button	191.817mph
Sec 3	S Vettel	33.413s	3	R Kubica	191.444mph	Sec 3	M Webber	33.094s	3	V Liuzzi	190.512mph

Jenson Button

"I struggled on inters, so we figured it was time for dries. As I pitted, I could see it was soaking, but I caught Sebastian, saved the tyres and built a useful gap."

Michael Schumacher

"I could have had a good race, so it was a pity I was hit right after the start. I had to take the rest of the race from last place, but I have to say that I was still having fun."

Sebastian Vettel

"I had sparks coming from the front-left wheel. Then, two corners before, I had huge vibrations and as soon as I touched the brakes, I had a failure into Turn 13."

Felipe Massa

"I managed not to spin the wheels and moved up to second. Then I lost places when I had grip problems, but thanks to the strategy, I was able to gain some."

Rubens Barrichello

"We should have finished seventh. We took the chance to change tyres. I thought everyone else would also come in, which is why I went for that route."

Robert Kubica

"I jumped Massa in the pits and came out ahead of Button, but I couldn't hold him off. The team said I didn't need to pit again if I could look after the tyres."

Lewis Hamilton

"This was one of the drives of my life. Maybe the decision to make a second stop wasn't right, but we usually get it right. It was disappointing to be hit by Webber."

Nico Rosberg

"I had a bad start and after that I lacked pace and struggled with the option tyre. We decided to go for a second stop for some fresh tyres to attack the group ahead."

Mark Webber

"At the end, we caught the leaders, but then we had the incident. I lost all front downforce when I got close to them, the car lifted and I slid into the back of Lewis."

Fernando Alonso

"I got an awful start, as I had wheelspin on a white line and was last after the first corner, after a collision with two other cars, so to finish fourth is significant."

Nico Hulkenberg

"It was disappointing. I was already in the corner when I was hit from behind by Kamui Kobayashi. It was a big impact, but I'm not sure what caused it."

Vitaly Petrov

"I made a good start to gain eight positions. Then we made a change to slicks, but I got caught out in the braking zone for Turn 3 and got stuck in the gravel."

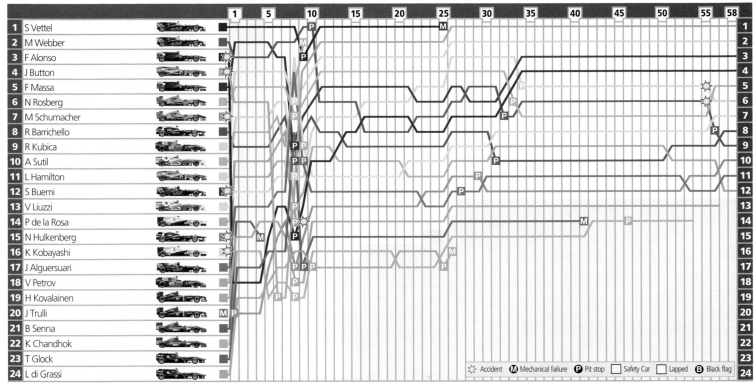

	Driver
1	S Vettel
2	M Webber
3	F Alonso
4	J Button
5	F Massa
6	N Rosberg
7	M Schumacher
8	R Barrichello
9	R Kubica
10	A Sutil
11	L Hamilton
12	S Buemi
13	V Liuzzi
14	P de la Rosa
15	N Hulkenberg
16	K Kobayashi
17	J Alguersuari
18	V Petrov
19	H Kovalainen
20	J Trulli
21	B Senna
22	K Chandhok
23	T Glock
24	L di Grassi

Key: ☆ Accident　Ⓜ Mechanical failure　Ⓟ Pit stop　▢ Safety Car　▢ Lapped　Ⓑ Black flag

QUALIFYING 3

	Driver	Time
1	S Vettel	1m23.919s
2	M Webber	1m24.035s
3	F Alonso	1m24.111s
4	J Button	1m24.675s
5	F Massa	1m24.837s
6	N Rosberg	1m24.884s
7	M Schumacher	1m24.927s
8	R Barrichello	1m25.217s
9	R Kubica	1m25.372s
10	A Sutil	1m26.036s

GRID

	Driver	Time
1	S Vettel	1m23.919s
2	M Webber	1m24.035s
3	F Alonso	1m24.111s
4	J Button	1m24.675s
5	F Massa	1m24.837s
6	N Rosberg	1m24.884s
7	M Schumacher	1m24.927s
8	R Barrichello	1m25.217s
9	R Kubica	1m25.372s
10	A Sutil	1m26.036s
11	L Hamilton	1m25.184s
12	S Buemi	1m25.638s
13	V Liuzzi	1m25.743s
14	P de la Rosa	1m25.747s
15	N Hulkenberg	1m25.748s
16	K Kobayashi	1m25.777s
17	J Alguersuari	1m26.089s
18	V Petrov	1m26.471s
19	H Kovalainen	1m28.797s
20	J Trulli	1m29.111s
21*	T Glock	1m29.592s
22*	L di Grassi	1m30.185s
23	B Senna	1m30.526s
24	K Chandhok	1m30.613s

*Started from pitlane

RACE

	Driver	Car	Laps	Time	Avg. mph	Fastest	Stops
1	J Button	McLaren-Mercedes MP4-25	58	1h33m36.531s	114.351	1m29.291s	1
2	R Kubica	Renault R30	58	1h33m48.565s	114.123	1m29.570s	1
3	F Massa	Ferrari F10	58	1h33m51.019s	114.076	1m29.537s	1
4	F Alonso	Ferrari F10	58	1h33m52.835s	114.042	1m29.707s	1
5	N Rosberg	Mercedes MGP W01	58	1h33m53.214s	114.035	1m28.489s	1
6	L Hamilton	McLaren-Mercedes MP4-25	58	1h34m06.429s	113.786	1m28.506s	2
7	V Liuzzi	Force India-Mercedes VJM03	58	1h34m36.378s	113.225	1m29.685s	1
8	R Barrichello	Williams-Cosworth FW32	58	1h34m37.067s	113.212	1m29.210s	2
9	M Webber	Red Bull-Renault RB6	58	1h34m43.850s	113.086	1m28.358s	3
10	M Schumacher	Mercedes MGP W01	58	1h34m45.922s	113.047	1m29.195s	3
11	J Alguersuari	Toro Rosso-Ferrari STR5	58	1h34m47.832s	113.012	1m29.713s	2
12	P de la Rosa	BMW Sauber-Ferrari C29	58	1h34m50.615s	112.960	1m30.587s	1
13	H Kovalainen	Lotus-Cosworth T127	56	1h34m49.139s	109.091	1m33.638s	1
14	K Chandhok	HRT-Cosworth F110	53	1h33m38.174s	104.465	1m35.045s	2
R	T Glock	Virgin-Cosworth VR-01	41	Suspension	-	1m34.230s	1
R	L di Grassi	Virgin-Cosworth VR-01	26	Hydraulics	-	1m36.607s	2
R	S Vettel	Red Bull-Renault RB6	25	Wheel	-	1m35.556s	1
R	A Sutil	Force India-Mercedes VJM03	9	Engine	-	1m43.132s	0
R	V Petrov	Renault R30	9	Spun off	-	1m43.223s	1
R	B Senna	HRT-Cosworth F110	4	Hydraulics	-	2m27.276s	0
R	S Buemi	Toro Rosso-Ferrari STR5	0	Accident			0
R	N Hulkenberg	Williams-Cosworth FW32	0	Accident			0
R	K Kobayashi	BMW Sauber-Ferrari C29	0	Accident			0
NS	J Trulli	Lotus-Cosworth T127	0	Hydraulics			0

CHAMPIONSHIP

	Driver	Pts
1	F Alonso	37
2	F Massa	33
3	J Button	31
4	L Hamilton	23
5	N Rosberg	20
6	R Kubica	18
7	S Vettel	12
8	M Schumacher	9
9	V Liuzzi	8
10	M Webber	6
11	R Barrichello	5

	Constructor	Pts
1	Ferrari	70
2	McLaren-Mercedes	54
3	Mercedes	29
4	Renault	18
5	Red Bull-Renault	18
6	Force India-Mercedes	8
7	Williams-Cosworth	5

Fastest lap
M Webber 1m28.358s
(134.282mph) on lap 47

Fastest speed trap
L Hamilton 192.811mph
Slowest speed trap
K Kobayashi 103.210mph

Fastest pit stop
1 M Webber 23.517s
2 M Webber 23.986s
3 N Rosberg 23.990s

Adrian Sutil
"We seemed to have a problem with the engine early on. I was driving on just four cylinders and then lost the power. It was a shame as we were looking good."

"Today went really badly for me, as I was involved in someone else's accident on the opening lap. I guess Kobayashi must have braked really late."

Jarno Trulli
"We couldn't start the race because we had a hydraulic failure on the grid and, despite the team's best efforts, we could not fix it in time to make the race."

Karun Chandhok
"To finish was extremely difficult, and all the more satisfying because of that. This is a great step forward. I am proud to have recorded our first finish."

Pedro de la Rosa
"We underestimated tyre degradation. In the end, I really had no rear tyres left. For the last 15 laps, it was just a question of how to keep the car on the track."

Timo Glock
"I was able to catch Chandhok and some others and we had fun fighting Michael. So it was a shame when I began to feel something wrong with the car."

Vitantonio Liuzzi
"I struggled on the intermediate tyres and lost a few positions. However, after I pitted for the dry tyres I was able to recover and stay on the race pace."

"I had a long fight with Michael, which was nice. I was under pressure, but was able to keep him behind me until I made a small mistake at Turn 13."

Heikki Kovalainen
"Our target was to finish and we were comfortably ahead of the new teams. When Glock dropped, I focused on keeping up a decent rhythm, not making mistakes."

Bruno Senna
"I didn't intend my second grand prix to end with hydraulic failure, but that's racing! I made a good start and was running in 14th place after the big crash in front."

Kamui Kobayashi
"It looks as if I touched a kerb or another car in Turn 3. I had no worries about the front wing, but a few corners later it went off and became stuck under the car."

Lucas di Grassi
"We didn't time the strategy well to change to slicks. So it's a shame that we were hit by another problem – a hydraulic problem – and we had to retire."

2010 FORMULA 1 PETRONAS MALAYSIAN GRAND PRIX
KUALA LUMPUR

FAST FROM THE START

The sprint from the grid to the first corner was the key to Sebastian Vettel's victory as he managed to dislodge pole-starting team-mate Mark Webber to lead home a Red Bull 1–2

He had a broken spark plug in Bahrain, and a loose wheel in Australia. On both occasions, Sebastian Vettel led from pole position, only to see victory snatched away. In Malaysia, everything finally came together for Red Bull Racing, and the mercurial German driver led team-mate Mark Webber home in a crushing 1–2 display.

The scene was very different to the way it was in Melbourne as Red Bull Team Principal Christian Horner hugged and congratulated everyone he came across in the garage. The sense of relief was palpable. This time it was McLaren and Ferrari who'd made bad calls in screwing up qualifying, while Ferrari (Fernando Alonso's engine) and Mercedes (with Michael Schumacher's loose rear wheel) endured costly problems in the race.

After taking so much flak – and putting up with conspiratorial suggestions that the broken spark plug in Bahrain was a cover for a fuel consumption problem – Horner had a right to look relieved.

"It was the perfect way to silence critics," he smiled. "Arguably, this is one of the hardest circuits on the cars. We saw a couple of teams have reliability issues, yet our cars ran impeccably from start to finish,

good at all, but he redeemed himself during a soaking-wet qualifying session, gambling by switching from wet tyres to intermediate tyres in the closing minutes. He duly took pole position ahead of the Mercedes of Nico Rosberg and team-mate Vettel.

Alas, Webber's great performance was overshadowed by drama elsewhere. Poor judgement of the deteriorating conditions early on left the McLaren and Ferrari drivers in the pits at the wrong time. They finished way down the order, with Jenson Button qualifying 17th, Hamilton 19th, Fernando Alonso 20th and Felipe Massa 21st. It would clearly be a hard slog for all of them come Sunday...

Against expectations, it was dry for the start of the race and, for the first time all week, there was no afternoon monsoon. We'd seen in the past that, wet or dry, Vettel was at his best when leading from the front. He didn't get pole this time, but he might as well have done. As Rosberg suffered excessive wheelspin on the dirty side of the track, Vettel surged into second, dragged up behind Webber and then flicked to the inside to claim the lead.

"I realised straight away that I had a good start and passed Nico, who was alongside," said Vettel. "Then I got the tow from Mark, so I was able to gain, gain, gain. It's a long sprint to Turn 1 and I clearly had an advantage over him and then I took the chance I had into Turn 1.

"It was quite late, so I just made it. Then Mark had a better exit out of Turn 2, through Turn 3 and it's very slippery and we both tried to push."

"Our drivers were firm but fair with each other," said Horner. "That's all I asked in the briefing before the race: please don't take each other off into Turn 1. Mark gave Seb the space and vice versa. Seb picked up the tow down the straight. If it had been the other way around, Mark would have won the race. There was just nothing to split them by today."

It was a decisive move, and one for which Webber had no response. For the rest of the race, the dark blue cars remained close together but, without the strategic

ABOVE Mark Webber and Red Bull Racing read the conditions in qualifying better than their rivals

BELOW Lewis Hamilton goes around the outside of Vitaly Petrov's Renault into Turn 1, as he works his way up the race order from 19th

OPPOSITE However quick Fernando Alonso's pit stop was, it was never going to turn him into a winner after he qualified 21st

so it's testimony to a brilliant team effort. We worked tremendously hard and had people who gave up their holiday during the Easter break to ensure that we had two reliable cars for here.

"I feel great relief and considerable satisfaction for all the hard work that's gone in from the crew here and in Milton Keynes, and from the drivers. We've got a great car and this result puts us right back in there in the championship."

Red Bull Racing was certainly under considerable pressure to get a result going into Sepang, as was Webber. The crash with Lewis Hamilton in the closing laps of his home race in Australia did his reputation no

INSIDE LINE
SEBASTIAN VETTEL
RED BULL RACING DRIVER

"After the disappointments in Bahrain and Melbourne, it was great to get the win under my belt here and stay within a couple of points of the championship lead.

The start of the race was key, with Mark on pole position and me third on the grid, and I realised straight away that I'd made a good one. I overtook Rosberg and then got the tow from Mark.

It's a long run to Turn 1 and I clearly had an advantage over him and took the chance.

The move was quite late. I just made it, and then Mark had a better exit out of Turn 2 and through Turn 3, which was slippery.

We're here to fight each other, but you should keep the respect and I think we both had that respect for each other. If Mark had been in my position, I'm sure he would have done the same.

After that, it was just a question of getting away from our competitors. I could see that Mark and I were more or less going at the same pace, although I think he was a little bit quicker than me in the early stages of the race.

I was trying to save my tyres, and it worked so that I could pull away a bit before my pit stop, and the second stint was very long. It's extremely hot here and I didn't stop sweating. Fortunately, I didn't run out of drinks in the car.

I was trying not to be too extreme in the beginning, but Malaysia is always tough and very physical and at some stage I was hoping for rain, just to cool down!

But, what a grand prix! Qualifying was extremely difficult with the wet conditions, but in the race it stayed dry and we had a magnificent car. The key was to pace yourself and to watch your tyres. Bridgestone did a good job bringing two compounds that worked well.

It was a fantastic result for us, especially for me, after two races in which I didn't finish where I wanted to be. It's very important not to panic and to stay relaxed, as it's a long season, but getting up on the top step of the podium here on Sunday, having won the race, was the best result we could get and one I needed.

On top of that, having Mark in second place was a big, big plus for the team. Under the new scoring system that meant 43 points, and I'm delighted."

element provided by fuel stops, their track positions were never going to change.

As had become the norm, the strategy of the drivers at the front was determined by that of their main opposition. Rosberg finally blinked and pitted on lap 22, so Vettel followed a lap later. Webber went the longest on the soft tyre of the frontrunners who started the race on it, without apparent problem. His 24-lap opening stint was exceeded by the 26 of Hamilton and 30 of Alonso on softs in the second half of the race, both having started on the harder tyre from their lowly grid spots. But, of course, they did those longer stints with less fuel on board.

"We weren't struggling on the option. We just wanted to make sure we covered Rosberg with both cars," Horner explained. "They went a remarkable distance on the option tyre without any issue. There were really no issues at all, we were just trying to look after the tyres in the second half of the race."

For the second race in succession, Webber had had to wait for Vettel to pit, a by-product of new rules which meant that fuel played no part in the decision to pit. The bottom line is that if your two cars are close together, you can't pit them on the same lap.

In Australia, Webber wanted to come in but had to wait for Vettel. That extra lap cost him vital time on a drying track, and a few places. In Malaysia, he again had to wait, although the delay wasn't as expensive.

"In that situation, it's only fair to give priority to the leader," related Horner. "As soon as Rosberg was in, we covered with Seb, and then a lap later with Mark. He had a sticking front-right wheel socket that delayed him a couple of seconds, but it made no difference to the result."

That extra delay in the pits was a little unfortunate, and it's worth noting that not one but two sceptical drivers from rival teams suggested that Webber had been held up deliberately for a few seconds, to prevent him from charging out of the pits and into a potential conflict with his team-mate. One driver even called it a 'Ferrari pit stop'!

Such mischievous gossip may be a little far-fetched, but nevertheless one can understand if Mark was a little frustrated at having to wait his turn, even if there was some logic to the team's choice.

Indeed, that frustration may have been a little evident towards the end of the race, when Mark set the race's fastest lap. Naturally, the potential to go

OPPOSITE TOP Force India's Adrian Sutil holds off Lewis Hamilton as he heads for fifth place

OPPOSITE BOTTOM HRT's Karun Chandhok was second best of the new team drivers, albeit finishing three laps down

BELOW Jenson Button and Fernando Alonso fight for position in the early stages of the race

TALKING POINT
BIG BOYS GET IT WRONG

Ferrari and McLaren paid a heavy price for a senseless gamble in the Malaysian Grand Prix.

When you're in Malaysia, close to mountains, where predicting rain patterns is nigh on impossible, how is it that the two most experienced teams in the sport failed to put in banker laps and found themselves

eliminated in the first of the three qualifying sessions?

They then suffered a dry race from the back of the grid in which even Lewis Hamilton's brio could salvage only sixth place.

Red Bull Racing said 'thank you very much', tapped in the open goal and took a maximum 43-point haul, 31 more than their closest major competitor.

So, what was the thinking that led to reliance on radar weather forecasting overcome the basic instinct of putting in an insurance lap at the start of a wet session?

"We should have done that," McLaren Team Principal Martin Whitmarsh admitted. "The drivers were sitting in the car and the team simply got it wrong.

"The radar had been pretty reliable

and we had watched the storms track in and track out again. We saw it coming, the rain started when the radar said it would, but it was also predicted to pass through and we thought that it would be dry by the end of qualifying one."

But why take the risk?

"If you send a car out to do a banker, there's always a risk as well," continued Whitmarsh. "These cars aren't at all easy to drive in tricky conditions and, thinking it was going to dry out, we didn't believe the banker lap was the right approach."

Mercedes GP Team Principal Ross Brawn elaborated: "The radar was so definitive – a little bit of rain at the start and then that would be it for the rest of the session. I think that somehow the clouds just disappear before they come over the mountains

nearby, then reform instantly and dump on the circuit."

But if it's so unpredictable, why no insurance lap?

"I'm sure that's what will happen next time..." smiled Brawn. "We're all the same, and I include myself – if we go with the technology, we've got something to blame. If we go with our intuition, we're the ones at fault.

"In truth, if you get it right more than 50% of the time you're doing well."

The man who really got it right was Mark Webber, who was the only one who risked intermediate tyres instead of extreme wets in the third qualifying session. It was a ballsy, fabulous pole effort, but then, with outboard mirrors, Vettel got in his blind spot off the line at the start of the race and mugged him into Turn 1...

faster was there as fuel loads dropped, but the Aussie wasn't exactly under threat from behind.

Horner explained: "With 15 laps to go we said 'OK, we've had a few reliability issues, let's look after the engines, they've still got to go a long way.' So they turned the engines down and then started doing purple sectors… And Mark set fastest lap with the engine turned right down, which was quite surprising. Sebastian was close to his time as well. I just made sure the engineers passed on the message that there's no point in chasing fastest lap…"

Vettel was delighted with his afternoon's work. "It was just a question about getting away from our competitors," said the German. "I could see Mark and I were more or less having the same pace, I think he was a little bit quicker in the beginning. I was trying to save my tyres. It worked, so before the stop I could pull away a little bit and the second stint was extremely long. It's extremely hot here and I didn't stop sweating."

Rosberg, meanwhile, had a lonely race to third place and the first podium for the rebadged Mercedes GP team. Once again, he outshone team-mate Michael Schumacher in qualifying, and the former World Champion had a frustrating race, stopping early when a rear wheel worked loose.

Robert Kubica had another good drive for Renault, marking himself as 'best of the rest' with fourth place. Adrian Sutil impressed with a good wet qualifying performance, which he turned into fifth come Sunday. For the last third of the race, the Force India driver successfully held off Hamilton, who put in a typically charging drive from the back, but had used up his tyres by the time he caught the German.

From their poor grid spots, Massa moved up to seventh and Button to eighth. The reigning World Champion showed that variety in race strategy was possible by making a very early pit stop and then going 47 laps on his second set of tyres, although ultimately it didn't help him much. In the closing laps, Button held off Alonso, who had struggled throughout the race with a downshift problem and then stopped with a blown engine just two laps from home.

Although it stayed dry through the race, this was a far more entertaining race than the season-opener in Bahrain, and the fact that the McLaren and Ferrari drivers were out of position after qualifying, so had to charge through the field, spiced up the action.

Reports of the death of F1 seemed to have been exaggerated, as was borne out by the points table. Although he had yet to win, Massa was on top and the first five drivers were covered by just four points – the equivalent, under the new-for-2010 scoring system, of just a humble eighth place.

LEFT TOP Red Bull Racing's pitcrew celebrates as Sebastian Vettel flashes past the chequered flag for victory, heading a team 1–2

LEFT BOTTOM Nico Rosberg pulls into *parc fermé* after finishing in third place for Mercedes GP

SNAPSHOT FROM
MALAYSIA

CLOCKWISE FROM RIGHT
Malaysian driver Fairuz Fauzy had his first run as Lotus's test driver; burnt rubber signatures on the grid; Vitaly Petrov made it three retirements from three in the second Renault, after a gearbox problem; Adrian Newey knew that champagne in the eyes hurt and Sebastian Vettel proved it; Lotus had Colin Chapman's famous cap on hand to celebrate in the unlikely event of a victory; when it rains in the tropics, it really rains; it was just like the old days when Michael Schumacher's name appeared at the top of the timesheets; one of the marshals displayed a weird sense of humour; the drivers keeping busy at the autograph session for the fans

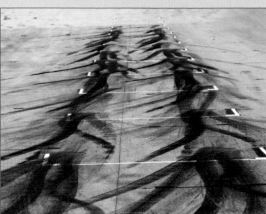

		BEST LAP	
1	3	MSC	1:50.611
2	11	KUB	1:50.749
3	10	HUL	1:51.148
4	5	VET	1:51.814
5	6	WEB	1:51.922
6	14	SUT	1:53.080
7	22	DLR	1:53.215
8	15	LIU	1:53.730
9	12	PET	1:53.751

RACE RESULTS
MALAYSIA
SEPANG

RACE DATE April 4th
CIRCUIT LENGTH 3.444 miles
NO. OF LAPS 56
RACE DISTANCE 192.864 miles
WEATHER Sunny & dry, 32°C
TRACK TEMP 44°C
ATTENDANCE 97,864
LAP RECORD Juan Pablo Montoya,
1m34.223s, 131.991mph, 2004

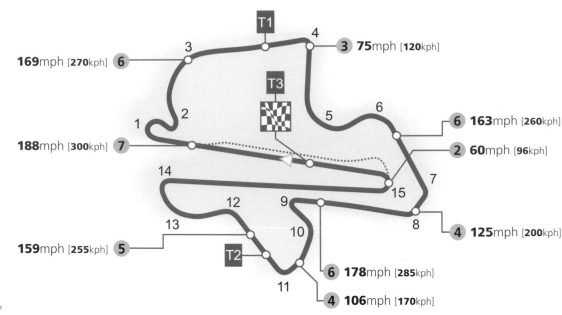

169mph [270kph] 6
188mph [300kph] 7
159mph [255kph] 5
3 75mph [120kph]
6 163mph [260kph]
2 60mph [96kph]
4 125mph [200kph]
6 178mph [285kph]
4 106mph [170kph]

PRACTICE 1			
	Driver	Time	Laps
1	L Hamilton	1m34.921s	19
2	N Rosberg	1m35.106s	19
3	J Button	1m35.207s	25
4	M Schumacher	1m35.225s	14
5	R Kubica	1m35.402s	22
6	M Webber	1m35.479s	22
7	A Sutil	1m35.955s	20
8	F Alonso	1m35.959s	20
9	S Vettel	1m36.043s	19
10	S Buemi	1m36.100s	20
11	F Massa	1m36.451s	22
12	K Kobayashi	1m36.503s	28
13	J Alguersuari	1m36.645s	18
14	V Petrov	1m36.712s	9
15	P di Resta	1m36.891s	25
16	P de la Rosa	1m36.899s	24
17	N Hulkenberg	1m37.802s	27
18	R Barrichello	1m38.278s	18
19	J Trulli	1m39.460s	21
20	T Glock	1m39.755s	17
21	L di Grassi	1m40.159s	25
22	F Fauzy	1m40.721s	19
23	B Senna	1m41.832s	27
24	K Chandhok	1m41.966s	24

PRACTICE 2			
	Driver	Time	Laps
1	L Hamilton	1m34.175s	27
2	S Vettel	1m34.441s	28
3	N Rosberg	1m34.443s	30
4	J Button	1m34.538s	24
5	M Schumacher	1m34.674s	30
6	R Kubica	1m35.148s	34
7	F Alonso	1m35.581s	34
8	S Buemi	1m35.660s	39
9	V Petrov	1m35.872s	20
10	A Sutil	1m35.957s	32
11	K Kobayashi	1m36.018s	38
12	V Liuzzi	1m36.221s	34
13	P de la Rosa	1m36.325s	33
14	J Alguersuari	1m36.325s	39
15	F Massa	1m36.602s	30
16	R Barrichello	1m36.813s	26
17	N Hulkenberg	1m37.415s	19
18	J Trulli	1m38.454s	34
19	H Kovalainen	1m38.530s	32
20	M Webber	1m38.786s	13
21	T Glock	1m39.061s	23
22	L di Grassi	1m39.158s	29
23	K Chandhok	1m41.084s	27
24	B Senna	1m41.481s	32

PRACTICE 3			
	Driver	Time	Laps
1	M Webber	1m33.542s	17
2	L Hamilton	1m33.559s	14
3	S Vettel	1m33.587s	17
4	F Alonso	1m33.751s	19
5	M Schumacher	1m33.992s	15
6	N Rosberg	1m34.090s	13
7	J Button	1m34.113s	16
8	F Massa	1m34.174s	15
9	R Barrichello	1m34.540s	13
10	R Kubica	1m34.549s	17
11	A Sutil	1m34.623s	11
12	S Buemi	1m34.673s	19
13	N Hulkenberg	1m34.882s	13
14	V Liuzzi	1m34.957s	16
15	J Alguersuari	1m35.026s	16
16	V Petrov	1m35.076s	17
17	P de la Rosa	1m35.477s	18
18	K Kobayashi	1m36.404s	19
19	T Glock	1m37.299s	15
20	J Trulli	1m37.369s	16
21	H Kovalainen	1m38.161s	18
22	L di Grassi	1m38.783s	13
23	B Senna	1m39.868s	19
24	K Chandhok	1m39.895s	16

QUALIFYING 1		
	Driver	Time
1	R Kubica	1m46.283s
2	P de la Rosa	1m47.153s
3	S Vettel	1m47.632s
4	V Petrov	1m47.952s
5	K Kobayashi	1m48.467s
6	J Alguersuari	1m48.655s
7	S Buemi	1m48.945s
8	A Sutil	1m49.479s
9	N Hulkenberg	1m49.664s
10	V Liuzzi	1m49.922s
11	R Barrichello	1m50.301s
12	M Webber	1m51.886s
13	J Button	1m52.211s
14	M Schumacher	1m52.239s
15	T Glock	1m52.398s
16	N Rosberg	1m52.560s
17	H Kovalainen	1m52.875s
18	J Trulli	1m52.884s
19	F Alonso	1m53.044s
20	L Hamilton	1m53.050s
21	F Massa	1m53.283s
22	K Chandhok	1m56.299s
23	B Senna	1m57.269s
24	L di Grassi	1m59.977s

QUALIFYING 2		
	Driver	Time
1	S Vettel	1m46.828s
2	R Kubica	1m46.951s
3	A Sutil	1m47.085s
4	N Hulkenberg	1m47.346s
5	N Rosberg	1m47.417s
6	K Kobayashi	1m47.792s
7	M Webber	1m48.210s
8	V Liuzzi	1m48.238s
9	R Barrichello	1m48.371s
10	M Schumacher	1m48.400s
11	V Petrov	1m48.760s
12	P de la Rosa	1m48.771s
13	S Buemi	1m49.207s
14	J Alguersuari	1m49.464s
15	H Kovalainen	1m52.270s
16	T Glock	1m52.520s
17	J Button	No time

Best sectors – Practice			Speed trap – Practice			Best sectors – Qualifying			Speed trap – Qualifying	
Sec 1	F Alonso	26.411s	1	L Hamilton	188.399mph	Sec 1	R Kubica	26.411s	1	L Hamilton	178.33mph
Sec 2	S Vettel	36.453s	2	M Webber	186.411mph	Sec 2	M Schumacher	36.453s	2	R Kubica	177.525mph
Sec 3	L Hamilton	38.187s	3	J Button	185.790mph	Sec 3	R Kubica	42.400s	3	M Schumacher	177.525mph

Jenson Button
"I got stuck behind Alonso, so pitted to get a clear track. I made up ground, but was on primes so long that it was hard to hold back cars that were 2s a lap faster."

Michael Schumacher
"It was a shame I couldn't finish, but the wheel nut on the left rear was lost. The car became very unstable in Turn 6 and I could hardly steer and had no drive."

Sebastian Vettel
"I had a good start past Nico, then able to gain on Mark, so took a chance into Turn 1 and just made it through! We're here to fight, but you should keep respect."

Felipe Massa
"Down the straights, Button could pull away, but when he made a mistake at the last corner, I was able to get close enough to pass under braking for Turn 1."

Rubens Barrichello
"I don't know what happened at the start. From there, I went to the back of the field. We tried a different strategy, but our car was just not competitive today."

Robert Kubica
"The start was vital, as I managed to get ahead of Hulkenberg, and then I got a good exit from Turn 2, which helped me to overtake Sutil. Fourth is a good result."

Lewis Hamilton
"I had a great start and got past a lot of cars. I even nearly got past Vettel after his pit stop. After my stop, I tried to pass Sutil, but he was too fast down the straights."

Nico Rosberg
"It's fantastic to achieve our first podium at the home race for Petronas. I had wheelspin and once I was third, I knew it would be hard to follow the leaders."

Mark Webber
"I got wheelspin and Seb got a tow into Turn 1. I didn't know where Nico was, so braked late. I had a better exit from Turn 2 and the fight with Seb went to Turn 4."

Fernando Alonso
"I had a gearbox problem from the start and had to drive without a clutch almost all race. On the positive side, at least the engine failure only cost me two points."

Nico Hulkenberg
"I picked up a point, maybe because our car was more reliable. It was a tough race, as we just don't have the pace at the moment. We have work to do."

Vitaly Petrov
"It was great fun and I enjoyed especially the battle with Hamilton. Then, in the middle of the race, the car just stopped and I think it was a gearbox problem."

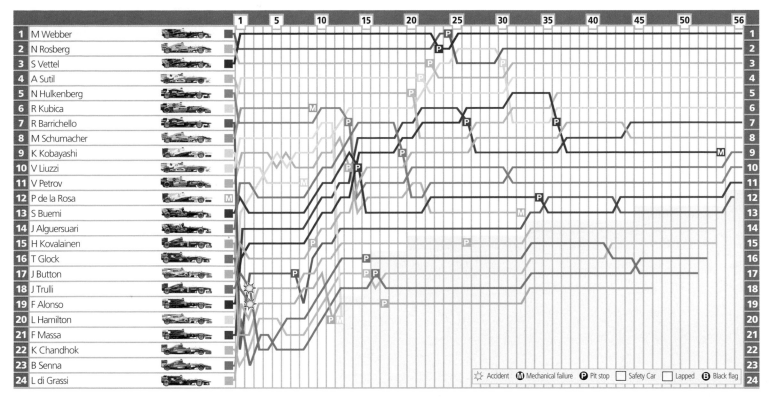

	1	5	10	15	20	25	30	35	40	45	50	56
1 M Webber												
2 N Rosberg												
3 S Vettel												
4 A Sutil												
5 N Hulkenberg												
6 R Kubica												
7 R Barrichello												
8 M Schumacher												
9 K Kobayashi												
10 V Liuzzi												
11 V Petrov												
12 P de la Rosa												
13 S Buemi												
14 J Alguersuari												
15 H Kovalainen												
16 T Glock												
17 J Button												
18 J Trulli												
19 F Alonso												
20 L Hamilton												
21 F Massa												
22 K Chandhok												
23 B Senna												
24 L di Grassi												

☆ Accident Ⓜ Mechanical failure Ⓟ Pit stop ☐ Safety Car ☐ Lapped Ⓑ Black flag

QUALIFYING 3

	Driver	Time
1	M Webber	1m49.327s
2	N Rosberg	1m50.673s
3	S Vettel	1m50.789s
4	A Sutil	1m50.914s
5	N Hulkenberg	1m51.001s
6	R Kubica	1m51.051s
7	R Barrichello	1m51.511s
8	M Schumacher	1m51.717s
9	K Kobayashi	1m51.767s
10	V Liuzzi	1m52.254s

GRID

	Driver	Time
1	M Webber	1m49.327s
2	N Rosberg	1m50.673s
3	S Vettel	1m50.789s
4	A Sutil	1m50.914s
5	N Hulkenberg	1m51.001s
6	R Kubica	1m51.051s
7	R Barrichello	1m51.511s
8	M Schumacher	1m51.717s
9	K Kobayashi	1m51.767s
10	V Liuzzi	1m52.254s
11	V Petrov	1m48.760s
12	P de la Rosa	1m48.771s
13	S Buemi	1m49.207s
14	J Alguersuari	1m49.464s
15	H Kovalainen	1m52.270s
16	T Glock	1m52.520s
17	J Button	No time
18	J Trulli	1m52.884s
19	F Alonso	1m53.044s
20	L Hamilton	1m53.050s
21	F Massa	1m53.283s
22	K Chandhok	1m56.299s
23	B Senna	1m57.269s
24	L di Grassi	1m59.977s

RACE

	Driver	Car	Laps	Time	Avg. mph	Fastest	Stops
1	S Vettel	Red Bull-Renault RB6	56	1h33m48.412s	123.358	1m37.813s	1
2	M Webber	Red Bull-Renault RB6	56	1h33m53.261s	123.252	1m37.054s	1
3	N Rosberg	Mercedes MGP W01	56	1h34m01.916s	123.063	1m38.129s	1
4	R Kubica	Renault R30	56	1h34m07.001s	122.952	1m38.074s	1
5	A Sutil	Force India-Mercedes VJM03	56	1h34m09.471s	122.898	1m38.160s	1
6	L Hamilton	McLaren-Mercedes MP4-25	56	1h34m11.883s	122.846	1m37.745s	1
7	F Massa	Ferrari F10	56	1h34m15.480s	122.768	1m37.784s	1
8	J Button	McLaren-Mercedes MP4-25	56	1h34m26.330s	122.533	1m38.501s	1
9	J Alguersuari	Toro Rosso-Ferrari STR5	56	1h34m59.014s	121.830	1m39.489s	1
10	N Hulkenberg	Williams-Cosworth FW32	56	1h35m01.811s	121.770	1m39.124s	1
11	S Buemi	Toro Rosso-Ferrari STR5	56	1h35m07.350s	121.652	1m37.610s	2
12	R Barrichello	Williams-Cosworth FW32	55	1h34m30.307s	120.260	1m39.428s	2
13	F Alonso	Ferrari F10	54	Engine	-	1m37.231s	1
14	L di Grassi	Virgin-Cosworth VR-01	53	1h35m03.483s	115.213	1m43.224s	1
15	K Chandhok	HRT-Cosworth F110	53	1h35m21.231s	114.856	1m44.790s	1
16	B Senna	HRT-Cosworth F110	52	1h34m17.980s	113.747	1m45.334s	1
17	J Trulli	Lotus-Cosworth T127	51	1h34m15.642s	111.606	1m43.753s	1
NC	H Kovalainen	Lotus-Cosworth T127	46	1h33m55.297s	101.206	1m42.701s	2
R	V Petrov	Renault R30	32	Gearbox	-	1m40.693s	1
R	V Liuzzi	Force India-Mercedes VJM03	12	Throttle	-	1m42.594s	0
R	M Schumacher	Mercedes MGP W01	9	Wheel nut	-	1m42.084s	0
R	K Kobayashi	BMW Sauber-Ferrari C29	8	Engine	-	1m43.340s	0
R	T Glock	Virgin-Cosworth VR-01	2	Spun off	-	1m46.388s	0
NS	P de la Rosa	BMW Sauber-Ferrari C29	0	Engine	-	-	

CHAMPIONSHIP

	Driver	Pts
1	F Massa	39
2	F Alonso	37
3	S Vettel	37
4	J Button	35
5	N Rosberg	35
6	L Hamilton	31
7	R Kubica	30
8	M Schumacher	24
9	A Sutil	10
10	M Schumacher	9
11	V Liuzzi	8
12	R Barrichello	5
13	J Alguersuari	2
14	N Hulkenberg	1

	Constructor	Pts
1	Ferrari	76
2	McLaren-Mercedes	66
3	Red Bull-Renault	61
4	Mercedes	44
5	Renault	30
6	Force India-Mercedes	18
7	Williams-Cosworth	6
8	Toro Rosso-Ferrari	2

Fastest lap
M Webber 1m37.054s
(127.763mph) on lap 53

Fastest speed trap
L Hamilton 186.784mph
Slowest speed trap
J Trulli 174.232mph

Fastest pit stop
1 N Rosberg 21.802s
2 R Barrichello 22.329s
3 F Alonso 22.350s

Adrian Sutil
"The race was exciting, and fifth place was a great result. It was very close with Lewis in the closing stages but I knew if I didn't make any mistakes I'd be okay."

Sebastian Buemi
"My front wing was damaged on lap 1 when I made contact with Kobayashi. From then on, I lacked grip. Once it was changed I was able to put in some very fast laps."

Jarno Trulli
"I made a good start, but on lap 2 I was hit by Glock, which made me spin, and from then on my race was compromised. Despite that, I still got the car home."

Karun Chandhok
"I am fantastically happy to have finished my second race after our difficult debut in Bahrain. On lap 45, though, I had a tricky moment, passing Trulli's Lotus."

Pedro de la Rosa
"This race is one you prepare for all year due to the physical demands and you really want to be driving in it. The failure was unusual, unexpected and unlucky."

Timo Glock
"I dropped behind Jarno and was quicker than him. I tried to overtake but locked the rears, and for some reason the anti-stall didn't kick in. Sadly, I hit Jarno."

Vitantonio Liuzzi
"I had a good start from 10th, and was in seventh and had a good pace, although I was stuck behind Hulkenberg. Unluckily, I had a problem with the throttle."

Jaime Alguersuari
"I am very happy to have scored, and have to say I never expected to do it so early in the season. Towards the end, I was worried about how the tyres would last."

Heikki Kovalainen
"I got into a good rhythm, then I tried to make a move on di Grassi, but clipped his front wing when I was going past and damaged my left-rear tyre, so had to pit."

Bruno Senna
"I had a good start and gained as much as I could. To have finished the race with both cars, it has been another positive weekend for the team, taking a good step."

Kamui Kobayashi
"The retirement came as a total surprise to me as after Turn 1 I suddenly had no more power. This is really bad luck. I was in a good position to fight for points."

Lucas di Grassi
"I had a great start and made up five places on lap 1. We had good early pace and continued to be strong, despite losing an endplate when Heikki tried to pass me."

2010 FORMULA 1
CHINESE GRAND PRIX
SHANGHAI

COME RAIN
OR SHINE

Jenson Button read the changing conditions to perfection to make it two wins from his first four starts for McLaren, but he was made to work for it as a safety car bunched the field

This was supposed to be the year during which Jenson Button's decision to take on Lewis Hamilton at McLaren was revealed as unwise. In fact, after winning for the second time in four races, Button's standing after China was arguably greater than at any previous time in his career.

As in Australia, an inspired call on tyres put him in a prime position, and thereafter he drove superbly to take full advantage of the situation to bring his car home in front. Great tactical decisions in the wet by Button laid the groundwork for both his victories.

However, having got himself into a winning position, he still had to finish the job. He'd done that brilliantly, running faultlessly over a marathon second stint in Australia, and surviving the tricky conditions and enormous pressure in China. On both occasions, he managed his tyres to perfection, showing what a savvy driver he is.

"It was a fantastic result," beamed McLaren boss Martin Whitmarsh. "Both guys were fantastic, they were both instrumental in calling the strategies. If we'd run the opposite way on the two guys, that probably wouldn't have worked, so I think we got the right strategies with those drivers in those conditions.

"I think there was a lot of negative reaction after the Bahrain GP, which was understandable after the build-up, but it was important that we didn't have a knee-jerk reaction. The subsequent races have been hugely entertaining and the Chinese GP was another one.

Much of the paddock was wrapped up in how they were going to get home again, with all travel disrupted by the volcanic ash cloud billowing away from Iceland. As much as the personnel, it was the freight that was a concern, and the knock-on it might've had on the Spanish GP with everyone scheduling significant upgrades.

However, the race focused everyone's attention, and the impending rain was again the main issue as the start approached. The Red Bulls were very quick in dry qualifying, but the conditions reminded you of Melbourne and once again Jenson called the race perfectly.

There was a lot of interest pre-season when we announced that he was joining Lewis, meaning we had two successive British World Champions in the same team. They're evenly matched and are driving fantastically well. If you look through practice, Jenson would be quickest in one session, then Lewis in another. In Q1 and Q2, Lewis was quicker. In Q3, Jenson got it. I'm convinced that we have the strongest driver line-up in F1.

Jenson got a reasonable start from fifth and it was clear that Alonso had jumped the start and would be penalised. Then there was the first-lap safety car and, with the rain spitting, most of the field took the opportunity to pit to put on intermediates. The decision for Lewis to come in was last-minute, but Jenson was firm in his decision to stay out.

When the track started to dry, the inters, which are a softer compound, started to wear quite quickly and everyone on them started piling back in to go back onto slicks. Jenson therefore looked very good and moved ahead of Rosberg to take the lead, but later lost most of his margin when a second safety car allowed the others back into it, Lewis among them.

Lewis produced another fabulously aggressive drive and at one point I was being asked, 'shouldn't we be slowing them down now?', but we decided to let them race. It was heart-in-the-mouth stuff as the inters wore again towards the end, but Jenson did a great job under a lot of pressure. It was a fantastic drive."

But it was very, very difficult. Mid-race, someone said we're only halfway through, and I thought we'd been running for four hours…"

Button has always had a sure touch in wet conditions, and both his wins had resulted from him being a little bit more confident than others about his ability to deal with a slippery track on dry tyres, although the circumstances were different each time.

In qualifying, this looked like a standard 2010 race, as Sebastian Vettel and Mark Webber planted their Red Bulls on the front row, ahead of Fernando Alonso and Nico Rosberg. McLaren had looked good all the way to Q3, and indeed Hamilton was fastest in Q1 and Q2. Yet, when it counted, he couldn't better sixth, a place behind his team-mate.

Everyone knew that it could all prove academic come Sunday, as for days rain had been forecast. Equally, bad weather wasn't a worry for Red Bull Racing, as a year earlier Vettel and Webber left the rest trailing in a soaking wet race, and there was no reason not to expect a repeat. In fact, race day turned into a disaster for the 2010 favourites.

The rain came as scheduled, minutes before the start, as happened in Australia. But while in

Melbourne it was a no-brainer for everyone to start on intermediates, this time slicks were the right call. However, in the few minutes between the final deadline for that decision and the formation lap, the rain began to fall more heavily. So when a first-lap crash brought out the safety car, a few drivers in the midfield pitted for inters. Next time around, under yellow, most of the field came charging in.

At McLaren, Hamilton pitted, but Button stayed out. It was a choice that would win him the race.

In Australia, it was a case of being the first to go to slicks after the rain eased, while in Shanghai he was one of just six drivers who had the nous to stay out on dries on the basis that the call for inters was so marginal that it wasn't worth stopping. It was interesting to note that two of the others who made that call – Rosberg and Robert Kubica – had, like Button, massively enhanced their reputations since the start of the year.

"We asked Jenson about it," said Whitmarsh. "I said to them before, you've both got to give us information. They were both given the option to stop. Lewis decided to come in, Jenson to stay out. As I say, I think they got it about right for both of them."

OPPOSITE TOP Sebastian Vettel gets away from pole, with Fernando Alonso powering past Mark Webber. But the Ferrari driver had jumped the start and would be penalised

OPPOSITE BOTTOM Drizzle before the start brought out the umbrellas in the grandstands

ABOVE Nico Hulkenberg ended up a lapped 15th in his Williams, and still needed a decent result to get his maiden season up and running

TALKING POINT
EMERGENCE OF BUTTON

It seems anomalous to speak of the reigning World Champion 'emerging', but four grands prix into the new season there was no doubt that Jenson Button's stock had risen.

Many of the sport's insiders had doubted the wisdom of Jenson venturing into the lion's den, which is how McLaren was viewed after Lewis

Hamilton had been able to gather an F1 title and three years of experience with the team that mentored him through karting and the junior single-seater formulae.

Without even considering too deeply the fall-out from that 2007 season alongside Fernando Alonso, McLaren was seen as Lewis's team and he is widely held to be the fastest natural driver.

Jenson, though, was hugely impressed by what he saw at the McLaren Technology Centre when he visited, and settled quickly.

At first, his seating position wasn't quite right, but that was quickly sorted. It seemed almost inconceivable that Jenson would win two races before Lewis won one in 2010, but that's the way it happened.

Fair enough, it wasn't outright

pace that helped Jenson claim the pair of wins, but shrewd, experienced calls in changeable conditions. In Melbourne, it had been Jenson's call to come in early for slick tyres and in Shanghai it was his decision not to stop for intermediates when most of the front-runners did.

At the root of both decisions was Jenson's natural feel for grip, which has allowed him to do great things in slippery conditions over the years, even if they largely went under the radar because they were not being done in frontrunning cars. The task of keeping control of a slick-shod F1 car on a wet track does not, for him, hold the same fears as it does for most of his contemporaries.

McLaren was happy for Jenson to make the calls, to trust his judgement, and that, in turn, did much to make

him feel at home, so soon. Lewis was driving spectacularly, performing 90% of the overtaking moves in those early races. Yet, for Jenson, overtaking moves galore weren't necessary as he won in Melbourne and Shanghai fairly effortlessly, without risking the car.

Off-track, Lewis had split with his father and looked a little isolated. And, of course, he knew Jenson's father, John, from karting days when Button Sr used to prepare Lewis's engines, and Button Jr, five years his elder, was someone to be looked up to. It was certainly a very different dynamic from 2007, when the Alonso faction sat in one corner of McLaren's Brand Centre and the Hamilton faction in the other.

Jenson was off to a good start with his new team and, amazingly, Lewis didn't seem to mind.

Although the drivers made the call, it was in fact the ideal scenario for the team, given the uncertain conditions. "We had one in each camp," said Whitmarsh. "Did we know at every moment of that race we'd got it right? No, because you can't. But did we make a lot of considered judgements under pressure? I think we called it right. For both of them, that was probably the best way to get to the end of the race, and they finished within a second of each other.

"At the start of the race, you probably thought 'take a flier and go on inters', but here, in two laps, if it wasn't wet enough, you'd destroy an inter. Intermediate tyre wear was very difficult. It's very difficult for the guys to see [the tyres] as well, and it's wear which both takes away the tread and takes away heat from the tyres."

As noted, just six drivers stayed out, led by Rosberg, Button and Kubica. When the track went green, the guys on inters briefly appeared to have an advantage, but it was soon clear that the track was drying, so they had to pit again for slicks. Those who had not stopped were thus left with a huge advantage.

Later, though, the rain returned. Button got past

LEFT Lewis Hamilton and Sebastian Vettel carried on their racing in the pitlane and were both duly reprimanded

BELOW Jenson Button and Nico Rosberg are led around by the safety car that came out on lap 22, after Jaime Alguersuari collided with Bruno Senna's HRT, scattering debris

BOTTOM Battle of the yellow helmets. Nico Rosberg and Lewis Hamilton run side-by-side as the McLaren driver attempts to wrest second place away from the Mercedes driver

ABOVE Vitaly Petrov waves to the crowd after taking his first F1 finish and scoring his first F1 points

BELOW Red Bull's Mark Webber and Sebastian Vettel appear tired rather than happy after the race

Rosberg for the lead just before everyone went to inters, and the guys who hadn't stopped remained miles out in front. Hamilton worked his way to the front of this group, and by passing Rosberg, got up to second.

Having lost ground at the start, Hamilton put in a typically charging drive, passing anyone who came into his sights. Along the way, he had a moment in the pitlane with Vettel, both men getting reprimands after a drag race to the exit.

Hamilton's charge into second was mighty but, like others who'd made that early call for inters, only to have to swap back, he gained hugely from the safety car that was dispatched when Jaime Alguersuari's front wing came adrift.

Before that happened, Hamilton was 48s down on Button. After the restart, the gap was 5.5s. In other words, Hamilton was given a huge bonus. Had the race run uninterrupted to the flag, he wouldn't have got anywhere near Button, whose strategy call would've looked even more impressive.

Instead, he chased Button down to the flag. Just to add to the excitement, both were struggling to keep their tyres alive, with Hamilton seemingly struggling more with the fronts, Button with the rears.

On lap 51, Button had a little excursion that cost him 4s and, with seven laps to go, Hamilton had even more motivation to push on. And, according to Whitmarsh, they really were racing.

"It added to the tension!" grinned Whitmarsh. "Lewis was bearing down and then, given the information, responded and closed the gap. I think that we did the right thing. We let them race without going crazy.

"We had a dilemma! We could have said to our guys quite a few laps out, now pace yourself back, both of you. But I think we tried to get them to have a go at racing. They really do have a good relationship. I think they're sensible people, and I think you've got to trust the drivers in those circumstances, and they could drive within their own limits."

"We were giving them the information, Jenson was getting the gap to Lewis, Lewis likewise was getting the gap, and he knew... Believe me, with five laps to go, Lewis wanted to win that race and he knew that he could catch Jenson. I think both their sets of tyres were pretty worn at the end, and we could have run a safer strategy."

Rosberg held on to finish third, while Alonso put in a brilliant drive – after taking a drive-through penalty for jumping the start – to salvage fourth place, ahead of Kubica's Renault.

An opportunistic lunge by Alonso down the inside of his team-mate Felipe Massa on the way into the pits – in order to give himself first call in the stacked pit stops – reminded onlookers of Michael Schumacher's last-lap passing move of Rubens Barrichello for seventh place at Monaco in 2005. On that occasion, the German took advantage of the fact that the car in front was his team-mate, and was obliged to not close the door. After the Chinese GP, Massa didn't look very happy at all.

So what then of Red Bull Racing? Both drivers blew it when they joined the early rush into the pits for intermediate tyres. Webber was in front and hit the jack, costing him time and damaging his wing, while Vettel had to wait behind him in the pit lane and dropped as low as 15th in the running order. He fought back to finish in sixth place, while Webber could not better eighth.

Meanwhile, Massa had a low-key drive to ninth, but he still beat his former Ferrari team-mate Michael Schumacher, who was the final point scorer, having a frustrating day in 10th as he again struggled to get the tyres to work. It could only get better from here for the seven-time World Champion...

SNAPSHOT FROM CHINA

CLOCKWISE FROM RIGHT The suburbs of Shanghai move ever closer to the circuit; Jenson Button's helmet design is even more patriotic than in 2009; Sebastian Vettel sneaks a look at Jenson Button's McLaren; there were furry animals in the pitlane...; ...and a furry prancing horse in the grandstands; Fernando Alonso flashes past the cameramen at pit exit; banners were flown marking a wager between Virgin Racing's Richard Branson and Lotus's Tony Fernandes that one of them would dress up as an air stewardess on their rival's airline if their team ranked below their rival's over the season; Force India pit or *Star Wars* Millennium Falcon?; Michael Schumacher checks out a Ferrari

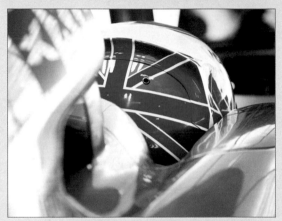

RACE RESULTS
CHINA SHANGHAI

Official Results © [2010]
Formula One Administration Limited,
6 Princes Gate, London, SW7 1QJ.
No reproduction without permission.
All copyright and database rights reserved.

RACE DATE April 18th
CIRCUIT LENGTH 3.390 miles
NO. OF LAPS 56
RACE DISTANCE 189.680 miles
WEATHER Overcast then rain, 21°C
TRACK TEMP 25°C
ATTENDANCE 155,000
LAP RECORD Michael Schumacher, 1m32.238s, 132.202mph, 2004

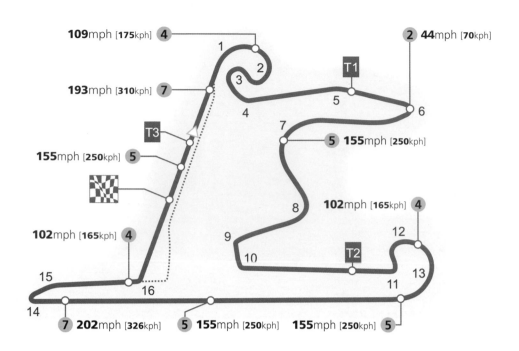

109mph [175kph] ④
193mph [310kph] ⑦
155mph [250kph] ⑤
102mph [165kph] ④
202mph [326kph] ⑦
44mph [70kph] ②
155mph [250kph] ⑤
102mph [165kph] ④
155mph [250kph] ⑤
155mph [250kph] ⑤
155mph [250kph] ⑤

PRACTICE 1			PRACTICE 2			PRACTICE 3			QUALIFYING 1		QUALIFYING 2	
Driver	**Time**	**Laps**	**Driver**	**Time**	**Laps**	**Driver**	**Time**	**Laps**	**Driver**	**Time**	**Driver**	**Time**
1 J Button	1m36.677s	15	1 L Hamilton	1m35.217s	26	1 M Webber	1m35.323s	16	1 L Hamilton	1m35.641s	1 L Hamilton	1m34.928s
2 N Rosberg	1m36.748s	17	2 N Rosberg	1m35.465s	22	2 L Hamilton	1m35.564s	12	2 N Rosberg	1m35.952s	2 M Webber	1m35.100s
3 L Hamilton	1m36.775s	19	3 J Button	1m35.593s	26	3 S Vettel	1m35.691s	14	3 M Webber	1m35.978s	3 N Rosberg	1m35.134s
4 M Schumacher	1m37.509s	14	4 M Schumacher	1m35.602s	28	4 J Button	1m35.747s	14	4 F Alonso	1m35.987s	4 F Alonso	1m35.235s
5 S Vettel	1m37.601s	20	5 S Vettel	1m35.791s	30	5 F Alonso	1m35.857s	13	5 F Massa	1m36.076s	5 S Vettel	1m35.280s
6 R Kubica	1m37.716s	17	6 M Webber	1m35.995s	29	6 N Rosberg	1m35.913s	12	6 J Button	1m36.122s	6 F Massa	1m35.290s
7 V Petrov	1m37.745s	25	7 A Sutil	1m36.254s	31	7 M Schumacher	1m36.262s	10	7 S Vettel	1m36.317s	7 J Button	1m35.443s
8 M Webber	1m37.980s	17	8 J Alguersuari	1m36.377s	43	8 R Kubica	1m36.343s	16	8 R Kubica	1m36.348s	8 R Kubica	1m35.550s
9 A Sutil	1m38.008s	13	9 R Kubica	1m36.389s	29	9 F Massa	1m36.416s	11	9 M Schumacher	1m36.484s	9 A Sutil	1m35.665s
10 F Massa	1m38.098s	19	10 F Alonso	1m36.604s	33	10 K Kobayashi	1m36.634s	16	10 J Alguersuari	1m36.618s	10 M Schumacher	1m35.715s
11 J Alguersuari	1m38.161s	19	11 F Massa	1m36.944s	36	11 J Alguersuari	1m36.879s	17	11 R Barrichello	1m36.664s	11 R Barrichello	1m35.748s
12 K Kobayashi	1m38.375s	21	12 V Petrov	1m36.986s	27	12 V Liuzzi	1m37.031s	16	12 A Sutil	1m36.671s	12 J Alguersuari	1m36.047s
13 P de la Rosa	1m38.421s	19	13 P de la Rosa	1m37.421s	32	13 S Buemi	1m37.192s	18	13 S Buemi	1m36.793s	13 S Buemi	1m36.149s
14 N Hulkenberg	1m38.569s	20	14 K Kobayashi	1m37.431s	33	14 A Sutil	1m37.240s	18	14 V Petrov	1m37.031s	14 V Petrov	1m36.311s
15 P di Resta	1m38.618s	26	15 R Barrichello	1m37.657s	30	15 V Petrov	1m37.339s	13	15 K Kobayashi	1m37.044s	15 K Kobayashi	1m36.422s
16 R Barrichello	1m38.678s	17	16 V Liuzzi	1m37.804s	31	16 R Barrichello	1m37.585s	13	16 N Hulkenberg	1m37.049s	16 N Hulkenberg	1m36.647s
17 S Buemi	1m39.939s	5	17 N Hulkenberg	1m37.867s	29	17 P de la Rosa	1m37.664s	19	17 P de la Rosa	1m37.050s	17 P de la Rosa	1m37.020s
18 J Trulli	1m41.531s	22	18 J Trulli	1m39.624s	35	18 N Hulkenberg	1m37.784s	14	18 V Liuzzi	1m37.161s		
19 H Kovalainen	1m41.779s	23	19 H Kovalainen	1m39.947s	30	19 T Glock	1m39.579s	15	19 T Glock	1m39.278s		
20 T Glock	1m41.830s	19	20 T Glock	1m40.233s	27	20 H Kovalainen	1m39.616s	17	20 J Trulli	1m39.399s		
21 L di Grassi	1m42.181s	27	21 K Chandhok	1m41.008s	32	21 L di Grassi	1m39.749s	13	21 H Kovalainen	1m39.520s		
22 B Senna	1m43.875s	23	22 L di Grassi	1m41.107s	28	22 J Trulli	1m39.776s	15	22 L di Grassi	1m39.783s		
23 K Chandhok	1m43.949s	20	23 B Senna	1m41.345s	32	23 B Senna	1m40.316s	19	23 B Senna	1m40.469s		
24 F Alonso	No time	6	24 S Buemi	No time	0	24 K Chandhok	1m41.141s	18	24 K Chandhok	1m40.578s		

Best sectors – Practice			Speed trap – Practice			Best sectors – Qualifying			Speed trap – Qualifying	
Sec 1	L Hamilton	25.018s	1	F Massa	196.415mph	Sec 1	S Vettel	24.816s	1 N Hulkenberg	192.625mph
Sec 2	M Webber	28.220s	2	F Alonso	195.980mph	Sec 2	M Webber	27.875s	2 R Barrichello	192.500mph
Sec 3	J Button	41.803s	3	K Kobayashi	194.302mph	Sec 3	S Vettel	41.811s	3 L Hamilton	192.190mph

 Jenson Button
"Every race you win becomes your best, but this was extremely special in tough conditions. From strategy calls to pit stops, you must get everything just right."

 Michael Schumacher
"In the last 10 laps, my tyres seemed more slicks than inters. I was one of those who'd gone onto the last set early, and we should've done that differently."

 Sebastian Vettel
"It was a difficult race – on nearly every second lap there was a car to pass or I got passed. I lost time with the first stop, but we fought our way back and ended up sixth."

 Felipe Massa
"From the start, it was hard to make the right tyre choice. I hit a puddle out of the hairpin and Alonso managed to get inside, passing me going into the pits."

 Rubens Barrichello
"I was called into the pits for intermediates early on. It was a hard call and the race developed from there. We then made good calls but it was too late to recover."

 Robert Kubica
"I made a bad start and lost a lot of positions, but we made the right decision to stay out on slicks when it started to rain, and I was able to advance to third place."

 Lewis Hamilton
"I made a very late call and pitted when I was halfway round the final corner! Unluckily, it wasn't the right choice and I needed to stop again, this time for dries."

 Nico Rosberg
"Following advice from the team, I stayed on slicks when the showers hit. It was the right call. When it started raining again, I suffered from degradation on the inters."

 Mark Webber
"We weren't quick enough, simple as that. There were very changeable conditions, and our cars are very sensitive when it's not going one way or the other."

 **Fernando Alonso**
"We did five tyre stops. My reflexes let me down and I left early at the start. It's never happened before. Despite the penalty, I managed to come fourth."

Nico Hulkenberg
"It was good experience for me to complete the race and experience all the conditions we faced. In particular, it was helpful to see how the car and tyres handled."

Vitaly Petrov
"I'm happy to get my first finish. It wasn't easy to make the right decisions. When I changed to my second set of inters, I knew it would be vital to look after them."

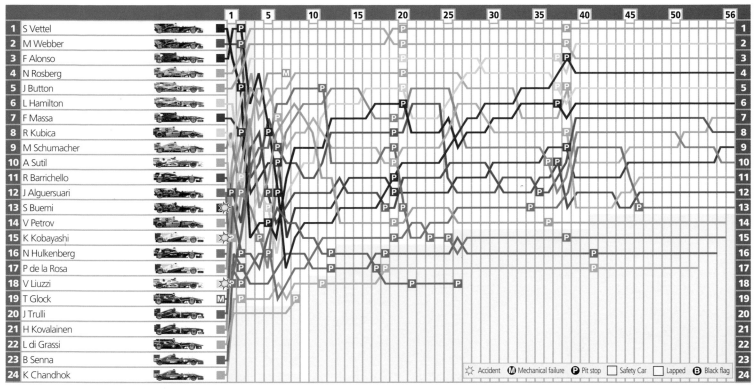

Key: ☆ Accident | Ⓜ Mechanical failure | Ⓟ Pit stop | □ Safety Car | □ Lapped | Ⓑ Black flag

QUALIFYING 3

	Driver	Time
1	S Vettel	1m34.558s
2	M Webber	1m34.806s
3	F Alonso	1m34.913s
4	N Rosberg	1m34.923s
5	J Button	1m34.979s
6	L Hamilton	1m35.034s
7	F Massa	1m35.180s
8	R Kubica	1m35.364s
9	M Schumacher	1m35.646s
10	A Sutil	1m35.963s

GRID

	Driver	Time
1	S Vettel	1m34.558s
2	M Webber	1m34.806s
3	F Alonso	1m34.913s
4	N Rosberg	1m34.923s
5	J Button	1m34.979s
6	L Hamilton	1m35.034s
7	F Massa	1m35.180s
8	R Kubica	1m35.364s
9	M Schumacher	1m35.646s
10	A Sutil	1m35.963s
11	R Barrichello	1m35.748s
12	J Alguersuari	1m36.047s
13	S Buemi	1m36.149s
14	V Petrov	1m36.311s
15	K Kobayashi	1m36.422s
16	N Hulkenberg	1m36.647s
17	P de la Rosa	1m37.020s
18	V Liuzzi	1m37.161s
19	T Glock	1m39.278s
20	J Trulli	1m39.399s
21	H Kovalainen	1m39.520s
22*	L di Grassi	1m39.783s
23	B Senna	1m40.469s
24*	K Chandhok	1m40.578s

* Started from pitlane.

RACE

	Driver	Car	Laps	Time	Avg. mph	Fastest	Stops
1	J Button	McLaren-Mercedes MP4-25	56	1h46m42.163s	106.659	1m42.886s	2
2	L Hamilton	McLaren-Mercedes MP4-25	56	1h46m43.693s	106.633	1m42.061s	4
3	N Rosberg	Mercedes MGP W01	56	1h46m51.647s	106.501	1m43.245s	2
4	F Alonso	Ferrari F10	56	1h46m54.032s	106.467	1m44.134s	5
5	R Kubica	Renault R30	56	1h47m04.376s	106.290	1m43.630s	2
6	S Vettel	Red Bull-Renault RB6	56	1h47m15.473s	106.107	1m42.358s	4
7	V Petrov	Renault R30	56	1h47m29.763s	105.872	1m43.801s	2
8	M Webber	Red Bull-Renault RB6	56	1h47m34.335s	105.797	1m42.609s	4
9	F Massa	Ferrari F10	56	1h47m39.959s	105.705	1m44.594s	4
10	M Schumacher	Mercedes MGP W01	56	1h47m43.912s	105.640	1m44.298s	4
11	A Sutil	Force India-Mercedes VJM03	56	1h47m45.037s	105.622	1m44.364s	4
12	R Barrichello	Williams-Cosworth FW32	56	1h47m45.828s	105.609	1m45.559s	4
13	J Alguersuari	Toro Rosso-Ferrari STR5	56	1h47m53.579s	105.482	1m43.755s	6
14	H Kovalainen	Lotus-Cosworth T127	55	1h47m52.460s	103.615	1m47.141s	2
15	N Hulkenberg	Williams-Cosworth FW32	55	1h48m01.537s	103.470	1m44.549s	6
16	B Senna	HRT-Cosworth F110	54	1h48m28.179s	101.171	1m48.219s	4
17	K Chandhok	HRT-Cosworth F110	52	1h47m39.011s	98.252	1m48.788s	4
R	J Trulli	Lotus-Cosworth T127	26	Hydraulics	-	1m49.675s	4
R	L di Grassi	Virgin-Cosworth VR-01	8	Clutch	-	1m53.185s	0
R	P de la Rosa	BMW Sauber-Ferrari C29	7	Engine	-	1m47.739s	0
R	S Buemi	Toro Rosso-Ferrari STR5	0	Accident	-	-	0
R	K Kobayashi	BMW Sauber-Ferrari C29	0	Accident	-	-	0
R	V Liuzzi	Force India-Mercedes VJM03	0	Accident	-	-	0
NS	T Glock	Virgin-Cosworth VR-01	-	Engine	-	-	-

CHAMPIONSHIP

	Driver	Pts
1	J Button	65
2	N Rosberg	50
3	F Alonso	49
4	L Hamilton	48
5	S Vettel	45
6	F Massa	41
7	R Kubica	40
8	M Webber	28
9	A Sutil	10
10	M Schumacher	10
11	V Liuzzi	8
12	V Petrov	6
13	R Barrichello	5
14	J Alguersuari	2
15	N Hulkenberg	1

	Constructor	Pts
1	McLaren-Mercedes	109
2	Ferrari	90
3	Red Bull-Renault	73
4	Mercedes	60
5	Renault	46
6	Force India-Mercedes	18
7	Williams-Cosworth	6
8	Toro Rosso-Ferrari	2

Fastest lap
L Hamilton 1m42.061s
(119.478mph) on lap 13

Fastest speed trap
L Hamilton 197.596mph
Slowest speed trap
P de la Rosa 178.333mph

Fastest pit stop
1 A Sutil 21.722s
2 M Schumacher 21.763s
3 F Massa 22.047s

Adrian Sutil
"I started on dries, pitted for inters on lap 1, then it eased and I went to dries but there was more rain. On the second set of inters, I was able to fight with the top guys."

Jarno Trulli
"When you start from the middle of the pack, the risk of an accident is greater. I don't want to blame anyone for the crash, but Liuzzi lost his car and hit me."

"I was enjoying myself, but I had more hydraulics issues which brought me in. The team got me back out, but the problems struck again and I had to retire."

Karun Chandhok
"I'm fantastically happy to have finished again, and it wasn't easy with the rain. Because of a change of hydraulic components, I had to start from the pit lane."

Pedro de la Rosa
"I started on slicks and managed to stay out in the drizzle. I enjoyed overtaking and then I was in fourth. I felt something wrong with the engine and stopped."

Timo Glock
"Everything was going well until late into the grid procedure, so the engine problem came out of the blue and there was nothing we could do to make the start."

Vitantonio Liuzzi
"I had a problem warming the brakes on the formation lap due to the cold and the rain. When I went into Turn 4 and braked, the rear locked and I went off."

"I made a mistake lapping a Hispania, but he moved from side to side. I tried to get by on the right, but he came back and touched my wing, which is how I lost it."

Heikki Kovalainen
"We had the correct strategy in tricky conditions. We decided to stay out on dry tyres, as it wasn't wet enough to come in and the cars on wets were struggling."

Bruno Senna
"We had no experience in really wet conditions like today and the car was a bit difficult to drive as, overall, my visor was a bit too dark for those conditions."

Kamui Kobayashi
"It's such a shame. I'm sure we would have scored points today. My start was good, but after a few corners Liuzzi's car just flew into mine and I was out."

Lucas di Grassi
"This is not a great way to end our weekend and is very frustrating as we had very good days on Friday and Saturday. We'll work hard to identify the problems."

FORMULA 1 GRAN PREMIO
DE ESPAÑA TELEFÓNICA 2010
CATALUNYA

FROM POLE TO FLAG

A dominant performance by a Red Bull driver was hardly a surprise, but few expected Mark Webber to leave team-mate Sebastian Vettel trailing. And yet that's exactly what the Australian veteran did

After three frustrating races and a second place behind Sebastian Vettel in Malaysia, Mark Webber did everything right and put in a masterful display with a car that was clearly the class of the field.

Rivals hoped that the update packages they introduced for the first European race of the campaign would allow them to close the gap to the Red Bulls, but they were to be disappointed, as the circuit's fast, sweeping curves played to the aero strengths of the RB6. In qualifying, nearest rival Lewis Hamilton was a huge 0.834s behind pole man Webber. The Australian edged out Vettel in a straight fight, having earlier beaten him with a slick-tyre gamble in the Malaysian rain. This time it was about pure speed.

"I don't think there was anything between the set-ups," said Webber's race engineer, Ciaron Pilbeam. "There was almost nothing between them all the way through qualifying, just a tenth here and there. It looks like it was in the last sector most of the time. Nothing else to it I think. It was just Mark's day."

Behind Hamilton on the grid, Fernando Alonso cheered up the home fans by qualifying fourth. Ferrari was using its F-duct, and it clearly helped with straightline speed. Jenson Button was fifth in the

ABOVE Making sure he wasn't caught out again, Mark Webber keeps Sebastian Vettel outside him on the dash to the first corner

OPPOSITE TOP BMW Sauber's Kamui Kobayashi was forced off the track on lap 1 and eventually finished down in 12th place

OPPOSITE BOTTOM Timo Glock reached the finish for Virgin for the first time in five attempts

other McLaren, while Michael Schumacher was much happier with the revised Mercedes, qualifying sixth.

Webber had been outfoxed on the run to Turn 1 by his team-mate in the Malaysian GP, and so his pole went to waste. This time, an FIA rule change gave him a hand. At Sepang, he 'lost' Vettel in his car's flimsy bargeboard-mounted mirrors. Those had now been banned, and by the Spanish GP mirrors had to be attached firmly to the cockpit. So this time Webber ably defended his position on the run to the first corner, not just from Vettel but Hamilton too.

"They got pretty close into the first corner," said Red Bull's relieved principal Christian Horner. "They

both did what they were asked, which was to give each other enough room to play with, and they managed to keep Hamilton from coming through."

One interesting aspect of the way the race played out was that Vettel – as the man running second – was given the first pit stop. Webber had suffered previously in 2010, notably in Australia, by having to cede the first go to his race-leading team-mate. There was nothing sinister about things being swapped this time, though, as Vettel went first simply because he was under threat from Hamilton. Also, in terms of the big picture, it was obvious that he should stop at the optimum time.

INSIDE LINE
MARK WEBBER
RED BULL RACING DRIVER

"All wins are good, but this one feels great. Obviously, Brazil last year was overshadowed by Jenson winning the title, but it was my day today. I'm happy and satisfied that I was able to get pole position and could control the race. That's the first time this year that someone's

won from pole, even if it's the 10th time in a row here…

It was a crucial pole. I said to some people that when I win a race this year I'll do something different, so it was nice to throw my helmet into the crowd and give a present back to the fans, because they don't always get the best treatment.

I knew after qualifying that I was in a great position, but it's a long run to the first corner here and we had cars behind with strong top speed. It was quite tight into there, then I just settled into a rhythm, looking after the tyres, making sure that we got the option tyre through. We had a pretty good idea that the option tyres would behave themselves, but you never know.

I was a bit surprised that I was

able to pull away from Seb, as sometimes I wasn't particularly happy with the laps I was doing. It was a surprise then, but a pleasant one and it made life easier.

After the pit stop, I had Lewis behind me and we just controlled the gap. The team have been incredible this week, getting the cars ready, with long, long nights for the guys and an incredible amount of effort at the factory.

It started on the way back from Shanghai after all the ash-cloud problems. A lot of people were out of position for a long time. There were some astronomical hours being worked and huge intensity – people were just doing things without question – boom, boom, everyone on the same channel, pushing hard.

Then there were so many new parts, and the guys trackside were fabulous. Kenny (Handkammer, chief mechanic) was up on the podium today, which was nice to see. He's been in F1 a long time and he's won many, many races as the chief bolt, so it was some reward for he and his soldiers for all the hours that they've done."

"Sebastian pitted as Hamilton was close," said Pilbeam. "It's more important that we get first and second..."

Unfortunately for Vettel, it all went wrong when the pitcrew had a problem.

"We had an issue at the pit stop with the right front," Horner explained. "We stopped Seb at exactly the right time to make sure we didn't get undercut by Lewis, but unfortunately the stop was too long, we had to hold the car for a Ferrari and for another car.

"Despite Seb 'going purple' on his out lap – and Lewis having his own problems at his stop with the right rear – we lost time, which was just enough to put him behind Lewis. Then, obviously, overtaking around here is very difficult and he couldn't get close enough to have a proper go. Also, with the F-duct that McLaren has, the straightline advantage, there was never going to be an overtaking manoeuvre."

After the identity of his pursuer changed, it was pretty much plain sailing for Webber, because Hamilton – even though he was fast – was never going to be as big a threat as Vettel. Thereafter, Webber put in a perfect drive to score his third grand prix win.

"It was a special victory," said the Australian. "The first one is good, but this one is right up there with it. I had to work very hard in qualifying, not that you don't ever when you're at the front in F1, but it was a crucial pole. I felt very good in the car. The car wasn't easy at the start, but it was always nice to see the gap going away and that helps. It gave me good confidence from there and off we went."

That doesn't mean the race wasn't stressful for Webber, or indeed engineer Pilbeam: "When you come out of the first pit stop a few seconds up the road, it looks like a long time to the finish, with 49 laps to go. It's a long time just to watch the car going around, but it's never quite that simple."

Indeed, Webber could well have suffered the sort of problem that tripped up Vettel late in the race, when he hit an unexpected brake-disc drama, coincidentally again with the right front.

"We had to manage a brake problem with about 15 laps to go, which caused him to run wide," said Horner. "So we brought him in immediately. We could see that the disc was still there, but that the carbon was damaged. There was no warning at all, and the brake temperatures weren't high, so it was quite strange.

"We put some new tyres on it and then he 'went purple' on his out lap in the middle sector… So we knew the brakes must still be there. Then it was just a matter of managing that problem, which he did very well, until the end of the race."

The stop dropped Vettel one spot to fourth, behind Alonso but ahead of Schumacher's Mercedes. The last few laps were touch-and-go. Vettel was encouraged to slow, and informed that the situation was becoming critical. At one point, he was even told that it was all over, and yet still he kept going, even putting in respectable times. Vettel was helped by the fact that he had brand new soft tyres, which basically flattered his lap times.

"It was then a matter of building in enough of a margin," said Horner. "We struggled to slow him down enough because, while he was putting massive margins into his braking distance, his corner speeds were very high on his soft set of tyres, so that made the lap time still competitive with Michael."

Vettel insisted that even if his quick lap times scared his engineers, he was running well below his potential. "I had fresh tyres, and if I had been at full pace I should have been in the 1m21s or something like that," he explained. "Obviously, when I was doing 1m25s or 1m26s, I went massively slower. From the pit wall, it's more difficult to judge how fast you go or not. You tend probably to underestimate compared to the others how quick your car or driver is going.

"Clearly, you need to consider as I said a fresh set of tyres which allowed me to go much quicker in the corners and on acceleration. Yet, for the last 10 laps I wasn't pushing, and for the last five laps I didn't use any brakes at all. Even before, I was backing off massively early and downshifting early in order to slow the car down for the corners."

Vettel got a bonus, when just two laps from home Hamilton crashed out of second place after his

BELOW Fernando Alonso was delighted, and so were the fans, when he benefited from Vettel's and Hamilton's problems to finish second

BOTTOM Sebastien Buemi guides his Toro Rosso past Jarno Trulli's Lotus as he recovers from a lap 1 pit stop for a replacement nose

OPPOSITE Michael Schumacher got ahead of Jenson Button during the pit stops and the McLaren just couldn't find a way back past

TALKING POINT
RED BULL'S MARGIN

The Red Bull RB6 had established itself as the car to beat in the opening four flyaway grands prix, even if it had won only one of these. The chasing pack hoped that their Barcelona upgrades would close the gap, but the reality was somewhat different...

While most had been beavering away on a workable F-duct, Red Bull Racing turned up at the Circuit de Catalunya with a car featuring different body surfaces just about everywhere other than the wings.

There may have been a couple of tenths of a second to be had from an F-duct, but that wasn't going to close the chasm between Red Bull Racing and the rest after qualifying. For the rival teams, the time sheet was depressing: pole position, Mark Webber, 1m19.995s; second on the grid, Sebastian Vettel, 1m20.101s; third, Lewis Hamilton's McLaren, 1m20.829s; fourth, Fernando Alonso's Ferrari, 1m20.937s. The Red Bull Racing advantage was impressive and, to the other 11 teams, depressing.

Adrian Newey has long been acknowledged as the best aerodynamicist in F1, and the Circuit de Catalunya, with its fast, sweeping turns, could not have been better suited to the Red Bull RB6. Vettel admitted that Webber had been 'unbeatable' in qualifying and the Aussie's face told the story. "Flat in sixth through Turn 9!" he beamed.

The Red Bulls were a gear up on everyone else at that part of the circuit, the best part of 10mph quicker than anything else. As well as a superb base chassis, the performance was a direct result of a huge update push that was not scuppered by the best efforts of the volcanic ash cloud emanating from Iceland, post-China.

Webber was quick to pay tribute to the effort and the sleepless nights: "The effort from the guys translated into lap time, no doubt about that. Christian Horner said to me 'You won't get to drive a car this good too often, so go out and enjoy it'. And I did."

The bodywork modifications allied to a new floor had given the RB6 even more downforce, as confirmed by team principal Horner: "The team is pushing hard all the time to get components from the drawing board to the car. The regulations are still relatively immature and there are reasonable gains to be found. I expect that we will see the usual ebb and flow throughout the season."

Red Bull's rivals were certainly hoping so. Michael Schumacher pointed out that Barcelona always gives the biggest payback to an aero advantage and said that it would be interesting to see what the position was next time out in Monte Carlo, a very different type of track. The rest were left hoping that the RB6 would not be quite so formidable there, otherwise it would be a long season...

McLaren's left-front wheel rim failed, sending the McLaren hard into the tyre wall. It was very similar to the accident his former team-mate Heikki Kovalainen suffered at the same track two years earlier.

To the delight of the partisan crowd, Alonso was gifted second place, while Vettel gratefully accepted third. It was a great effort by the young German, the sort of salvage job of which former champions Schumacher or Alonso would have been proud.

"That was a very mature drive by him," said Horner. "He managed the problem well, and those were very important points."

Meanwhile, second place was a real gift for Alonso, who was now second in the World Championship, three points behind Button.

"I feel extremely happy after the result today," said Alonso. "When you gain two positions in the last part of the race, and unexpected positions as well, it feels great, and you have a fantastic feeling. Fourth in qualifying was a good performance, and second in the race is fantastic for the team. But, as I said, we need to improve.

"Sometimes we know we will be first, sometimes fifth, sometimes we will be first hopefully, so as much as we do 100 per cent every weekend, we are happy with the job and need to be satisfied with today's race."

Behind Vettel, Schumacher had the best result yet of his comeback with fourth place. He jumped Button at the pit stops when the Briton had a tardy getaway, and thereafter the veteran managed to keep the 2009 World Champion behind with some clever defensive driving. Despite having a quicker car, Button could do nothing about it.

Struggling with a lack of grip – and a front wing damaged in contact with backmarker Karun Chandhok – Felipe Massa followed them for much of the race in the other Ferrari and finished sixth.

Adrian Sutil had a good run to seventh place for Force India, finishing ahead of Robert Kubica, Rubens Barrichello and Jaime Alguersuari.

Nico Rosberg had a terrible race in the second Mercedes, losing time with a botched pit stop and eventually finishing 13th. Yet, like the others who had endured frustrating weekends, he could at least turn his attention to Monaco where, just four days after the Spanish GP, the F1 cars would be practising on the streets of the principality.

TOP LEFT Mark Webber does nothing to disguise his delight after scoring the first win of his campaign

BOTTOM LEFT Lewis Hamilton was all set for second place when his McLaren suffered wheel failure and crashed with just two laps to go

SNAPSHOT FROM
SPAIN

CLOCKWISE FROM RIGHT The main difference in 2010 was that the crowd had swapped Renault caps for Ferrari ones in support of Fernando Alonso; Jenson Button, Pedro de la Rosa and Lewis Hamilton chat during the circuit's 20th anniversary celebrations; McLaren has 12 drivers' titles and wants more; welcome to Spain; Mark Webber celebrates victory by giving away his helmet; Alonso shows allegiance to Spain and to Italy too, for Ferrari; the Williams HQ looks clean cut and corporate; Button had his own 'barmy army' out in support; rallying great Carlos Sainz was present to watch his son race in Formula BMW; Rubens Barrichello sported yet another new helmet livery

RACE RESULTS
SPAIN
BARCELONA

RACE DATE May 9th
CIRCUIT LENGTH 2.892 miles
NO. OF LAPS 66
RACE DISTANCE 190.872 miles
WEATHER Sunny & dry, 22°C
TRACK TEMP 35°C
ATTENDANCE 226,303
LAP RECORD Kimi Räikkönen,
1m21.670s, 127.500mph, 2008

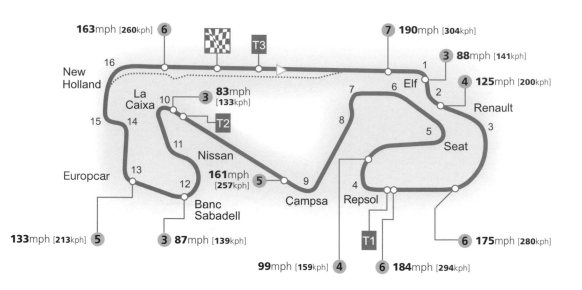

PRACTICE 1

	Driver	Time	Laps
1	L Hamilton	1m21.134s	21
2	J Button	1m21.672s	14
3	M Schumacher	1m21.716s	12
4	M Webber	1m22.011s	27
5	S Vettel	1m22.026s	22
6	N Rosberg	1m22.070s	19
7	R Kubica	1m22.202s	22
8	F Alonso	1m22.258s	19
9	V Petrov	1m22.397s	23
10	K Kobayashi	1m22.492s	26
11	S Buemi	1m22.588s	24
12	F Massa	1m22.975s	22
13	P di Resta	1m23.030s	21
14	J Alguersuari	1m23.110s	31
15	V Liuzzi	1m23.284s	19
16	R Barrichello	1m23.312s	22
17	N Hulkenberg	1m23.471s	20
18	H Kovalainen	1m25.329s	17
19	J Trulli	1m26.244s	20
20	T Glock	1m26.340s	23
21	L di Grassi	1m26.694s	24
22	C Klien	1m27.250s	26
23	B Senna	1m27.752s	27
24	P de la Rosa	No time	3

PRACTICE 2

	Driver	Time	Laps
1	S Vettel	1m19.965s	24
2	M Webber	1m20.175s	35
3	M Schumacher	1m20.757s	28
4	F Alonso	1m20.819s	30
5	L Hamilton	1m21.191s	23
6	R Kubica	1m21.202s	36
7	N Rosberg	1m21.271s	27
8	F Massa	1m21.302s	25
9	J Button	1m21.364s	26
10	A Sutil	1m21.518s	32
11	P de la Rosa	1m21.672s	37
12	V Liuzzi	1m21.904s	32
13	K Kobayashi	1m21.931s	29
14	S Buemi	1m22.184s	37
15	R Barrichello	1m22.192s	33
16	V Petrov	1m22.435s	35
17	J Alguersuari	1m22.449s	34
18	N Hulkenberg	1m23.765s	7
19	J Trulli	1m24.209s	26
20	H Kovalainen	1m24.894s	22
21	L di Grassi	1m25.066s	30
22	K Chandhok	1m25.972s	23
23	B Senna	1m26.152s	25
24	T Glock	1m26.596s	21

PRACTICE 3

	Driver	Time	Laps
1	S Vettel	1m20.528s	15
2	M Webber	1m21.232s	11
3	L Hamilton	1m21.348s	14
4	J Button	1m21.376s	16
5	M Schumacher	1m21.583s	14
6	F Massa	1m21.749s	16
7	N Rosberg	1m22.013s	14
8	F Alonso	1m22.091s	15
9	R Kubica	1m22.242s	20
10	A Sutil	1m22.377s	12
11	S Buemi	1m22.400s	18
12	K Kobayashi	1m22.412s	11
13	P de la Rosa	1m22.527s	20
14	N Hulkenberg	1m22.634s	16
15	J Alguersuari	1m22.926s	20
16	R Barrichello	1m22.953s	16
17	V Liuzzi	1m23.597s	12
18	V Petrov	1m23.896s	5
19	J Trulli	1m24.610s	14
20	H Kovalainen	1m24.745s	11
21	T Glock	1m25.722s	15
22	L di Grassi	1m25.855s	14
23	K Chandhok	1m26.611s	18
24	B Senna	1m30.246s	6

QUALIFYING 1

	Driver	Time
1	M Webber	1m21.412s
2	S Vettel	1m21.680s
3	L Hamilton	1m21.723s
4	J Button	1m21.915s
5	F Alonso	1m21.957s
6	P de la Rosa	1m22.211s
7	N Rosberg	1m22.419s
8	R Kubica	1m22.488s
9	M Schumacher	1m22.528s
10	F Massa	1m22.564s
11	K Kobayashi	1m22.577s
12	J Alguersuari	1m22.593s
13	A Sutil	1m22.628s
14	S Buemi	1m22.699s
15	N Hulkenberg	1m22.857s
16	V Petrov	1m22.976s
17	V Liuzzi	1m23.084s
18	R Barrichello	1m23.125s
19	J Trulli	1m24.674s
20	H Kovalainen	1m24.748s
21	T Glock	1m25.475s
22	L di Grassi	1m25.556s
23	K Chandhok	1m26.750s
24	B Senna	1m27.122s

QUALIFYING 2

	Driver	Time
1	M Webber	1m20.655s
2	S Vettel	1m20.772s
3	J Button	1m21.168s
4	L Hamilton	1m21.415s
5	F Alonso	1m21.549s
6	M Schumacher	1m21.557s
7	R Kubica	1m21.599s
8	K Kobayashi	1m21.725s
9	F Massa	1m21.841s
10	N Rosberg	1m21.867s
11	A Sutil	1m21.985s
12	P de la Rosa	1m22.026s
13	N Hulkenberg	1m22.131s
14	V Petrov	1m22.139s
15	S Buemi	1m22.191s
16	J Alguersuari	1m22.207s
17	V Liuzzi	1m22.854s

Best sectors – Practice

Sec 1	F Alonso	22.436s
Sec 2	S Vettel	29.793s
Sec 3	M Webber	27.512s

Speed trap – Practice

1	L Hamilton	193.930mph
2	F Massa	193.805mph
3	F Alonso	193.432mph

Best sectors – Qualifying

Sec 1	S Vettel	22.438s
Sec 2	M Webber	29.843s
Sec 3	M Webber	27.681s

Speed trap – Qualifying

1	F Alonso	193.805mph
2	F Massa	193.743mph
3	V Petrov	192.190mph

Jenson Button
"During the opening laps, my dashboard readout failed. Then at my first stop there was a problem with the clutch dragging, so the guys couldn't get the wheel on."

Michael Schumacher
"It was quite an entertaining race for me, even if we knew from the very beginning that there would not be any chance for us to compete for a podium place."

Sebastian Vettel
"The start was okay, but there was no chance to pass Mark. I then had a slow stop and had to wait for the Ferrari to drive past and then Jenson coming in."

Felipe Massa
"The main difficulty was a lack of grip, especially in the third sector: every time it looked as though I might close on Button, he was able to get away from me there."

Rubens Barrichello
"I had a great start, passing five cars, and was able to stay with the Renaults and the Force Indias. I think we were on the verge of a tyre issue in the last five laps."

Robert Kubica
"I was fighting with Massa in Turn 1, but the car went sideways when I got on the power. Then, in Turn 3, I touched Kobayashi which damaged my front wing."

Lewis Hamilton
"I was looking good to split the Red Bulls. I was nursing the car to the finish, then felt the steering go, and there was immediately a failure on the left-front corner."

Nico Rosberg
"When I tried for the gap by Robert at the start, he didn't see me so I was pushed wide. Then we had a problem at my first stop which dropped me back again."

Mark Webber
"I was happy to capitalise on pole. It's an aggressive run in to Turn 1 with the slipstream and headwind, but I had that covered then settled into the race."

Fernando Alonso
"I'm happy with second place in front of my fans. We knew we could expect a difficult race, as on tracks like this we still don't have enough aerodynamic downforce."

Nico Hulkenberg
"I felt like I was always in the wrong place at the wrong time on lap 1. After the first stop, I went offline and damaged the car, limiting its downforce."

Vitaly Petrov
"At the start of the race, I decided it was better to be cautious, as the first corner was busy. I didn't gain any places but I knew I needed to avoid damaging the car."

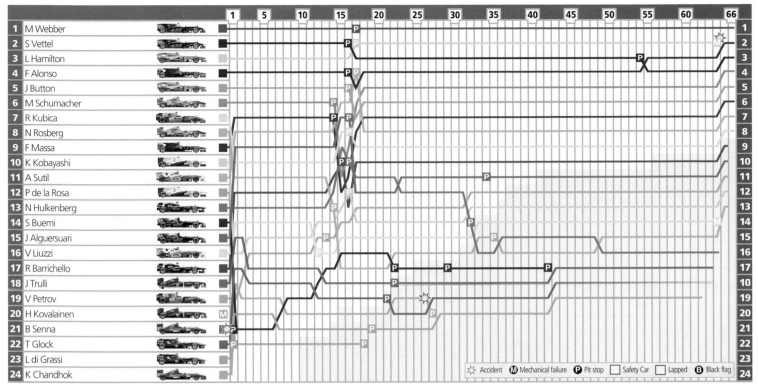

	Driver		
1	M Webber		1
2	S Vettel		2
3	L Hamilton		3
4	F Alonso		4
5	J Button		5
6	M Schumacher		6
7	R Kubica		7
8	N Rosberg		8
9	F Massa		9
10	K Kobayashi		10
11	A Sutil		11
12	P de la Rosa		12
13	N Hulkenberg		13
14	S Buemi		14
15	J Alguersuari		15
16	V Liuzzi		16
17	R Barrichello		17
18	J Trulli		10
19	V Petrov		19
20	H Kovalainen		20
21	B Senna		21
22	T Glock		22
23	L di Grassi		23
24	K Chandhok		24

☆ Accident Ⓜ Mechanical failure Ⓟ Pit stop ☐ Safety Car ☐ Lapped Ⓑ Black flag

QUALIFYING 3

	Driver	Time
1	M Webber	1m19.995s
2	S Vettel	1m20.101s
3	L Hamilton	1m20.829s
4	F Alonso	1m20.937s
5	J Button	1m20.991s
6	M Schumacher	1m21.294s
7	R Kubica	1m21.353s
8	N Rosberg	1m21.408s
9	F Massa	1m21.585s
10	K Kobayashi	1m21.984s

GRID

	Driver	Time
1	M Webber	1m19.995s
2	S Vettel	1m20.101s
3	L Hamilton	1m20.829s
4	F Alonso	1m20.937s
5	J Button	1m20.991s
6	M Schumacher	1m21.294s
7	R Kubica	1m21.353s
8	N Rosberg	1m21.408s
9	F Massa	1m21.585s
10	K Kobayashi	1m21.984s
11	A Sutil	1m21.985s
12	P de la Rosa	1m22.026s
13	N Hulkenberg	1m22.131s
14	S Buemi	1m22.191s
15	J Alguersuari	1m22.207s
16	V Liuzzi	1m22.854s
17	R Barrichello	1m23.125s
18	J Trulli	1m24.674s
19*	V Petrov	1m22.139s
20	H Kovalainen	1m24.748s
21	B Senna	1m27.122s
22^	T Glock	1m25.475s
23^	L di Grassi	1m25.556s
24*	K Chandhok	1m26.750s

* Five-place grid penalty for gearbox change.
^Five-place grid penalty for failing to notify FIA of gear ratios

RACE

	Driver	Car	Laps	Time	Avg. mph	Fastest	Stops
1	M Webber	Red Bull-Renault RB6	66	1h35m44.101s	119.596	1m24.828s	1
2	F Alonso	Ferrari F10	66	1h36m08.166s	119.126	1m24.846s	1
3	S Vettel	Red Bull-Renault RB6	66	1h36m35.439s	118.566	1m25.176s	2
4	M Schumacher	Mercedes MGP W01	66	1h36m46.296s	118.344	1m25.529s	1
5	J Button	McLaren-Mercedes MP4 25	66	1h36m47.829s	118.313	1m25.166s	1
6	F Massa	Ferrari F10	66	1h36m49.868s	118.271	1m25.497s	1
7	A Sutil	Force India-Mercedes VJM03	66	1h36m57.042s	118.125	1m25.845s	1
8	R Kubica	Renault R30	66	1h36m57.778s	118.110	1m25.466s	1
9	R Barrichello	Williams-Cosworth FW32	65	1h36m04.378s	117.398	1m25.728s	1
10	J Alguersuari	Toro Rosso-Ferrari STR5	65	1h36m13.288s	117.217	1m25.655s	1
11	V Petrov	Renault R30	65	1h36m20.307s	117.075	1m25.470s	1
12	K Kobayashi	BMW Sauber-Ferrari C29	65	1h36m21.168s	117.057	1m26.083s	1
13	N Rosberg	Mercedes MGP W01	65	1h36m41.080s	116.656	1m25.155s	2
14	L Hamilton	McLaren-Mercedes MP4-25	64	Accident		1m24.357s	1
15	V Liuzzi	Force India-Mercedes VJM03	64	Engine	-	1m25.924s	1
16	N Hulkenberg	Williams-Cosworth FW32	64	1h35m44.518s	115.992	1m26.863s	2
17	J Trulli	Lotus-Cosworth T127	63	1h37m09.713s	112.955	1m29.564s	1
18	T Glock	Virgin-Cosworth VR-01	63	1h37m11.174s	112.927	1m29.776s	1
19	L di Grassi	Virgin-Cosworth VR-01	62	1h37m00.618s	110.898	1m29.904s	1
R	S Buemi	Toro Rosso-Ferrari STR5	42	Hydraulics	-	1m26.724s	2
R	K Chandhok	HRT-Cosworth F110	27	Suspension	-	1m32.041s	1
R	P de la Rosa	BMW Sauber-Ferrari C29	18	Accident damage	-	1m30.411s	1
R	B Senna	HRT-Cosworth F110	0	Accident	-	-	0
NS	H Kovalainen	Lotus-Cosworth T127	-	-	-	-	0

CHAMPIONSHIP

	Driver	Pts
1	J Button	70
2	F Alonso	67
3	S Vettel	60
4	M Webber	53
5	N Rosberg	50
6	L Hamilton	49
7	F Massa	49
8	R Kubica	44
9	M Schumacher	22
10	A Sutil	16
11	V Liuzzi	8
12	R Barrichello	8
13	V Petrov	6
14	J Alguersuari	3
15	N Hulkenberg	1

	Constructor	Pts
1	McLaren-Mercedes	119
2	Ferrari	116
3	Red Bull-Renault	113
4	Mercedes	72
5	Renault	50
6	Force India-Mercedes	24
7	Williams-Cosworth	8
8	Toro Rosso-Ferrari	3

Fastest lap
L Hamilton 1m24.357s
(123.444mph) on lap 59

Fastest speed trap
F Massa   193.992mph
Slowest speed trap
B Senna   180.384mph

Fastest pit stop
1 M Schumacher   20.104s
2 F Massa   20.314s
3 F Alonso   20.396s

Adrian Sutil
"I had a great start, moving from 11th to 8th, and wasn't far behind Massa. I had to push a lot, though, as for about 40 laps Kubica was close behind."

Jarno Trulli
"I was trying to pass de la Rosa down the left side and he moved towards me. The impact broke my front wing, so I had to pit. Then I collected a drive-through."

Karun Chandhok
"I'm pleased we finished easily ahead of Virgin, even though the car felt difficult to drive. I don't know why. Despite that, we showed good race pace."

Pedro de la Rosa
"I kept out of Jaime's way, held the car straight and he just turned left into me. Though we changed the front wing, the damage to my suspension was too much."

Timo Glock
"I had a good start, but I got hit by a Toro Rosso which caused a rear-tyre puncture. I pitted for a tyre change but the damage to the car made it undriveable."

"I had a race-long battle with Jarno, but the traffic we came across made it difficult. Out of 66 laps, only 15 were in free air and the rest were full of blue flags."

Vitantonio Liuzzi
"It was hard starting from so far behind. We suffered understeer then snap oversteer with the softer tyres, but the balance with the hard tyres was better."

"I am happy with a point, even if my race was a mess, with the problem at the pit stop with a wheel nut, then the penalty after my collision with Chandhok."

Heikki Kovalainen
"I had a gearbox problem while we were firing up on the grid. The gearbox selected two gears, as there was some sort of software issue that caused it to fail."

Bruno Senna
"I made a great start and made up a few places. I was in 17th and it was a good opportunity but, at Turn 4, the car caught me out and unluckily my race ended there."

Kamui Kobayashi
"I was hit by Robert in Turn 3. I left him enough room, but he said he had understeer. I came back from the gravel in 15th. Without this, I would have scored points."

Lucas di Grassi
"My race was very tough: we opted to start on the prime tyres and it was tricky to drive the car. When we switched to options, I was able to do some good laps."

FORMULA 1 GRAND PRIX
DE MONACO 2010
MONTE CARLO

MARK DOES IT AGAIN

Mark Webber controlled the Monaco GP to make it two wins in two weekends and move level on points at the top of the table with his Red Bull Racing team-mate Sebastian Vettel

Mark Webber made it two wins in eight days when he added a superb victory in Monaco to his earlier success in Spain, not putting a foot wrong as he outran his team-mate Sebastian Vettel.

The result meant that the two Red Bull Racing drivers were tied at the top of the table on 78 points apiece, but Webber had become the man of the moment, and his two faultless performances forced a lot of people to reassess him.

His blinding form shouldn't have come as a surprise. Some drivers just click with Monaco, and given the constraints of their equipment, always shine there. Webber won here in his F3000 days, and since then had put in some noteworthy performances that had to some extent passed under the radar.

In 2005, he finished third with Williams, albeit frustrated by a strategy that saw him beaten by team-mate Nick Heidfeld. In 2006, he qualified on the front row, only to suffer a frustrating retirement. With Red Bull, he finished fourth and fifth in 2007 and 2008 from starting positions that didn't reflect his potential.

Days after the race came the news that Red Bull had found an issue with Vettel's chassis, and the team confirmed that it would be changed for Turkey. That

absolutely been on top of his game the last couple of races, no doubt about that."

Webber secured pole position with a brilliant lap, beating Robert Kubica by 0.3s and leaving Vettel in third. Having been only 10th in practice on Thursday, Webber found the lap time when it mattered.

Kubica was the dark horse, as his Renault proved to be more competitive on pure speed than it had been previously. Indeed, he looked a good bet for pole until Webber popped up with his lap. Vettel ended up 0.4s down – a huge amount by Monaco standards. However, by starting third on the cleaner side of the track he had a good chance of getting past Kubica.

Felipe Massa qualified fourth, while it was a frustrating day for McLaren too, as past winners Lewis Hamilton and Jenson Button had to settle for fifth and eighth places on the grid.

The big news was the absence of Fernando Alonso from qualifying. The Spaniard had a huge crash at the entry to Casino Square at the start of Saturday practice. As anyone who changes a chassis can't run again on the same day, he had to start from the pitlane.

Webber held his advantage into the first corner, while Vettel successfully jumped Kubica.

A safety car then came out before the end of the lap after Nico Hulkenberg crashed his Williams in the tunnel, having dislodged his front wing in earlier contact. Meanwhile, there was more drama when Button stopped almost immediately with a spectacular engine failure. It was a self-inflicted wound, as a mechanic had forgotten to remove a radiator cover, and the engine had overheated on the way to the grid.

Webber soon began to build up an advantage. After his compulsory pit stop, he was chased by Nico Rosberg, who had chosen to pit later than most other frontrunners. When the German driver finally came in, Webber had Vettel behind him once again.

Another safety-car period was needed after Rubens

ABOVE Mark Webber leads into Ste Devote on lap 1, with Vettel having moved past Kubica

BELOW The beginning of the end for Jenson Button, as his McLaren's engine blows on the opening lap

OPPOSITE Webber kept his cool to stay ahead after three post-safety-car restarts to score a famous win

put a slightly different perspective on things. If Vettel was saddled with below-par equipment for Spain and Monaco, it couldn't have helped his prospects.

However, the discovery certainly should not have detracted from what was a brilliant performance from Webber. Even with a great car, you still have to get the job done and bring the thing home in one piece.

"Monaco is never easy, to be honest," said Adrian Newey as the celebrations began in the garage. "So much is down to the driver: getting the car to work with the driver is the big thing. I think Mark was very smart. He played himself in and got quicker and quicker as he got comfortable with the car. Mark has

INSIDE LINE
SAM MICHAEL
WILLIAMS TECHNICAL DIRECTOR

"There's always something in F1, and at the moment it's the exhaust-blown diffuser. Monte Carlo is not the kind of place you'd want to introduce it, but pretty much all the leading teams are working on it.

All the systems are different, and ours is probably most like Red Bull's when you look at exhaust exits and how we will work the diffuser. The Mercedes one, Ferrari and to an extent McLaren, are different. They all vary by where they blow the diffuser. You only have a certain amount of energy in the exhaust, so you can't try and blow it all because there's not enough puff. You have to choose where you blow it. Red Bull's is obviously fully optimised and it made sense to have a look at what they were doing.

It's not a new concept, as there were blown floors on the ground-effect Williams FW14/15s, but it was a different concept back then. There were two types of blowing: you could take the exhaust right out of the top of the tunnel, and there were also ones that blew in the centre tunnels. You can't get into

that part now. Well, you can, but it's not a good way of doing it. It's a completely different aero study now and the materials we use didn't exist back in the early 1990s.

People have been scratching their heads about Red Bull's qualifying speed, and wondering whether perhaps they are using a trail-throttle system in qualifying to produce more stable downforce. It's very easy from a chassis point-of-view, but the problem is doing it without damaging the engine.

You've got to retard the ignition significantly so that you get the gas to fire in the exhaust system and produce a lot of high-energy air coming out of the exhaust, but for very low torque for the engine. Doing it places considerable strain on the exhaust valves. We're into trying it

with Cosworth on the dyno, but we haven't got anything signed off yet.

Judging by the Red Bull pace, you'd probably say they are the only ones doing it. Mind you, Renault is using the same engine, so they've probably got something.

A blown exhaust also increases the fuel consumption, and so it's not something you would do in the race, only in qualifying. It's only for one-and-a-half seconds when you hit the brakes, so it's not like running a retarded mixture all the time. It's pretty realistic to get it done."

TALKING POINT
EMERGENCE OF WEBBER

Two wins inside a week put Mark Webber into the lead of the World Championship as the F1 circus left Monte Carlo. For the first time, people started to talk about the Australian as a potential champion.

"Mark's chances are pretty good," said Australia's finest, three-time World Champion Jack Brabham.

"He has proved that he can deal with [Sebastian] Vettel, who is his greatest opponent."

Certainly, this was not in the script as far as Vettel was concerned, the young German's body language very revealing as he contemplated his team-mate's second successive win from pole position.

It was not just that, it was the manner of a very special day for Webber in the Principality. His pole position time had been four-tenths of a second quicker than third-placed Vettel's best lap, although Sebastian had been caught in traffic when his tyres were at their best. He was still hopeful of a strong race and managed to jump front-row starter Robert Kubica into the first corner.

Yet, still there was no holding Webber. Despite three safety-car

periods wiping out nearly 25s of Webber's advantage, as soon as they departed the scene, Webber simply drove away again.

"We have to look at why, especially at the beginning and after the restarts, I wasn't able to keep up," Vettel said. "When I finally felt the grip after a few laps, I wasn't too far off, but he'd already be down the road by then."

Last year notwithstanding, this is the first time in his F1 career that Webber has driven a truly front-running car. In 2009, he was still hampered by the broken leg and shoulder sustained in his charity Tasmanian Challenge event less than four months before the start of the season. He'd still been strong enough to win at the Nürburgring in July and at Interlagos, but this time he was

properly ready for the challenge.

The seeds of a delicate intra-team situation at Red Bull were sown by Webber's supremely accomplished drive in Monaco. In the following week, the team announced that a problem had been found with Vettel's chassis and that he would have a replacement in time for the following round at Istanbul.

Webber, meanwhile, was being mentioned as a possible Ferrari team-mate for Fernando Alonso, as the team took time confirming an extension to Felipe Massa's contract. The Australian, though, said he was happy where he is – it's not every day that you come upon a race-winning F1 car from a design team led by Adrian Newey. Webber intends making the most of it, so a new Red Bull deal was his priority.

Barrichello crashed the other Williams on the way up the hill from Ste Devote. No one knew at the time, but some days later the team confirmed that he'd suffered a failure after running over a loose drain cover.

This yellow period again trimmed Webber's lead over Vettel, and it happened a third time when another safety car was dispatched for attention to a loose drain cover before Casino.

Webber continued after each restart to open up a gap on Vettel. Then, in the closing laps, backmarkers Jarno Trulli and Karun Chandhok collided at Rascasse. It was the last lap by the time the mess was cleared up, but green flags flew at the last corner for a final dash across the finish line.

The race had played out perfectly for Webber, although the safety-car periods didn't help. He was 15.3s clear of Vettel the lap before the second (Barrichello) safety car came out, 4.8s ahead for the third (drain cover) safety car, and was 4.1s in front when Trulli and Chandhok did their thing in front of him in the closing laps. In others words, 25s went astray in total. Yet at no stage did he let it get to him.

"The safety cars are a focus thing more than anything," said Newey. "To lose a 15s lead at one point was frustrating."

"The start was good and that's the first hurdle," said Webber's engineer, Ciaron Pilbeam. "Mark left in the lead, and pulled out a good gap which meant that the pit stop was not dramatic. The safety car is a bit less tricky than it used to be when everybody is already fuelled to the end of the race, but still he had a 15s lead the first time, and to have that reduced to nothing and start again is quite tough.

"All three times he pulled out the gap again, though, so he was clearly quick enough to win the race. Seb had Kubica on him for most of the race, so I guess that occupied him a little bit.

"We didn't score all the points we should have

done in the early races, for various reasons, but it's nice to have had two dry, trouble-free weekends where we scored good results with both cars. Mark is driving very well, and these last two races he's been on top of his game. Hopefully he can carry this forward."

It was a good effort too by the team to put earlier problems behind it and get two cars to the flag. The consensus in the pitlane was that no team was expending more effort in fast-tracking new parts through the system, and getting them onto the cars.

"After the brake issue that we had in Spain, there was a big effort from the factory to support us with a couple of small new parts, and it certainly helped,"

OPPOSITE Robert Kubica was left to rue a poor start and had to make do with third place for Renault

ABOVE In spite of the fireworks, Nico Rosberg endured a frustrating race to finish eighth, although this soon became seventh

BELOW It's thought that earlier contact led to Nico Hulkenberg's front wing collapsing and triggering his accident in the tunnel on lap 1

the season isn't necessarily the quickest at the end. It's really a question of whether we can continue to at least match our rivals."

Meanwhile, Kubica's third-place finish was a huge boost to Renault. "The team is somehow building up again with a bit of a different mentality, a bit of a different approach, and I think it's working," said the Pole. "Nobody, before the start of the season, would put one Euro on us. We've managed to finish on the podium twice in the first six races. We showed good pace, especially here in Monaco. We are bringing along quite a lot of new parts for the car. All the guys in the factory are working really hard to improve the car. I think that we are getting better direction than maybe in the past and it seems to be giving results."

Massa had a quiet run to fourth, while Hamilton gave McLaren scant reward with fifth place. From the pitlane, Alonso made his tyre change at the end of the first lap under yellows. After that, and with his stop out of the way, he gained ground rapidly. He was set to cross the line in sixth when Michael Schumacher cheekily passed him when the field was released at the last corner after the final safety-car period.

After the race, there was a debate about whether Schumacher was allowed to pass. In fact, the rulebook appeared to contradict itself. As of 2010, drivers were allowed to pass between the safety-car line at the last corner and the chequered flag, once the field was released. However, elsewhere, the old rule about a single-file finish under a last-lap safety car still applied.

The stewards duly deemed that passing was not permitted, and Schumacher was docked a costly 20s, dropping him to 12th place. Alonso thus regained his sixth ahead of Rosberg, Adrian Sutil, Vitantonio Liuzzi and Sebastien Buemi.

Mercedes GP then lodged an appeal, but some days after the race the team announced that it had accepted the original decision. The rules were later clarified.

ABOVE Fernando Alonso holds off Michael Schumacher, but he was to be passed out of the final corner, earning the Mercedes driver a 20s penalty and the loss of six places

BELOW Two wins in two races gave Webber every reason to unleash his party tricks into the Red Bull Racing swimming pool

Christian Horner noted. "We had no issues at all, at arguably one of the toughest circuits on the calendar. Seventy-eight laps around here is pretty gruelling, pretty tough on the cars, so it's testimony to the hard work that's going on within the team. A result like today's is about the team working as a group."

"I've given up predicting what circuits we'll be good at and what circuits we won't be good at," said design chief Newey. "The RB6 has proved to be very quick everywhere but, as I keep saying, we're the second year in from a very big regulation change, so the progress rate is extremely high. And, as was proved last year, the car that's quickest at the start of

SNAPSHOT FROM MONACO

CLOCKWISE FROM RIGHT
Robert Kubica's Renault flashes into Massenet with the harbour and Hotel Hermitage as a backdrop; the Branson family enjoys the view; Felipe Massa guides his Ferrari through Portier; there's only one Bernie Ecclestone...; Michael Schumacher arrives at 'the office'; central Monte Carlo offers a backdrop like no other; Fernando Alonso's weekend received a setback when he shunted into the barriers at Massenet on Saturday morning; massed celebrations at Red Bull, with Christian Horner and Adrian Newey in the pool with Mark Webber; the tool of Lewis Hamilton's trade – his McLaren's steering wheel

RACE RESULTS

RACE DATE May 16th
CIRCUIT LENGTH 2.075 miles
NO. OF LAPS 78
RACE DISTANCE 161.850 miles
WEATHER Sunny & dry, 22°C
TRACK TEMP 35°C
ATTENDANCE Not available
LAP RECORD Michael Schumacher,
1m14.439s, 100.373mph, 2004

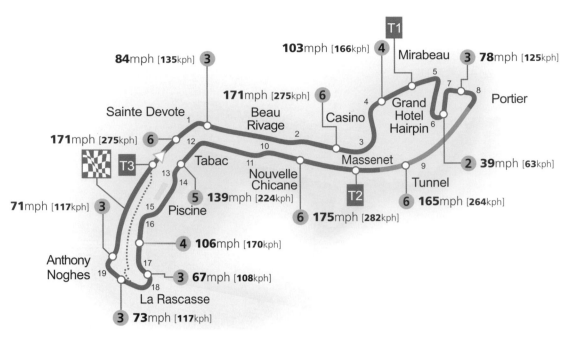

	PRACTICE 1				PRACTICE 2				PRACTICE 3				QUALIFYING 1			QUALIFYING 2	
	Driver	Time	Laps		Driver	Time	Laps		Driver	Time	Laps		Driver	Time		Driver	Time
1	F Alonso	1m15.927s	32	1	F Alonso	1m14.904s	36	1	R Kubica	1m14.806s	26	1	F Massa	1m14.757s	1	N Rosberg	1m14.375s
2	S Vettel	1m16.000s	27	2	N Rosberg	1m15.013s	40	2	F Massa	1m14.852s	22	2	M Webber	1m15.035s	2	F Massa	1m14.405s
3	R Kubica	1m16.016s	28	3	S Vettel	1m15.099s	48	3	M Webber	1m14.945s	25	3	R Kubica	1m15.045s	3	M Webber	1m14.462s
4	M Webber	1m16.382s	25	4	F Massa	1m15.120s	45	4	L Hamilton	1m15.038s	25	4	S Vettel	1m15.110s	4	L Hamilton	1m14.527s
5	F Massa	1m16.517s	30	5	M Schumacher	1m15.143s	38	5	S Vettel	1m15.046s	26	5	N Rosberg	1m15.188s	5	R Kubica	1m14.549s
6	M Schumacher	1m16.589s	21	6	R Kubica	1m15.192s	39	6	M Schumacher	1m15.236s	22	6	V Liuzzi	1m15.397s	6	S Vettel	1m14.568s
7	L Hamilton	1m16.647s	32	7	L Hamilton	1m15.249s	32	7	N Rosberg	1m15.252s	20	7	A Sutil	1m15.445s	7	M Schumacher	1m14.691s
8	J Button	1m16.692s	30	8	A Sutil	1m15.460s	42	8	S Buemi	1m15.537s	22	8	V Petrov	1m15.482s	8	V Liuzzi	1m15.061s
9	A Sutil	1m16.805s	23	9	J Button	1m15.619s	38	9	A Sutil	1m15.659s	14	9	R Barrichello	1m15.590s	9	R Barrichello	1m15.083s
10	S Buemi	1m16.857s	31	10	M Webber	1m15.620s	28	10	J Button	1m15.682s	22	10	J Button	1m15.623s	10	J Button	1m15.150s
11	N Rosberg	1m17.149s	15	11	V Petrov	1m15.746s	44	11	V Liuzzi	1m15.691s	19	11	M Schumacher	1m15.649s	11	N Hulkenberg	1m15.317s
12	R Barrichello	1m17.331s	28	12	S Buemi	1m16.276s	46	12	J Alguersuari	1m15.769s	27	12	L Hamilton	1m15.676s	12	A Sutil	1m15.318s
13	V Liuzzi	1m17.704s	27	13	N Hulkenberg	1m16.348s	48	13	N Hulkenberg	1m16.164s	24	13	P de la Rosa	1m15.908s	13	S Buemi	1m15.413s
14	V Petrov	1m17.718s	39	14	R Barrichello	1m16.522s	38	14	R Barrichello	1m16.232s	21	14	S Buemi	1m15.961s	14	V Petrov	1m15.576s
15	J Alguersuari	1m17.991s	37	15	V Liuzzi	1m16.528s	42	15	V Petrov	1m16.240s	27	15	J Alguersuari	1m16.021s	15	P de la Rosa	1m15.692s
16	N Hulkenberg	1m18.397s	39	16	P de la Rosa	1m16.599s	36	16	F Alonso	1m16.266s	6	16	N Hulkenberg	1m16.030s	16	K Kobayashi	1m15.992s
17	P de la Rosa	1m18.434s	38	17	K Kobayashi	1m16.818s	46	17	K Kobayashi	1m16.644s	26	17	K Kobayashi	1m16.175s	17	J Alguersuari	1m16.176s
18	K Kobayashi	1m18.547s	32	18	J Alguersuari	1m17.023s	28	18	P de la Rosa	1m16.696s	23	18	H Kovalainen	1m17.094s			
19	T Glock	1m19.527s	24	19	H Kovalainen	1m18.184s	48	19	H Kovalainen	1m17.782s	18	19	J Trulli	1m17.134s			
20	H Kovalainen	1m19.606s	32	20	L di Grassi	1m18.478s	38	20	J Trulli	1m17.865s	26	20	T Glock	1m17.377s			
21	J Trulli	1m19.902s	31	21	J Trulli	1m18.667s	13	21	L di Grassi	1m18.063s	25	21	L di Grassi	1m17.864s			
22	L di Grassi	1m20.566s	18	22	T Glock	1m18.721s	42	22	B Senna	1m19.720s	25	22	B Senna	1m18.509s			
23	B Senna	1m21.688s	28	23	K Chandhok	1m20.313s	36	23	K Chandhok	1m19.781s	21	23	K Chandhok	1m19.559s			
24	K Chandhok	1m21.853s	6	24	B Senna	1m22.148s	11	24	T Glock	No time	3	24	F Alonso	No time			

Best sectors – Practice			Speed trap – Practice			Best sectors – Qualifying			Speed trap – Qualifying		
Sec 1	L Hamilton	19.676s	1	L Hamilton	178.271mph	Sec 1	R Kubica	19.393s	1	R Kubica	178.892mph
Sec 2	S Vettel	34.571s	2	R Kubica	178.147mph	Sec 2	M Webber	34.162s	2	A Sutil	178.147mph
Sec 3	M Webber	20.308s	3	V Petrov	177.215mph	Sec 3	M Webber	20.098s	3	L Hamilton	177.960mph

 Jenson Button

"There was a cooling cover left on the left-hand sidepod, where the radiator is. My car began to overheat and I started losing engine power, so I turned it off."

 Michael Schumacher

"Our understanding was that the 'safety car in, track clear' message meant we were back to racing conditions, so I went for it and overtook Fernando."

Sebastian Vettel

"We achieved our optimum from third on the grid. I had good acceleration at the start and dived down the inside to get into the first corner ahead of Robert."

 Felipe Massa

"I ran almost all race behind Vettel and Kubica, and finished in the same position I had started. As passing is so hard, I don't think I could have done more."

 Rubens Barrichello

"I had a good start, but the car began to feel strange after the pit stop. The steering wheel didn't feel normal. It continued to get worse and then I crashed."

 Robert Kubica

"Nobody expected us to finish third. I lost a place to Vettel at the start as I got wheelspin and it was too late to close the door. I also had to defend from Felipe."

 Lewis Hamilton

"After the Spanish GP, I didn't want any further mishaps, so just looked after the car and went for the points, and fifth place was the maximum possible."

 Nico Rosberg

"I'm disappointed that I could achieve only seventh place. We had the speed for a front-row position and that should have given us a podium finish."

 Mark Webber

"It's the greatest day of my life. As an F1 driver, you hope that you win races and if you have a choice then the blue-riband event is very, very special for any driver."

Fernando Alonso

"The team chose an aggressive strategy and worked hard to build the car for the race. To finish a race like this without problems is the result of a super job."

Nico Hulkenberg

"There was a problem with the clutch before the start. I'm not sure what happened in the tunnel. The car felt odd one second and the next I was in the wall."

Vitaly Petrov

"I felt something wrong at the rear, so the team decided to stop me. Unluckily, my race was also affected by a puncture, that had earlier put me a lap down."

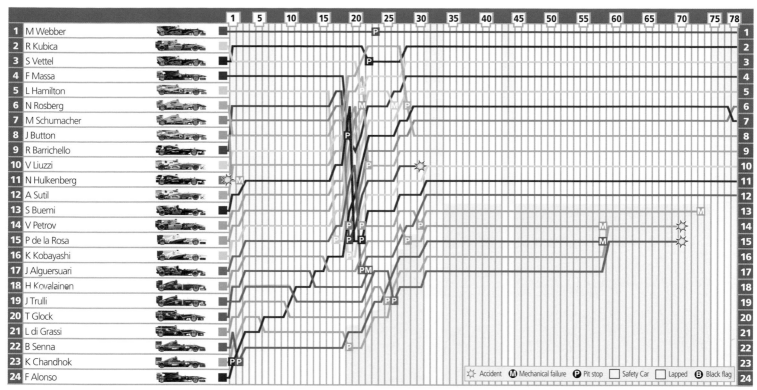

	Driver		1	5	10	15	20	25	30	35	40	45	50	55	60	65	70	75	78	
1	M Webber																			1
2	R Kubica																			2
3	S Vettel																			3
4	F Massa																			4
5	L Hamilton																			5
6	N Rosberg																			6
7	M Schumacher																			7
8	J Button																			8
9	R Barrichello																			9
10	V Liuzzi																			10
11	N Hulkenberg																			11
12	A Sutil																			12
13	S Buemi																			13
14	V Petrov																			14
15	P de la Rosa																			15
16	K Kobayashi																			16
17	J Alguersuari																			17
18	H Kovalainen																			18
19	J Trulli																			19
20	T Glock																			20
21	L di Grassi																			21
22	B Senna																			22
23	K Chandhok																			23
24	F Alonso																			24

☆ Accident Ⓜ Mechanical failure Ⓟ Pit stop ☐ Safety Car ☐ Lapped Ⓑ Black flag

QUALIFYING 3

	Driver	Time
1	M Webber	1m13.826s
2	R Kubica	1m14.120s
3	S Vettel	1m14.227s
4	F Massa	1m14.283s
5	L Hamilton	1m14.437s
6	N Rosberg	1m14.544s
7	M Schumacher	1m14.590s
8	J Button	1m14.637s
9	R Barrichello	1m14.901s
10	V Liuzzi	1m15.170s

GRID

	Driver	Time
1	M Webber	1m13.826s
2	R Kubica	1m14.120s
3	S Vettel	1m14.227s
4	F Massa	1m14.283s
5	L Hamilton	1m14.432s
6	N Rosberg	1m14.544s
7	M Schumacher	1m14.590s
8	J Button	1m14.637s
9	R Barrichello	1m14.901s
10	V Liuzzi	1m15.170s
11	N Hulkenberg	1m15.317s
12	A Sutil	1m15.318s
13	S Buemi	1m15.413s
14	V Petrov	1m15.576s
15	P de la Rosa	1m15.692s
16	K Kobayashi	1m15.992s
17	J Alguersuari	1m16.176s
18	H Kovalainen	1m17.094s
19	J Trulli	1m17.134s
20	T Glock	1m17.377s
21	L di Grassi	1m17.864s
22	B Senna	1m18.509s
23	K Chandhok	1m19.559s
24*	F Alonso	No time

* Started from pitlane

RACE

	Driver	Car	Laps	Time	Avg. mph	Fastest	Stops
1	M Webber	Red Bull-Renault RB6	78	1h50m13.355s	88.104	1m15.318s	1
2	S Vettel	Red Bull-Renault RB6	78	1h50m13.803s	88.098	1m15.192s	1
3	R Kubica	Renault R30	78	1h50m15.030s	88.081	1m15.353s	1
4	F Massa	Ferrari F10	78	1h50m16.021s	88.068	1m15.503s	1
5	L Hamilton	McLaren-Mercedes MP4-25	78	1h50m17./18s	88.045	1m16.219s	1
6	F Alonso	Ferrari F10	78	1h50m19.696s	88.019	1m15.905s	1
7	N Rosberg	Mercedes MGP W01	78	1h50m20.006s	88.015	1m15.959s	1
8	A Sutil	Force India-Mercedes VJM03	78	1h50m20.325s	88.011	1m15.963s	1
9	V Liuzzi	Force India-Mercedes VJM03	78	1h50m20.660s	88.006	1m16.142s	1
10	S Buemi	Toro Rosso-Ferrari STR5	78	1h50m21.554s	87.994	1m16.493s	1
11	J Alguersuari	Toro Rosso-Ferrari STR5	78	1h50m22.490s	87.982	1m16.381s	1
12	M Schumacher	Mercedes MGP W01	78	1h50m39.067s*	87.762	1m15.580s	1
13	V Petrov	Renault R30	73	Suspension	-	1m16.405s	2
14	K Chandhok	HRT-Cosworth F110	70	Accident	-	1m19.553s	1
15	J Trulli	Lotus-Cosworth T127	70	Accident	-	1m19.340s	1
R	H Kovalainen	Lotus-Cosworth T127	58	Steering	-	1m18.401s	1
R	B Senna	HRT-Cosworth F110	58	Hydraulics	-	1m20.130s	1
R	R Barrichello	Williams-Cosworth FW32	30	Suspension	-	1m19.074s	1
R	K Kobayashi	BMW Sauber-Ferrari C29	26	Gearbox	-	1m18.775s	0
R	L di Grassi	Virgin-Cosworth VR-01	25	Wheel	-	1m22.255s	1
R	T Glock	Virgin-Cosworth VR-01	22	Suspension	-	1m20.775s	0
R	P de la Rosa	BMW Sauber-Ferrari C29	21	Hydraulics	-	1m19.270s	1
R	J Button	McLaren-Mercedes MP4-25	2	Engine fire	-	2m14.285s	1
R	N Hulkenberg	Williams-Cosworth FW32	0	Wing failure	-	-	0

* Including 20s penalty for passing Alonso

CHAMPIONSHIP

	Driver	Pts
1	M Webber	78
2	S Vettel	78
3	F Alonso	75
4	J Button	70
5	F Massa	61
6	R Kubica	59
7	L Hamilton	59
8	N Rosberg	56
9	M Schumacher	22
10	A Sutil	20
11	V Liuzzi	10
12	R Barrichello	7
13	V Petrov	6
14	J Alguersuari	3
15	S Buemi	1
16	N Hulkenberg	1

	Constructor	Pts
1	Red Bull-Renault	156
2	Ferrari	136
3	McLaren-Mercedes	129
4	Mercedes	78
5	Renault	65
6	Force India-Mercedes	30
7	Williams-Cosworth	8
8	Toro Rosso-Ferrari	4

Fastest lap
S Vettel 1m15.192s
(99.368mph) on lap 71

Fastest speed trap
V Petrov   177.650mph
Slowest speed trap
T Glock   170.939mph

Fastest pit stop
1 M Schumacher   24.914s
2 S Vettel   25.115s
3 N Rosberg   25.140s

Adrian Sutil
"I had a great start and I made up two places on the first lap. We then had a good first stop where I gained a position to be ninth and then I could just do my own race."

Jarno Trulli
"It was a good race in that I was able to finish without accidents or technical problems and came ahead of my team-mate. It's also great to get my first point."

Karun Chandhok
"After a wheelgun problem, I was stuck behind the HRTs. Karun seemed slow, and I'd seen he was leaving room at Rascasse, so I tried to get by but we touched."

Pedro de la Rosa
"I managed to jump di Grassi and Trulli during the pit stop. After that, I was catching Senna until he retired, and was cruising when Jarno hit me out of nowhere."

"I stayed away from trouble and took care of the tyres. I was behind Petrov and waiting for my chance to push, but had a problem with the hydraulic system."

Timo Glock
"I could match Heikki's pace, but I had too much degradation on the rear and some problems with the brakes. Then the rear suspension failed at Casino Corner."

Vitantonio Liuzzi
"I was ninth after the start, but stopped a couple of laps early for my tyre change, which let Adrian pass us when he came in, but we got both cars in the top 10."

Heikki Kovalainen
"You can't expect more on this track as it's very hard to overtake, especially as the man ahead of me was my team-mate, so I just couldn't take such a risk."

"Just before I retired, I could feel the steering alignment was uneven, even in the tunnel, and it got to the point where the car didn't feel safe to drive any more."

Bruno Senna
"The team made a good call for me to make a tyre stop under the safety car, and I had a great run. We could have finished 13th but a hydraulic problem put me out."

Kamui Kobayashi
"My start was good. The first corner is never easy in Monaco, but it went alright, then I wasn't able to shift up anymore and I looked for a safe place to park."

Lucas di Grassi
"The first part of my race was good. I overtook Timo and had a good fight with Fernando for a couple of laps, but as soon as I pitted I had a wheel problem."

2010 FORMULA 1
TURKISH GRAND PRIX
ISTANBUL

GIVING IT AWAY

This was Red Bull Racing's nadir, when its drivers tussled over the lead, collided, and handed McLaren a 1–2 result, Lewis Hamilton just holding off Jenson Button

At times in 2010, it seemed that Red Bull Racing had been doing its best to throw away the World Championship and, on an astonishing afternoon in Istanbul, the drivers played their part when they collided while battling for the lead.

Should Sebastian Vettel have stayed riding shotgun for Mark Webber? Or should the Aussie, sensing he wasn't as fast at that point in the race, have invited his team-mate through to take advantage of a clear track? Opinions were divided.

The recriminations went deep into the following week and, while the RBR team management insisted that the matter had been consigned to history, the focus on the Webber v Vettel battle would become more intense than ever.

Webber arrived in Turkey on the back of his fabulous pair of wins in Spain and Monaco, while Vettel knew that he needed to get his title campaign back on track. Webber duly took his third straight pole, but it was a far from straightforward weekend thus far for the Australian. He suffered a blown Renault engine late on Friday and then lost track time on Saturday morning with a throttle problem that saw him crawl back to the pits on idle. He also had a spectacular spin at Turn 8. Yet, when it mattered in the afternoon, he got a lap together.

Vettel was stuck down in third after a scrappy session that saw him abort his final run. After the session, it was discovered that his car had a broken anti-roll bar. The dark blue cars were split by Lewis Hamilton, who put in a great effort for McLaren. Jenson Button qualified fourth, despite not improving on his final run, when yellow flags came out after Michael Schumacher spun.

Schumacher took fifth place despite his last-minute trip into the gravel at, where else, Turn 8. He was a place ahead of Mercedes team-mate Nico Rosberg as he continued on his path of silencing the critics. Conversely, Fernando Alonso admitted that he wasn't quick enough, and was stuck down in 12th.

Vettel briefly got ahead of Hamilton at the start, but the McLaren driver, aided by the straightline boost provided by McLaren's F-duct, got back past. In a gripping opening stint, Webber ran ahead of Hamilton and Vettel, with Button close behind in the other McLaren. It was real cat-and-mouse stuff, and the closest racing we'd seen for a while between the four frontrunning cars.

After the pit stops, Vettel jumped into second place, aided by a tardy stop for Hamilton. The top four continued to run close together, and it was evident that they were all walking a tightrope and that this race was far from over.

On lap 40, Vettel edged closer than ever, and then dodged to the outside of his rival at the exit of Turn 11, a fast sweeping righthander. On the following straight, Vettel pulled alongside and slightly ahead but, as he sought to move right to take the line for the next turn, Webber stood his ground. They touched and both spun wildly off the circuit. Vettel was out on the spot, while Webber continued, a damaged nose forcing a pit stop.

It later emerged that Webber had just had to switch to fuel-saving mode, and had asked that Vettel not pass. That presumably gave the management the impression that he couldn't outpace the German.

"We had that discussion on the pit wall," said team principal Christian Horner. "There was less than a second in it and, with McLaren's straightline speed advantage, we couldn't afford to back up into the McLarens. It was quite clear that, with the speed advantage that they had on the straight, it was inadvisable to fall back into them.

"Mark had requested the lap before to ask Sebastian to back off a bit, but there was no way you could do that because of the McLarens being right there."

Horner insisted that while a mixture change could have given Vettel a small lap-time advantage, it wasn't akin to a significant horsepower boost. He implied that the critical moment could well have been inspired by their relative tyre performance at that stage.

"It looked like Mark started to struggle with the rear tyres a bit more," said Horner. "That's what it looked like on the pit wall. Between laps 38 and 39,

BELOW It's tight in the midfield as Fernando Alonso tussles with fellow Spaniard Pedro de la Rosa on lap 1

BOTTOM Rubens Barrichello and Nico Hulkenberg fought hard for Williams, but failed to score

OPPOSITE Bruno Senna (right) drove well to pass Lucas di Grassi, then had to pull into retirement

Sebastian really closed up rapidly on Mark, and then obviously got a run on him on lap 40 and they both found themselves in a situation which they didn't want to be in.

"What I didn't see was what happened at Turn 9 or the chicane, because Sebastian obviously had an excellent exit from there, because he got a very clear run in the slipstream off Mark, who kept him to the left, and then Sebastian tried to work him back to the right. And the end result was contact."

By the time Webber emerged from the pits with a new nose, he was third, and the McLarens were long gone. However, anyone who thought that the

INSIDE LINE
CHRISTIAN HORNER
**RED BULL RACING
TEAM PRINCIPAL**

"It was massively close between us and McLaren in the race, and we'd managed to get ourselves ahead. Sebastian on the prime tyre felt slightly happier than Mark and, for a couple of laps, was looking pretty dangerous. He got a run on him and of course we all saw what happened.

To give away 28 points to McLaren on a plate is disappointing for all the guys who have put in so much hard work. It's very frustrating.

We need to sit down with both drivers and go through what happened, because we've got to bounce back.

It's inevitable when you've got two guys fighting at the front that occasionally you're going to get incidents, but what you don't expect is to see them within your own team. It's a problem that we will have to manage. They're both grown-ups and we need to look at it objectively and move on.

I'm annoyed that they got themselves into that situation. One car was quicker than the other at that stage of the race, and I think that Sebastian had a clear run and he was quicker at that point in the race, but got squeezed. Mark kept him on the dirty line and Seb came over arguably a bit too early so, yes, they're both at fault. You could see it coming for a couple of laps. One of the instructions I was giving was that I didn't want to see the two drivers fighting each other in that way.

McLaren was very strong at Istanbul and had a big advantage in a straight line, as you saw by Lewis dragging his way back past Sebastian after the start. They had a good straightline-speed advantage and we had to use the performance of our car in other areas. But it was very frustrating between two teams that were far ahead of the rest.

What's really frustrating is that we got all the calls right strategy-wise, we managed to get Sebastian ahead of Lewis, we had two good pit stops and got them into a commanding 1–2 position. To go from that to a third place and a DNF was hugely disappointing.

We speak before the race at every grand prix and the one request I have is for them to give each other respect and room. From the team point-of-view, it's the worst possible thing that you can see. As we saw with Lewis and Jenson, they fought hard and yet gave each other just enough room."

ABOVE Michael Schumacher started fifth for Mercedes and rose to fourth place when Sebastian Vettel limped into retirement

OPPOSITE Nightmare scenes for Red Bull Racing as Sebastian Vettel and Mark Webber arrive at Turn 12 after the clash that cost the team a potential 43-point scoop

fuel-saving chat on McLaren's radio was code for 'hold station' was to be proved wrong. At the end of lap 48, Button got past Hamilton in a move that had everyone on the McLaren pit wall holding their collective breath. He was only ahead for a few hundred metres before the situation was reversed, and thereafter, things ran smoothly to the flag.

Hamilton's demeanour afterwards was not that of a man delighted to receive the victory spoils after the guys in front had crashed out. He was far from happy, having been told after going to fuel-saving mode that Button wouldn't pass.

In an effort to clarify the situation, McLaren said later that while Hamilton's engineer had indeed given that message, it was not one that reflected the management position, and the same message hadn't been passed on to Button.

"We hadn't given any instructions to Jenson not to fight, just as we didn't to Lewis in China," team principal Martin Whitmarsh insisted. "There were those that held the view that we should do, but we didn't, and it was my decision. So they were allowed to do that. Lewis had short-shifted quite significantly. A grand prix driver these days has

to save tyres, brakes, engine, fuel, so anything you can do. This is why Lewis short-shifted quite significantly in Turn 8.

"That enabled Jenson to get close, and he's a racing driver, so he had a go. If he hadn't, you'd be disappointed in him... Lewis was quite robust in responding to that. Jenson then took a view on risk management, and made the right call thereafter.

"If you rely on the drivers to figure those things out, I think Jenson wanted to beat Lewis, and Lewis was determined to beat Jenson, but in a very positive way. There is actually a lot of respect between the guys, and they are racing drivers.

"At the time, there was a slight dampness occurring as well, and Lewis felt that it was under control, and he could start to look after his equipment. You don't expect an aggressive overtaking manoeuvre by your team-mate... But, in fairness to Jenson, he thought Lewis had made a mistake, missed a gear or had a problem, and thought, 'I'd better have a go at him'.

"I think it was what every racing driver would do if he had the opportunity, and what Lewis would have done if he was in the same position. Lewis

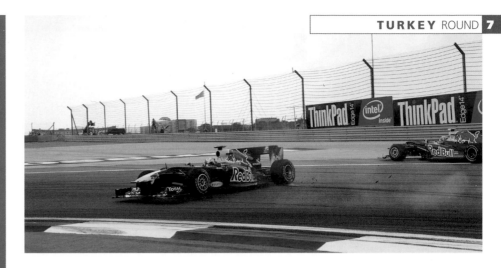

TALKING POINT
RED BULL
IMPLODES

Perhaps it was inevitable: two successive pole-to-flag victories for Mark Webber in Spain and Monaco followed by a third successive pole at Istanbul Park. Vettel was perplexed and on the back foot.

This one was different, though. The German, with a new chassis post-Monaco, had pipped Webber by a tenth in Q1 and Q2 and was on course to do it again in Q3 until a broken anti-roll bar prompted a lock-up and sentenced Vettel to third on the grid. There was no doubting that Vettel was quick though.

The Red Bulls were split by Lewis Hamilton on the grid, as McLaren was closer than expected. It was a game of cat and mouse. The Red Bull was devastatingly fast through the high-speed Turn 8, but the McLarens had much better straightline speed, leading to an opportunity to tee up an overtaking move into Turn 12.

What was surprising was that Webber, having been able to fend off an F-ducted McLaren, suddenly found himself much slower than his team-mate out of Turn 9 on the fateful 40th lap when the Red Bulls collided.

Asked about it in the press conference, Webber told journalists that they "would have to do some digging".

Did he have a problem? Had he been asked to turn the engine down? What was it? It transpired that the unexpectedly fast race pace had driven fuel consumption beyond the level expected. Webber had been told to turn to a more conservative fuel map, yet Vettel still had a lap or two remaining before he needed to.

The word was that the message went out to Webber's race engineer Ciaron Pilbeam that his driver should not resist Vettel, but Pilbeam had not passed it on at the point at which the accident happened.

Webber, obviously, was going to make it as hard for Vettel as he could, which meant pinning him on the dirty line so that he wouldn't be able to brake as effectively for the following turn. Vettel, wanting to get off it, carved right while Webber was still alongside and caused the crash.

They were the facts, but the body language of the major Red Bull Racing team players, Red Bull motorsport boss Helmut Marko in particular, made it clear that they were placing more blame at Webber's door.

The Red Bull PR machine went into damage-limitation mode, but the incident was damaging and one of the negatives that goes with running two number one drivers in a race-winning team. In the constructors' championship, what should have been a 43–27 advantage to Red Bull Racing translated into a 43–15 success for McLaren, which was the equivalent of a 43 point swing...

was then clearly very determined to rectify that manoeuvre, which he did."

McLaren ultimately secured an amazing 1–2 result, although that tussle had clearly created a little tension. It wasn't as much as we saw at Red Bull, though. The company's motorsport chief Helmut Marko immediately blamed Webber, while Horner felt both men had played a part in letting the team down, which seemed a fair assessment.

"It's not about one being right and one being wrong," said Horner. "I think both the guys, when they reflect on it, need to take responsibility."

It was a messy situation, one that Red Bull Racing didn't control very well and which really highlighted how hard it is for any team to balance the interests of two drivers who are gunning for the title. Whatever the rights and wrongs, though, it was great motor racing. However, the fuss detracted a little from a great race for McLaren.

"The satisfying thing for us, in fairness to Sebastian, is that he was under enormous pressure from Lewis," said Whitmarsh. "It was difficult for them to avoid the issue, and I think that's what we've got to do. At the moment, we aren't qualifying as quickly, but I think we actually had a quicker car in this particular race.

"So, had we got by the Red Bulls, by whatever means, I think we could have opened up a gap and had a comfortable race. It was difficult to get by them, but I think Lewis in particular did the right thing, to just keep the pressure on and see what happens then."

Behind Red Bull Racing and McLaren, Mercedes led the chase, albeit at a distance. Michael Schumacher finished a solid fourth, ahead of team-mate Rosberg. Robert Kubica took sixth for Renault, ahead of Felipe Massa, after a poor afternoon for Ferrari.

Fernando Alonso managed to climb up from 12th at the start to eighth, finally forcing his way past Vitaly Petrov. The Russian picked up a puncture after they touched, and fell out of the top 10, so the final points went to Adrian Sutil in ninth, and Kamui Kobayashi in 10th, this the first score of the season for the BMW Sauber team.

TOP LEFT Vitaly Petrov holds off Fernando Alonso in their battle for eighth place, but they would clash, giving the Renault driver a puncture

BOTTOM LEFT Lewis Hamilton and Jenson Button congratulate each other, but Hamilton was initially vexed that Button had overtaken him, before he managed to reverse their positions

SNAPSHOT FROM
TURKEY

CLOCKWISE FROM RIGHT The view from Turn 14 down the start/finish straight; three-time World Champion Niki Lauda; Adrian Sutil was caught up in World Cup fever; Fernando Alonso, Stefano Domenicali and Felipe Massa celebrate Ferrari's 800th grand prix; armed and ready for action; Rubens Barrichello gathers his thoughts; at 2.46m, the world's tallest man Sultan Kosen just isn't cut out for racing; air guns; McLaren celebrates its 1–2 result; a winning smile; Lewis Hamilton faces the media in the build-up to the weekend in McLaren's stylish Brand Centre

RACE RESULTS
TURKEY
ISTANBUL

Official Results © [2010]
Formula One Administration Limited,
6 Princes Gate, London, SW7 1QJ.
No reproduction without permission.
All copyright and database rights reserved.

RACE DATE May 30th
CIRCUIT LENGTH 3.317 miles
NO. OF LAPS 58
RACE DISTANCE 192.386 miles
WEATHER Sunny & dry, 29°C
TRACK TEMP 50°C
ATTENDANCE 110,400
LAP RECORD Juan Pablo Montoya, 1m24.770s, 138.056mph, 2005

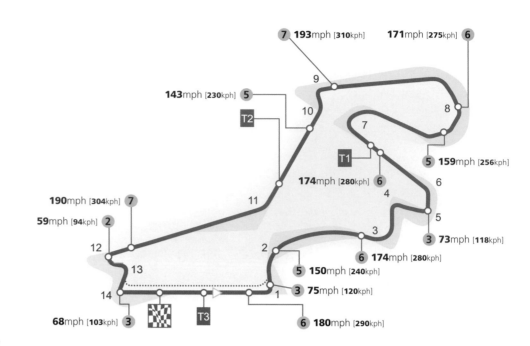

PRACTICE 1		
Driver	Time	Laps
1 L Hamilton	1m28.653s	20
2 J Button	1m29.615s	21
3 M Schumacher	1m29.750s	24
4 N Rosberg	1m29.855s	25
5 S Vettel	1m29.867s	30
6 R Kubica	1m30.061s	23
7 V Petrov	1m30.065s	24
8 M Webber	1m30.097s	26
9 F Alonso	1m30.294s	20
10 A Sutil	1m30.501s	17
11 K Kobayashi	1m30.615s	20
12 V Liuzzi	1m30.853s	21
13 F Massa	1m30.867s	22
14 S Buemi	1m31.011s	24
15 P de la Rosa	1m31.238s	18
16 N Hulkenberg	1m31.355s	23
17 R Barrichello	1m31.464s	19
18 J Alguersuari	1m31.735s	27
19 H Kovalainen	1m32.161s	24
20 J Trulli	1m32.990s	23
21 K Chandhok	1m34.876s	13
22 L di Grassi	1m35.137s	21
23 T Glock	1m35.583s	15
24 S Yamamoto	1m36.137s	26

PRACTICE 2		
Driver	Time	Laps
1 J Button	1m28.280s	30
2 M Webber	1m28.378s	24
3 S Vettel	1m28.590s	27
4 L Hamilton	1m28.672s	32
5 F Alonso	1m28.725s	30
6 N Rosberg	1m28.914s	22
7 M Schumacher	1m28.974s	22
8 R Kubica	1m29.225s	34
9 V Petrov	1m29.501s	36
10 F Massa	1m29.620s	26
11 A Sutil	1m29.629s	16
12 N Hulkenberg	1m29.987s	17
13 K Kobayashi	1m30.053s	34
14 P de la Rosa	1m30.176s	34
15 S Buemi	1m30.386s	32
16 V Liuzzi	1m30.627s	28
17 R Barrichello	1m30.766s	32
18 J Alguersuari	1m30.933s	37
19 H Kovalainen	1m31.610s	37
20 L di Grassi	1m33.013s	28
21 J Trulli	1m33.081s	11
22 T Glock	1m33.312s	29
23 B Senna	1m33.420s	35
24 K Chandhok	1m33.740s	25

PRACTICE 3		
Driver	Time	Laps
1 S Vettel	1m27.086s	18
2 N Rosberg	1m27.359s	16
3 L Hamilton	1m27.396s	14
4 M Webber	1m27.553s	15
5 R Kubica	1m27.784s	20
6 F Alonso	1m27.861s	18
7 M Schumacher	1m27.879s	16
8 J Button	1m27.963s	17
9 F Massa	1m27.969s	20
10 V Petrov	1m28.344s	18
11 S Buemi	1m28.610s	22
12 P de la Rosa	1m28.652s	21
13 J Alguersuari	1m28.734s	21
14 K Kobayashi	1m29.036s	20
15 N Hulkenberg	1m29.044s	18
16 V Liuzzi	1m29.211s	15
17 R Barrichello	1m29.305s	14
18 J Trulli	1m30.618s	19
19 H Kovalainen	1m30.884s	22
20 T Glock	1m31.341s	21
21 L di Grassi	1m32.180s	16
22 B Senna	1m32.230s	22
23 K Chandhok	1m32.762s	19
24 A Sutil	No time	1

QUALIFYING 1	
Driver	Time
1 S Vettel	1m27.067s
2 M Webber	1m27.500s
3 J Button	1m27.555s
4 V Petrov	1m27.620s
5 N Rosberg	1m27.649s
6 L Hamilton	1m27.667s
7 M Schumacher	1m27.756s
8 R Kubica	1m27.766s
9 F Alonso	1m27.857s
10 A Sutil	1m27.951s
11 F Massa	1m27.993s
12 P de la Rosa	1m28.147s
13 K Kobayayshi	1m28.158s
14 N Hulkenberg	1m28.227s
15 R Barrichello	1m28.336s
16 J Alguersuari	1m28.460s
17 S Buemi	1m28.534s
18 V Liuzzi	1m28.958s
19 J Trulli	1m30.237s
20 H Kovalainen	1m30.519s
21 T Glock	1m30.744s
22 B Senna	1m31.256s
23 L di Grassi	1m31.989s
24 K Chandhok	1m32.060s

QUALIFYING 2	
Driver	Time
1 S Vettel	1m26.729s
2 M Webber	1m26.818s
3 L Hamilton	1m27.013s
4 N Rosberg	1m27.141s
5 F Massa	1m27.200s
6 J Button	1m27.277s
7 V Petrov	1m27.387s
8 R Kubica	1m27.426s
9 K Kobayashi	1m27.434s
10 M Schumacher	1m27.438s
11 A Sutil	1m27.525s
12 F Alonso	1m27.612s
13 P de la Rosa	1m27.879s
14 S Buemi	1m28.273s
15 R Barrichello	1m28.392s
16 J Alguersuari	1m28.540s
17 N Hulkenberg	1m28.841s

Best sectors – Practice			Speed trap – Practice			Best sectors – Qualifying			Speed trap – Qualifying	
Sec 1	S Vettel	32.632s	1 J Button	195.297mph		Sec 1	L Hamilton	31.991s	1 J Button	199.087mph
Sec 2	S Vettel	30.365s	2 L Hamilton	194.551mph		Sec 2	S Vettel	30.000s	2 L Hamilton	198.901mph
Sec 3	R Kubica	24.004s	3 J Alguersuari	193.805mph		Sec 3	L Hamilton	23.937s	3 M Webber	195.110mph

Jenson Button
"I was stuck behind Lewis into Turn 1. Then Michael went around the outside. I got him back into Turn 12. Then it was four of us, two McLarens and two Red Bulls."

Michael Schumacher
"I caught Jenson at the start, but I didn't have a lot of grip which, combined with the top speed of the McLarens, meant that I couldn't hold Jenson behind me."

Sebastian Vettel
"I was on the inside going into the corner, ahead and focusing on the braking point and then we touched. Mark's car hit my rear-right wheel and I went off."

Felipe Massa
"It was a very boring race for me. I was always stuck behind Kubica and the two Mercedes. I often managed to get close, but never had a chance of passing Robert."

Rubens Barrichello
"I had a clutch problem, then pitted earlier than planned, as our pace was better than those in front. Our stop was slow as we had a front-wheel problem."

Robert Kubica
"Unfortunately, we started the race behind the Mercedes and I remained stuck behind them all afternoon, even though my car seemed to be quicker."

Lewis Hamilton
"I passed Sebastian into Turn 3, then challenged Mark before I lost time when my right rear took ages to go on. So then I had to battle two Red Bulls not one."

Nico Rosberg
"I'm reasonably happy with fifth. I was slightly faster than Michael, but it wasn't possible to overtake and I had to be careful as Robert was pushing hard behind me."

Mark Webber
"Sebastian had a top speed advantage, he went down the inside and we were side by side. I was surprised when he came right, as I was holding my line."

Fernando Alonso
"Our aim is to fight McLaren and Red Bull for the podium, not with a Renault for eighth. I attacked Petrov and hope the points this brought could prove useful."

Nico Hulkenberg
"Our race pace wasn't enough. I also had an incident on the first lap which meant that I had to pit early. We have to keep working hard to find more performance."

Vitaly Petrov
"My tyres were really worn when I was fighting with Alonso. He tried to go around the outside and my car pushed to the outside, so we made contact, causing a flat tyre."

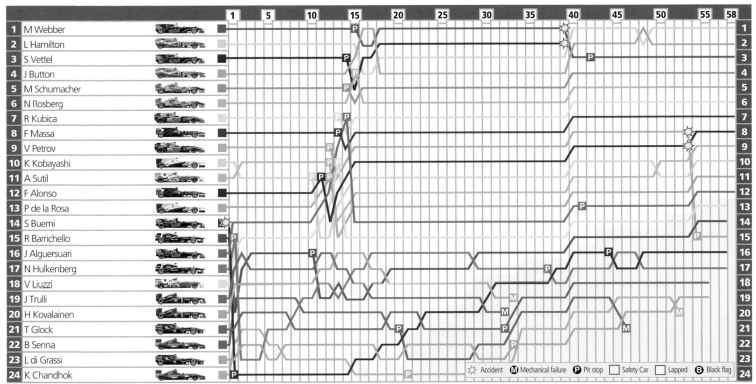

		1	5	10	15	20	25	30	35	40	45	50	55	58	
1	M Webber														1
2	L Hamilton														2
3	S Vettel														3
4	J Button														4
5	M Schumacher														5
6	N Rosberg														6
7	R Kubica														7
8	F Massa														8
9	V Petrov														9
10	K Kobayashi														10
11	A Sutil														11
12	F Alonso														12
13	P de la Rosa														13
14	S Buemi														14
15	R Barrichello														15
16	J Alguersuari														16
17	N Hulkenberg														17
18	V Liuzzi														18
19	J Trulli														19
20	H Kovalainen														20
21	T Glock														21
22	B Senna														22
23	L di Grassi														23
24	K Chandhok														24

☆ Accident Ⓜ Mechanical failure Ⓟ Pit stop ☐ Safety Car ☐ Lapped Ⓑ Black flag

QUALIFYING 3

	Driver	Time
1	M Webber	1m26.295s
2	L Hamilton	1m26.433s
3	S Vettel	1m26.760s
4	J Button	1m26.781s
5	M Schumacher	1m26.857s
6	N Rosberg	1m26.952s
7	R Kubica	1m27.039s
8	F Massa	1m27.082s
9	V Petrov	1m27.430s
10	K Kobayashi	1m28.122s

GRID

	Driver	Time
1	M Webber	1m26.295s
2	L Hamilton	1m26.433s
3	S Vettel	1m26.760s
4	J Button	1m26.781s
5	M Schumacher	1m26.857s
6	N Rosberg	1m26.952s
7	R Kubica	1m27.039s
8	F Massa	1m27.082s
9	V Petrov	1m27.430s
10	K Kobayashi	1m28.122s
11	A Sutil	1m27.525s
12	F Alonso	1m27.612s
13	P de la Rosa	1m27.879s
14	S Buemi	1m28.273s
15	R Barrichello	1m28.392s
16	J Alguersuari	1m28.540s
17	N Hulkenberg	1m28.841s
18	V Liuzzi	1m28.958s
19	J Trulli	1m30.237s
20	H Kovalainen	1m30.519s
21	T Glock	1m30.744s
22	B Senna	1m31.256s
23*	L di Grassi	1m31.989s
24	K Chandhok	1m32.060s

* Started from pitlane

RACE

	Driver	Car	Laps	Time	Avg. mph	Fastest	Stops
1	L Hamilton	McLaren-Mercedes MP4-25	58	1h28m47.620s	130.000	1m30.075s	1
2	J Button	McLaren-Mercedes MP4-25	58	1h28m50.265s	129.935	1m29.895s	1
3	M Webber	Red Bull-Renault RB6	58	1h29m11.905s	129.410	1m29.195s	2
4	M Schumacher	Mercedes MGP W01	58	1h29m18.730s	129.245	1m29.810s	1
5	N Rosberg	Mercedes MGP W01	58	1h29m19.886s	129.217	1m29.977s	1
6	R Kubica	Renault R30	58	1h29m20.444s	129.204	1m29.580s	1
7	F Massa	Ferrari F10	58	1h29m24.255s	129.112	1m29.996s	1
8	F Alonso	Ferrari F10	58	1h29m34.164s	128.874	1m30.011s	1
9	A Sutil	Force India-Mercedes VJM03	58	1h29m36.649s	128.814	1m29.959s	1
10	K Kobayashi	BMW Sauber-Ferrari C29	58	1h29m53.270s	128.417	1m30.891s	1
11	P de la Rosa	BMW Sauber-Ferrari C29	58	1h29m53.564s	128.410	1m30.421s	1
12	J Alguersuari	Toro Rosso-Ferrari STR5	58	1h29m55.420s	128.366	1m29.535s	2
13	V Liuzzi	Force India-Mercedes VJM03	57	1h28m56.806s	127.539	1m31.421s	1
14	R Barrichello	Williams-Cosworth FW32	57	1h28m59.057s	127.485	1m30.933s	1
15	V Petrov	Renault R30	57	1h29m25.954s	126.486	1m29.165s	2
16	S Buemi	Toro Rosso-Ferrari STR5	57	1h29m44.682s	126.405	1m29.588s	2
17	N Hulkenberg	Williams-Cosworth FW32	57	1h29m54.170s	126.182	1m30.620s	2
18	T Glock	Virgin-Cosworth VR-01	55	1h29m03.005s	122.921	1m32.265s	1
19	L di Grassi	Virgin-Cosworth VR-01	55	1h29m31.763s	122.263	1m33.257s	1
20	K Chandhok	HRT-Cosworth F110	52	Fuel system	-	1m34.585s	1
R	B Senna	HRT-Cosworth F110	46	Fuel pressure	-	1m34.247s	1
R	S Vettel	Red Bull-Renault RB6	39	Accident	-	1m30.181s	1
R	H Kovalainen	Lotus-Cosworth T127	33	Hydraulics	-	1m34.363s	0
R	J Trulli	Lotus-Cosworth T127	32	Hydraulics	-	1m34.463s	0

CHAMPIONSHIP

	Driver	Pts
1	M Webber	93
2	J Button	88
3	L Hamilton	84
4	F Alonso	79
5	S Vettel	78
6	R Kubica	67
7	F Massa	67
8	N Rosberg	66
9	M Schumacher	34
10	A Sutil	22
11	V Liuzzi	10
12	R Barrichello	7
13	V Petrov	6
14	J Alguersuari	3
15	S Buemi	1
16	K Kobayashi	1
17	N Hulkenberg	1

	Constructor	Pts
1	McLaren-Mercedes	172
2	Red Bull-Renault	171
3	Ferrari	146
4	Mercedes	100
5	Renault	73
6	Force India-Mercedes	32
7	Williams-Cosworth	8
8	Toro Rosso-Ferrari	4
9	BMW Sauber-Ferrari	1

Fastest lap
V Petrov 1m29.165s
(133.924mph) on lap 57

Fastest speed trap
L Hamilton   199.708mph
Slowest speed trap
H Kovalainen   186.846mph

Fastest pit stop
1 N Rosberg   21.085s
2 F Massa   21.246s
3 M Schumacher   21.463s

Adrian Sutil
"The only real downside was the pit stop when I lost a few seconds at a crucial time. That's where I lost two positions and had to fight back past Kobayashi."

Nico Hulkenberg
"Going into Turn 3, I tried to go round de la Rosa, but I went wide. When I came back, Hulkenberg got past and as I tried to retake him he clipped my right rear."

Jarno Trulli
"It was difficult with the harder tyres. Afterwards, I was pulling away from our competitors on the option tyres, but hydraulic failure put an end to my race."

Karun Chandhok
"Early in the race, the fuel pump failed and I was struggling for straightline speed. Unfortunately, I finished my race five laps before the chequered flag in the pits."

Pedro de la Rosa
"I had understeer early on, but the lighter the car became, the better the balance. I'd have been fighting at the end if it hadn't been my team-mate in front."

Timo Glock
"I stalled, which let Senna past, then was stuck behind him for 18 laps. Then I got him in Turn 12. Five laps from the end, I felt a drop in the power-steering assist."

Vitantonio Liuzzi
"It was a tough race. I tried to push at the beginning with the strategy, but we knew it would be a big job, as when you don't have the right grip it's really tough."

Rubens Barrichello
"The decision to make two tyre stops was the correct one, so that I could attack de La Rosa and Kobayashi. Sadly, I couldn't quite do it in the number of laps left."

Heikki Kovalainen
"I lost power steering due to a hydraulics failure. I thought I had a puncture, as the steering suddenly felt strange, but then I lost gearbox, clutch and throttle."

Bruno Senna
"The start was good and I gained some places, though I was later unlucky with traffic. In the end, I had a fuel system problem and that's why I had to retire."

Kamui Kobayashi
"The car was better on the harder tyre compound, so we did a short first stint on the softer ones. I pitted after 10 laps and drove the rest of the race with the same set."

Lucas di Grassi
"We have had a lot of problems during this weekend, especially regarding the engine, but we achieved our target of getting both cars to the finish."

FORMULA 1 GRAND PRIX
DU CANADA 2010
MONTREAL

TACTICAL TRIUMPH

Shrewd tactics suggested an early visit to the pits worked best and got the McLarens past Sebastian Vettel. Then Lewis Hamilton and Jenson Button worked their tyres best for another 1–2 result

After a year's absence, everyone was happy to be back in Montréal, now of course the venue for the sole North American event on the calendar. The city itself has always been popular, and the track invariably seems to produce action. In an era of asphalt run-offs, it's a rare venue with little margin.

This year's race was all about tyres and making the right strategic calls. For the first time under the 2010 no-refuelling rules, everyone had to make at least two pit stops, and that really spiced things up. The man who got it right was Lewis Hamilton, who propelled himself to the top of the World Championship as he led team-mate Jenson Button in a spectacular 1–2.

Hamilton did the difficult bit in qualifying by securing pole. He ran a lot of laps to do his time, and on his in-lap the team told him to switch off the engine in order to save enough fuel for the FIA sample that's taken after qualifying and the race.

Hamilton even stood up in the cockpit as the car freewheeled down the straight and, after getting out, tried pushing it for a few metres. The team was fined $10,000 for not completing the lap. Many thought it a lucky escape. The rules were later clarified to prevent drivers running down their fuel loads in this way.

Along with most people in the top 10, Hamilton qualified on the option tyres, and thus had to start on them, while in second and third behind him, Mark Webber and Sebastian Vettel were committed to primes, their team feeling that the harder tyre was the better bet for the race.

However, Red Bull's plans took a knock when the team suspected that Webber might have a gearbox problem. The unit was changed on Sunday morning, and the associated penalty dropped him five places to seventh. Fernando Alonso moved up to third for Ferrari, ahead of Jenson Button, Tonio Liuzzi, Felipe Massa and Webber.

From the start, Hamilton slotted into the lead ahead of Vettel, Alonso, Button and Webber, while there was chaos behind when Liuzzi clashed with Massa through the first two corners, forcing both into the pits for repairs.

As expected, the option tyre soon went off, and the pit stops started as early as lap 6 when Button came in. He was followed on the next lap by Hamilton and Alonso, the Spaniard getting in front of the McLaren after a race out of the pitlane.

All that activity left Vettel in the lead. However,

the harder tyre proved less durable than expected, and after just 13 laps Webber pitted from second place. He took a new set of primes, while a lap later Vettel came in and took on options.

The German was surprised to find that he had dropped to fourth, for the simple reason that after their early stops Alonso, Hamilton and Button had gained ground with their fresher primes.

Hamilton and Button were able to run quickly after their stops. While a team can plan around finding a gap, it also took some sheer good luck that handy spaces opened up for them.

"We hoped for it, we saw it on the timing screens and just went for the gaps," explained McLaren team principal Martin Whitmarsh. "That meant the drivers could just push at their pace throughout the whole race. I think the team got it right that way, and so did the drivers.

"With a safety-car deployment, it would have been easy, frankly. That didn't happen, so we then had to wait and pit as soon as we could when we were able to see a free space."

Vettel admitted that he was a little confused. "To be honest, I was lost in the beginning," said the German. "Because you come in first and then you come out behind cars that should be behind you, according to the plan. That was a surprise, and obviously you don't know where you are exactly, and how many times you have to stop.

"After a while, you can talk to the team and they can tell you. Obviously, when I noticed that I was fourth, and real position fourth, I wasn't too happy, but there's not much you can do by then.

"I think we did the right thing with the tyres, everything happened according to our plan. The others didn't survive for long on the soft tyres at the beginning, so they had to stop early, and they should come out in traffic and their race is over. It didn't seem to be the case, I think they were in clean air, and obviously when I came out of the pits, I got stuck behind them."

Immediately after Vettel returned to the track, there was drama at the front, as Hamilton found a way past Alonso to reclaim the lead.

At this stage, Vettel was on options. In a clever move, Red Bull decided to use the less-favoured tyres up sooner rather than later on his car, and he ran a handy 14-lap stint on them, helped by the fact

OPPOSITE TOP Fernando Alonso and the Ferrari crew prepare for action on the packed grid

OPPOSITE BOTTOM Turn left into Turn 1, but not yet... Pedro de la Rosa and Vitaly Petrov get it wrong

BELOW Lewis Hamilton fought with Fernando Alonso before and after his first pit stop *en route* to a famous win for McLaren

INSIDE LINE
LEWIS HAMILTON
McLAREN DRIVER

"This was one of the toughest races so far, but another great 1–2 for us… It was very close with Fernando, both in the pits and on the track.

I pitted quite a bit ahead of him, but clearly we didn't have the best of pit stops. I saw Alonso's Ferrari being released and as I pulled away he was right in my blind spot. I didn't even know he was there, but I tried to make sure that I had enough space to pull out.

All of a sudden, Alonso was right there with me and we raced all the way down towards the first corner and unfortunately he had the inside line there and so got ahead.

After that, he had great pace and put up a really good fight. The traffic was very difficult today and I capitalised on that.

The second pit stop was very good, which enabled us to finally get ahead of Fernando.

It was an interesting race. Nobody quite knew how the tyre situation was going to pan out, but it worked out in our favour.

Through the race, it was difficult to know how much to save your tyres and how much to push, and whether others were pushing or saving fuel. Clearly, Fernando could see when I was catching traffic and he would close the gap to me all of a sudden, so it showed that he had great pace.

For a while, my race was all about trying to get through the traffic without allowing him to pass me, and it was extremely difficult. I'd say that the traffic was almost as bad as it is at Monaco.

We are doing everything we can to close the gap to Red Bull Racing, and on the race weekends we are doing a better job.

This was a special day for me: I took my first grand prix win here, and to come back and repeat it after three years was a real pleasure.

You can see how tight this championship is. I don't know whether it's the new points-scoring system, but the field is so close and all the best drivers are in the top teams. It's the biggest challenge I've experienced in F1.

I don't know why I go well in Montréal, but it's a great track, a fantastic city, great food, great people and amazing support.

I've had pole every time I've been here and for me this is one of the best races of the whole season. I'm able to dial the car in and feel it a little bit better here than in other places, but we've got a long season ahead of us…"

TALKING POINT
TYRES, WHO GAMBLED?

Strategically, the Canadian GP was truly fascinating. McLaren got it tactics absolutely spot-on but on Saturday night, post-qualifying, few thought so.

McLaren produced quicker Q2 times than Red Bull Racing on both the option tyre and the prime, then elected to run the option in Q3,

while Red Bull Racing went for the prime, which looked much better-suited as a race tyre. A great lap from Hamilton got McLaren pole, but when they were nip-and-tuck on the prime, nobody could quite understand the 'gamble' of starting on the option.

Estimates of how long the option would last ranged from just five laps to around 12. The thinking was that with such a short stint there would be no way that McLaren would clear the midfield pack after its first stop, and would therefore have its race compromised, its cars caught in traffic. You suspected that they were gambling on an early safety-car intervention, so often a feature at Montréal, to get the option tyre stint out of the way cheaply.

"We had quite a debate about

which way to go," admitted team principal Martin Whitmarsh after qualifying. "We'll see if we're right..." Few thought that likely. Most thought they had handed Red Bull Racing a good win against the head at a track which its team principal Christian Horner admitted from the very beginning did not particularly suit the RB6.

Renault's Robert Kubica looked a threat, having qualified well on the harder tyre, and got himself into sixth place by lap 5, with only the Red Bulls ahead of him on the hard tyre. But, slightly to his dismay, the Pole was heading for the pits at the end of lap 9, even on the prime...

"The rears went away much more quickly than we thought," admitted Renault's chief race engineer Alan Permane. "We'd figured on getting

to lap 15–17 before having to stop, but there was no way."

What was surprising was the degree to which the tyre behaviour changed as the track rubbered in. It did so to the extent that Hamilton did 19 laps on his first set of primes, stopped on lap 26 for another set, and went to the end of the race on them, 44 laps later...

And he didn't limp there either, as Hamilton set what was then the fastest lap of the race on lap 62, with eight to go, on a set of primes that had run 36 laps...

Button summed it up: "We were struggling with graining on the prime tyre in Friday practice and I think had a good understanding of what would happen to it. We actually thought it was Red Bull that took the gamble in qualifying, not us..."

that the car was lighter and there was now more rubber down on the track.

No one was quite sure how the tyre situation would pan out, and on lap 26 Hamilton came in for a second set of primes. Button and Vettel stopped on lap 27, with Vettel giving up his options, which had lasted well. Then Alonso came in on lap 28. For the first time, Vettel was on the same strategy as the three cars ahead of him.

From the outside, no one could be sure what the top guys were up to, but radio traffic indicated that they were indeed going to run to the flag. That meant a marathon 44 laps for Hamilton, 43 for Button and Vettel, and 42 for Alonso.

Whitmarsh admitted that the team was concerned about the length of the stints: "Yes we were, and as you heard we were telling Lewis 'these tyres have got to last you'. He did a fantastic job to keep them going. I think we realised that fuel loads were coming off, the track would improve and we could go longer towards the end. Mind you, we really didn't want to go much more than 30 laps…

"I think it was a question that if you could get track position, even if your tyres were going off, you would be able to defend. As it happened, the durability of the tyres improved as the race went on, so that worked quite well."

In contrast, Webber ran a long middle stint on primes. He benefited several times from such a schedule in 2009, under different rules of course, but this time it didn't really achieve much.

"Sebastian was very quick in the second stint on the option," said Red Bull team principal Christian Horner. "He managed to make that work really well. We did the opposite with Mark: we put him onto the hard tyre, because strategically it was better to split them at that point. At the start of

his middle stint he was looking good on the prime, then they started to drop away too."

At one stage, Webber opened up a lead of around 12s on Hamilton, but it was clear that none of the Australian's pursuers were going to stop again. Then Hamilton gradually caught him and, when he finally passed, Red Bull decided to bring Webber in for his compulsory run to the flag on options, and he fell down the order.

Hamilton then enjoyed a serene run to the finish, while Button managed to get ahead of Alonso in traffic to secure second place. Vettel fell away in fourth as he had to nurse a gearbox issue, while Webber had to be content with fifth.

"I think it was a great team victory," said Whitmarsh. "The drivers did a fantastic job, and the team made the right calls in preparing the strategy and implementing it during the race. We had a lot of debate about what tyres we should qualify on, and Lewis was quite quick on the prime, but the mathematicians said this is the way to do it."

Down at Red Bull Racing, Horner had no regrets about the strategy: "We just weren't able to do the damage when we had clean air. I think we were right

OPPOSITE Mark Webber ran a different tyre strategy to his team-mate Sebastian Vettel, but ended up behind him, in fifth place

BELOW German civil war as Nico Hulkenberg clatters his Williams into the rear of Adrian Sutil's Force India

BOTTOM Hulkenberg then had to pit for a new nose, costing him any chance of scoring points

to give it a go, as the only way to beat McLaren was to do something different here. We tried it, it didn't work, but the end result is probably about the same."

Nico Rosberg had a good run to sixth place for Mercedes after being held up by the first-lap crash, while Robert Kubica finished seventh, setting fastest lap after making an extra stop for a set of fresh tyres towards the end. Sebastien Buemi took a good eighth for Toro Rosso after leading a lap when the leaders pitted, while Liuzzi and Adrian Sutil both passed a gripless Michael Schumacher on the last lap to gain points for Force India.

Meanwhile, Red Bull Racing was a little concerned about the next race, at Valencia, another race with straights and heavy braking. "We knew that both types of tracks are not our favourites," said Vettel. "But still we are surprised, as our pace is very good. Unfortunately, for some reasons, we couldn't show it today, but I think we were as quick as the leaders, and able to win. For strategy and many reasons it didn't happen, but we still took fourth and fifth, and need to look forward to the next race."

Red Bull Racing wasn't too happy that Alonso got between the dark blue cars and McLaren, though. He didn't just take points away from Webber and Vettel, he also kept himself in the title hunt...

SNAPSHOT FROM
CANADA

CLOCKWISE FROM RIGHT

This is the wonderful view from the grandstand facing L'Epingle; red for Ferrari; Adrian Sutil, Nico Rosberg and Michael Schumacher show their support for the German football team in the World Cup; Sebastian Vettel's eyes display the look of concentration; the Mounties were present in their distinctive uniforms; last-minute adjustments at Red Bull Racing; former team principal Ron Dennis shares the unbridled joy in the McLaren pit garage after a second straight 1–2; Robert Kubica's helmet, complete with an illustration of rain; Michael Schumacher's Mercedes seen through the trees at the back of the circuit

RACE RESULTS
CANADA
MONTREAL

RACE DATE June 13th
CIRCUIT LENGTH 2.710 miles
NO. OF LAPS 70
RACE DISTANCE 189.700 miles
WEATHER Sunny & dry, 28°C
TRACK TEMP 38°C
ATTENDANCE 300,000
LAP RECORD Rubens Barrichello,
1m13.622s, 132.511mph, 2004

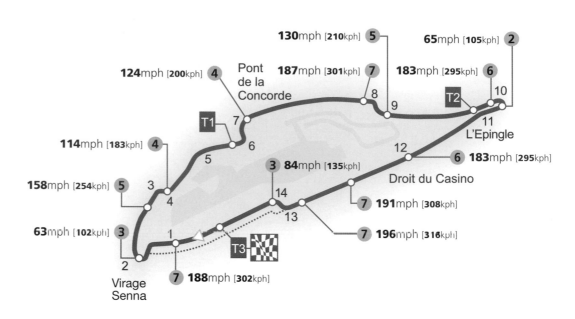

PRACTICE 1			
	Driver	Time	Laps
1	J Button	1m18.127s	23
2	M Schumacher	1m18.285s	19
3	L Hamilton	1m18.352s	19
4	N Rosberg	1m18.356s	23
5	S Vettel	1m18.549s	27
6	R Kubica	1m18.662s	19
7	F Alonso	1m18.726s	21
8	V Liuzzi	1m19.097s	25
9	N Hulkenberg	1m19.282s	31
10	R Barrichello	1m19.313s	19
11	A Sutil	1m19.373s	12
12	F Massa	1m19.511s	21
13	V Petrov	1m19.549s	24
14	M Webber	1m19.609s	26
15	K Kobayashi	1m20.186s	33
16	S Buemi	1m20.320s	27
17	P de la Rosa	1m20.584s	21
18	J Alguersuari	1m20.823s	28
19	H Kovalainen	1m21.869s	24
20	K Chandhok	1m21.977s	27
21	J Trulli	1m22.543s	12
22	B Senna	1m22.701s	28
23	T Glock	1m22.713s	20
24	L di Grassi	No time	4

PRACTICE 2			
	Driver	Time	Laps
1	S Vettel	1m16.877s	32
2	F Alonso	1m16.963s	35
3	N Rosberg	1m17.151s	34
4	M Webber	1m17.273s	33
5	F Massa	1m17.401s	33
6	A Sutil	1m17.415s	28
7	L Hamilton	1m17.522s	29
8	R Kubica	1m17.529s	36
9	M Schumacher	1m17.688s	34
10	V Liuzzi	1m17.903s	35
11	J Button	1m17.961s	33
12	R Barrichello	1m18.385s	27
13	N Hulkenberg	1m18.447s	41
14	V Petrov	1m18.582s	40
15	P de la Rosa	1m18.658s	34
16	K Kobayashi	1m19.142s	38
17	S Buemi	1m19.168s	32
18	J Alguersuari	1m19.274s	41
19	H Kovalainen	1m19.969s	35
20	K Chandhok	1m20.879s	29
21	B Senna	1m21.097s	31
22	J Trulli	1m21.346s	11
23	T Glock	1m21.488s	25
24	L di Grassi	1m21.577s	30

PRACTICE 3			
	Driver	Time	Laps
1	L Hamilton	1m16.058s	15
2	M Webber	1m16.340s	16
3	F Alonso	1m16.495s	19
4	M Schumacher	1m16.536s	15
5	S Vettel	1m16.582s	16
6	R Kubica	1m16.653s	15
7	A Sutil	1m16.673s	15
8	J Button	1m16.699s	16
9	V Liuzzi	1m16.814s	15
10	V Petrov	1m16.982s	18
11	N Hulkenberg	1m17.121s	16
12	F Massa	1m17.231s	16
13	J Alguersuari	1m17.331s	22
14	K Kobayashi	1m17.548s	20
15	P de la Rosa	1m17.609s	16
16	S Buemi	1m17.633s	21
17	R Barrichello	1m17.789s	18
18	N Rosberg	1m17.979s	4
19	J Trulli	1m19.013s	15
20	H Kovalainen	1m19.447s	16
21	T Glock	1m19.536s	22
22	L di Grassi	1m19.844s	20
23	B Senna	1m20.325s	18
24	K Chandhok	No time	1

QUALIFYING 1		
	Driver	Time
1	L Hamilton	1m15.889s
2	S Vettel	1m16.129s
3	F Alonso	1m16.171s
4	N Rosberg	1m16.350s
5	R Kubica	1m16.370s
6	J Button	1m16.371s
7	M Webber	1m16.423s
8	A Sutil	1m16.495s
9	V Petrov	1m16.569s
10	M Schumacher	1m16.598s
11	F Massa	1m16.673s
12	N Hulkenberg	1m16.770s
13	R Barrichello	1m16.880s
14	J Alguersuari	1m17.027s
15	V Liuzzi	1m17.086s
16	S Buemi	1m17.356s
17	P de la Rosa	1m17.611s
18	K Kobayashi	1m18.019s
19	H Kovalainen	1m18.237s
20	J Trulli	1m18.698s
21	T Glock	1m18.941s
22	B Senna	1m19.484s
23	L di Grassi	1m19.675s
24	K Chandhok	1m27.757s

QUALIFYING 2		
	Driver	Time
1	L Hamilton	1m15.528s
2	S Vettel	1m15.556s
3	F Alonso	1m15.597s
4	R Kubica	1m15.682s
5	M Webber	1m15.692s
6	J Button	1m15.742s
7	N Rosberg	1m16.001s
8	V Liuzzi	1m16.171s
9	A Sutil	1m16.295s
10	F Massa	1m16.314s
11	R Barrichello	1m16.434s
12	N Hulkenberg	1m16.438s
13	M Schumacher	1m16.492s
14	V Petrov	1m16.844s
15	S Buemi	1m16.928s
16	J Alguersuari	1m17.029s
17	P de la Rosa	1m17.384s

Best sectors – Practice			Speed trap – Practice		
Sec 1	M Webber	21.079s	1	L di Grassi	201.386mph
Sec 2	L Hamilton	24.434s	2	S Buemi	199.584mph
Sec 3	L Hamilton	30.370s	3	J Alguersuari	198.963mph

Best sectors – Qualifying			Speed trap – Qualifying		
Sec 1	L Hamilton	20.883s	1	V Petrov	201.075mph
Sec 2	M Webber	24.126s	2	S Buemi	200.827mph
Sec 3	L Hamilton	30.023s	3	R Kubica	199.770mph

Jenson Button
"I looked after my tyres and was able to pull out 5s on Sebastian. Then I focused on driving flat-out to catch Fernando. When we hit more traffic, I was able to pounce."

Michael Schumacher
"My first pit stop was perfectly timed. Then I had a puncture after I got together with Kubica, and that really decided my race. From there, I was stuck in traffic."

Sebastian Vettel
"I was surprised that I came in for my first stop as the leader, but came out fourth. Otherwise, I had a gearbox problem from halfway, which meant I had to slow."

Felipe Massa
"I had an accident at the first corner. I got a good start, but I was sandwiched between Button and Liuzzi, who touched me and you all saw how it ended up."

Rubens Barrichello
"Alguersuari covered his line and hit me very hard. The damage blocked my front-left brake duct and so I then lost the pedal and had to let cars by until I could pit."

Robert Kubica
"I had a lot of degradation, so pitted early, then the rears went in the second stint. But I had a battle with Michael after my first stop, then Sutil before my second."

Lewis Hamilton
"It was incredibly challenging, especially in the last 20 laps, when I was trying to look after my tyres while also keeping Jenson and Alonso behind me."

Nico Rosberg
"I was unlucky to lose so many places from the chaos in front of me on lap 1. From there, I was able to do some good overtaking and push to make up the places."

Mark Webber
"My first few laps took its toll on the tyres, so I pitted earlier than planned. In the second stint I was monitoring the gap to Lewis, but the tyres didn't want that pace."

Fernando Alonso
"I could have won, but we paid a heavy price for traffic. It was hard to manage the tyres: the softs suffered from degradation at the start, but even the hards grained."

Nico Hulkenberg
"My first problem occurred when I was fighting Sutil and damaged my front wing. Then, on my second stop I broke the speed limit, which meant a drive-through."

Vitaly Petrov
"I was trying to pass on the right at the start, when I got pushed onto the grass and spun. I was lucky I only damaged the front wing. Then I had drive-throughs."

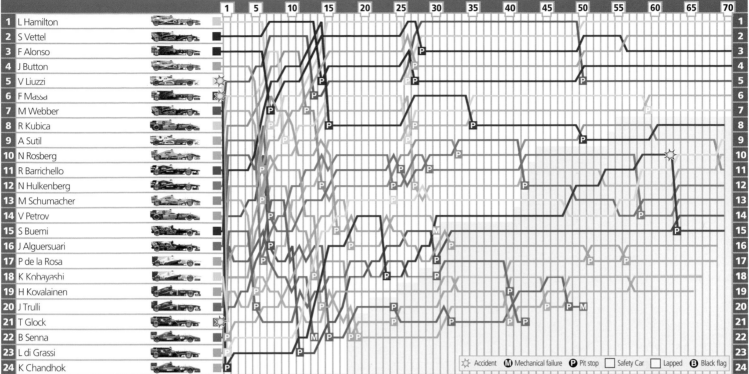

	Driver		1	5	10	15	20	25	30	35	40	45	50	55	60	65	70	
1	L Hamilton																	1
2	S Vettel																	2
3	F Alonso																	3
4	J Button																	4
5	V Liuzzi																	5
6	F Massa																	6
7	M Webber																	7
8	R Kubica																	8
9	A Sutil																	9
10	N Rosberg																	10
11	R Barrichello																	11
12	N Hulkenberg																	12
13	M Schumacher																	13
14	V Petrov																	14
15	S Buemi																	15
16	J Alguersuari																	16
17	P de la Rosa																	17
18	K Kobayashi																	18
19	H Kovalainen																	19
20	J Trulli																	20
21	T Glock																	21
22	B Senna																	22
23	L di Grassi																	23
24	K Chandhok																	24

☆ Accident   Ⓜ Mechanical failure   ℗ Pit stop   ☐ Safety Car   ☐ Lapped   Ⓑ Black flag

QUALIFYING 3

	Driver	Time
1	L Hamilton	1m15.105s
2	M Webber	1m15.373s
3	S Vettel	1m15.420s
4	F Alonso	1m15.435s
5	J Button	1m15.520s
6	V Liuzzi	1m15.648s
7	F Massa	1m15.688s
8	R Kubica	1m15.715s
9	A Sutil	1m15.881s
10	N Rosberg	1m16.071s

GRID

	Driver	Time
1	L Hamilton	1m15.105s
2	S Vettel	1m15.420s
3	F Alonso	1m15.435s
4	J Button	1m15.520s
5	V Liuzzi	1m15.648s
6	F Massa	1m15.688s
7*	M Webber	1m15.373s
8	R Kubica	1m15.715s
9	A Sutil	1m15.881s
10	N Rosberg	1m16.071s
11	R Barrichello	1m16.434s
12	N Hulkenberg	1m16.438s
13	M Schumacher	1m16.492s
14	V Petrov	1m16.844s
15	S Buemi	1m16.928s
16	J Alguersuari	1m17.029s
17	P de la Rosa	1m17.384s
18	K Kobayashi	1m18.019s
19	H Kovalainen	1m18.237s
20	J Trulli	1m18.698s
21	T Glock	1m18.941s
22	B Senna	1m19.484s
23	L di Grassi	1m19.675s
24*	K Chandhok	1m27.757s

* 5-place grid penalty for gearbox change

RACE

	Driver	Car	Laps	Time	Avg. mph	Fastest	Stops
1	L Hamilton	McLaren-Mercedes MP4-25	70	1h33m53.456s	121.216	1m17.806s	2
2	J Button	McLaren-Mercedes MP4-25	70	1h33m55.710s	121.168	1m18.144s	2
3	F Alonso	Ferrari F10	70	1h34m02.760s	121.018	1m18.207s	2
4	S Vettel	Red Bull-Renault RB6	70	1h34m31.273s	120.408	1m18.417s	2
5	M Webber	Red Bull-Renault RB6	70	1h34m32.747s	120.377	1m18.148s	2
6	N Rosberg	Mercedes MGP W01	70	1h34m49.540s	120.021	1m17.832s	2
7	R Kubica	Renault R30	70	1h34m50.756s	119.996	1m16.972s	3
8	S Buemi	Toro Rosso-Ferrari STR5	69	1h34m38.435s	118.538	1m19.784s	3
9	V Liuzzi	Force India-Mercedes VJM03	69	1h34m42.634s	118.451	1m19.349s	2
10	A Sutil	Force India-Mercedes VJM03	69	1h34m43.991s	118.423	1m19.530s	2
11	M Schumacher	Mercedes MGP W01	69	1h34m44.747s	118.406	1m19.577s	3
12	J Alguersuari	Toro Rosso-Ferrari STR5	69	1h34m46.635s	118.367	1m19.842s	3
13	N Hulkenberg	Williams-Cosworth FW32	69	1h34m47.422s	118.351	1m18.912s	3
14	R Barrichello	Williams-Cosworth FW32	69	1h34m48.538s	118.327	1m19.175s	3
15	F Massa	Ferrari F10	69	1h35m15.971s	117.760	1m18.325s	4
16	H Kovalainen	Lotus-Cosworth T127	68	1h35m04.808s	116.280	1m20.654s	3
17	V Petrov	Renault R30	68	1h35m05.361s	116.269	1m19.453s	2
18	K Chandhok	HRT-Cosworth F110	66	1h34m04.900s	114.058	1m21.884s	2
19	L di Grassi	Virgin-Cosworth VR-01	65	1h33m59.377s	112.440	1m21.937s	3
R	T Glock	Virgin-Cosworth VR-01	50	Accident damage	-	1m21.669s	4
R	J Trulli	Lotus-Cosworth T127	42	Vibration	-	1m20.791s	4
R	P de la Rosa	BMW Sauber-Ferrari C29	30	Engine	-	1m20.574s	1
R	B Senna	HRT-Cosworth F110	13	Gearbox	-	1m24.524s	0
R	K Kobayashi	BMW Sauber-Ferrari C29	1	Accident	-	-	0

CHAMPIONSHIP

	Driver	Pts
1	L Hamilton	109
2	J Button	106
3	M Webber	103
4	F Alonso	94
5	S Vettel	90
6	N Rosberg	74
7	R Kubica	73
8	F Massa	67
9	M Schumacher	34
10	A Sutil	23
11	V Liuzzi	12
12	R Barrichello	7
13	V Petrov	6
14	S Buemi	5
15	J Alguersuari	3
16	K Kobayashi	1
17	N Hulkenberg	1

	Constructor	Pts
1	McLaren-Mercedes	215
2	Red Bull-Renault	193
3	Ferrari	161
4	Mercedes	108
5	Renault	79
6	Force India-Mercedes	35
7	Toro Rosso-Ferrari	8
8	Williams-Cosworth	8
9	BMW Sauber-Ferrari	1

Fastest lap
R Kubica 1m16.972s
(126.738mph) on lap 67

Fastest speed trap
V Petrov   201.759mph
Slowest speed trap
T Glock   191.879mph

Fastest pit stop
1	F Alonso	21.277s
2	M Schumacher	21.579s
3	R Kubica	21.936s

Adrian Sutil
"Kubica and I touched at the first corner. I got a puncture and had to drive a long way to the pits, then had to fight past Hulkenberg and Schumacher to score points."

Rubens Barrichello
"I'm super happy to score four points. I enjoyed passing Schumacher which was hard as, even though we were on the same tyres, he is a real fighter."

Jarno Trulli
"It's such a shame I had to pull over – I had a great start and was flying. I was keeping up, but I felt a vibration that caused a problem with the braking system."

Karun Chandhok
"We were racing both Virgins and I was 8s ahead of Glock before he stopped, so I'm pleased. Realistically, we were only racing those three cars and were ahead."

Pedro de la Rosa
"Petrov spun on lap 1 and hit my car when he came back from the grass. I pitted for a new nose. Then on lap 31 I felt a sudden loss of speed on the straight."

Timo Glock
"Senna hit my car in Turn 8, which destroyed the rear of the car and cost me downforce, as well as pushing me off the track. Later, I had a steering-rack leak."

Vitantonio Liuzzi
"The door was closed on me in the first corner by Felipe. With Jenson right on the other side, there wasn't anything that I could do and I lost the front wing."

Michael Schumacher
"On the positive side, I finished the race. It was a tough afternoon that didn't go so well for me, even if I was involved in a lot of exciting incidents and moves."

Heikki Kovalainen
"It's great, as I finished in front of Petrov and lapped the other new guys. Although it was hard work managing the tyres, it's great to show just what we can do."

Bruno Senna
"We had a gearbox failure. Second gear was lost and there was no way to finish without it, so we decided to retire, which is really disappointing for us."

Kamui Kobayashi
"I fought Hulkenberg for ninth. In front of us was Schumacher. We were all braking late and I had nowhere to go. I hit the kerb, the car jumped and I had to stop."

Lucas di Grassi
"I got a good start, then got by Timo and Senna and was catching Trulli. The first stint was strong and I ran 10th, but then I had a loss of hydraulic pressure."

2010 FORMULA 1 TELEFÓNICA GRAND PRIX OF EUROPE
VALENCIA

BOTH RED BULLS FLY

Sebastian Vettel put his title bid back on course with victory, but the talking point was the crash that befell his team-mate Mark Webber, who was launched over Heikki Kovalainen's Lotus

Every now and again, Formula 1 witnesses an accident that makes onlookers gasp. Mark Webber's spectacular aerial accident was one such, but fortunately the Australian driver walked away unharmed. However, the incident triggered a safety-car period that shook up the order behind Sebastian Vettel and led to several drivers being hit with time penalties for infringements. In addition, through sheer bad luck, it compromised both Ferrari drivers.

Vettel and Webber locked out the front row, although the achievement came as a surprise even to the team, as it had been assumed that both Montréal and Valencia – tracks lacking any fast corners – weren't going to favour its RB6s. What's more, Ferrari, Renault and Mercedes all arrived with major updates, based around new exhaust packages that followed the blown-diffuser route pioneered by Red Bull.

Red Bull Racing also had a novelty for, having tested it on Friday in Turkey, the team ran its version of the F-duct all meeting for the first time, and it created a little extra benefit on the straights. In the end, Vettel pipped Webber for pole position by 0.075s.

McLaren proved to be the closest challengers, as Lewis Hamilton lined up third. Ferrari's package helped

Fernando Alonso qualify fourth, just ahead of Felipe Massa. Robert Kubica would line up sixth for Renault, which was something of a disappointment after the Pole had topped Q1. Jenson Button couldn't match Hamilton and so had to settle for seventh.

Vettel led away at the start, while from third on the grid Hamilton got ahead of Webber and very nearly stole the lead at Turn 2, the first proper corner. However, the English driver damaged his front wing against Vettel, picking up a vibration.

"It got quite close," said Vettel. "There wasn't much I could have done to go further left. I was quite lucky, as I felt the hit, but a couple of corners later felt there was nothing wrong with the car. I think Lewis hit the inside kerb, so there isn't much you can do."

After getting off the line badly, Webber found himself bundled down the order through the first few corners, falling to ninth. Stuck behind Nico Hulkenberg, he couldn't progress, so Red Bull decided to bring him for a very early tyre stop on lap 7. An attempt to find clean air faltered when the crew had a problem with a front wheel, so he lost time. Instead of emerging in an empty 11s window between Kamui Kobayashi and Heikki Kovalainen, the delay meant that

Webber came out behind the Lotus, and Kovalainen was lapping around 3.5s off the RB6's potential speed.

Keen to make up ground, Webber drew up behind the dark green Lotus, then appeared to misjudge how early the slower car was braking. The RB6 became airborne, struck an advertising hoarding over the track, and landed upside down, before flicking back over and sliding into the tyre wall. It was an horrific-looking incident, but Webber was unhurt. The team blamed Kovalainen for braking early and defending his place too aggressively.

"He caught Kovalainen extremely quickly," said RBR team principal Christian Horner, "and there was a huge performance difference between the cars. Unfortunately, an incident happened where Kovalainen's braking point took Mark completely by surprise. He was right in his slipstream and it was a very dramatic outcome, being launched over the back of his car. So it wasn't a very nice moment, and a great deal of relief for us that he was OK.

"To make his strategy work, Mark needed to go past Heikki quickly. Heikki was in the middle of the road and it wasn't clear whether he was going to defend to the right or go left. Mark felt he still had a

OPPOSITE TOP Lewis Hamilton tried his utmost to take the lead at Turn 2, but was just too far back

OPPOSITE BOTTOM Adrian Sutil advanced from 16th to sixth

BELOW There were plenty of yachts in the harbour, but the tifosi onboard couldn't will either Ferrari driver to a podium finish

INSIDE LINE
HEIKKI KOVALAINEN
LOTUS DRIVER

"Mark Webber's accident after he hit me on the straight was a big one and I was just mightily relieved that he was okay. I was always going to defend my position, as it wasn't as though Mark was lapping me, since he'd been delayed and we were fighting for position.

It may be true that I braked well before the point that he was used to, but that was down to the relative performance of the two cars. Also, if you think about it, whenever Mark has encountered one of the new team cars previously it has been in a lapping situation and not a racing situation, so they have been letting him go rather than fighting for position.

We checked my telemetry afterwards and it showed that I braked a little bit earlier than on a normal lap, but that's because I was off-line. I defended, but I didn't close the door on Mark while I was braking. I was trying to make him go around the outside.

I spoke to Mark about it afterwards and he said he wasn't sure which way to go and that he

didn't realise how early I had to brake. At various stages this season, mainly before Monaco, people have talked about the speed differentials between the frontrunning cars and the new team cars being dangerous, but I don't see that it's a factor. It was quite ironic that in Monaco, after all the talk of having split sessions because of the new team cars being so much slower, it was only the quick guys who ended up getting in each other's way...

I really don't see that it's an issue. It wasn't that Mark was catching me so quickly that there was nothing I could do. You always have to be careful when you're fighting with somebody under braking. I haven't felt this season, at any point, that the speed differential is dangerous. It was simply a misjudgement

on Mark's part and I honestly think it would have happened whoever was in front of him.

Still, it's never nice to see something like that and it was a relief to see the car come to rest on its wheels. It was a big one, but it's part of what we do.

When I had my accident at Barcelona last year, I was wearing a heart monitor, coincidentally. When I had the accident it was normal, at 170bpm, then it stopped for a few seconds before coming back at the same rate. I have the data on my laptop. That was pretty hard core!"

bit of time to decide before he got to the braking area, but Heikki braked half a kilometre before Mark even thought about braking!"

When the safety car was called for, leader Vettel was just passing the pit exit and, as it emerged, Hamilton just managed to overtake it. Behind him, the Ferraris of Alonso and Massa were obliged to fall into line behind it. Those behind the Ferraris had enough time to make snap decisions to dive into the pits, with Kubica, Button and Rubens Barrichello leading the charge.

So now there were in effect several groups of cars. Vettel and Hamilton ran around unhindered to the pit entry and stopped on the next lap. The Ferraris drove half a lap behind a very slow safety car, before being waved by just after the accident scene. The rest of the leading group followed on, having made their stops.

Vettel and Hamilton pitted and emerged still in front. But, having been held up behind the safety car, the Ferraris were swallowed up by the pack of those who'd made instant stops, falling down the order. Alonso tumbled to 10th, while Massa, who had to wait his turn behind him, fell to 17th. Neither driver had done anything wrong – they were just in the

wrong place at the wrong time. The same applied to Michael Schumacher. He had stayed out at first, then pitted a lap later, and it looked as though he might make a huge jump up the order. But Mercedes misjudged things and when he got to the pit exit the red light was on, so he had to wait for the field to pass by before he could rejoin.

The driver who gained the most was Kobayashi who, having started 18th, decided not to stop under the safety car. That promoted his BMW Sauber to third and, when the race restarted, he had no trouble staying there, happily holding off Button.

For the restart, Vettel had a new headache. His 4.1s margin over Hamilton had become nothing and, what's more, the McLaren driver had replaced the nose he'd damaged at the start, and thus now had improved performance, so there was also no guarantee that Vettel would still have the upper hand now that both men were on primes. Given that situation, he could perhaps be forgiven for locking up at the final corner before the restart, caught out by cold tyres and an understandable urgency to get going. Hamilton was 0.4s behind as they crossed the line, but Vettel stayed safely in front on the run down to Turn 2. However, he now had a flatspotted front tyre, and would have to carry the problem for another 43 laps. Meanwhile, Hamilton's passing of the safety car had attracted the attention of the FIA. Alonso had raved about it on his pit-to-car radio, and television replays eventually indicated that when he went past the safety car it had already passed the safety-car line and was therefore 'active'. It was only a fractional transgression, but the rule was clear: he should have backed off and stayed behind it.

Hamilton was eventually given a drive-through penalty. However, it proved to be academic as, by the time he'd been issued with it, he'd pulled such a gap on Kobayashi that he was able to emerge from

BELOW Jarno Trulli had great expectations, but his Lotus was hit on the first lap then clipped another car

BOTTOM A marshal surveys the scene as Mark Webber prepares to climb out of his battered Red Bull RB6 after its scary flight

OPPOSITE Making three stops while his rivals pitted once confined Michael Schumacher to 15th place

TALKING POINT
THE FIA GOT IT RIGHT

Fernando Alonso was furious. How had he observed the safety-car rules behind Lewis Hamilton, who did not and was penalised, yet still finished the race behind him?

When the safety car was deployed following Mark Webber's accident, Sebastian Vettel was starting his 10th lap, with a 4s lead over Hamilton,

and cleared the emerging safety car comfortably as it left the pit exit. Hamilton didn't quite make it, so his pass of the safety car was illegal. Alonso realised he wasn't going to make it and so fell in behind.

Ferrari had two issues: the delay in giving Hamilton his drive-through penalty and the fact that he was then able to serve it without losing track position.

However, there was less than a car's length between Hamilton and the safety car when the transgression happened, and no back-up timing loop at that point, so Race Director Charlie Whiting wanted to see footage of the incident. This, initially, was from an angle that was inconclusive and so there was a delay while aerial footage was sought. It confirmed that Hamilton appeared to

be guilty, but that it was a close call.

The relative positioning of timing transponders on the cars also needed to be checked. For instance, if one was at the back and the other at the front, you can have a situation where a car that appears to be ahead of another actually records the same time. So, when it's that tight, transponder installation positions have to be checked, times and distances noted and calculations made.

It was also touch-and-go as to whether a drive-through penalty was going to impact on Hamilton. The rules say that you have to serve it within three laps of notification, and McLaren used that leeway to tell Hamilton to get the hammer down before stopping. He emerged from the pits only just ahead of Kamui Kobayashi.

You might think that a stop-and-go penalty would have been better. The FIA is able to work out the probable impact of a penalty and so it would have cost Hamilton more time in the pits and punished him more in line with his crime. That was certainly a view, but the FIA tends to take into account precedent so that it limits the extent to which it is accused of inconsistency.

For instance, when Mark Webber scored his debut victory at the Nürburgring in 2009, he was able to serve a drive-through penalty for weaving at Barrichello off the start, without losing his lead. Had the stewards deviated from that, they may have found themselves dubbed 'Ferrari International Assistance' again. So they're damned if they do, damned if they don't...

ABOVE Karun Chandhok finished 18th, two laps down, in the second of Hispania Racing's home races

BELOW Rubens Barrichello had a great run from ninth on the grid to fourth for Williams, resisting Robert Kubica's Renault

the pits still in second place, an outcome that left rivals – especially Ferrari – scratching their heads, and frustrated that the stewards had taken so long to come to a decision.

Had Hamilton been able to maintain the pressure, Vettel's flatspotted tyre might have become more of an issue, but the penalty – which he took with 30 laps to go when was just 1.7s behind – gave Vettel breathing space. So, while Hamilton didn't drop any positions when he took his penalty, he did lose a clear opportunity to push Vettel and possibly tip that damaged tyre over the edge. Instead, Vettel had a safe margin and could pace himself. The gap subsequently

fell from as much as 14.5s after the penalty to 3.8s on the penultimate lap, before Hamilton backed off.

"It was obviously a bit easier when Lewis had to come in and lost about 15s," said Vettel, "so I could control my pace and carry the car home. Obviously, I never really tried to push hard, as I didn't want to try anything stupid. Looking at the first stint and then after the restart, when I was pushing, I was very happy. The pace seemed to be strong and we were able to pull away a bit more initially at the start of the race and afterwards at the rate of two- or three-tenths a lap, something like that."

Button picked up third place when Kobayashi finally made his compulsory pit stop four laps from the flag. Barrichello moved up to fourth place after a superb race for Williams, while Kubica and Adrian Sutil completed the top six.

Kobayashi's late stop dropped him to ninth place. However, with new soft tyres, he had more speed than those ahead and, after first passing Alonso, he then ousted Sebastien Buemi's STR on the very last corner to claim seventh. It was a brilliant effort by both the driver and the Sauber team, and it was good to see someone try a different strategy and make it work.

After the race, all nine of the drivers who'd dived straight into the pits when the safety car came out, including Button, were given 5s penalties for going too fast under safety-car conditions. In truth, most had little chance to slow, because the safety car came out as they were approaching pit entry. In the end, the only ones who lost points were Buemi, who fell from eighth to ninth behind Alonso, and Pedro de la Rosa, who lost 10th place to Nico Rosberg.

It was another nightmare race for Schumacher, who finished a lowly 15th, which is where he'd qualified. The new diffuser package hadn't worked, and Mercedes had hurriedly revised the car for Saturday, the weekend proving to be a struggle.

SNAPSHOT FROM VALENCIA

CLOCKWISE FROM RIGHT "Do you think that Hamilton made it past before the safety car came out?"; some bubbly for the winner; Rubens Barrichello's patriotic yellow and green racing boots; Adrian Newey chats with his former McLaren colleague Martin Whitmarsh; Jarno Trulli and Mike Gascoyne front up Lotus's celebration of its 500th grand prix, with a 1958 Lotus 12 facing this year's T127; diffusers remain as much a dark art as ever to the casual observer; a marshal throws himself into keeping Mark Webber's broken Red Bull from swinging on the hoist; a Lotus team member snuggles up to some Air Asia girls; when in Spain, have a paella in the likeness of Pedro de la Rosa...

RACE RESULTS

EUROPE
VALENCIA

Official Results © [2010]
Formula One Administration Limited,
6 Princes Gate, London, SW7 1QJ.
No reproduction without permission.
All copyright and database rights reserved.

RACE DATE June 27th
CIRCUIT LENGTH 3.367 miles
NO. OF LAPS 57
RACE DISTANCE 191.919 miles
WEATHER Sunny & dry, 27°C
TRACK TEMP 45°C
ATTENDANCE 162,785
LAP RECORD Timo Glock,
1m38.683s, 122.837mph, 2009

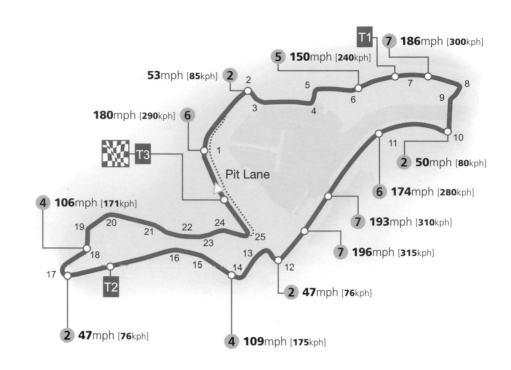

PRACTICE 1				PRACTICE 2				PRACTICE 3				QUALIFYING 1			QUALIFYING 2	
	Driver	Time	Laps		Driver	Time	Laps		Driver	Time	Laps		Driver	Time		Driver	Time
1	N Rosberg	1m41.175s	16	1	F Alonso	1m39.283s	33	1	S Vettel	1m38.052s	14	1	R Kubica	1m38.132s	1	S Vettel	1m38.015s
2	L Hamilton	1m41.339s	19	2	S Vettel	1m39.339s	27	2	R Kubica	1m38.154s	17	2	S Vettel	1m38.324s	2	M Webber	1m38.041s
3	J Button	1m41.383s	21	3	M Webber	1m39.427s	29	3	M Webber	1m38.313s	13	3	J Button	1m38.360s	3	F Massa	1m38.046s
4	R Kubica	1m41.715s	20	4	N Rosberg	1m39.650s	22	4	A Sutil	1m38.500s	17	4	R Barrichello	1m38.449s	4	R Kubica	1m38.062s
5	F Massa	1m42.182s	21	5	L Hamilton	1m39.749s	24	5	F Alonso	1m38.513s	18	5	F Alonso	1m38.472s	5	L Hamilton	1m38.158s
6	S Vettel	1m42.216s	24	6	R Kubica	1m39.880s	28	6	R Barrichello	1m38.623s	15	6	M Webber	1m38.549s	6	F Alonso	1m38.179s
7	M Webber	1m42.275s	17	7	F Massa	1m39.947s	22	7	V Liuzzi	1m38.676s	17	7	F Massa	1m38.657s	7	R Barrichello	1m38.326s
8	M Schumacher	1m42.312s	18	8	A Sutil	1m40.020s	30	8	F Massa	1m38.686s	16	8	L Hamilton	1m38.697s	8	J Button	1m38.399s
9	F Alonso	1m42.421s	22	9	J Button	1m40.029s	27	9	J Button	1m38.769s	15	9	N Rosberg	1m38.752s	9	N Hulkenberg	1m38.523s
10	R Barrichello	1m42.463s	21	10	R Barrichello	1m40.174s	33	10	L Hamilton	1m38.816s	15	10	N Hulkenberg	1m38.843s	10	V Petrov	1m38.552s
11	N Hulkenberg	1m42.707s	23	11	M Schumacher	1m40.287s	24	11	N Rosberg	1m38.822s	15	11	V Liuzzi	1m38.969s	11	S Buemi	1m38.586s
12	V Petrov	1m42.962s	17	12	V Liuzzi	1m40.387s	33	12	S Buemi	1m39.050s	16	12	M Schumacher	1m38.994s	12	N Rosberg	1m38.627s
13	S Buemi	1m43.310s	23	13	V Petrov	1m40.618s	29	13	N Hulkenberg	1m39.105s	15	13	P de la Rosa	1m39.003s	13	A Sutil	1m38.851s
14	V Liuzzi	1m43.380s	19	14	K Kobayashi	1m40.906s	34	14	V Petrov	1m39.113s	16	14	V Petrov	1m39.004s	14	V Liuzzi	1m38.884s
15	P de la Rosa	1m43.397s	21	15	P de la Rosa	1m40.945s	30	15	M Schumacher	1m39.222s	14	15	A Sutil	1m39.021s	15	M Schumacher	1m39.234s
16	P di Resta	1m43.437s	18	16	S Buemi	1m41.115s	35	16	J Alguersuari	1m39.392s	18	16	S Buemi	1m39.096s	16	P de la Rosa	1m39.264s
17	K Kobayashi	1m43.729s	21	17	N Hulkenberg	1m41.371s	30	17	K Kobayashi	1m39.527s	16	17	J Alguersuari	1m39.128s	17	J Alguersuari	1m39.458s
18	J Alguersuari	1m44.183s	21	18	J Alguersuari	1m41.457s	36	18	P de la Rosa	1m39.699s	16	18	K Kobayashi	1m39.343s			
19	H Kovalainen	1m44.491s	21	19	H Kovalainen	1m42.467s	31	19	H Kovalainen	1m41.303s	19	19	J Trulli	1m40.658s			
20	T Glock	1m45.653s	23	20	J Trulli	1m42.993s	30	20	J Trulli	1m41.428s	20	20	H Kovalainen	1m40.882s			
21	B Senna	1m47.123s	17	21	T Glock	1m43.811s	14	21	T Glock	1m41.955s	17	21	L di Grassi	1m42.086s			
22	J Trulli	1m47.285s	18	22	L di Grassi	1m43.854s	27	22	L di Grassi	1m42.354s	18	22	T Glock	1m42.140s			
23	C Klien	1m47.343s	14	23	B Senna	1m44.095s	24	23	B Senna	1m42.611s	18	23	K Chandhok	1m42.600s			
24	L di Grassi	1m47.356s	24	24	K Chandhok	1m44.566s	21	24	K Chandhok	1m42.622s	19	24	B Senna	1m42.851s			

Best sectors – Practice			Speed trap – Practice				Best sectors – Qualifying			Speed trap – Qualifying		
Sec 1	S Vettel	26.048s	1	J Button	195.856mph		Sec 1	F Massa	26.005s	1	J Button	194.427mph
Sec 2	A Sutil	44.664s	2	S Buemi	195.483mph		Sec 2	L Hamilton	44.421s	2	F Massa	193.992mph
Sec 3	M Webber	27.148s	3	L Hamilton	195.110mph		Sec 3	S Vettel	27.083s	3	F Alonso	193.867mph

Jenson Button

"I was very close to the pit entry when the safety car came out, so I dived in. There was no room to lift or hit the brakes, so I can't see why I was called to the stewards."

Michael Schumacher

"We'd like to have clarification about the safety-car situation, as the red light on the exit from my first stop ruined a race that would have offered good possibilities."

Sebastian Vettel

"On a circuit where we didn't expect to be that strong, we were fast enough to pull away, find the gap, then guide it home, but it wasn't as easy as expected."

Felipe Massa

"On the lap of Mark's accident, we were coming into the final corner. Then the safety car came out, the cars behind us pitted and our chance of a podium went."

Rubens Barrichello

"It was great fun. We seem to be heading in the right direction with the car's development, and I hope this improved performance continues for the rest of the year."

Robert Kubica

"Jenson and I spent half a lap side by side. Then I was braking for the last corner when the safety car came out. I was the first to pit, but the third to leave."

Lewis Hamilton

"I outbraked Seb into Turn 1, but we touched and my wing was damaged. When the safety car came out, the team did a top job to change the nosebox and tyres."

Nico Rosberg

"It wasn't a great race. I had little grip and had to work really hard to save my brakes, which took away the ability to challenge and try to make up positions."

Mark Webber

"I was a lot faster than Heikki. Then 80m before the braking point he braked, and at that point I'm a passenger. The car, thank God, was very safe and I'm OK."

Fernando Alonso

"I was third, a metre behind Hamilton when the safety car came out. At the chequered flag, he was second and I was ninth, even with the same strategy."

Nico Hulkenberg

"I was 10th before the safety car. But, when it came in, I couldn't keep Alonso behind me. After that, it was processional until something caught fire on my car."

Vitaly Petrov

"At the start, I got wheel spin and lost a lot of positions. After that, I tried to keep up good pace and to attack de la Rosa, but he had very good speed on the straight."

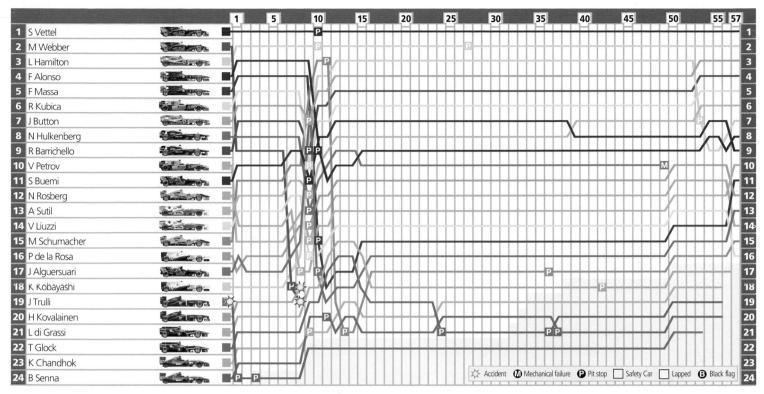

	Driver		1	5	10	15	20	25	30	35	40	45	50	55	57	
1	S Vettel															1
2	M Webber															2
3	L Hamilton															3
4	F Alonso															4
5	F Massa															5
6	R Kubica															6
7	J Button															7
8	N Hulkenberg															8
9	R Barrichello															9
10	V Petrov															10
11	S Buemi															11
12	N Rosberg															12
13	A Sutil															13
14	V Liuzzi															14
15	M Schumacher															15
16	P de la Rosa															16
17	J Alguersuari															17
18	K Kobayashi															18
19	J Trulli															19
20	H Kovalainen															20
21	L di Grassi															21
22	T Glock															22
23	K Chandhok															23
24	B Senna															24

☆ Accident　Ⓜ Mechanical failure　Ⓟ Pit stop　☐ Safety Car　☐ Lapped　Ⓑ Black flag

QUALIFYING 3

	Driver	Time
1	S Vettel	1m37.587s
2	M Webber	1m37.662s
3	L Hamilton	1m37.969s
4	F Alonso	1m38.075s
5	F Massa	1m38.127s
6	R Kubica	1m38.137s
7	J Button	1m38.210s
8	N Hulkenberg	1m38.428s
9	R Barrichello	1m38.428s
10	V Petrov	1m38.523s

GRID

	Driver	Time
1	S Vettel	1m37.587s
2	M Webber	1m37.662s
3	L Hamilton	1m37.969s
4	F Alonso	1m38.075s
5	F Massa	1m38.127s
6	R Kubica	1m38.137s
7	J Button	1m38.210s
8	N Hulkenberg	1m38.428s
9	R Barrichello	1m38.428s
10	V Petrov	1m38.523s
11	S Buemi	1m38.586s
12	N Rosberg	1m38.627s
13	A Sutil	1m38.851s
14	V Liuzzi	1m38.884s
15	M Schumacher	1m39.234s
16	P de la Rosa	1m39.264s
17	J Alguersuari	1m39.458s
18	K Kobayashi	1m39.343s
19	J Trulli	1m40.658s
20	H Kovalainen	1m40.882s
21	L di Grassi	1m42.086s
22	T Glock	1m42.140s
23	K Chandhok	1m42.600s
24	B Senna	1m42.851s

RACE

	Driver	Car	Laps	Time	Avg. mph	Fastest	Stops
1	S Vettel	Red Bull-Renault RB6	57	1h40m29.571s	114.587	1m39.141s	1
2	L Hamilton	McLaren-Mercedes MP4-25	57	1h40m34.613s	114.491	1m39.156s	2
3	J Button	McLaren-Mercedes MP4-25	57	1h40m42.229s*	114.347	1m38.766s	1
4	R Barrichello	Williams-Cosworth FW32	57	1h40m55.198s*	114.102	1m39.489s	1
5	R Kubica	Renault R30	57	1h40m56.693s*	114.074	1m39.542s	1
6	A Sutil	Force India-Mercedes VJM03	57	1h40m59.739s*	114.016	1m39.803s	1
7	K Kobayashi	BMW Sauber-Ferrari C29	57	1h41m00.536s	114.001	1m39.517s	1
8	F Alonso	Ferrari F10	57	1h41m02.380s	113.967	1m39.889s	1
9	S Buemi	Toro Rosso-Ferrari STR5	57	1h41m05.870s*	113.901	1m40.084s	1
10	N Rosberg	Mercedes MGP W01	57	1h41m13.953s	113.793	1m39.878s	1
11	F Massa	Ferrari F10	57	1h41m16.192s	113.707	1m40.208s	1
12	P de la Rosa	BMW Sauber-Ferrari C29	57	1h41m16.985s*	113.693	1m40.430s	1
13	J Alguersuari	Toro Rosso-Ferrari STR5	57	1h41m17.810s	113.677	1m40.327s	1
14	V Petrov	Renault R30	57	1h41m17.858s*	113.676	1m40.100s	1
15	M Schumacher	Mercedes MGP W01	57	1h41m18.397s	113.666	1m38.968s	3
16	V Liuzzi	Force India-Mercedes VJM03	57	1h41m20.461s*	113.628	1m40.305s	1
17	L di Grassi	Virgin-Cosworth VR-01	56	1h41m59.858s	110.916	1m42.414s	1
18	K Chandhok	HRT-Cosworth F110	55	1h40m37.870s	110.414	1m43.820s	1
19	T Glock	Virgin-Cosworth VR-01	55	1h40m53.767s**	110.124	1m42.319s	2
20	B Senna	HRT-Cosworth F110	55	1h41m07.902s	109.868	1m42.927s	2
21	J Trulli	Lotus-Cosworth T127	53	1h41m42.171s	105.278	1m41.770s	2
R	N Hulkenberg	Williams-Cosworth FW32	49	Exhaust	-	1m40.790s	1
R	H Kovalainen	Lotus-Cosworth T127	8	Accident	-	1m46.130s	0
R	M Webber	Red Bull-Renault RB6	8	Accident	-	1m44.064s	1

* Including 5s penalty for driving too fast behind the safety car. ** Including 20s penalty for ignoring blue flags

CHAMPIONSHIP

	Driver	Pts
1	L Hamilton	127
2	J Button	121
3	S Vettel	115
4	M Webber	103
5	F Alonso	98
6	R Kubica	83
7	N Rosberg	75
8	F Massa	67
9	M Schumacher	34
10	A Sutil	31
11	R Barrichello	19
12	V Liuzzi	12
13	K Kobayashi	7
14	S Buemi	7
15	V Petrov	6
16	J Alguersuari	3
17	N Hulkenberg	1

	Constructor	Pts
1	McLaren-Mercedes	248
2	Red Bull-Renault	218
3	Ferrari	165
4	Mercedes	109
5	Renault	89
6	Force India-Mercedes	43
7	Williams-Cosworth	20
8	Toro Rosso-Ferrari	10
9	BMW Sauber-Ferrari	7

Fastest lap
J Button 1m38.766s
(123.089mph) on lap 54

Fastest speed trap
J Button 194.427mph
Slowest speed trap
T Glock 189.145mph

Fastest pit stop
1 F Alonso 20.649s
2 M Schumacher 20.737s
3 S Vettel 21.197

 Adrian Sutil

"When the safety car went out, I was in the last sector and pitted straight away, then moved up the order when the front guys came in. Then I passed Buemi on track."

Sebastien Buemi

"I could have finished sixth, but made two mistakes. I knew Kobayashi was closing fast, but at the final corner, I didn't think he could brake that late."

 Jarno Trulli

"At the start, I got away from the mess at the front, but was hit from the back and at the same time lost my front wing. I went back out, but had a gearbox problem."

Karun Chandhok

"I struggled with the option tyres. We pitted under the safety car and switched to primes. I was then able to settle into a rhythm and pull away from Bruno."

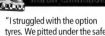 **Pedro de la Rosa**

"The strategy paid off and the car was really good. For most of the race I was stuck in traffic. The last 12 laps were difficult as I had a big flat spot on my front right."

Timo Glock

"I was behind Lucas for ages. Then I had a lock-up and ruined the front right, but when I overtook Senna I touched his front wing and destroyed the rears."

 Vitantonio Liuzzi

"It was a shame we couldn't make more of the safety car as Adrian did, but we came in at the same time and as he was ahead on the road I had to wait for him."

Jaime Alguersuari

"I never had 100% control of the car, never having quite the right feeling with the brakes, and that was my issue. The situation improved a bit during the race."

 Heikki Kovalainen

"I didn't do anything wrong, but Mark just ran into me. I think he just missed his braking point and ran into me. I'm absolutely fine, and glad Mark is too."

Bruno Senna

"It was frustrating. Unluckily, there was the incident with Glock when my wing was damaged. This happened during the blue flag we got for a lapping car."

 **Kamui Kobayashi**

"I started on the harder tyres and didn't pit with everybody else, but later I had four laps to make use of my fresh tyres and it was a risk to pass Alonso and Buemi."

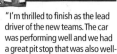 **Lucas di Grassi**

"I'm thrilled to finish as the lead driver of the new teams. The car was performing well and we had a great pit stop that was also well-timed to manage the traffic."

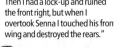

2010 FORMULA 1 SANTANDER BRITISH GRAND PRIX
SILVERSTONE

PROVING A POINT

Mark Webber used the word karma, and that seemed an appropriate way to sum up his victory. He also made his point on the radio, telling his team boss that it was "not bad for a number two"

Having weathered the storm after the Turkish GP, Red Bull Racing sailed into another one at its home race. This time it appeared that Sebastian Vettel had been handed a technical advantage in qualifying, only for fortune to turn the other way on race day when the German driver's race was ruined at the first corner, and Mark Webber was left to win as he pleased.

The controversy began because the team had two new-spec front wings. Vettel's suffered some damage on Saturday morning when the nose worked loose, and the wing dragged along the ground. In the break before qualifying, RBR tech chief Adrian Newey decided to give the remaining new wing – which had been on Webber's car – to the German. Only later did the team come up with the explanation that Vettel had priority, as he was ahead in the World Championship.

The two dark blue cars dominated the session, as expected, and Vettel pipped his team-mate to pole by 0.148s. Asked about the situation, Webber alerted the media to what had transpired.

Fernando Alonso led the chase for Ferrari, despite hitting traffic on his run. Lewis Hamilton did a good job for McLaren to qualify fourth after the team took off its new blown diffuser update package overnight, and

At the time, it certainly looked as though Webber had left his team-mate with nowhere to go, but further viewings suggested that Vettel made it look a little closer to the edge than it actually was. Neither the team nor Vettel himself had any complaints afterwards.

"They're competitive drivers, they're going for the World Championship," said Red Bull Racing team principal Christian Horner. "They did what I asked, in that they gave each other enough space. Mark was ahead into the first corner, and I've got absolutely no problems with that..."

"Not much to say," shrugged Vettel when quizzed. "I think we were a little bit out of the window with the clutch. I had a bad start, lots of wheelspin, so I lost the immediate pull away. I tried probably a bit too hard, but that's life, you try always to get the optimum and then into Turn 1 I had to let Mark past.

"From my point of view, he had a better start. Obviously I moved to the right, trying to defend, and he was already there. I knew that because I couldn't see him in the mirror and I knew he didn't stall. I knew he was there, so there was no point to do something stupid. The race is longer than one corner. It's a shame I couldn't fight him, but it's good for the team, so I'm happy for the team.

"People said that Lewis touched me, but I didn't feel anything. Only he achieved this time what he didn't achieve in Valencia! Surely it wasn't his intention to give me a puncture. With a puncture that early in the race and especially during the lap, obviously it's a big minus, so I had to come back slowly to the pits."

The race wasn't just about Red Bull Racing, of course. From fourth place, Hamilton had got up to second, ahead of Robert Kubica, Nico Rosberg and Alonso. The Spaniard lost two places and had a tangle with Ferrari team-mate Felipe Massa that gave the Brazilian a puncture, and ensured that, like Vettel, he too dropped down the field on the first lap.

ABOVE Mark Webber was looking the wrong way when his front wing was swapped to his team-mate's car

BELOW Mark Webber claims the inside line to take the lead at Copse, with Lewis Hamilton looking to follow him past Sebastian Vettel, ahead of the chasing pack

OPPOSITE Rubens Barrichello followed fourth in Valencia with an excellent fifth place at Silverstone

had to start afresh on set-up, Hamilton saying that he drove as "if my life depended on it". Meanwhile, his team-mate and title rival Jenson Button called his car "undriveable" and was stuck in Q2 in 14th place.

Not for the first time in 2010, the Red Bulls swapped positions on the run from the start, Webber helped by the fact that Vettel didn't get away as well as he should have, blaming the clutch settings.

Things got a bit tight at the first corner, Copse, with Vettel running wide and, more significantly, picking up a puncture after a slight touch from Hamilton. He dropped right to the back of the field after a long crawl back to the pits.

INSIDE LINE
MARK WEBBER
RED BULL RACING DRIVER

"Coming here to the British GP at Silverstone after what happened in Valencia was not ideal. Then there was the qualifying stuff. Maybe there is a bloke upstairs every now and again...

In truth, I enjoyed it. It was a good fight with Lewis, particularly during the first part of the grand prix. People don't always see you having a battle if you aren't right together on the circuit, but it was a case of watching the pit boards to check how each other was getting on. Lewis drove a sensational race. We pushed each other as hard as we could.

I think it's fair to say that I had a better car here, and that I used it to the maximum and managed to pull away. We controlled the race well and took care of business.

The pit stops are always crucial, and the team did a great job at mine. I came back out onto the track still in front and got my head down on the prime tyres. I made sure that they were comfortable for the whole stint. The safety car then gave them a chance to recover a fraction and the car was faultless all day.

I made a good start to the race. The dirty side of the grid didn't prove to be that dirty in the end. There's sometimes quite a big discrepancy left to right on the grid, but thank God we had quite a few support races, which helped.

I was very keen to make it my first corner and it worked out. We need to try and keep consolidating on weekends like this. We were very strong, and that's proof of the development that's gone on. Everyone at Milton Keynes has done an incredible job. The guys have pushed hard with the F-duct, which isn't an easy thing to get on top of.

Ann said to me at the start of the year, 'if you don't do anything else this year, bloody win Monaco and the British Grand Prix.' I have now, but hope I have more victories as the season goes on. This is a very special one. I won here in Formula Ford, F3000, sportscars and now F1, so it's been a special track to me. To get the F1 victory in the company of these guys is a highlight.

I heard over the loudspeaker something about Jack Brabham. He won here half a century ago in 1960. A lot of amazing grands prix have taken place here. It had the new layout and it was very special to win here in the UK. The team is down the road with a lot of English employees and it was a great day for them."

Once in front, Webber did an exemplary job. Hamilton might not have had as good a car at Silverstone, but he's not an easy guy to have in your mirrors, and Webber drove faultlessly throughout. He was 6s ahead when a safety car was called out on lap 27 to allow debris – parts of Pedro de la Rosa's rear wing – to be removed from the track.

It was not a huge amount, but a handy cushion nonetheless. As in Monaco, Webber saw his advantage thrown away. And, as in Monaco, he simply went about rebuilding it, stretching the gap to Hamilton to around 7s until easing back before the flag.

"That's the most important thing, we've won the race today," said a mightily relieved Horner, trying to steer clear of the controversy. "Mark drove a fantastic race, no mistakes. He got a good start, then excellent pit stops and good strategy were enough to win the grand prix reasonably comfortably ahead of McLaren."

Horner wasn't upset by Webber's "number two" comment: "I think he was trying to make a point with his Australian humour," he smiled. "He was obviously unhappy about the front-wing decision, but when you've got one, one into two doesn't go, unless you chop it in half. But he drove a great race and he can be

BELOW Slick pitwork helped Kamui Kobayashi move up the order at Michael Schumacher's expense

OPPOSITE TOP Brake problems resulted in Jaime Alguersuari ending his race in the Luffield gravel

OPPOSITE BOTTOM Vitaly Petrov's Renault flashes by the frame of Silverstone's new pit buildings as he heads towards Club corner

TALKING POINT
RED BULL GIVES YOU WINGS...

...but only if you're Sebastian Vettel!

Red Bull Racing won the British Grand Prix, but its team principal Christian Horner spent most of his weekend fending off charges of favouritism towards Vettel.

Red Bull Racing had a new front wing at Silverstone, which both drivers back-to-back tested on Friday and then had fitted to their cars in final Saturday practice. Halfway through that session, Vettel's front wing broke and, just ahead of qualifying, the decision was taken to take the front wing off Webber's car and put it on Vettel's.

With the lack of in-season testing in 2010, tech chief Adrian Newey's desire to run the new wing – reckoned to be worth 0.07s a lap – was understandable and, according to Horner, the remaining wing went to the man who was faster in the third free practice session (Vettel by a fraction of a second) and who was also ahead in the championship.

Webber, however, was unaware of any significance to his free practice 3 time, and was also oblivious to the fact that his front wing had gone to his team-mate, until his engineer Ciaron Pilbeam told him just before he climbed in to go out to qualify.

Vettel pipped Webber to pole position by 0.14s, so the new wing was probably not decisive, but that wasn't the point.

At the post-qualifying press conference, Webber was stony-faced. "The team will be very happy with the result," he said pointedly.

Vettel didn't help when he said that the ability to continue with the same wing had been 'key', but without acknowledging that it came from his team-mate's car. He was trying to be discreet, but Webber's face let the cat out of the bag.

At the start of the race, Vettel moved across to defend his pole, but there was no way that Webber was going to be denied, surface grip willing. It was, and the Australian was well ahead by the time they turned in to Copse. Vettel kept coming on the outside, meaning that he had to back off on the exit, putting himself in the position where his rear tyre was punctured within the first few hundred yards.

To many, Webber's victory was justice being served and the post-race applause around the circuit on his slowing down lap spelled out just how popular a win it had been.

"Not bad for a number two driver..." Mark said to Horner over the radio on the slowing down lap. Then, at the post-race press conference, he made it clear that had he known he was going to receive that kind of treatment, he wouldn't have signed an extension to his contract. It was not a happy camp...

very happy and should be very happy with the job he's done and the job the team's done today.

"We're in a very fortunate situation, and it's a nice headache to have. Many teams would dream of having the situation where we've got two world-class drivers who are doing an excellent job.

"Both the guys drive for the team. And the team is bigger than any individual. All we can do is keep pushing, keep trying to add performance to the car. So far up to this weekend we've managed to do it the same across both cars."

Webber could gain extra satisfaction from the fact that he had the legs on Vettel for most of the race. Of course, the German lost some performance from aero damage due to the flailing tyre, and he basically had to do the whole race on a set of primes. He eventually recovered to seventh, helped by the safety car closing up the pack. Nevertheless, Webber made his point.

After his first-lap tyre change, Vettel was 1m23s behind Webber, with a completely clear track ahead and nothing to lose by just pressing on. And yet when Mark stopped 15 laps later, the margin had extended to 1m33s. With both men now running to the flag, the new gap after Mark's stop was 1m13s,

ABOVE Nico Rosberg prepares to put another lap on Heikki Kovalainen's Lotus *en route* to third

BELOW Christian Horner and Adrian Newey share Mark Webber's delight after his famous victory

and by the time the safety car came out, it was back up to 1m20s.

In other words, Vettel lost around 17s to Webber on the road over those first 26 or so racing laps. Fate played him a hand when the safety car came out, and at the restart he was only 10s behind Webber and, more importantly, in a position to work his way up the top 10. In the end, six points for seventh place was handy damage limitation.

"If you have a puncture in the first corner, you know your race is pretty much over," said Vettel. "I was praying for a safety car, it came, and it allowed me to score some points, which was good."

But obviously if you have the car to win, finishing seventh is not ideal. But still I had, especially in the last 20 laps, quite an entertaining race. I enjoyed passing people here and there, so it was good fun."

"These things tend to even out over the course of the championship," said Horner. "After the first lap, seventh seemed an awfully long way away. But he managed to achieve that with some good moves. It was a like a battle of the Germans at one point! At a track where overtaking is supposed to be difficult, he did a good job."

Hamilton couldn't match Webber on pace, but did a faultless job to take second and more useful points. Rosberg ran a strong race to take third for Mercedes, running fast all day and holding off Button in the last part of the race. From 14th, Button had made a great start and, by pitting later than just about everyone else, he jumped up the order in determined style.

Rubens Barrichello had another good run for Williams to fifth, while Kamui Kobayashi again scored well in sixth. As noted, the safety car allowed Vettel to catch the pack and he was finally able to gain some significant places, but he could not better seventh. Fellow Germans Adrian Sutil, Michael Schumacher and Nico Hulkenberg completed the top 10.

Massa never recovered from his first-lap puncture and, after a late spin forced another tyre change, he finished 15th. That was one place behind Alonso, who received a drive-through penalty for crossing a chicane to overtake Kubica, even though the Pole had retired by the time it was assessed.

The Spaniard's penalty was amplified, because just before Alonso could take it, the safety car came out, the field bunched up and he duly dropped to the rear of the field. Later on, Alonso made an extra tyre stop and set a token fastest lap on new rubber. After the frustration of Valencia, Ferrari was beginning to feel that the FIA was trying to make a point. More trouble was to come at Hockenheim...

SNAPSHOT FROM
GREAT BRITAIN

CLOCKWISE FROM RIGHT Fans at Copse await the start; there was huge support for Lewis and Jenson; Sebastian Vettel works the crowds; Sakon Yamamoto took over Senna's HRT seat; Lewis Hamilton was in constant demand; Vitaly Petrov finds time for tricks in the paddock; Hazel, wife of Lotus founder Colin Chapman, and Nigel Mansell join Tony Fernandes for a celebration; the Red Arrows astounded as always; as did the ebullient Stirling Moss; the BRDC connection lives on; marshal art

RACE RESULTS
GREAT BRITAIN SILVERSTONE

RACE DATE 11th July
CIRCUIT LENGTH 3.666 miles
NO. OF LAPS 52
RACE DISTANCE 190.632 miles
WEATHER Sunny & dry, 22°C
TRACK TEMP 37°C
ATTENDANCE 305,000
LAP RECORD Fernando Alonso,
1m30.874s, 145.011mph, 2010

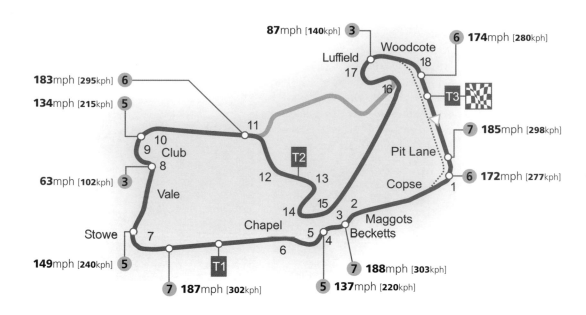

PRACTICE 1				PRACTICE 2				PRACTICE 3				QUALIFYING 1			QUALIFYING 2	
	Driver	Time	Laps		Driver	Time	Laps		Driver	Time	Laps		Driver	Time		Driver	Time
1	S Vettel	1m32.280s	22	1	M Webber	1m31.234s	15	1	S Vettel	1m30.958s	14	1	S Vettel	1m30.841s	1	M Webber	1m30.114s
2	L Hamilton	1m32.614s	16	2	F Alonso	1m31.626s	26	2	M Webber	1m30.992s	15	2	M Webber	1m30.858s	2	S Vettel	1m30.480s
3	R Kubica	1m32.725s	21	3	S Vettel	1m31.875s	25	3	F Alonso	1m31.101s	10	3	F Alonso	1m30.997s	3	F Alonso	1m30.700s
4	M Webber	1m32.747s	23	4	F Massa	1m32.099s	25	4	N Rosberg	1m31.188s	15	4	A Sutil	1m31.109s	4	F Massa	1m31.010s
5	A Sutil	1m32.968s	18	5	N Rosberg	1m32.166s	29	5	F Massa	1m31.240s	16	5	L Hamilton	1m31.297s	5	M Schumacher	1m31.022s
6	N Rosberg	1m33.318s	21	6	M Schumacher	1m32.660s	28	6	R Kubica	1m31.519s	18	6	F Massa	1m31.313s	6	N Rosberg	1m31.085s
7	N Hulkenberg	1m33.377s	19	7	V Petrov	1m32.745s	28	7	L Hamilton	1m31.549s	16	7	R Barrichello	1m31.424s	7	L Hamilton	1m31.118s
8	J Button	1m33.519s	20	8	L Hamilton	1m32.757s	22	8	M Schumacher	1m31.555s	14	8	J Button	1m31.435s	8	R Barrichello	1m31.126s
9	M Schumacher	1m33.955s	18	9	A Sutil	1m32.787s	27	9	P de la Rosa	1m31.559s	18	9	P de la Rosa	1m31.533s	9	P de la Rosa	1m31.327s
10	R Barrichello	1m34.016s	17	10	R Barrichello	1m32.967s	33	10	R Barrichello	1m31.581s	16	10	N Rosberg	1m31.626s	10	R Kubica	1m31.344s
11	S Buemi	1m34.132s	21	11	R Kubica	1m33.019s	30	11	V Petrov	1m31.698s	17	11	V Petrov	1m31.638s	11	A Sutil	1m31.399s
12	V Petrov	1m34.365s	22	12	N Hulkenberg	1m33.164s	29	12	J Button	1m31.703s	16	12	R Kubica	1m31.680s	12	K Kobayashi	1m31.421s
13	F Alonso	1m34.490s	20	13	J Button	1m33.200s	24	13	N Hulkenberg	1m31.867s	17	13	K Kobayashi	1m31.851s	13	N Hulkenberg	1m31.635s
14	P di Resta	1m34.580s	22	14	K Kobayashi	1m33.402s	23	14	K Kobayashi	1m31.947s	16	14	S Buemi	1m31.901s	14	J Button	1m31.699s
15	K Kobayashi	1m34.710s	16	15	V Liuzzi	1m33.728s	27	15	A Sutil	1m31.994s	13	15	M Schumacher	1m32.058s	15	V Liuzzi	1m31.708s
16	P de la Rosa	1m34.901s	17	16	S Buemi	1m33.836s	36	16	S Buemi	1m32.235s	18	16	N Hulkenberg	1m32.144s	16	V Petrov	1m31.796s
17	F Massa	1m35.037s	21	17	P de la Rosa	1m34.051s	29	17	J Alguersuari	1m32.331s	20	17	V Liuzzi	1m32.226s	17	S Buemi	1m32.012s
18	J Alguersuari	1m35.318s	27	18	J Alguersuari	1m34.643s	36	18	V Liuzzi	1m32.723s	18	18	J Alguersuari	1m32.430s			
19	H Kovalainen	1m36.747s	16	19	H Kovalainen	1m35.465s	25	19	H Kovalainen	1m34.339s	20	19	H Kovalainen	1m34.405s			
20	T Glock	1m37.330s	11	20	L di Grassi	1m36.237s	24	20	L di Grassi	1m35.479s	17	20	T Glock	1m34.775s			
21	L di Grassi	1m37.518s	15	21	T Glock	1m36.553s	21	21	J Trulli	1m36.098s	11	21	J Trulli	1m34.864s			
22	K Chandhok	1m38.735s	21	22	K Chandhok	1m37.019s	27	22	K Chandhok	1m36.286s	16	22	L di Grassi	1m35.212s			
23	F Fauzy	1m39.510s	11	23	S Yamamoto	1m38.303s	32	23	T Glock	1m36.640s	6	23	K Chandhok	1m36.576s			
24	S Yamamoto	1m39.673s	27	24	J Trulli	1m42.901s	3	24	S Yamamoto	1m37.178s	18	24	S Yamamoto	1m36.968s			

Best sectors – Practice			Speed trap – Practice			Best sectors – Qualifying			Speed trap – Qualifying	
Sec 1	S Vettel	25.107s	1	J Button	186.908mph	Sec 1	M Webber	24.909s	1	A Sutil	189.083mph
Sec 2	M Webber	29.318s	2	A Sutil	186.784mph	Sec 2	S Vettel	29.008s	2	J Button	187.716mph
Sec 3	S Vettel	36.033s	3	L Hamilton	186.411mph	Sec 3	S Vettel	35.633s	3	L Hamilton	187.343mph

Jenson Button
"I made up six places off the start, then had to push on the option. That worked and I came out behind Fernando, who had a drive-through, so I took fourth."

Michael Schumacher
"I was in traffic for most of the race. After my pit stop, I made a mistake out of a slow corner which put me off the track and that cost me two positions."

Sebastian Vettel
"I had a lot of wheelspin at the start. Then I had the puncture and got a bit of damage to the car which lost me performance, but I was able to recover to score."

Felipe Massa
"I have to find a way of getting rid of my bad luck! Today, my race was over when I touched Fernando and got a puncture that dropped me to the back."

Rubens Barrichello
"I gained some places early on without much trouble. Then, around the stops and the safety car, I gained a place from Alonso and lost one to Jenson."

Robert Kubica
"After my stop, Alonso passed me by cutting Turn 8. He was on the outside, all four wheels off the track. Before he had to give back the place, I had driveshaft failure."

Lewis Hamilton
"I'm so happy: considering how far behind we were in practice. I was able to jump Fernando, then chased Mark all race, but the Red Bull was 0.4–0.5s a lap faster."

Nico Rosberg
"I was fourth on lap 1, with Robert holding me up and Fernando pushing hard. I then had a great lap and quick stop, to get me out ahead of Robert."

Mark Webber
"It's great to win, as Silverstone has got such a lot of history. The start was ideal, when I got to the first corner I was ahead and thought, 'let's get on with it'."

Fernando Alonso
"The instruction to hand back the place came when I'd passed another car and Kubica was slowing. It coincided with the safety car and so I lost 12 places or so."

Nico Hulkenberg
"I lost places at the start and Petrov passed me down the Hangar Straight. That, combined with not being able to get past Michael at the end, meant 10th."

Vitaly Petrov
"I made up three places on lap 1. It was possible to finish in the points, but I had some bad luck with a puncture after the safety-car period which cost me time."

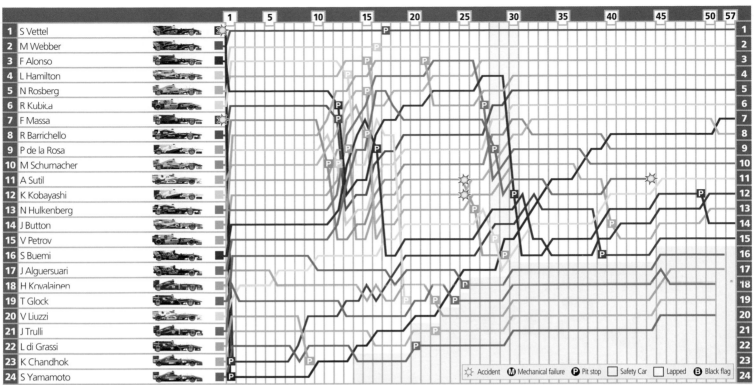

Accident | M Mechanical failure | P Pit stop | Safety Car | Lapped | B Black flag

	1	5	10	15	20	25	30	35	40	45	50 57
1	S Vettel										
2	M Webber										
3	F Alonso										
4	L Hamilton										
5	N Rosberg										
6	R Kubica										
7	F Massa										
8	R Barrichello										
9	P de la Rosa										
10	M Schumacher										
11	A Sutil										
12	K Kobayashi										
13	N Hulkenberg										
14	J Button										
15	V Petrov										
16	S Buemi										
17	J Alguersuari										
18	H Kovalainen										
19	T Glock										
20	V Liuzzi										
21	J Trulli										
22	L di Grassi										
23	K Chandhok										
24	S Yamamoto										

QUALIFYING 3

	Driver	Time
1	S Vettel	1m29.615s
2	M Webber	1m29.758s
3	F Alonso	1m30.426s
4	L Hamilton	1m30.556s
5	N Rosberg	1m30.625s
6	R Kubica	1m31.040s
7	F Massa	1m31.172s
8	R Barrichello	1m31.175s
9	P de la Rosa	1m31.274s
10	M Schumacher	1m31.430s

GRID

	Driver	Time
1	S Vettel	1m29.615s
2	M Webber	1m29.758s
3	F Alonso	1m30.426s
4	L Hamilton	1m30.556s
5	N Rosberg	1m30.625s
6	R Kubica	1m31.040s
7	F Massa	1m31.172s
8	R Barrichello	1m31.175s
9	P de la Rosa	1m31.274s
10	M Schumacher	1m31.430s
11	A Sutil	1m31.399s
12	K Kobayashi	1m31.421s
13	N Hulkenberg	1m31.635s
14	J Button	1m31.699s
15	V Petrov	1m31.796s
16	S Buemi	1m32.012s
17	J Alguersuari	1m32.430s
18	H Kovalainen	1m34.405s
19	T Glock	1m34.775s
20*	V Liuzzi	1m31.708s
21	J Trulli	1m34.864s
22	L di Grassi	1m35.212s
23	K Chandhok	1m36.576s
24	S Yamamoto	1m36.968s

*5-place grid penalty for impeding Hulkenberg

RACE

	Driver	Car	Laps	Time	Avg. mph	Fastest	Stops
1	M Webber	Red Bull-Renault RB6	52	1h24m38.200s	134.892	1m32.364s	1
2	L Hamilton	McLaren-Mercedes MP4-25	52	1h24m39.560s	134.856	1m32.758s	1
3	N Rosberg	Mercedes MGP W01	52	1h24m59.507s	134.328	1m32.952s	1
4	J Button	McLaren-Mercedes MP4-25	52	1h25m00.186s	134.310	1m33.003s	1
5	R Barrichello	Williams-Cosworth FW32	52	1h25m09.656s	134.062	1m33.615s	1
6	K Kobayashi	BMW Sauber-Ferrari C29	52	1h25m10.371s	134.043	1m33.558s	1
7	S Vettel	Red Bull-Renault RB6	52	1h25m14.934s	133.923	1m31.967s	1
8	A Sutil	Force India-Mercedes VJM03	52	1h25m19.132s	133.813	1m34.337s	1
9	M Schumacher	Mercedes MGP W01	52	1h25m19.799s	133.796	1m34.171s	1
10	N Hulkenberg	Williams-Cosworth FW32	52	1h25m20.212s	133.785	1m33.989s	1
11	V Liuzzi	Force India-Mercedes VJM03	52	1h25m20.659s	133.774	1m34.018s	1
12	S Buemi	Toro Rosso-Ferrari STR5	52	1h25m25.827s	133.639	1m32.980s	1
13	V Petrov	Renault R30	52	1h25m37.574s	133.333	1m32.484s	2
14	F Alonso	Ferrari F10	52	1h25m40.585s	133.255	1m30.874s	3
15	F Massa	Ferrari F10	52	1h25m45.689s	133.123	1m31.646s	1
16	J Trulli	Lotus-Cosworth T127	51	1h26m13.365s	129.863	1m36.519s	1
17	H Kovalainen	Lotus-Cosworth T127	51	1h26m13.616s	129.857	1m36.251s	1
18	T Glock	Virgin-Cosworth VR-01	50	1h24m38.350s	129.699	1m36.415s	1
19	K Chandhok	HRT-Cosworth F110	50	1h25m36.238s	128.236	1m38.798s	1
20	S Yamamoto	HRT-Cosworth F110	50	1h25m36.857s	128.221	1m38.309s	1
R	J Alguersuari	Toro Rosso-Ferrari STR5	44	Spun off	-	1m33.748s	1
R	P de la Rosa	BMW Sauber-Ferrari C29	29	Crash damage	-	1m35.883s	2
R	R Kubica	Renault R30	19	Driveshaft	-	1m36.846s	1
R	L di Grassi	Virgin-Cosworth VR-01	9	Hydraulics	-	1m40.641s	0

CHAMPIONSHIP

	Driver	Pts
1	L Hamilton	145
2	J Button	133
3	M Webber	128
4	S Vettel	121
5	F Alonso	98
6	N Rosberg	90
7	R Kubica	83
8	F Massa	67
9	M Schumacher	36
10	A Sutil	35
11	R Barrichello	29
12	K Kobayashi	15
13	V Liuzzi	12
14	S Buemi	8
15	V Petrov	6
16	J Alguersuari	3
17	N Hulkenberg	2

	Constructor	Pts
1	McLaren-Mercedes	278
2	Red Bull-Renault	249
3	Ferrari	165
4	Mercedes	126
5	Renault	89
6	Force India-Mercedes	47
7	Williams-Cosworth	31
8	BMW Sauber-Ferrari	15
9	Toro Rosso-Ferrari	10

Fastest lap
F Alonso 1m30.874s
(145.011mph) on lap 52

Fastest speed trap
S Vettel 186.970mph
Slowest speed trap
L di Grassi 176.593mph

Fastest pit stop
1 R Kubica 18.970s
2 M Schumacher 19.124s
3 M Webber 19.164s

Adrian Sutil
"I didn't have enough grip, so came in early for the soft tyre. I fought Schumacher and defended against Vettel until the last lap when he drove into me."

Sebastian Buemi
"After my stop, I came out behind Liuzzi who hadn't pitted, so spent 10 laps behind him, using my fronts a lot and, when the safety car went in, I had graining."

Jarno Trulli
"When you consider that I didn't have a chance to work on set-up changes, and had to get used to the new track section in qualifying, I did a pretty good job."

Karun Chandhok
"I pushed early on to open a 15s gap to Sakon. After the pit stop, I ran over some debris which damaged the bargeboard and the sidepod, costing downforce."

Pedro de la Rosa
"Rubens pushed me wide in Turn 1, losing me two places. I was still racing for points when Sutil hit me from behind and the damage proved too bad to go on."

Timo Glock
"I lost out at the start to Jarno and Heikki. When Heikki pitted, I had two good laps and came out in front. Then I followed Jarno but hit a bump and Heikki got by."

Vitantonio Liuzzi
"In the first part of the race, with the hard tyres, I had understeer. We have to work it out, as on the softs I was performing very well and just missed out on points."

Jaime Alguersuari
"I'm disappointed not to have finished, but was happy up to then, as the pace was there, I felt comfortable with the car and I was getting faster all race."

Heikki Kovalainen
"My pace was good all race, but there was constant traffic in front of me. I lost my position on the first lap, which was frustrating, as I then got held up quite a bit."

Sakon Yamamoto
"It was a good experience to race in F1 again. I improved all weekend and got a better feeling for the car. I want to thank the team for giving me the chance."

Kamui Kobayashi
"I'm happy, but don't have much to tell. I had a very good start from 12th, the team did a great pit stop, and the race pace was as good as I thought it would be."

Lucas di Grassi
"We didn't have a good day. The car was good at the start, but we lost hydraulic pressure which ended my race. I'm disappointed, but the car is showing progress."

FORMULA 1 GROSSER PREIS SANTANDER
VON DEUTSCHLAND 2010
HOCKENHEIM

FURY AT FERRARI

A Ferrari 1–2 should have been good news,
and it would have had a sentimental value too,
had Felipe Massa not been asked to pull aside
and let Fernando Alonso through to victory

Ferrari finally made good on the promise that its F10 chassis had shown since the blown-diffuser package was introduced in Valencia back at the end of June, following a couple of weekends when little had gone right for the team.

A 1–2 race finish should have been cause for celebration for the team and its fans the world over, but instead the men from Maranello found themselves under siege and under threat from heavier sanctions from the FIA than the token $100,000 fine announced on Sunday evening. Why? Because Felipe Massa handed the lead of the race to Fernando Alonso, and was made to settle for second place.

Some six weeks later, an FIA World Motor Sport Council hearing in Paris decided that there should be no further penalty, and that the result should stand. Nevertheless, the WMSC supported the decision of the original stewards, confirming that the team had broken the rule that states team orders that affect the result of a race are banned, and that it had brought the sport into disrepute.

Sebastian Vettel gave Red Bull Racing another pole, but this time it was close, as he only just

managed to pip Alonso. After rain on Friday and at the start of the Saturday morning practice session, it stayed dry in the afternoon. Alonso was quickest after the first runs, but when the drivers completed their final laps, Vettel went ahead. Then, with the very last lap of the session, the Spaniard got within 0.002s of the local hero.

Massa underlined Ferrari's resurgence by claiming third place on the grid. As race day marked the first anniversary of his accident in qualifying for the 2009 Hungarian GP, he was hoping for a change of luck after a frustrating season. "I'd love to be there fighting for first position in the championship," said the Brazilian driver. "Anyway, there's nothing to say that we have a number one and number two. We don't have that. It's pretty clear..."

What was clear from the start of the weekend, even in Friday's rain, was that Ferrari was right on the pace. Massa even went off the road a few times as he explored the limits, but there was a real spring in his step at Hockenheim.

Mark Webber had to settle for fourth, while Ferrari had leapfrogged McLaren. Jenson Button did a good job to get ahead of team-mate Lewis

Hamilton to qualify fifth. In Hamilton's defence, a crash in the wet on Friday morning cost him track time and he had struggled to catch up.

The rain stayed away on Sunday, but in front of his home crowd Vettel had a truly disastrous opening lap. Off the line, he moved to the right to keep Alonso behind him, but from third Massa charged around the outside and, by taking a wide line into Turn 1, swept into the lead.

Alonso kept the pressure on Massa through the early laps, and the Spaniard became the first driver to pit, as early as lap 13. Massa came in next time around and stayed ahead, but he struggled on his first few laps on the harder tyre, which gave Alonso a chance to really apply the pressure.

When the Ferrari duo came up to backmarkers on lap 20, Alonso launched an attack and almost made it past, but Massa somehow managed to stay ahead. An angry Alonso then made his feelings clear on the radio. He dropped 3s back from his Brazilian team-mate for a while, taking the opportunity to save his machinery.

As the race developed and Alonso dropped back, it looked as if Ferrari was going to claim a perfectly

OPPOSITE TOP Felipe Massa pounces to take the lead after Fernando Alonso had been preoccupied with Sebastian Vettel

OPPOSITE BOTTOM Sebastian Vettel was pumped up to deliver at his home grand prix, but couldn't match the Ferraris

BELOW Opening lap embarrassment for Force India, as Adrian Sutil takes to the grass and Vitantonio Liuzzi spins after contact from his team-mate

INSIDE LINE
FERNANDO ALONSO
FERRARI DRIVER

"I think we really deserved this result. There were no proper points for either Felipe or me in Valencia and Silverstone, with a competitive car, for different reasons, and some very bad luck. We came here with some upgrades and they seemed to work really well. From Friday

morning, we felt competitive. We felt happy with the car, so were just concentrating on finishing and doing a good race on Sunday.

This is a long championship and we need to remain very focused for 10 months. Today was very important for the team, for the motivation of all the guys, and especially for the technical people that keep working day and night to improve the car. This result is thanks to them.

My start was very good. I felt I had a better start than Sebastian on pole, who lost a bit of ground in the first few metres. Then I was very close to the wall and this battle lost me a couple of metres and one position to Felipe. Later, there was a moment when we were side-by-side into Turn 6, with the people we

were lapping, which was tight.

People need to think not just about the result, but about the fact that I had a very strong performance all weekend and if the final thought of the weekend is negative, it's because maybe you didn't see the whole practice, qualifying and the race. You need to consider the performance of the team and the car this weekend.

We tried to do our race as well as we could. We're professional drivers, we try to work in a team and try to do the best we can every day, not only here on the track but also between the races, at the factory, preparing for the races. I think we've been doing a good job over the last couple of races and finally we got a strong

Sunday with a strong result. We're happy with this, although some will want to write all sorts of other things.

As I said, I was very competitive on Friday: first position. I qualified second by 12cm and today I set the fastest lap, so I don't think I was very slow this weekend... As Felipe said, we work for companies, we work for teams. Sometimes, as we saw this year, there are crashes between team-mates and the loss of many points for the team. Today, Ferrari put 43 in their pocket, so I think it's what we're here for."

TALKING POINT
TEAM ORDERS OR STRATEGIES?

Fact: Felipe Massa moved over to let Fernando Alonso win the German Grand Prix, round 11 of a 19-race championship. Fact: Alonso was the only Ferrari driver in with a realistic shot at the World Championship. Fact: Alonso had been almost half a second quicker than Massa all weekend and was only behind his team-mate because, off the grid, he'd had to lift off to avoid contact with Sebastian Vettel or the pitwall. Fact: a certain number of casual fans who don't have a feel for the history of F1, were affronted. Question: should anyone care?

Obviously, from the moment engineer Rob Smedley came on the radio to Massa and said, pointedly: "OK, so Fernando is faster than you... confirm you understood that message?" it was obvious what was going to happen, especially when Smedley added, after Alonso had been let by, "good lad."

Fact: the team orders situation in F1 has been a bit of a mess ever since the FIA introduced a ban on them after Ferrari's cynicism in Austria in 2002. The then Ferrari chief Jean Todt had ordered Rubens Barrichello to move over for Michael Schumacher, despite the fact that Ferrari were vastly superior to everyone, we were just a third of the way into the season, and Schumacher had won all bar one of the races. It was unnecessary.

There was an outcry then, but so what? If that's the way Ferrari wanted to operate its race team, that was up to them. It was not illegal at the time Todt did it, and Ferrari's $1m fine was for confusing the dignitaries at the podium ceremony when an embarrassed Schumacher ushered Barrichello onto the top step.

Previously, there was concern over possible collusion between Williams and McLaren at Jerez in 1997, after which the FIA brought in a rule that banned anything prejudicial to the interests of competition. They clarified, however, that it was perfectly legitimate for a team to decide that one driver was its main championship contender, but that anything outside that which affected the result of a race was unacceptable.

That all changed post-Austria 2002, however, and team orders were applied with more subtlety, using such tactics as slower pit stops, which enabled Massa to hand Kimi Räikkönen the 2007 championship while winning his home grand prix at Interlagos. However, now that Ferrari had been such poor actors, the FIA elected at a World Motor Sport Council inquiry just prior to Monza to get the Sporting Working Group to look into the team orders ban.

acceptable result, and one that would have been massively positive for the sport. A win for Massa on the anniversary of his accident would have been a great story, and proof that he was back to his best. Ferrari would have got maximum constructors' points, and the result would have demonstrated that its faith in the Brazilian, recently signed up for two more years, was justified.

Crucially, Massa would have the boost he so clearly needed, and would head into the rest of the season with his confidence fully restored, in a position to help pile up the points. And the world would know that, like Red Bull Racing and McLaren, Ferrari had drivers who were allowed to race each other and were both capable of winning.

The only negative in this situation would be seven fewer points for Alonso relative to those at the front of the World Championship, and thus a grumpy Spaniard in the camp.

However, Alonso then began to close the gap. The TV relayed a message from engineer Rob Smedley to Massa saying, "Fernando is faster than you… confirm you understood that message?"

It was an indication to let Alonso past, and in fact the discussion had been going on for some time before the world was made aware of it. Sure enough, a lap later, Massa slowed on the exit of a corner and let Fernando accelerate into the lead. Thereafter, Alonso had a comfortable run to the chequered flag. A disappointed Massa followed him home to claim second, with his feelings then all too clear on the podium.

When he was grilled after the race, Alonso made the point to the media that he had been quick all weekend, implying that we hadn't noticed. Some observers agreed that Alonso had the 'right' to the win by virtue of the fact that he had been quicker than Massa in qualifying.

Yet Sunday is what counts. Massa took his chance at the start, overcame the brief crisis after the switch to hard tyres and even managed to survive locking up a few times. Then he did what he always does best, which is just enough to bring the thing home in front. Except, this time he wasn't allowed to.

The team had to go through the charade of claiming that Massa made his own generous call based on information supplied, as if this example was reminiscent of Peter Collins handing his car to Juan Manuel Fangio at Monza in 1956.

Alonso had to field a barrage of questions, but refused to concede that the team had done anything wrong, or that his win was in anyway devalued by the way it was achieved (see 'Inside Line' sidebar).

"Look at the overall races," he said. "There are a lot of points that we win sometimes and a lot of points that we lose sometimes. As I said, today was a good day, some other races were bad days for us, disappointing but, as I said before, we need to remain focused, keep working, keep developing the car, not to be too excited when we win, not to be too down when we lose.

"In November, [we need to] try to be in the fight

OPPOSITE Nico Rosberg had a troubled race, but made sure that he was the top-ranked Mercedes driver

BELOW Sebastien Buemi's race ended on the opening lap, after his Toro Rosso team-mate, Jaime Alguersuari, ran into the back of him

BOTTOM Robert Kubica had a quiet run, finishing where he started, in seventh place

ABOVE Felipe Massa was pressed but not passed by Alonso (right) until he heeded team instructions

BELOW Felipe Massa's rueful look and Fernando Alonso's stony countenance tell it all in the post-race press conference

for the championship, not forgetting that Red Bull has so far been very dominant, not scoring many points on Sunday, or the points that they should have scored on Sunday, but remain very strong, and McLaren as well, leading both championships, so there is still a long way to go for us."

Alonso's less-than-optimum points total prior to Germany was not due to Ferrari shortcomings or errors, and it's not as if the team owed him a huge favour for letting him down. Yes, he had a technical problem in Malaysia, and yes, he had bad luck with the safety car in Valencia, although Massa came off a lot worse that day.

However, Alonso got involved in a first-lap skirmish in Australia, jumped the start in China, and totalled a car in practice in Monaco. His penalty at Silverstone, while it was made worse by the unfortunate timing of the safety car, was ultimately self-inflicted.

The really sad thing is that Ferrari is supposed to be the team steeped in passion and emotion. And we would have surely seen a lot of both had Felipe got that vital win on the anniversary of his terrible accident in Hungary in 2009.

"For sure we know that it's very important for Felipe," said Ferrari team principal Stefano Domenicali, "and I'm sure he will deserve a victory very soon. Because he has shown, you know, that he is keeping up. I would like next time to share with him the victory."

The fuss completely overshadowed the rest of the race. Vettel couldn't quite match the pace of the Ferraris, but remained in touch with Massa to take third place and valuable points. Hamilton made a good start to get up to fourth, and was still there at the chequered flag, which ensured that his championship lead remained intact.

Button dropped to sixth at the start, but managed to get ahead of Webber by staying out for a very late pit stop, which meant he led for a few laps. Webber had an oil consumption problem which forced him to ease off for the second half of the race, but he held onto sixth place.

Robert Kubica was seventh in qualifying and was in the same position at the end of the race. Contrastingly, Mercedes GP had a frustrating day, as the silver cars were off the pace, not helped by the fact that their new floors were affected by the heat of the exhausts. The final point went to Renault's Vitaly Petrov, who drove a solid race and finished ahead of Kamui Kobayashi and Rubens Barrichello.

SNAPSHOT FROM GERMANY

CLOCKWISE FROM RIGHT

The Ferrari team cheers beneath the podium, but not everyone else was so happy; a sight not seen before in F1, support for Vitaly Petrov; BMW's leading act wowed the crowds...; ...and he wasn't the only one; Lucas di Grassi wishes that his weekend would improve; the cars line up to head out for qualifying; Bruno Senna enjoys a different set of wheels; Rubens Barrichello wanted to let everyone know how he got on when he appeared on *Top Gear*; McLaren drivers Lewis Hamilton and Jenson Button hit the campsites, literally...

RACE RESULTS
GERMANY
HOCKENHEIM

Official Results © [2010]
Formula One Administration Limited,
6 Princes Gate, London, SW7 1QJ.
No reproduction without permission.
All copyright and database rights reserved.

RACE DATE July 25th
CIRCUIT LENGTH 2.842 miles
NO. OF LAPS 67
RACE DISTANCE 190.414 miles
WEATHER Sunny & dry, 21°C
TRACK TEMP 33°C
ATTENDANCE Not available
LAP RECORD Kimi Räikkönen,
1m14.917s, 138.685mph, 2004

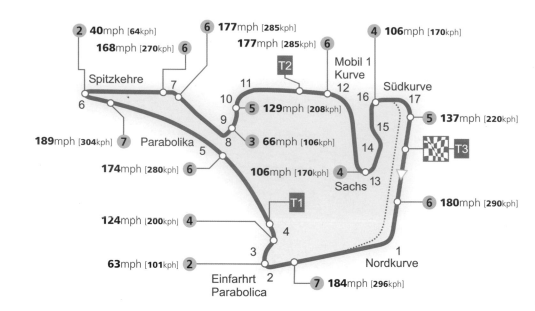

PRACTICE 1				PRACTICE 2				PRACTICE 3				QUALIFYING 1			QUALIFYING 2	
	Driver	Time	Laps		Driver	Time	Laps		Driver	Time	Laps		Driver	Time		Driver	Time
1	A Sutil	1m25.701s	20	1	F Alonso	1m16.265s	35	1	S Vettel	1m15.103s	18	1	F Alonso	1m14.808s	1	F Alonso	1m14.081s
2	F Massa	1m26.850s	27	2	S Vettel	1m16.294s	26	2	F Alonso	1m15.387s	21	2	S Vettel	1m15.152s	2	S Vettel	1m14.249s
3	J Button	1m26.936s	16	3	F Massa	1m16.438s	37	3	M Webber	1m15.708s	16	3	F Massa	1m15.216s	3	M Webber	1m14.340s
4	R Barrichello	1m26.947s	21	4	M Webber	1m16.585s	40	4	F Massa	1m15.854s	20	4	M Webber	1m15.334s	4	F Massa	1m14.478s
5	V Petrov	1m26.948s	21	5	N Rosberg	1m16.827s	32	5	N Rosberg	1m16.046s	20	5	L Hamilton	1m15.505s	5	L Hamilton	1m14.488s
6	N Rosberg	1m27.448s	20	6	M Schumacher	1m16.971s	20	6	L Hamilton	1m16.207s	13	6	R Kubica	1m15.736s	6	R Barrichello	1m14.698s
7	S Buemi	1m28.114s	31	7	L Hamilton	1m17.004s	10	7	M Schumacher	1m16.473s	16	7	J Button	1m15.823s	7	J Button	1m14.716s
8	N Hulkenberg	1m28.193s	24	8	R Kubica	1m17.009s	37	8	R Barrichello	1m16.481s	23	8	K Kobayashi	1m15.951s	8	R Kubica	1m14.835s
9	V Liuzzi	1m28.300s	19	9	R Barrichello	1m17.056s	37	9	R Kubica	1m16.646s	20	9	S Buemi	1m16.029s	9	N Hulkenberg	1m14.943s
10	P de la Rosa	1m28.486s	23	10	N Hulkenberg	1m17.204s	44	10	N Hulkenberg	1m16.743s	17	10	M Schumacher	1m16.084s	10	N Rosberg	1m15.018s
11	S Vettel	1m28.735s	21	11	K Kobayashi	1m17.336s	44	11	K Kobayashi	1m16.882s	19	11	N Rosberg	1m16.178s	11	M Schumacher	1m15.026s
12	T Glock	1m28.735s	21	12	V Petrov	1m17.547s	35	12	S Buemi	1m16.990s	21	12	A Sutil	1m16.220s	12	K Kobayashi	1m15.084s
13	R Kubica	1m28.903s	20	13	P de la Rosa	1m17.573s	39	13	J Button	1m17.037s	15	13	N Hulkenberg	1m16.387s	13	V Petrov	1m15.307s
14	M Webber	1m29.048s	13	14	A Sutil	1m17.701s	38	14	V Petrov	1m17.148s	20	14	R Barrichello	1m16.398s	14	A Sutil	1m15.467s
15	J Trulli	1m29.280s	17	15	J Button	1m17.739s	36	15	P de la Rosa	1m17.220s	19	15	P de la Rosa	1m16.450s	15	P de la Rosa	1m15.550s
16	J Alguersuari	1m29.366s	34	16	V Liuzzi	1m17.871s	33	16	J Alguersuari	1m17.341s	21	16	V Petrov	1m16.521s	16	J Alguersuari	1m15.588s
17	L Hamilton	1m29.429s	8	17	S Buemi	1m18.147s	45	17	V Liuzzi	1m17.538s	22	17	J Alguersuari	1m16.664s	17	S Buemi	1m15.974s
18	L di Grassi	1m29.500s	19	18	J Alguersuari	1m19.327s	48	18	H Kovalainen	1m19.193s	11	18	J Trulli	1m17.583s			
19	F Alonso	1m29.684s	15	19	T Glock	1m19.553s	30	19	J Trulli	1m19.607s	10	19	H Kovalainen	1m18.300s			
20	K Kobayashi	1m29.690s	17	20	J Trulli	1m20.008s	34	20	B Senna	1m20.533s	9	20	T Glock	1m18.343s			
21	F Fauzy	1m30.938s	27	21	L di Grassi	1m20.106s	31	21	S Yamamoto	1m21.538s	14	21	B Senna	1m18.592s			
22	B Senna	1m31.720s	23	22	H Kovalainen	1m20.377s	37	22	L di Grassi	1m23.444s	10	22	V Liuzzi	1m18.952s			
23	M Schumacher	1m32.450s	13	23	B Senna	1m21.988s	37	23	T Glock	1m23.873s	7	23	S Yamamoto	1m19.844s			
24	S Yamamoto	1m32.791s	26	24	S Yamamoto	1m23.066s	37	24	A Sutil	No time	2	24	L di Grassi	No time			

Best sectors – Practice			Speed trap – Practice			Best sectors – Qualifying			Speed trap – Qualifying		
Sec 1	M Webber	16.390s	1	L Hamilton	197.720mph	Sec 1	F Alonso	16.125s	1	J Button	197.285mph
Sec 2	S Vettel	35.873s	2	V Liuzzi	197.347mph	Sec 2	F Alonso	35.181s	2	L Hamilton	196.788mph
Sec 3	S Vettel	22.786s	3	J Button	195.545mph	Sec 3	S Vettel	22.298s	3	V Liuzzi	196.104mph

 Jenson Button

"I got away well, but we got to Turn 1 and Sebastian, who was fighting the Ferraris, braked early, and I had to avoid him, hit the brakes and lost three places."

 Michael Schumacher

"I had a pretty good start, then was aiming to stay out long, but changed the strategy to react to circumstances, and maybe I could have finished slightly higher."

 **Sebastian Vettel**

"I didn't stall at the start, but lost momentum and the Ferraris came by. They were a tenth quicker and it was hard to keep up, so I can be proud of third."

Felipe Massa

"This wasn't team orders: my engineer informed me what was going on, especially when I was struggling on hards: so I decided to do the best thing for the team."

Rubens Barrichello

"On the option and prime, our pace was much the same as the cars in front but, having lost track position, there wasn't enough pace differential to move ahead."

Robert Kubica

"I was fighting to pass Hamilton into Turn 2 when he braked early, and ended up losing positions to Button and Webber. After my stop, I had a battle with Michael."

 Lewis Hamilton

"I managed to make up two places. We hoped the gap would be closer than in qualifying, and it was, but we've got to make up some pace on our main rivals."

 Nico Rosberg

"Achieving eighth is damage limitation really and we were able to minimise the loss to Robert in terms of points, but it has been a struggle here."

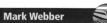 **Mark Webber**

"When I pitted, I thought Lewis might pit, but he stayed out a lap longer. It was a gamble to try and jump Lewis, but I came out in traffic and lost ground to him."

Fernando Alonso

"I was pushed against the wall by Vettel. I tried to stay close to Felipe and when he had troubles, I got past: I'm sure he was thinking of the good of the team."

 **Nico Hulkenberg**

"The race was defined by the start, which wasn't good, and the places lost couldn't be recovered. I ran a long first stint on options, but it was hard to make progress."

Vitaly Petrov

"This was an interesting race and I'm happy to have scored my first point in dry conditions – especially as I thought I'd come 11th, so it was an even better surprise."

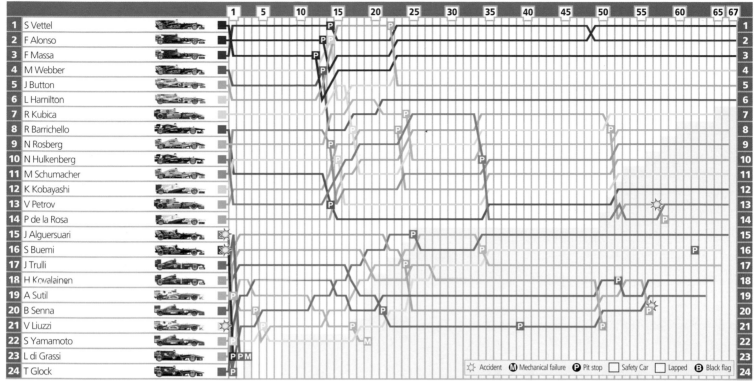

		1	5	10	15	20	25	30	35	40	45	50	55	60	65 67	
1	S Vettel															1
2	F Alonso															2
3	F Massa															3
4	M Webber															4
5	J Button															5
6	L Hamilton															6
7	R Kubica															7
8	R Barrichello															8
9	N Rosberg															9
10	N Hulkenberg															10
11	M Schumacher															11
12	K Kobayashi															12
13	V Petrov															13
14	P de la Rosa															14
15	J Alguersuari															15
16	S Buemi															16
17	J Trulli															17
18	H Kovalainen															18
19	A Sutil															19
20	B Senna															20
21	V Liuzzi															21
22	S Yamamoto															22
23	L di Grassi															23
24	T Glock															24

☆ Accident ⓜ Mechanical failure ⓟ Pit stop ☐ Safety Car ☐ Lapped ⓑ Black flag

QUALIFYING 3

	Driver	Time
1	S Vettel	1m13.791s
2	F Alonso	1m13.793s
3	F Massa	1m14.290s
4	M Webber	1m14.347s
5	J Button	1m14.427s
6	L Hamilton	1m14.566s
7	R Kubica	1m15.079s
8	R Barrichello	1m15.109s
9	N Rosberg	1m15.179s
10	N Hulkenberg	1m15.339s

GRID

	Driver	Time
1	S Vettel	1m13.791s
2	F Alonso	1m13.793s
3	F Massa	1m14.290s
4	M Webber	1m14.347s
5	J Button	1m14.427s
6	L Hamilton	1m14.566s
7	R Kubica	1m15.079s
8	R Barrichello	1m15.109s
9	N Rosberg	1m15.179s
10	N Hulkenberg	1m15.339s
11	M Schumacher	1m15.026s
12	K Kobayashi	1m15.084s
13	V Petrov	1m15.307s
14	P de la Rosa	1m15.550s
15	J Alguersuari	1m15.588s
16	S Buemi	1m15.974s
17	J Trulli	1m17.583s
18	H Kovalainen	1m18.300s
19*	A Sutil	1m15.467s
20	B Senna	1m18.592s
21	V Liuzzi	1m18.952s
22	S Yamamoto	1m19.844s
23*	L di Grassi	No time
24*	T Glock	1m18.343s

* 5-place grid penalty for gearbox change

RACE

	Driver	Car	Laps	Time	Avg. mph	Fastest	Stops
1	F Alonso	Ferrari F10	67	1h27m38.864s	130.356	1m15.880s	1
2	F Massa	Ferrari F10	67	1h27m43.060s	130.246	1m16.097s	1
3	S Vettel	Red Bull-Renault RB6	67	1h27m43.985s	130.223	1m15.824s	1
4	L Hamilton	McLaren-Mercedes MP4-25	67	1h28m05.760s	129.686	1m16.503s	1
5	J Button	McLaren-Mercedes MP4-25	67	1h28m08.346s	129.623	1m16.451s	1
6	M Webber	Red Bull-Renault RB6	67	1h28m22.470s	129.278	1m16.678s	1
7	R Kubica	Renault R30	66	1h27m40.899s	128.354	1m17.166s	1
8	N Rosberg	Mercedes MGP W01	66	1h27m47.541s	128.192	1m16.609s	1
9	M Schumacher	Mercedes MGP W01	66	1h27m50.738s	128.115	1m17.088s	1
10	V Petrov	Renault R30	66	1h27m55.114s	128.008	1m17.198s	1
11	K Kobayashi	BMW Sauber-Ferrari C29	66	1h27m56.373s	127.978	1m17.100s	1
12	R Barrichello	Williams-Cosworth FW32	66	1h27m58.027s	127.938	1m17.029s	1
13	N Hulkenberg	Williams-Cosworth FW32	66	1h27m58.676s	127.922	1m16.836s	1
14	P de la Rosa	BMW Sauber-Ferrari C29	66	1h28m22.985s	127.336	1m16.527s	2
15	J Alguersuari	Toro Rosso-Ferrari STR5	66	1h28m40.457s	126.917	1m16.971s	2
16	V Liuzzi	Force India-Mercedes VJM03	65	1h27m52.031s	126.143	1m16.596s	3
17	A Sutil	Force India-Mercedes VJM03	65	1h28m02.328s	125.897	1m16.687s	3
18	T Glock	Virgin-Cosworth VR-01	64	1h28m22.856s	123.480	1m18.211s	1
19	B Senna	HRT-Cosworth F110	63	1h28m10.760s	121.829	1m20.861s	2
R	H Kovalainen	Lotus-Cosworth T127	56	Collision	-	1m20.664s	1
R	L di Grassi	Virgin-Cosworth VR-01	50	Spun off	-	1m20.703s	0
R	S Yamamoto	HRT-Cosworth VR-01	19	Gearbox	-	1m23.541s	1
R	J Trulli	Lotus-Cosworth T127	3	Gearbox	-	2m14.452s	1
R	S Buemi	Toro Rosso-Ferrari STR5	1	Collision	-	-	0

CHAMPIONSHIP

	Driver	Pts
1	L Hamilton	157
2	J Button	143
3	M Webber	136
4	S Vettel	136
5	F Alonso	123
6	N Rosberg	94
7	R Kubica	89
8	F Massa	85
9	M Schumacher	38
10	A Sutil	35
11	R Barrichello	29
12	K Kobayashi	15
13	V Liuzzi	12
14	V Petrov	7
15	S Buemi	7
16	J Alguersuari	3
17	N Hulkenberg	2

	Constructor	Pts
1	McLaren-Mercedes	300
2	Red Bull-Renault	272
3	Ferrari	208
4	Mercedes	132
5	Renault	96
6	Force India-Mercedes	47
7	Williams-Cosworth	31
8	BMW Sauber-Ferrari	15
9	Toro Rosso-Ferrari	10

Fastest lap
S Vettel 1m15.824s
(134.940mph) on lap 67

Fastest speed trap
J Button 198.528mph
Slowest speed trap
L di Grassi 188.151mph

Fastest pit stop
1	N Rosberg	17.992s
2	M Schumacher	18.052s
3	M Webber	18.060s

Adrian Sutil
"There was confusion, as Tonio had radioed that he was coming in for a front-wing change and, as we both arrived at the same time, the tyre sets got mixed up."

Jarno Trulli
"When we came to the hairpin on lap 1, I was braking mid-corner and my team-mate came from a long way back and ended up driving onto the top of my car."

Sakon Yamamoto
"I made a very good start and then suddenly lost the gearbox and sadly that was it. We tried to reset it in the pit and I went out again, but it didn't work."

Pedro de la Rosa
"The race weekend was better than Silverstone and I got more experience with the car. We tried adjustments on the set-up that will help us for future races."

Timo Glock
"After my late stop I was on fresh tyres, but the backmarkers were a serious problem, and I crashed into one who'd opened the door for Rubens but closed it again."

"I had a really good start and overtook both HRTs in Turn 1, but in Turn 2 I lost everything again. It felt as if someone pushed me and I ran wide and was last again."

Vitantonio Liuzzi
"I had contact on lap 1 and thought I'd damaged the front wing, so I pitted, but there was a mix-up in the stop with the tyres so I had to come back in again."

Nico Rosberg
"I was on the inside into Turn 6 and braked well, but the cars ahead slowed more than normal. I braked again, but it wasn't enough and I hit Sebastien."

Heikki Kovalainen
"It was one of those things that can happen when you're letting cars past. I thought I was letting the Williams by, and did not see the Sauber so closed the door."

Bruno Senna
"We were having a good race and were very competitive, but then I had a slow puncture and had to do an unplanned pit stop that ended our challenge."

Kamui Kobayashi
"I tried to pass Schumacher, who was held up by a backmarker. We ended up fighting on the straight and this isn't a strength of our car. Later, I tried to fight Petrov."

Lucas di Grassi
"I gained four places on lap 1 and ran with Heikki. I was confident I could beat Lotus after the switch to the option, but I hit a bump that damaged the suspension."

FORMULA 1 ENI
MAGYAR NAGYDÍJ 2010
BUDAPEST

A MATTER OF TIME

The outcome of this race was as unpredictable
as so many were in 2010, and it was Sebastian
Vettel who turned potential victory into abject
disappointment as Mark Webber triumphed

M ark Webber scored his fourth win of the season,
but only after a silly misjudgement under a safety-
car situation tripped up his Red Bull Racing team-mate
Sebastian Vettel.

By the end of the grand prix, the grateful Australian
driver claimed the World Championship lead heading
into the summer break and, with five drivers separated
by just 20 points – the equivalent of eight points in 'old
money' – things were starting to look really interesting.

The fuss over the Ferrari team orders affair in Germany
had barely died down by the time the teams arrived
in Budapest just four days later. However, it was business
as usual on the track, as Vettel made it four poles in
a row. Indeed, the margin of superiority was so huge
relative to the close competition in the previous event,
that it seemed barely credible so little time had passed.

Vettel set the fastest-ever qualifying lap here, and
then did another time that was also good enough for
pole. Webber looked fast in the early part of qualifying,
but couldn't match his team-mate when it mattered.
In the end, he was a not insignificant 0.4s off, and like
Vettel, didn't improve on his second lap.

As expected, Ferrari led the chase, but there was a
large margin to the Red Bulls. Fernando Alonso qualified

INSIDE LINE
RUBENS BARRICHELLO

WILLIAMS DRIVER

"Michael had already been closing the door, but on the lap I passed him he was slow out of the final corner and I got a run on him. He was watching his mirrors and he knew where I was.

I like fair battles, but that was horrible. He should have been black-flagged. It was a go-kart manoeuvre. If he wants to get to heaven before I do, then please do... But it was one of the most enjoyable overtakes of my career.

Spa will be my 300th grand prix, which is quite a milestone and I'm pleased I'm going to make it! I feel great about it, as it's a privilege to be involved in F1 for that time. But I still feel powerful. When I was in F1 five years I always felt that the holidays weren't long enough. But now, after one week of the summer break I wanted to be driving the car again. I was getting up at 4am to work out and get back on European time. I think sometimes my wife worries that I am going to drive forever...

Someone pointed out that I've competed in a third of all the World Championship races, which is quite impressive! I don't regret anything. You might say 'you didn't win the championship yet'. Yeah, I didn't. But the reason I'm still working in F1 is that I still aim to be champion. You would never have said that with a Honda in 2008 I would finish on a podium, but I did!

People say I had a bad time at Ferrari... but I had a great time with everyone. Obviously, I fought to have the same treatment, and the day that I felt 'right, they're not going to give me that' was the day I decided to leave. However, even in those years, when the car was better than the others, I still had a chance to win, even with Michael there. I had so much fun and pleasure when I raced for Jordan and Stewart, but the cars weren't good enough to win grands prix.

Incidents like the one with Michael don't make you think about doing something safer. Honestly, I saw the wall for the first time on TV. In the car, my measure was Michael and not the wall. I saw that he was coming and coming and coming, but I would never have backed off. I didn't feel any fear because I was just going to make that happen. I didn't care what was coming."

third and at least had the benefit of starting on the clean side of the track, while Felipe Massa was alongside him in fourth. After the team struggled from the start of practice, Lewis Hamilton achieved McLaren's stated target by qualifying fifth, but Jenson Button had a terrible time, just missing out on getting out of Q2 and ending up 11th on the grid.

Vettel rocketed away at the start, while Webber had a difficult time off the dirty side of the front row and was beaten away by Alonso. The Ferrari couldn't match the pace of the leader, so Webber found himself stuck behind the Spaniard, unable to do anything about his flying team-mate up ahead.

The race appeared to have settled into a procession, when a safety car was dispatched on lap 15 due to debris left behind by the Force India of Vitantonio Liuzzi. A dramatic series of events would then turn the race on its head. Vettel led the charge into the pits – he had to cut across the pit entry kerbing as the call came so late – but Red Bull left Webber out. That seemed like a strange idea at the time, but the logic soon became apparent.

Vettel was happy with the way things were going at this point: "The start was fine. It was a long way to the first corner, so Fernando got the tow but I was able to defend. After that, I had a very good first stint in which I could use my speed.

"Then, with the safety car it was a very late call, so I just managed to pit, and after that usually it would be an easy race from there, as we knew we had the pace advantage."

The rest of the field followed Vettel into the tight confines of the pitlane, and chaos ensued. Due to a mistake by the crew, Robert Kubica was signalled to leave just as Adrian Sutil pulled across his bows to enter his own pit box. The pair made heavy contact, and the Force India was out on the spot. Kubica continued after a check for damage, but he was soon hit with a penalty, and later retired.

At the same time, there was more drama when the right-rear wheel wasn't fitted properly on Nico Rosberg's car. The Mercedes jack man saw a waved hand, but rather than being the signal that all was OK, it was someone trying to solve the problem. The jack went down, the green light went on, and Rosberg got the signal to go. As he accelerated away, the wheel parted company with the car, before bouncing right through the Sauber pit and striking a Williams mechanic, who fortunately wasn't seriously hurt. Rosberg had to retire at the end of the pitlane. Mercedes was duly fined $50,000.

Out on the track, Webber was at the head of

OPPOSITE Fernando Alonso had no answer to the pace of the Red Bulls, but came away with second

ABOVE Jaime Alguersuari's race was a short one as his engine blew on the opening lap

BELOW Jenson Button made a poor start and found himself battling with Force India's Vitantonio Liuzzi

When Michael Schumacher and Rubens Barrichello, team-mates for six years at Ferrari, encountered each other in the closing laps at Hungaroring, Michael was on a set of medium-compound Bridgestones that had done 50 laps. Relatively gripless, he was lapping in the high 1:25s.

Rubens, meanwhile, had started on the primes in a move that Williams conceded hadn't worked well for them. Having run those primes to lap 55, he was on a brand new set of supersofts when he caught the Mercedes. He was flying and ultimately set a fastest lap only 0.16s slower than race winner Mark Webber's.

Rubens and Michael had 560 grands prix between them and a combined age of 80, and there was a single point on the table for 10th place. But it was also about those six long years at Ferrari, Austria 2002, that uncompromising last-lap pass by Michael at Monaco, and the frustration of having to play second fiddle. Here, with no orders, Barrichello was going to have that last point.

But, so long as Schumacher could get out of the last turn and rely on his Mercedes horses down the straight, he could hang on. When he was slow out of the final corner though, we got the horror show, Michael all but putting Rubens into the pit wall at nearly 200mph. The margins were tiny and, given the speed, you shuddered at the potential consequences of wheel-over-wheel contact.

The ex-driver in the stewarding hot seat was Derek Warwick. "Throwing the black flag would have shown a better example to our young drivers but, by the time we got the video evidence, we ran out of time," he explained.

Schumacher apologised for the manoeuvre via his German website and then sent Rubens a text at Spa, but Warwick hadn't been impressed by the seven-time champion's explanation, when he claimed that his move to the right had been an attempt to force Barrichello to pass him on the left.

"It was kind of disappointing how Michael handled it," said Warwick, "and we had no option but to give him a 10-place grid penalty for Spa. You could disqualify him from the next grand prix, two grands prix, whatever, but we felt that grid penalty effectively put him out of the race at Spa. Hopefully he'll learn from that and remember that the new stewards will not tolerate that sort of driving."

It was good to see something done to address intimidatory driving that was seriously dangerous. However, the widespread feeling was still that Schumacher escaped lightly.

the queue, in front of Vettel, and so Red Bull's strategy became clear. By not pitting with Vettel, Webber had avoided losing ground by being stacked behind his team-mate. Now, with a clear track, he'd be able to use his superior pace to pull away from third-placed Alonso. The intention was that Webber would come back out in second place after making his late compulsory pit stop for prime tyres, still behind Vettel, but safely ahead of the Ferrari.

The plan worked out better for Webber than he expected as, after the restart, the stewards decreed that Vettel had dropped too far behind his team-mate when they were running behind the safety car.

The rules state clearly that a driver has to stay within 10 lengths of the car ahead, which the FIA equates to around 50 metres. Officials in race control could see that Vettel had dropped more than that distance behind. On checking GPS recordings before confirming the penalty, the gap was determined to be as much 110 metres, or 22 lengths.

By dropping so far back, Vettel had given Webber a much bigger advantage over Alonso and his other pursuers, so it did actually make a difference.

Vettel had no idea that he had broken the rules and expressed his displeasure when he got the news of a drive-through penalty. "I didn't understand what was going on and why I was penalised," he said. "It was a question mark for me. I didn't understand at the time. Now, after the race, people told me what happened.

"At the restart I was sleeping. I was probably relying too much on the radio, but somewhere in the first stint I lost the radio connection and didn't hear anything. I saw the safety-car boards and was waiting for instruction when the safety car would wihdraw. I didn't see the lights.

"Usually the leader, when he does the restart, tries to drop back and then dictates the pace. Mark was very close and I was warming up my car. I was sure we had another lap, so I didn't really understand. Then I saw Mark and the safety car at the second-last corner, with quite a big gap to myself.

"I noticed the safety car going into the pits, so that must be the restart and I was caught out, so I lost momentum and lost a lot in the first couple of laps which was not the intention. Then I got the drive-through. Pretty unlucky..."

Meanwhile, Webber put in some great laps as he stayed out for an amazing 43 laps on the option tyres

OPPOSITE TOP Sebastian Vettel drives into the pits for his drive-through penalty

OPPOSITE BOTTOM Polish flags were waving for Robert Kubica, but Nico Hulkenberg had little time to notice as he swept to sixth place

ABOVE Vitaly Petrov had scored just twice in the first 11 races, then everything went right and he collected fifth place in Hungary

on which he'd started. Sure enough, he opened up more than enough of a gap to stay safely in front of Alonso when he finally pitted, and had no problems bringing the car home in front.

"We knew that we needed around 20 seconds over Alonso," Webber explained. "But I told the guys 'let's get a bit more of a buffer to make sure that the guys have less pressure in the pit stop'. They were on it anyway, though. The front-left tyre was completely finished and it was pretty difficult with the grip that we had finishing that stint.

"In the end, I knew once I got the prime tyres on, these guys had already done 20-odd laps on theirs and the race was pretty much in the bag. I knew that Seb had some difficulties on the restart and it was a bit of a gift today for me."

Vettel spent the second half of the race chasing Alonso hard, but was never really in a position to pass, and thus had to settle for a frustrated third place.

Massa had a relatively quiet run to fourth place in the wake of the previous week's controversy. Hamilton should have been fifth, but he stopped with a transmission problem early on, thus losing his championship lead to Webber after his second retirement of the season.

Instead, a surprise fifth went to Renault's Vitaly Petrov after a great effort by the Russian rookie, who had outperformed Kubica for most of the weekend. Enjoying his best run to date, Nico Hulkenberg took sixth, ahead of Pedro de la Rosa. Title contender Jenson Button could salvage only eighth after making a bad start from 11th, while Kamui Kobayashi was ninth.

If all the safety-car-related action wasn't enough, there was more major drama towards the end when Rubens Barrichello relieved Michael Schumacher of a humble 10th place. When the Brazilian took a run on him on the pit straight, the former World Champion swept over to the right, all but putting Barrichello into the pit wall. Arguably it was only the fact that the two most experienced drivers in the field were involved in this crazy moment that ensured contact was avoided, and they made it to the end of the race in one piece.

"I have two little mirrors from where I try to judge the situation," said Schumacher. "As a driver, you have the ability to change the line once. That's what I was driving to. Obviously, there was space enough to go through. We didn't touch, so I guess I just left enough space for him to come through..."

Barrichello was furious and, after the race, Schumacher was handed a 10-place grid penalty for the next event at Spa-Francorchamps. His comeback season was going from bad to worse...

LEFT TOP Pedro de la Rosa enjoyed the best run of his season to finish in seventh place

LEFT BOTTOM Mark Webber and Fernando Alonso showed their delight on the podium, but Sebastian Vettel was less than happy

SNAPSHOT FROM
HUNGARY

CLOCKWISE FROM RIGHT Sebastian Vettel was in dominant form, until the race...; a track sweeper, Hungarian style; the grid girls were as pretty as ever; Timo Glock sports yet another helmet livery; Sauber celebrated the team's 300th appearance; racing at the Hungaroring is always thirsty work; happiness at a pit stop well done; happiness in the form of a bar of chocolate; Ferrari flags are still the most popular in the grandstands; Heikki Kovalainen's Lotus claimed 14th

RACE RESULTS
HUNGARY
HUNGARORING

Official Results © [2010]
Formula One Administration Limited,
6 Princes Gate, London, SW7 1QJ.
No reproduction without permission.
All copyright and database rights reserved.

RACE DATE August 1st
CIRCUIT LENGTH 2.722 miles
NO. OF LAPS 70
RACE DISTANCE 190.540 miles
WEATHER Hot & sunny, 28°C
TRACK TEMP 46°C
ATTENDANCE 182,000
LAP RECORD Michael Schumacher,
1m19.071s, 123.828mph, 2004

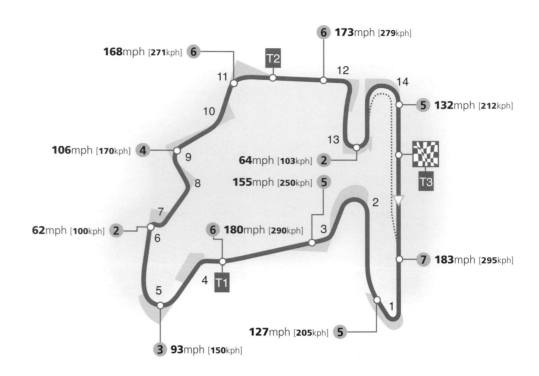

PRACTICE 1				PRACTICE 2				PRACTICE 3				QUALIFYING 1			QUALIFYING 2	
	Driver	Time	Laps		Driver	Time	Laps		Driver	Time	Laps		Driver	Time		Driver	Time
1	S Vettel	1m20.976s	29	1	S Vettel	1m20.087s	33	1	M Webber	1m19.574s	17	1	S Vettel	1m20.417s	1	M Webber	1m19.531s
2	M Webber	1m21.106s	27	2	F Alonso	1m20.584s	34	2	S Vettel	1m20.058s	15	2	M Webber	1m21.132s	2	S Vettel	1m19.573s
3	R Kubica	1m22.072s	21	3	M Webber	1m20.597s	36	3	F Alonso	1m20.724s	19	3	R Kubica	1m21.159s	3	F Alonso	1m20.237s
4	J Button	1m22.444s	17	4	F Massa	1m20.986s	33	4	R Kubica	1m21.066s	19	4	N Rosberg	1m21.212s	4	V Petrov	1m20.797s
5	R Barrichello	1m22.601s	25	5	V Petrov	1m21.195s	33	5	F Massa	1m21.264s	16	5	F Alonso	1m21.278s	5	N Rosberg	1m20.811s
6	P de la Rosa	1m22.764s	24	6	L Hamilton	1m21.308s	30	6	L Hamilton	1m21.376s	17	6	F Massa	1m21.299s	6	F Massa	1m20.857s
7	F Alonso	1m22.772s	25	7	R Kubica	1m21.375s	37	7	V Petrov	1m21.399s	15	7	J Button	1m21.422s	7	R Kubica	1m20.867s
8	N Rosberg	1m22.777s	25	8	N Hulkenberg	1m21.623s	41	8	N Rosberg	1m21.422s	18	8	L Hamilton	1m21.455s	8	L Hamilton	1m20.877s
9	M Schumacher	1m22.792s	26	9	J Button	1m21.730s	33	9	J Button	1m21.473s	18	9	R Barrichello	1m21.478s	9	P de la Rosa	1m21.273s
10	N Hulkenberg	1m22.966s	25	10	M Schumacher	1m21.773s	31	10	N Hulkenberg	1m21.513s	18	10	V Petrov	1m21.558s	10	N Hulkenberg	1m21.275s
11	A Sutil	1m23.003s	19	11	P de la Rosa	1m21.809s	38	11	R Barrichello	1m21.705s	19	11	N Hulkenberg	1m21.598s	11	J Button	1m21.292s
12	F Massa	1m23.007s	26	12	R Barrichello	1m21.844s	36	12	M Schumacher	1m21.939s	15	12	V Liuzzi	1m21.789s	12	R Barrichello	1m21.331s
13	V Petrov	1m23.249s	24	13	N Rosberg	1m22.039s	28	13	P de la Rosa	1m22.151s	21	13	M Schumacher	1m21.840s	13	A Sutil	1m21.517s
14	K Kobayashi	1m23.327s	23	14	K Kobayashi	1m22.212s	37	14	K Kobayashi	1m22.337s	20	14	P de la Rosa	1m21.891s	14	M Schumacher	1m21.630s
15	P di Resta	1m23.520s	19	15	J Alguersuari	1m22.469s	43	15	J Alguersuari	1m22.427s	19	15	J Alguersuari	1m21.978s	15	S Buemi	1m21.897s
16	S Buemi	1m23.780s	22	16	A Sutil	1m22.507s	22	16	S Buemi	1m22.508s	22	16	S Buemi	1m21.982s	16	V Liuzzi	1m21.927s
17	J Alguersuari	1m23.868s	28	17	S Buemi	1m22.602s	38	17	A Sutil	1m22.918s	14	17	A Sutil	1m22.080s	17	J Alguersuari	1m21.998s
18	L Hamilton	1m24.075s	15	18	V Liuzzi	1m23.138s	36	18	V Liuzzi	1m23.708s	8	18	K Kobayashi	1m22.222s			
19	J Trulli	1m25.032s	22	19	J Trulli	1m24.553s	37	19	L di Grassi	1m24.547s	19	19	T Glock	1m24.050s			
20	H Kovalainen	1m25.210s	23	20	T Glock	1m25.376s	35	20	J Trulli	1m24.576s	22	20	H Kovalainen	1m24.120s			
21	T Glock	1m25.990s	21	21	L di Grassi	1m25.669s	32	21	H Kovalainen	1m24.623s	22	21	J Trulli	1m24.199s			
22	L di Grassi	1m26.686s	17	22	B Senna	1m26.745s	34	22	T Glock	1m24.805s	17	22	L di Grassi	1m25.118s			
23	B Senna	1m26.990s	34	23	S Yamamoto	1m26.798s	32	23	B Senna	1m26.479s	21	23	B Senna	1m26.391s			
24	S Yamamoto	1m28.157s	24	24	H Kovalainen	1m27.705s	5	24	S Yamamoto	1m27.176s	21	24	S Yamamoto	1m26.453s			

Best sectors – Practice			Speed trap – Practice			Best sectors – Qualifying			Speed trap – Qualifying		
Sec 1	M Webber	29.124s	1	A Sutil	186.349mph	Sec 1	S Vettel	28.803s	1	V Liuzzi	182.993mph
Sec 2	M Webber	27.949s	2	J Button	184.112mph	Sec 2	S Vettel	27.521s	2	A Sutil	182.931mph
Sec 3	M Webber	22.447s	3	P di Resta	182.248mph	Sec 3	S Vettel	22.312s	3	N Hulkenberg	180.197mph

Jenson Button
"I got a good start, but went four abreast into Turn 1 and got stuck on the outside, losing about four or five places. So, from that position, eighth wasn't too bad."

Michael Schumacher
"Regarding the manoeuvre with Rubens, I indicated pretty early that I would move towards the inside. It was a hard fight, and this is what we're here for."

Sebastian Vettel
"Mark was close to the safety car, so I thought we had another lap. Then I saw it come in and was caught out. I lost a lot of momentum. Then I got the drive-through."

Felipe Massa
"I didn't have much grip on the dirty side of the track at the start. The decision to pit under the safety car was right: we couldn't have done the same as Webber."

Rubens Barrichello
"Taking the chance to start on primes left us liable to a safety car. It came too early for the option, so I had to stay out until we found a point to make it work."

Robert Kubica
"I was stuck behind Rosberg until the safety car came out and we pitted. That's when I had the crash with Sutil. I saw the lollipop go up and started to go but we hit."

Lewis Hamilton
"I was accelerating out of Turn 1 when I felt a vibration then a loss of drive. I thought it was a driveshaft failure, but it appears that it was a gearbox problem."

Nico Rosberg
"I didn't have a good start as I was on the dirty side. I needed to have a good stop to stay ahead of Kubica, but I had the problem with the right-rear wheel."

Mark Webber
"When the safety car came out and I was told to stay out, I hoped Fernando would pit. When I saw him go in, I settled on the soft and worked on getting a 20s lead."

Fernando Alonso
"Luck owed us a lot and it made a payment. When the safety car came in, it was vital not to make mistakes. After that, it wasn't easy fighting Vettel for 30 laps."

Nico Hulkenberg
"I was in the right place to make a gain from the safety car, but the car had good pace and I didn't make any mistakes. The result is a good way to go into the break."

Vitaly Petrov
"I feel great, as I made a good start and passed Rosberg and Hamilton into Turn 1. After that, I didn't try and block Lewis, as I had a problem with tyre warm-up."

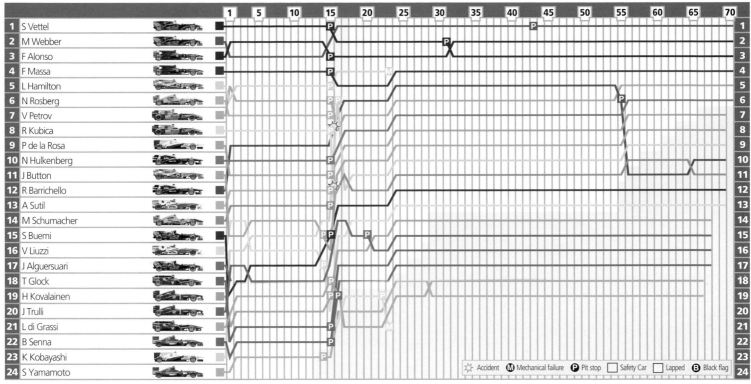

	Driver								
1	S Vettel								
2	M Webber								
3	F Alonso								
4	F Massa								
5	L Hamilton								
6	N Rosberg								
7	V Petrov								
8	R Kubica								
9	P de la Rosa								
10	N Hulkenberg								
11	J Button								
12	R Barrichello								
13	A Sutil								
14	M Schumacher								
15	S Buemi								
16	V Liuzzi								
17	J Alguersuari								
18	T Glock								
19	H Kovalainen								
20	J Trulli								
21	L di Grassi								
22	B Senna								
23	K Kobayashi								
24	S Yamamoto								

☆ Accident Ⓜ Mechanical failure Ⓟ Pit stop ☐ Safety Car ☐ Lapped Ⓑ Black flag

QUALIFYING 3

	Driver	Time
1	S Vettel	1m18.773s
2	M Webber	1m19.184s
3	F Alonso	1m19.987s
4	F Massa	1m20.331s
5	L Hamilton	1m20.499s
6	N Rosberg	1m21.082s
7	V Petrov	1m21.229s
8	R Kubica	1m21.328s
9	P de la Rosa	1m21.411s
10	N Hulkenberg	1m21.710s

GRID

	Driver	Time
1	S Vettel	1m18.773s
2	M Webber	1m19.184s
3	F Alonso	1m19.987s
4	F Massa	1m20.331s
5	L Hamilton	1m20.499s
6	N Rosberg	1m21.082s
7	V Petrov	1m21.229s
8	R Kubica	1m21.328s
9	P de la Rosa	1m21.411s
10	N Hulkenberg	1m21.710s
11	J Button	1m21.292s
12	R Barrichello	1m21.331s
13	A Sutil	1m21.517s
14	M Schumacher	1m21.630s
15	S Buemi	1m21.897s
16	V Liuzzi	1m21.927s
17	J Alguersuari	1m21.998s
18	T Glock	1m24.050s
19	H Kovalainen	1m24.120s
20	J Trulli	1m24.199s
21	L di Grassi	1m25.118s
22	B Senna	1m26.391s
23*	K Kobayashi	1m22.222s
24	S Yamamoto	1m26.453s

*5-place grid penalty for failing to stop for weighing at end of Q1

RACE

	Driver	Car	Laps	Time	Avg. mph	Fastest	Stops
1	M Webber	Red Bull-Renault RB6	70	1h41m05.571s	113.083	1m22.651s	1
2	F Alonso	Ferrari F10	70	1h41m23.392s	112.751	1m23.195s	1
3	S Vettel	Red Bull-Renault RB6	70	1h41m24.823s	112.725	1m22.362s	2
4	F Massa	Ferrari F10	70	1h41m33.045s	112.572	1m23.329s	1
5	V Petrov	Renault R30	70	1h42m18.763s	111.734	1m23.799s	1
6	N Hulkenberg	Williams-Cosworth FW32	70	1h42m22.294s	111.670	1m24.204s	1
7	P de la Rosa	BMW Sauber-Ferrari C29	69	1h41m06.407s	111.451	1m24.342s	1
8	J Button	McLaren-Mercedes MP4-25	69	1h41m07.854s	111.425	1m24.205s	1
9	K Kobayashi	BMW Sauber-Ferrari C29	69	1h41m08.856s	111.406	1m24.282s	1
10	R Barrichello	Williams-Cosworth FW32	69	1h41m10.638s	111.374	1m22.811s	1
11	M Schumacher	Mercedes MGP W01	69	1h41m30.110s	111.018	1m25.372s	1
12	S Buemi	Toro Rosso-Ferrari STR5	69	1h41m36.709s	110.897	1m25.449s	1
13	V Liuzzi	Force India-Mercedes VJM03	69	1h41m37.358s	110.885	1m25.358s	1
14	H Kovalainen	Lotus-Cosworth T127	67	1h41m07.636s	108.199	1m27.457s	1
15	J Trulli	Lotus-Cosworth T127	67	1h41m08.524s	108.182	1m27.429s	1
16	T Glock	Virgin-Cosworth VR-01	67	1h41m35.185s	107.710	1m27.674s	1
17	B Senna	HRT-Cosworth F110	67	1h42m04.467s	107.194	1m28.093s	1
18	L di Grassi	Virgin-Cosworth VR-01	66	1h42m03.173s	105.617	1m27.287s	2
19	S Yamamoto	HRT-Cosworth F110	66	1h42m33.460s	105.097	1m29.278s	1
R	L Hamilton	McLaren-Mercedes MP4-25	23	Gearbox	-	1m26.258s	1
R	R Kubica	Renault R30	23	Crash damage	-	1m26.825s	2
R	N Rosberg	Mercedes MGP W01	15	Wheel	-	1m27.954s	1
R	A Sutil	Force India-Mercedes VJM03	15	Collision	-	1m28.177s	0
R	J Alguersuari	Toro Rosso-Ferrari STR5	1	Engine	-	-	0

CHAMPIONSHIP

	Driver	Pts
1	M Webber	161
2	L Hamilton	157
3	S Vettel	151
4	J Button	147
5	F Alonso	141
6	F Massa	97
7	N Rosberg	94
8	R Kubica	89
9	M Schumacher	38
10	A Sutil	35
11	R Barrichello	30
12	V Petrov	17
13	K Kobayashi	17
14	V Liuzzi	12
15	N Hulkenberg	10
16	S Buemi	7
17	P de la Rosa	6
18	J Alguersuari	3

	Constructor	Pts
1	Red Bull-Renault	312
2	McLaren-Mercedes	304
3	Ferrari	238
4	Mercedes	132
5	Renault	106
6	Force India-Mercedes	47
7	Williams-Cosworth	40
8	BMW Sauber-Ferrari	23
9	Toro Rosso-Ferrari	10

Fastest lap
S Vettel 1m22.362s
(118.987mph) on lap 70

Fastest speed trap
V Liuzzi 182.372mph
Slowest speed trap
J Alguersuari 162.364mph

Fastest pit stop
1 J Button 20.682s
2 M Webber 20.688s
3 S Vettel 20.700s

Adrian Sutil
"I made up two places and was behind de la Rosa. Then the safety car came out and I pitted. I was driving into my area when the Renault came out in front of me."

[Sebastian Buemi]
"Michael pushed me left on the way to Turn 1 and I had to hit the brakes. Then I had to fight back as I was behind a Lotus, although I was able to pass Trulli easily."

Jarno Trulli
"Once I got ahead of Timo, it was easy staying in front. I lost out to Heikki in the strategy call in the safety-car period, but that was in the best interests of the team."

Sakon Yamamoto
"We decided to have a different strategy, as we started on prime tyres. This was good because we could get different data, which we can use for the next races."

Pedro de la Rosa
"After the start, it was hard for me, but the safety car came out at a good time and the team did well calling me in. After my stop, it was about keeping position."

Timo Glock
"I took the wrong line into Turn 1 and lost out. When the safety car came out, I queued behind Lucas. Then I was behind Kovalainen, but Trulli came out in front."

Vitantonio Liuzzi
"Starting from that far back, it's hard to make up places. I lost a piece of front wing at Turn 1. Then I had to come in for a change, which dropped me back."

[Jaime Alguersuari]
"I'm not sure what the problem was, as I saw no alarms on my dash. I felt that I was beginning to lose torque and power and the pit wall told me to stop the car."

Heikki Kovalainen
"I dropped a few places at the start, but when the safety car came in I was brought straight in to pit and it worked out well, as I jumped a couple of guys ahead."

Bruno Senna
"It was a hard race and to race with the other teams was very difficult. But in the end, both cars finished the race and I want to thank the team for a good job."

Kamui Kobayashi
"My start was good. Then, after the safety-car period, it was vital that I passed Michael, as otherwise Rubens would have caught me before the end."

Lucas di Grassi
"I had a good first lap. When the safety car came out, we decided to pit, but there was a problem with one of the wheels and I had to come in again on the next lap."

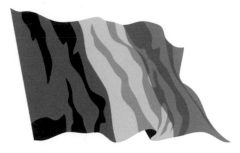

2010 FORMULA 1
BELGIAN GRAND PRIX
SPA-FRANCORCHAMPS

TURNING POINT

Lewis Hamilton took the World Championship lead after a superb victory in the Belgian GP, the McLaren man coming out on top on a day when three of his title rivals failed to score any points

Hamilton enjoyed a dose of luck when, having initially stayed out on slicks in a late shower, he managed to steer himself away from the tyre wall and out of the gravel trap. However, other drivers made more expensive mistakes and, having twice suffered a mechanical retirement this year, few could begrudge him a bit of good fortune.

"He had a slight excursion," smiled relieved McLaren team principal Martin Whitmarsh, "which was a bit tingling for a moment... But, overall, it was a pretty commanding and impressive drive. It's pleasing for the team. Our drivers are great, but it's very easy to get it wrong, get panicked, and I think the pit-wall crew has done a good job."

As is usual at Spa-Francorchamps, rain fell throughout the weekend. A brief shower in Q1 and another late in Q3 made qualifying exciting. It was business as usual at the front, though, as Mark Webber took pole for Red Bull Racing, but it should have been Hamilton.

Through the three practice sessions, Hamilton had been second, third and second, and he clearly had some performance up his sleeve. However, life was made difficult for the McLaren drivers in Q3

INSIDE LINE
LEWIS HAMILTON
McLAREN DRIVER

"That was a great weekend and a very tough race. I was praying for a race that went smoothly, but when it started to rain so early you lose temperature in the tyres and don't really know how much you can push in each corner, which is tough when you're leading.

There were a couple of 'moments'. The first was at the final corner on the first lap, when we all went wide and off the circuit. It had just started to rain and I went quite deep and just couldn't get back across. It was impossible, but everyone behind me did exactly the same and went off the track as well.

The bigger moment was in the closing stages at Turn 8. The Lord definitely had his hand over me there when I got away with that. I made it all the way out to the wall and just clipped it with the edge of my wing. I was very fortunate. It was so slippery out there and there's nothing you can do.

The team did a great job this weekend. We are constantly pushing, but in some places we're just not as fast as the Red Bull Racing guys and have to make sure that we capitalise whenever we are. So I'm proud of the job we did and so happy to finally get on the top step of the podium at Spa.

I thought I'd done it in 2008 but, now that I have, I'm delighted. It's one of those classic races you want to win, like Monaco and Silverstone, and I can tick it off now!

Everyone has seen in the past few races how quickly everything can change, and we still have quite a long way to go in the championship and there are still many points to be grabbed. My closest rival is Mark [Webber] in terms of points, but I still think it's open.

Jenson was very unfortunate in the incident with Vettel. He'd done a fantastic job to get up to second place and those points would have been very valuable. I did happen to see it on the screen and it wasn't his fault.

I don't expect any preferential treatment in the last five or six races, even though I'm 35 points ahead of Jenson now. I get the same treatment and vice versa and that enables us both to score maximum points, so I don't feel there should be preferential treatment. The team does the maximum for both of us."

because they both had only one set of new option tyres left for that final session, so they went out for their initial runs on used tyres.

When they put on the superior new sets, drizzle was already falling, and it seemed highly unlikely that anyone would improve. Yet Hamilton leapt from fourth on the grid to second, and Jenson Button improved from sixth to fifth.

Robert Kubica qualified an excellent third for Renault, ahead of Sebastian Vettel, Button and Felipe Massa. Fernando Alonso was stuck down in 10th, but was confident that he'd have a good race.

Webber made a terrible start from pole, and was passed immediately by Hamilton, Button, Kubica, Vettel and Massa. With perfect timing, spots of rain had begun to fall at the start of the race, and at the end of the first lap nearly every driver in the field slid off at the chicane. There was a mad scramble across the asphalt run-off, but all of those in the leading group regained the track intact.

A little further back, Alonso was hit hard by an out-of-control Rubens Barrichello, who ended his 300th grand prix on the spot, although Alonso was able to continue. Some backmarkers who had

suffered damage dived into the pits to gamble on a change to intermediates, and Alonso joined them.

It looked as though the misfortune of being rammed might now play in his favour, but a safety car was deployed, and that meant the leaders could stay out on slicks and wait for what turned out to be a brief shower to pass by. Those who had already changed tyres, including Alonso, soon had to pit again to change back.

Hamilton pulled away from Button at the restart. The latter had front wing damage from the first-lap chaos – probably from a clash with Kubica as they straightlined the chicane – and couldn't match his team-mate's pace. Instead, he soon came under strong pressure from Vettel, while Kubica and Webber weren't far behind.

Vettel was keen to overtake Button and attack Hamilton, but he tried a little too hard. On lap 16, he lost control at the chicane, got out of shape and hit the McLaren hard in the side. Button had to retire on the spot, while Vettel ducked into the pits and continued after a nose change. Shortly afterwards, he lost more ground with a drive-through penalty for causing that collision.

OPPOSITE LEFT Pedro de la Rosa blasts through the rain that, as ever, fell in varying intensities

OPPOSITE RIGHT Belgian fans know to bring their rain gear

ABOVE Traffic chaos at La Source on lap 1 as Sebastian Vettel chases after Robert Kubica, while team-mate and poleman Mark Webber finds himself back behind Felipe Massa

TALKING POINT
HARD GOING FOR VETTEL

When Mark Webber converted pole position into sixth place on lap 1, it was an unexpected bonus for Sebastian Vettel, who came to Belgium on the back of four successive poles, but still 10 points behind his Red Bull team-mate.

Vettel himself was up a place to third at the end of the first lap.

If Webber had led and Vettel had found himself behind Lewis Hamilton and Robert Kubica – two of the toughest racers on the grid – it could have been a long afternoon.

You would have thought Vettel's head might now have gone into consolidation mode. The important thing as far as his championship challenge was concerned, was that Webber was behind him.

Instead, he had an accident trying to pass Jenson Button for second. It bore all the hallmarks of a driver caught out by the man in front braking early, which is the observation Christian Horner made, albeit not accusingly.

Vettel himself admitted: "I lost the car going over a bump under braking. I'm not proud of it, but what happened, happened."

Would it turn out to be the pivotal moment in the championship? Button's challenge was dealt a potentially fatal blow, the reigning champion finding himself 35 points behind team-mate Hamilton.

"It's not what you'd expect to see in F1," McLaren's Martin Whitmarsh said. "It was more reminiscent of the junior formulae and a drive-through penalty seemed a pretty light punishment to me."

Vettel dropped to 12th place and was then stuck behind Tonio Liuzzi's Force India. The rules say that you must serve a drive-through within three laps of notification, but the skies and the weather radars were indicating imminent rain.

If Vettel stayed out and the rain arrived on the lap he stopped to serve his penalty, he wouldn't be able to change tyres at the same time, and could have faced a lap on slicks in teeming rain. The team told him to come in immediately.

And yet, Vettel was still diving around behind Liuzzi, knowing he was about to stop. When he rejoined, he re-caught Liuzzi and made contact with the Force India trying to go inside at the Bus Stop, puncturing his left-rear tyre in the process.

The German's Red Bull had to crawl around another lap before pitting for the fourth of five stops during a chaotic afternoon. Jackie Stewart used to talk about 'good mind management' and this was a poor example of it. It was the fourth time in seven races that Vettel had made errors of judgement. Many questioned whether he was quite ready to win the championship.

When the Vettel/Button clash happened, Hamilton had built up a handy lead of around 10s.

"It was a shame that Jenson had that [front wing] damage," rued Martin Whitmarsh. "That hurt him, but I think he would have had a good chance of still getting second place in any case, as by the time we got to the first stop, we would have either adjusted it or changed it.

"The crash was deeply frustrating for him, completely innocent in a situation where a rival was presumably thinking he was going down the inside with a gap that didn't exist, then outbraking himself, having a tankslapper and T-boning you. It's not exactly what you expect in F1, is it?

"Lewis then controlled the pace, having opened up a buffer of about 10 seconds. It was difficult out there, and he needed to be careful. He controlled the race, we weren't going to take any risks, and so to an extent we had to cover other people, although we didn't need to once we had that buffer."

Hamilton had a big enough lead to ensure that he just had to wait and see what his immediate pursuers did, and take the least risky reaction.

"It was a matter of trying to build as big a lead as we could," said McLaren engineering head Paddy Lowe. "What you're wondering about was whether there would be rain at a moment when you could avoid running the prime. When the other guys went for the prime, they took the gamble that there wouldn't be any more rain, otherwise we could have all stayed out and just gone on the inter. But we had to cover them. The option tyre could have done the whole race."

Indeed, after Webber, Kubica and Massa had pitted for primes, Hamilton followed them in on lap 24, knowing that his lead was not at risk. Now it was a question of waiting for rain to come before the end. It finally arrived during lap 34, with 10 laps

to go. And yet Hamilton sailed right past the pits. What was perhaps more surprising was that the three drivers behind him did the same.

However, Adrian Sutil ducked in from fifth for a change. Everyone behind him followed suit. It looked like the right call, as the rain fell more heavily as that lap progressed. Hamilton then had a lucky escape when he ran through a gravel trap at Rivage, but he drove his way out of it and got safely back to the pits for a tyre change. Meanwhile, Kubica had a bad stop, misaligning his car and surprising his mechanics, which gifted second to Webber.

"In the pitlane, I had to change a few things on my steering wheel for the wet tyres and wing settings," said Kubica. "I got distracted and when I was done with all the switches it was too late. I jumped on the brakes and locked the front wheels and unfortunately it took some guys on my front wing. I hope they are fine. I lost second place there, but that's racing."

Despite his excursion, Hamilton was still safely in front after his pit stop. A second safety car then came out after Alonso crashed with seven laps to go while running in eighth, ending what had been

OPPOSITE **Nico Rosberg qualified down in 14th, but advanced to sixth**

BELOW **Heikki Kovalainen and Lucas di Grassi scrap over the honour of being highest placed of the new team runners**

BOTTOM **Sebastian Vettel gets it wrong and slams into Jenson Button's McLaren at the Bus Stop**

a frustrating and fruitless race for the Spaniard.

The green flags flew again for a four-lap sprint to the chequered flag, and Hamilton successfully stayed ahead of Webber and Kubica.

"I was hoping the safety car would stay out longer," said Hamilton. "But fortunately it didn't rain anymore and the track got a little bit better. At the end, it was just about nursing the car home and bringing it back in one piece. I was just trying to keep a small gap between myself and Mark to try to bag those points. It's not many times that you're in this position."

In the end, he made it look easy, but clearly

it wasn't. Once again McLaren won a weather-affected race on a day when drivers and team had to get everything just right. In addition, for the first time since the Canadian GP in June, McLaren had the fastest car in both qualifying and the race, even if the history books will show that Red Bull Racing earned another pole position.

"I think we did have the quickest car," agreed Whitmarsh. "We should have had pole. I think there were a few races where we had the quickest race car, but not the quickest qualifying car. Whereas we had both here, and in Canada we had both."

Massa gave Ferrari some compensation with fourth: "It was a very difficult race," explained the Brazilian. "To stay on the track and to finish wasn't easy. I think we did a good strategy, a good job on the tyres, and also we were a bit lucky with the accident in front of me, but it's part of racing."

Sutil had a good run to fifth for Force India, while Nico Rosberg headed home Mercedes team-mate Michael Schumacher in sixth after the pair had fought each other for much of the race. The top 10 was completed by Kamui Kobayashi, Vitaly Petrov and Vitantonio Liuzzi. The last named moved up after Jaime Alguersuari received a penalty for cutting a chicane with two laps to go, and was demoted from 10th to 13th.

Having managed to claw his way back into the points, Vettel suffered a rear puncture after late contact with Liuzzi at the chicane. He lost a lot of time by running a full lap back to the pits, in a repeat of the fate he suffered on the first lap at Silverstone. He eventually finished 15th, a 'nothing-to-lose' tyre gamble during the final shower finally putting paid to any remote chance of grabbing some points. It was a disastrous day for the German who, as in Turkey, found himself under fire for his impetuosity. This time, however, he accepted the blame.

SNAPSHOT FROM
BELGIUM

CLOCKWISE FROM RIGHT

McLarens to the fore as Lewis Hamilton leads from Jenson Button and Robert Kubica; Ferrari personnel consider just when the rain might arrive, while protecting their car from prying eyes; a bright smile on a grey day; the drivers turned out in force to celebrate Rubens Barrichello's 300th grand prix; Rubens Barrichello accepts a gift from Bernie Ecclestone for his 300th grand prix; even though not at the front, Michael Schumacher attracted the microphones; Ron Dennis and the team applaud Lewis Hamilton's victory; Timo Glock has the right visor for rain; Jarno Trulli checks out a visor; intermediate tyres steam away after use on a drying track

RACE RESULTS
BELGIUM
SPA-FRANCORCHAMPS

RACE DATE August 29th
CIRCUIT LENGTH 4.352 miles
NO. OF LAPS 44
RACE DISTANCE 191.488 miles
WEATHER Dry, then rain showers, 16°C
TRACK TEMP 20°C
ATTENDANCE 60,000
LAP RECORD Sebastian Vettel,
1m47.263s, 146.065mph, 2009

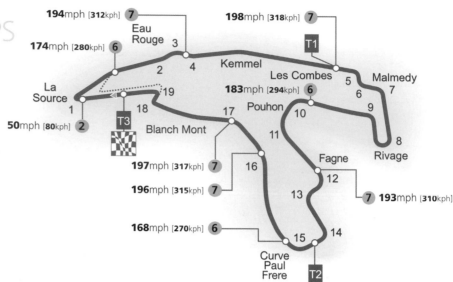

PRACTICE 1			
	Driver	Time	Laps
1	F Alonso	2m00.797s	17
2	L Hamilton	2m01.567s	7
3	R Kubica	2m02.081s	14
4	S Vettel	2m02.450s	11
5	A Sutil	2m02.646s	14
6	J Button	2m02.913s	6
7	M Webber	2m02.926s	11
8	K Kobayashi	2m03.401s	17
9	R Barrichello	2m03.424s	7
10	M Schumacher	2m03.489s	9
11	F Massa	2m03.601s	17
12	N Hulkenberg	2m03.649s	17
13	N Rosberg	2m03.654s	16
14	P de la Rosa	2m03.851s	17
15	V Liuzzi	2m04.145s	12
16	J Alguersuari	2m04.250s	16
17	V Petrov	2m04.690s	13
18	S Buemi	2m05.680s	6
19	T Glock	2m05.697s	18
20	L di Grassi	2m06.695s	14
21	J Trulli	2m07.189s	15
22	B Senna	2m07.737s	15
23	H Kovalainen	2m07.955s	15
24	S Yamamoto	2m10.507s	18

PRACTICE 2			
	Driver	Time	Laps
1	F Alonso	1m49.032s	25
2	A Sutil	1m49.157s	17
3	L Hamilton	1m49.248s	14
4	R Kubica	1m49.282s	20
5	F Massa	1m49.588s	23
6	S Vettel	1m49.689s	19
7	J Button	1m49.755s	20
8	P de la Rosa	1m50.081s	27
9	R Barrichello	1m50.128s	22
10	K Kobayashi	1m50.200s	24
11	V Petrov	1m50.251s	24
12	M Schumacher	1m50.341s	23
13	N Rosberg	1m50.382s	21
14	J Alguersuari	1m50.682s	25
15	N Hulkenberg	1m50.831s	20
16	V Liuzzi	1m51.520s	17
17	S Buemi	1m51.523s	25
18	M Webber	1m51.636s	19
19	H Kovalainen	1m53.480s	15
20	J Trulli	1m53.639s	21
21	L di Grassi	1m54.325s	17
22	B Senna	1m55.751s	24
23	S Yamamoto	1m56.039s	21
24	T Glock	2m03.179s	3

PRACTICE 3			
	Driver	Time	Laps
1	M Webber	1m46.106s	10
2	L Hamilton	1m46.223s	17
3	S Vettel	1m46.396s	12
4	J Button	1m46.397s	17
5	R Kubica	1m46.492s	17
6	F Alonso	1m46.627s	11
7	F Massa	1m46.962s	10
8	A Sutil	1m47.064s	15
9	N Hulkeneberg	1m47.160s	16
10	K Kobayashi	1m47.296s	17
11	P de la Rosa	1m47.388s	15
12	V Petrov	1m47.406s	15
13	R Barrichello	1m47.512s	14
14	M Schumacher	1m47.695s	16
15	N Rosberg	1m47.837s	9
16	S Buemi	1m47.905s	20
17	J Alguersuari	1m47.981s	18
18	V Liuzzi	1m48.692s	8
19	J Trulli	1m50.600s	14
20	B Senna	1m51.133s	9
21	H Kovalainen	1m51.384s	14
22	L di Grassi	1m51.517s	13
23	T Glock	1m51.669s	16
24	S Yamamoto	1m52.001s	13

QUALIFYING 1		
	Driver	Time
1	N Rosberg	1m54.826s
2	N Hulkenberg	1m55.442s
3	R Barrichello	1m55.757s
4	R Kubica	1m56.041s
5	M Schumacher	1m56.313s
6	L Hamilton	1m56.706s
7	F Alonso	1m57.023s
8	M Webber	1m57.352s
9	J Button	1m57.981s
10	F Massa	1m58.323s
11	S Vettel	1m58.487s
12	A Sutil	1m58.730s
13	J Alguersuari	1m58.944s
14	S Buemi	2m00.386s
15	V Liuzzi	2m01.102s
16	T Glock	2m01.316s
17	H Kovalainen	2m01.343s
18	J Trulli	2m01.491s
19	K Kobayashi	2m02.284s
20	B Senna	2m03.612s
21	S Yamamoto	2m03.941s
22	P de la Rosa	2m05.294s
23	L di Grassi	2m18.754s
24	V Petrov	No time

QUALIFYING 2		
	Driver	Time
1	L Hamilton	1m46.211s
2	J Button	1m46.790s
3	S Vettel	1m47.245s
4	M Webber	1m47.253s
5	A Sutil	1m47.292s
6	R Kubica	1m47.320s
7	F Massa	1m47.322s
8	F Alonso	1m47.544s
9	R Barrichello	1m47.797s
10	N Hulkenberg	1m47.821s
11	M Schumacher	1m47.874s
12	N Rosberg	1m47.885s
13	J Alguersuari	1m48.267s
14	V Liuzzi	1m48.680s
15	S Buemi	1m49.209s
16	H Kovalainen	1m50.980s
17	T Glock	1m52.049s

Best sectors – Practice			Speed trap – Practice		
Sec 1	L Hamilton	31.066s	1	L Hamilton	190.885mph
Sec 2	M Webber	45.629s	2	J Button	190.761mph
Sec 3	L Hamilton	28.746s	3	F Alonso	190.512mph

Best sectors – Qualifying			Speed trap – Qualifying		
Sec 1	L Hamilton	31.093s	1	F Massa	194.427mph
Sec 2	S Vettel	45.493s	2	S Vettel	191.258mph
Sec 3	L Hamilton	28.500s	3	J Button	191.009mph

 **Jenson Button**

"I had an incident with Sebastian. I didn't brake early, then felt a bang in the sidepod, which ripped the radiator out. It's a huge blow to my title hopes."

 Michael Schumacher

"I met Nico twice today. The first time, I had the better go in a duel and the second time was after the restart, where I had to lift into Eau Rouge and Nico flew past."

 Sebastian Vettel

"What happened, happened and we can't change it. I'm not proud of it, I lost the car over the bump as I was braking and unluckily hit Jenson, so he couldn't continue."

 **Felipe Massa**

"This is a positive result and, given the Vettel/Button incident, we were a bit lucky. Our set-up was more efficient in the dry, while we suffered a bit in the wet."

 **Rubens Barrichello**

"It was wet at Blanchimont. I was closing the door on Rosberg and when I touched the brakes it wasn't enough and the car went straight on into Alonso."

 Robert Kubica

"Webber stopped before me to change onto the prime, but the team got me out ahead. Next time in, I was changing controls, locked up and hit the mechanics."

 Lewis Hamilton

"Spa is one of the trickiest races, and I'm ecstatic that I'm able to tick it off. When the conditions changed, I ran wide at Rivage, so I was so relieved to cross the line."

 Nico Rosberg

"My rain set-up worked towards the end and I made up two places on the restart. Sixth is the most we could have hoped for. Michael and I had a couple of battles."

 Mark Webber

"The start was a mess, it wasn't ideal to lose that many places, but luckily it's not Monaco, so I was able to get some of them back. To get second was a good result."

Fernando Alonso

"I made up places, but Rubens crashed into me. I pitted to check the car and we fitted inters. Then I went off when I ran over a kerb and that was my race over."

 **Nico Hulkenberg**

"I had a throttle-control problem, so pitted, but the engine died and had to be restarted. I then had to cope without full engine control, which caused some spins."

Vitaly Petrov

"Scoring points was the target. I pushed hard to come through the field, which is what I did. I also had the F-duct, which helped me in my battle with Rosberg."

1	M Webber	
2	L Hamilton	
3	R Kubica	
4	S Vettel	
5	J Button	
6	F Massa	
7	R Barrichello	
8	A Sutil	
9	N Hulkenberg	
10	F Alonso	
11	J Alguersuari	
12	V Liuzzi	
13	H Kovalainen	
14	N Rosberg	
15	J Trulli	
16	S Buemi	
17	K Kobayashi	
18	B Senna	
19	S Yamamoto	
20	T Glock	
21	M Schumacher	
22	P de La Rosa	
23	L di Grassi	
24	V Petrov	

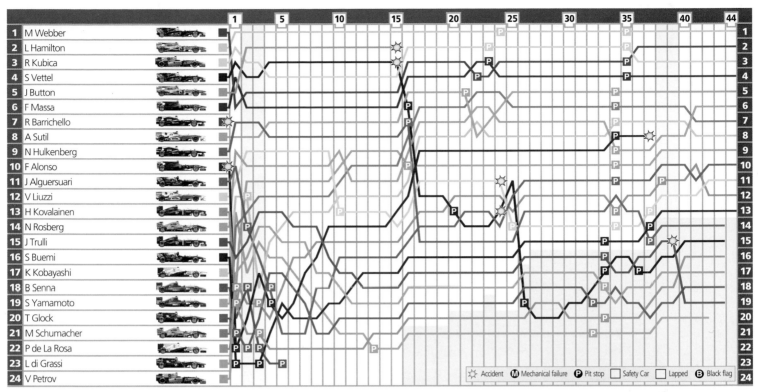

☆ Accident · M Mechanical failure · P Pit stop · ▢ Safety Car · ▢ Lapped · B Black flag

QUALIFYING 3

	Driver	Time
1	M Webber	1m45.778s
2	L Hamilton	1m45.863s
3	R Kubica	1m46.100s
4	S Vettel	1m46.127s
5	J Button	1m46.206s
6	F Massa	1m46.314s
7	R Barrichello	1m46.602s
8	A Sutil	1m46.659s
9	N Hulkenberg	1m47.053s
10	F Alonso	1m47.441s

GRID

	Driver	Time
1	M Webber	1m45.778s
2	L Hamilton	1m45.863s
3	R Kubica	1m46.100s
4	S Vettel	1m46.127s
5	J Button	1m46.206s
6	F Massa	1m46.314s
7	R Barrichello	1m46.602s
8	A Sutil	1m46.659s
9	N Hulkenberg	1m47.053s
10	F Alonso	1m47.441s
11	J Alguersuari	1m48.267s
12	V Liuzzi	1m48.680s
13	H Kovalainen	1m50.980s
14*	N Rosberg	1m47.885s
15	J Trulli	2m01.491s
16^	S Buemi	1m49.209s
17	K Kobayashi	2m02.284s
18	B Senna	2m03.612s
19	S Yamamoto	2m03.941s
20†	T Glock	1m52.049s
21‡	M Schumacher	1m47.874s
22	L di Grassi	2m18.754s
23	V Petrov	No time
24°	P de La Rosa	2m05.294s

* 5-place grid penalty for gearbox change; ^3-place penalty for impeding Rosberg; 15-place penalty for impeding Yamamoto; †10-place penalty for dangerous move on Barrichello in Hungarian GP; ‡10-place penalty for engine change

RACE

	Driver	Car	Laps	Time	Avg. mph	Fastest	Stops
1	L Hamilton	McLaren-Mercedes MP4-25	44	1h29m04.268	128.940	1m49.069s	2
2	M Webber	Red Bull-Renault RB6	44	1h29m05.839s	128.903	1m49.395s	2
3	R Kubica	Renault R30	44	1h29m07.761s	128.856	1m49.807s	2
4	F Massa	Ferrari F10	44	1h29m12.532s	128.741	1m50.111s	2
5	A Sutil	Force India-Mercedes VJM03	44	1h29m13.362s	128.721	1m50.477s	2
6	N Rosberg	Mercedes MGP W01	44	1h29m16.627s	128.643	1m51.688s	1
7	M Schumacher	Mercedes MGP W01	44	1h29m19.816s	128.566	1m51.914s	1
8	K Kobayashi	BMW Sauber-Ferrari C29	44	1h29m20.946s	128.539	1m51.749s	2
9	V Petrov	Renault R30	44	1h29m28.119s	128.368	1m51.175s	2
10	V Liuzzi	Force India-Mercedes VJM03	44	1h29m33.725s	128.233	1m52.267s	4
11	P de La Rosa	BMW Sauber-Ferrari C29	44	1h29m39.099s	128.105	1m52.537s	4
12	S Buemi	Toro Rosso-Ferrari STR5	44	1h29m40.287s	128.077	1m52.966s	4
13	J Alguersuari	Toro Rosso-Ferrari STR5	44	1h29m44.163s*	127.985	1m51.576s	3
14	N Hulkenberg	Williams-Cosworth FW32	43	1h29m25.271s	125.515	1m51.864s	2
15	S Vettel	Red Bull-Renault RB6	43	1h29m30.159s	125.401	1m50.868s	5
16	H Kovalainen	Lotus-Cosworth T127	43	1h29m44.538s	125.066	1m55.797s	3
17	L di Grassi	Virgin-Cosworth VR-01	43	1h29m46.318s	125.025	1m55.705s	1
18	T Glock	Virgin-Cosworth VR-01	43	1h29m52.280s	124.887	1m55.268s	3
19	J Trulli	Lotus-Cosworth T127	43	1h30m06.854s	124.550	1m55.103s	1
20	S Yamamoto	HRT-Cosworth F110	42	1h29m57.404s	121.866	1m55.484s	2
R	F Alonso	Ferrari F10	37	Accident	-	1m51.374s	3
R	J Button	McLaren-Mercedes MP4-25	15	Accident	-	1m52.879s	0
R	B Senna	HRT-Cosworth F110	5	Suspension	-	2m20.201s	2
R	R Barrichello	Williams-Cosworth FW32	0	Accident	-	-	0

* Including 20s penalty for cutting a chicane to overtake Liuzzi

CHAMPIONSHIP

	Driver	Pts
1	L Hamilton	182
2	M Webber	179
3	S Vettel	151
4	J Button	147
5	F Alonso	141
6	F Massa	109
7	R Kubica	104
8	N Rosberg	102
9	A Sutil	45
10	M Schumacher	44
11	R Barrichello	30
12	K Kobayashi	21
13	V Petrov	19
14	V Liuzzi	13
15	N Hulkenberg	10
16	S Buemi	7
17	P de la Rosa	6
18	J Alguersuari	3

	Constructor	Pts
1	Red Bull-Renault	330
2	McLaren-Mercedes	329
3	Ferrari	250
4	Mercedes	146
5	Renault	123
6	Force India-Mercedes	58
7	Williams-Cosworth	40
8	BMW Sauber-Ferrari	27
9	Toro Rosso-Ferrari	10

Fastest lap
L Hamilton 1m49.069s
(143.647mph) on lap 32

Fastest speed trap
F Massa 189.580mph
Slowest speed trap
B Senna 167.894mph

Fastest pit stop
1 M Webber 20.597s
2 R Kubica 20.727s
3 F Massa 20.935s

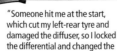

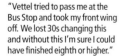
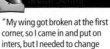

Adrian Sutil
"Another fifth place, so I'm very pleased as I started eighth. When the rain came, it was light in places, heavy in others and I had to concentrate to drive it home."

Sebastien Buemi
"Someone hit me at the start, which cut my left-rear tyre and damaged the diffuser, so I locked the differential and changed the wing settings to compensate."

Jarno Trulli
"I went wide to avoid Heikki and lost two places. At the restart, the visibility was poor and I made an error on a high-speed corner, touched the white line and spun."

Sakon Yamamoto
"It was hard to push on the options, so I changed to primes. Near the end, the rain came back and I gambled on wets, but they got used too hard and grained."

Pedro de la Rosa
"I shouldn't moan about 12th, but two laps before the end I was 10th. I was on wets, but they went off and when I tried to catch Petrov I went into the gravel."

Timo Glock
"When Barrichello and Alonso had their incident, I went through the 50m board. I had to pit, then catch Trulli and Lucas again, and gambled on having wet tyres."

Vitantonio Liuzzi
"Vettel tried to pass me at the Bus Stop and took my front wing off. We lost 30s changing this and without this I'm sure I could have finished eighth or higher."

Jaime Alguersuari
"It was difficult to make the right tyre choice. I think within our team's potential, today's result wasn't too bad and I'm delighted to have crossed the line 10th."

Heikki Kovalainen
"I damaged my front wing in the last turn, so had to pit. We took a gamble with inters, but the rain stopped, so I had to pit again and lost out to the group ahead of me."

Bruno Senna
"My wing got broken at the first corner, so I came in and put on inters, but I needed to change back as the rain stopped. One lap later, the rear suspension failed."

Kamui Kobayashi
"The team chose the right tyres at the right time. The conditions were changing every lap, so I'm happy I brought the car home and scored four more points."

Lucas di Grassi
"They were difficult conditions due to the weather changing through the race. The team did a great job calling me at the correct moment and choosing the tyres."

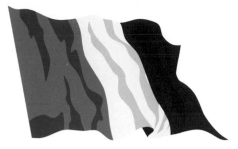

FORMULA 1 GRAN PREMIO
SANTANDER D'ITALIA 2010
MONZA

ALONSO IN CONTROL

Fernando Alonso had his pit crew to thank, as a perfect pit stop got him back out ahead of Jenson Button to win in front of the *tifosi* in a race from which Lewis Hamilton crashed out

To the delight of the *tifosi*, Fernando Alonso put his World Championship challenge back on track by triumphing on Ferrari's home ground at Monza. However, it was far from a straightforward victory, as the Spaniard had to spend the first part of the race behind McLaren's Jenson Button, before jumping him at the pit stops.

Monza was a track that should have suited McLaren, and the team knew that it had to come away with a big haul of points. Given the circumstances, a first-lap retirement for Lewis Hamilton, after an unnecessary tangle with Felipe Massa, was potentially extremely expensive.

Alonso staked his claim for victory by taking pole position. He set his best time in the first part of Q3, and neither he nor anyone else came close to it. It was only the second time that a Red Bull driver had not been fastest thus far in 2010.

Alonso's closest challenger was Button. There was a fascinating contrast in set-ups at McLaren, as the World Champion elected to run the F-duct and a big rear wing, while Hamilton did without the F-duct, using a traditional ultra-low-downforce Monza wing. Button appeared to have made the

better choice, at least in qualifying. Down in fifth, Hamilton was hoping that his straightline speed would allow him to pass come race day.

Massa qualified third, while Mark Webber was happy to be fourth for Red Bull Racing at a track that the team always expected to be difficult for its RB6s. Behind Hamilton, Sebastian Vettel qualified a frustrated sixth. For both Red Bull Racing drivers, this was to be a weekend of damage limitation.

Button made a great start, and muscled his way past Alonso before they reached the first chicane. Behind him, the Ferrari drivers got a little close through the first right/left, but they managed to avoid contact. However, Alonso gave Button a nudge, damaging the McLaren's diffuser and poking a hole in the Ferrari's nose.

There was a more serious drama at the second chicane, when Hamilton dived down the inside of Massa. There appeared to be no room, and the two made wheel-to-wheel contact, which snapped Hamilton's front-right suspension. He carried on, seemingly oblivious, but at the first Lesmo the wheel folded inwards and the erstwhile points leader speared into the gravel trap. It was

Hamilton's third retirement of 2010, but the first time that he'd lost points with a serious mistake.

It's worth recalling that Hamilton had tapped Vettel at the start at both Valencia and Silverstone. The first time, he was able to change his tweaked front wing under safety-car conditions, thus without penalty, and the second time he escaped unharmed and sent the German into the pits for a new rear tyre. Monza was thus a case of three strikes and you're out...

"He had a great chance to get up there," said McLaren team principal Martin Whitmarsh. "He was attacking for third place, that's what you've got to do if you're a racing driver. There was wheel contact, a pure racing incident. Unfortunately, it broke Lewis's track rod.

"You can't take no risks and score the points. Lewis is a racing driver, he's going to push, that's a hallmark of what makes him the great driver he is. With hindsight, conserving the points would have been the right thing to do. But, if you drive like that it affects your mentality, and Lewis wouldn't be the winner that he is."

The first part of the race turned into a game of cat and mouse, with Button and Alonso running together, and Massa keeping an eye on them from third. The Ferrari was potentially faster, but there was no way that Alonso could get past. It was clear that everything would depend on the pit stops.

Monza races have traditionally been about a single late pit stop, although in the past, fuel loads have of course been a factor. This time, it was only about tyres, and that's what drove McLaren to bring Button into the pits first.

Between them, the pit wall crew and the strategists back at McLaren's Woking base determined that new hard tyres were faster, giving an instant advantage to anyone pitting before their rivals. Whether they were guaranteed to work as early as the first lap out of the pits, which is when Button needed a boost, was less clear.

McLaren didn't have too many samples to draw on in terms of the quick cars. The key ones were Robert Kubica and Sebastien Buemi. When they pitted on lap 33, the new-tyre advantage was apparent, and that's what led McLaren into a three-lap countdown to Button's stop on lap 36.

With clear air ahead, Alonso was finally able to

OPPOSITE TOP Jenson Button leads through the first chicane, with Fernando Alonso and Felipe Massa scrapping for second behind him

OPPOSITE BOTTOM Lewis Hamilton's McLaren sits with its front-right suspension broken by its clash with Felipe Massa's Ferrari

BELOW Williams's Nico Hulkenberg had an eventful race, holding back Mark Webber's Red Bull for a while

INSIDE LINE
FERNANDO ALONSO
FERRARI DRIVER

"Winning in a Ferrari at Monza is special. The only comparable feeling was winning my home grand prix at Barcelona in 2006.

This was a tough race. The first lap was stressful, even from pole. Jenson had a much better start and I touched the nose on his left rear in the first chicane, and the car jumped a little in the air. When I landed, I touched Felipe on the right and I thought something was probably damaged. Thankfully, it was okay.

I attacked Jenson hard. Our car was quicker on the straights than the McLaren, so I knew that out of Parabolica if I was close enough maybe I had a chance. I was pushing all race for that, but Jenson was driving superbly and it wasn't possible. He wasn't making a single mistake the whole lap.

It was therefore a case of waiting for the pit stops and there were two possibilities: stop one lap earlier than him or run one lap longer. When we saw him come in, we knew that we had only one lap to push as, after that, the prime tyre was quicker. I pushed 100 per cent and I think the lap was more or less okay, nothing special, but the pit stop was superb. We won the race in the pits. When I saw the green light, I didn't even have first gear in. It was a surprise how quick it was. It was a perfect job.

With Webber only sixth and Hamilton having a problem, it was very important for the championship in terms of the points gap. But our championship chances won't depend on what the others do, as we need to find some consistency. This was a good weekend, but the Belgian GP was a bad one and we can't afford any more of them.

Any good result gives you extra confidence and is good motivation for the whole team to keep working hard and not give up.

We know that one race, good or bad, can change the positions in the championship a lot with the new points system.

I will be in Maranello on Monday and Tuesday, to say thanks to the whole team. To be on the podium with all those fans below was amazing. I won here in 2007 for McLaren, but they were not saying very nice things because McLaren was fighting for the championship against Ferrari then… Today was different and the whole weekend has been great for both Felipe and myself."

do one lap at his true pace, before coming in for his own set of hard tyres. The team carried out a perfect stop – he gained 0.9s in the pitlane – and when he emerged he'd done just enough to slip ahead of the McLaren. Having struggled a little with grip on his out-lap, Button tried to get back in front on the run to the first chicane, but he fell short.

It was easy to criticise the team's strategy, and Button asked the question and got a clear explanation from his engineer. McLaren had done the sums, but it just didn't work out for them.

"The new tyres were quicker, so had Ferrari stopped before us they would have been further ahead after we stopped," said Whitmarsh. "So we had to play that card. It would have been nice if they'd come in and raced us in the pitlane, but that would have been the wrong thing for them to do, and sadly they didn't do the wrong thing!

"The facts are the facts. They were quicker than us, they were behind, and the new tyres were quicker. What were the three scenarios there? They could have stopped in front of us, got onto the quicker tyre, and been further ahead. They could have stopped at the same time, which they weren't

likely to do. They had the luxury of knowing when we were going to stop, and they were going to cover it, or not cover it I should say. They had to stop quickly after we stopped.

"It was touch and go. If we'd stayed out another three laps, they'd have stayed out another three laps, or if they'd jumped in before us, then they'd have been further ahead. When you're racing a car that's quicker than you, it's quite difficult to outdo that, unless they make a mistake. They didn't make the mistake of coming in with us, which would have been nice."

Alonso explained it from Ferrari's perspective: "The possibilities were two, coming in one lap earlier or one lap later. We had to find the right choice and the right moment. When we saw Jenson coming in, it was one of the two possibilities we had. There was one lap to push and [then] rely on the mechanics."

Once in front, Alonso edged slightly away from Button, who had no choice but to settle for second place and a useful helping of points. Massa kept the pressure on the McLaren driver, who also had to keep an eye on fuel consumption.

BELOW LEFT Vitantonio Liuzzi ended up just 2s outside the points

BELOW RIGHT Michael Schumacher runs wide out of Ascari as he chases a minor points placing

BOTTOM Fernando Alonso was able to resist Jenson Button's passing move after emerging from the pits

OPPOSITE Robert Kubica rose from ninth to fifth, but a slow pit stop dropped him to eighth place

TALKING POINT
McLAREN WINGS IT

Now that the old Hockenheim is no more, Monza stands alone in demanding an ultra-low-downforce set-up. With straightline speed a major factor, you would have imagined that the F-duct would be particularly key. But it wasn't that simple, even for the team that pioneered it.

The McLaren drivers, in fact, adopted entirely different F-duct strategies. Both ran with a blown wing in practice on Friday morning. Jenson Button stuck with it on Friday afternoon, but Lewis Hamilton was keen to try a conventional low-downforce Monza set-up. He did so in the afternoon session and elected to run without the F-duct for the rest of the weekend.

With his conventional Monza mini-wing, Hamilton was third fastest through the speed trap in qualifying, at 214mph. Button, towing a barn door behind him by comparison, was 10mph slower and quicker only than the two HRTs. Of course, with so much more downforce, Button was much quicker in the corners, especially the Lesmos and Parabolica.

McLaren's simulations showed that both approaches should have added up to pretty much the same lap time. It just depended what you preferred. Button would get the tyres working more quickly and should also have been in a better position to look after them on Sunday afternoon. Hamilton, by contrast, would have straightline speed in his favour and should have been in a position to overtake.

After qualifying second, it was Button who was smiling, three slots and 0.6s better off than Lewis. But the real difference was less clear cut, as Hamilton had messed up his best qualifying lap. Trying to get a tow, he got too close to Mark Webber, leading to a moment at the Roggia chicane and a lack of front downforce through Parabolica. Still, Hamilton hoped he would come good in the race.

Sadly, he didn't find out. Knowing that the first lap was a vital opportunity to make progress, he was too optimistic in a bid to go inside Massa at the second chicane and was out on lap 1. The ball was now in Button's court as far as McLaren's hopes were concerned. He got a great start, beating Alonso's pole-sitting Ferrari into the first turn and then found, as he'd hoped, that his additional downforce meant that Alonso had a hard time getting close enough to pass. Ultimately, the Spaniard only managed it at the pit stop to take the narrowest of victories.

"I think I made the right choice," said Button. "I was able to keep Alonso behind the whole race, but we pitted one lap earlier than them, which was possibly a mistake."

ABOVE For once, the Red Bull RB6 wasn't the car to have, and Sebastian Vettel had to settle for fourth place

BELOW The *tifosi* erupts as Fernando Alonso celebrates giving them a win on their home patch

Button was frustrated to have lost his lead, but admitted that it was always going to be hard to keep Alonso behind.

"These are difficult situations when you've got 0.5s lead, whether you stop a lap earlier or whether you stop a lap later," said the English driver. "I don't feel that it worked for us today but, even so, we've got a good result out of it and hopefully we will be as strong in Singapore."

There was plenty of action going on behind the top three. From fourth and sixth on the grid, the Red Bulls of Vettel and Webber dropped to seventh and ninth respectively after scrappy first laps, and knew

that it would be a notably tough job to recover a decent points haul.

Webber soon got in front of Michael Schumacher and began chasing Vettel, finally getting by his team-mate when the German mysteriously lost performance for one lap. He thought at first that it was the engine, but it turned out that the brake pedal wasn't returning fully. After the problem solved itself, Vettel got back up to speed.

Vettel stayed out on the track when the cars ahead of him pitted, and thus he gradually moved up the race order. In fact, Red Bull Racing decided to leave his compulsory tyre change to the start of the final lap, in an attempt to get Vettel ahead of as many cars as possible.

This unusual plan worked better than expected, as he climbed to fourth before coming in for hard tyres at the end of lap 52, and was able to come back out in the same position.

Vettel just pipped Nico Rosberg, who had run in fourth place before his own stop but lost precious seconds with a mistake in the closing laps.

Webber finished in sixth place, having lost ground when his car was stuck behind the Williams of Nico Hulkenberg. The Williams driver cut chicanes three times while staying ahead, but was deemed to have not gained an advantage, and thus didn't get hit with a penalty. Webber finally got by the German with four laps to go.

Kubica was in the points again for Renault in eighth place, after losing time at his pit stop. Four years on from his retirement announcement here, Schumacher finished ninth, while Rubens Barrichello completed the top 10 for Williams.

Despite finishing only sixth, Webber regained the championship lead, just edging ahead of Hamilton, while the other three contenders had closed the gap. Heading to Singapore, it was still wide open.

SNAPSHOT FROM
ITALY

CLOCKWISE FROM RIGHT
Packed grandstands have a great view over the entry to the first chicane; Ferrari fan Hugh Grant dropped in; yet another new helmet livery for Vitantonio Liuzzi; Fernando Alonso takes a snapshot of his winning team on the podium; one of Formula One Television's high-definition TV cameras; with Alonso's win, there was no need to be embarrassed about being a Ferrari fan; British band Kasabian made an appearance on the starting grid; Jarno Trulli is congraulated by his Lotus crew after claiming the team's best qualifying position of the year, in 18th place; where would F1 fans rather be, Lesmo or California? No contest...

RACE RESULTS

ITALY
MONZA

Official Results © [2010]
Formula One Administration Limited,
6 Princes Gate, London, SW7 1QJ.
No reproduction without permission.
All copyright and database rights reserved.

RACE DATE 12th September
CIRCUIT LENGTH 3.600 miles
NO. OF LAPS 53
RACE DISTANCE 190.800 miles
WEATHER Sunny & dry, 25°C
TRACK TEMP 36°C
ATTENDANCE 130,000
LAP RECORD Rubens Barrichello,
1m21.046s, 159.909mph, 2004

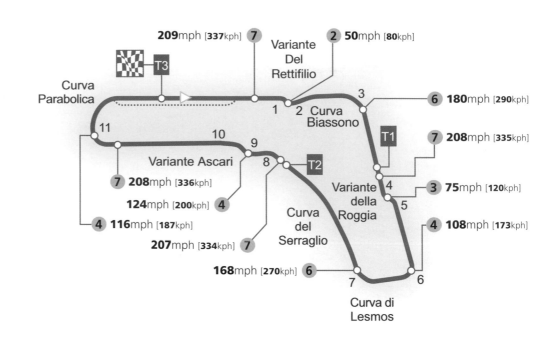

	PRACTICE 1		
	Driver	Time	Laps
1	J Button	1m23.693s	28
2	S Vettel	1m23.790s	27
3	L Hamilton	1m23.967s	25
4	R Kubica	1m24.120s	25
5	N Rosberg	1m24.129s	30
6	M Webber	1m24.446s	26
7	V Liuzzi	1m24.512s	19
8	F Alonso	1m24.543s	24
9	F Massa	1m24.648s	22
10	M Schumacher	1m24.756s	26
11	N Hulkenberg	1m24.841s	28
12	P di Resta	1m24.923s	23
13	V Petrov	1m25.292s	25
14	S Buemi	1m25.318s	29
15	P de la Rosa	1m25.320s	20
16	K Kobayashi	1m25.334s	24
17	J Alguersuari	1m25.897s	19
18	T Glock	1m26.772s	19
19	J Trulli	1m26.898s	12
20	L di Grassi	1m26.956s	17
21	H Kovalainen	1m27.374s	14
22	B Senna	1m28.256s	8
23	R Barrichello	1m28.516s	4
24	S Yamamoto	1m29.870s	17

	PRACTICE 2		
	Driver	Time	Laps
1	S Vettel	1m22.839s	27
2	F Alonso	1m22.915s	32
3	F Massa	1m23.061s	20
4	L Hamilton	1m23.154s	22
5	J Button	1m23.210s	38
6	M Webber	1m23.415s	23
7	R Barrichello	1m23.708s	31
8	R Kubica	1m23.709s	32
9	N Hulkenberg	1m23.852s	30
10	N Rosberg	1m23.857s	29
11	A Sutil	1m24.181s	35
12	V Liuzzi	1m24.380s	36
13	V Petrov	1m24.407s	21
14	M Schumacher	1m24.448s	29
15	S Buemi	1m24.517s	35
16	P de la Rosa	1m24.547s	32
17	K Kobayashi	1m24.785s	31
18	J Alguersuari	1m25.106s	24
19	J Trulli	1m26.204s	38
20	H Kovalainen	1m26.306s	41
21	L di Grassi	1m26.631s	31
22	T Glock	1m26.676s	25
23	S Yamamoto	1m29.498s	5
24	B Senna	No time	3

	PRACTICE 3		
	Driver	Time	Laps
1	L Hamilton	1m22.498s	19
2	S Vettel	1m22.545s	21
3	F Alonso	1m22.644s	15
4	F Massa	1m22.648s	16
5	J Button	1m22.724s	19
6	N Rosberg	1m22.946s	17
7	M Webber	1m23.082s	9
8	N Hulkenberg	1m23.129s	18
9	R Kubica	1m23.209s	20
10	A Sutil	1m23.303s	19
11	R Barrichello	1m23.450s	19
12	S Buemi	1m23.673s	20
13	M Schumacher	1m23.896s	21
14	K Kobayashi	1m23.908s	24
15	J Alguersuari	1m23.909s	17
16	V Petrov	1m23.967s	19
17	P de la Rosa	1m24.191s	19
18	V Liuzzi	1m24.439s	15
19	J Trulli	1m25.788s	14
20	H Kovalainen	1m25.925s	16
21	T Glock	1m26.434s	18
22	L di Grassi	1m26.682s	19
23	B Senna	1m27.471s	18
24	S Yamamoto	1m28.730s	14

	QUALIFYING 1	
	Driver	Time
1	F Massa	1m22.421s
2	F Alonso	1m22.646s
3	L Hamilton	1m22.830s
4	J Button	1m23.085s
5	R Kubica	1m23.234s
6	S Vettel	1m23.235s
7	M Webber	1m23.431s
8	A Sutil	1m23.493s
9	N Hulkenberg	1m23.516s
10	N Rosberg	1m23.529s
11	R Barrichello	1m23.695s
12	S Buemi	1m23.744s
13	M Schumacher	1m23.840s
14	J Alguersuari	1m24.083s
15	V Petrov	1m24.086s
16	K Kobayashi	1m24.273s
17	P de la Rosa	1m25.442s
18	J Trulli	1m25.540s
19	H Kovalainen	1m25.742s
20	V Liuzzi	1m25.774s
21	T Glock	1m25.934s
22	L di Grassi	1m25.974s
23	B Senna	1m26.847s
24	S Yamamoto	1m27.020s

	QUALIFYING 2	
	Driver	Time
1	F Alonso	1m22.297s
2	J Button	1m22.354s
3	L Hamilton	1m22.394s
4	F Massa	1m22.610s
5	S Vettel	1m22.701s
6	M Webber	1m22.706s
7	R Kubica	1m22.880s
8	N Hulkenberg	1m22.989s
9	N Rosberg	1m23.055s
10	R Barrichello	1m23.142s
11	A Sutil	1m23.199s
12	M Schumacher	1m23.388s
13	K Kobayashi	1m23.659s
14	S Buemi	1m23.681s
15	V Petrov	1m23.819s
16	J Alguersuari	1m23.919s
17	P de la Rosa	1m24.044s

Best sectors – Practice			Speed trap – Practice			Best sectors – Qualifying			Speed trap – Qualifying		
Sec 1	N Rosberg	26.866s	1	J Alguersuari	215.988mph	Sec 1	F Alonso	26.825s	1	J Alguersuari	216.672mph
Sec 2	J Button	27.865s	2	S Buemi	215.491mph	Sec 2	J Button	27.694s	2	S Buemi	215.243mph
Sec 3	S Vettel	27.493s	3	K Kobayashi	215.118mph	Sec 3	F Alonso	27.327s	3	L Hamilton	213.938mph

Jenson Button

"It was a tough race, holding off the challenge from behind. Maybe it was the wrong call to pit when I did, but the team felt the new primes were faster."

Michael Schumacher

"My race was action-packed with lots of fighting. Annoyingly, I had to give away two positions to Sebastian and Mark as I just couldn't keep them behind me."

Sebastian Vettel

"Our strategy was a risk after I had a bad start. It was hard to pass from there, as we don't have extra speed on the straights, so we had to fight in the corners."

Felipe Massa

"I got a good start, but didn't have good traction out of Turn 2. Then I felt a knock and it was Lewis who had hit my car. Luckily, there was no damage."

Rubens Barrichello

"Coming into Turn 1, I took the outside line and we bunched up behind Vettel and I lost a part of my nose. Worse, I fell behind Buemi and that dictated my race."

Robert Kubica

"Hulkenberg came out of the pits level with me, then took a defensive line through the chicane, which meant Webber also got a run on me, so I lost two places."

Lewis Hamilton

"I made a good start, got up to fourth, and perhaps should have stayed there, but I put my car inside Felipe, trying to get third, and that was a bit too much."

Nico Rosberg

"Fifth was OK, except for losing the place to Sebastian at the end. I pushed to the maximum, firstly with Robert at the start and then with Sebastian towards the end."

Mark Webber

"I could have got more points, but lost out on the start. I lost a lot of time behind Nico, who seemed to spend every second lap going through the chicane."

Fernando Alonso

"Jenson's start was better. I could keep up with him and we were working out what might be best, then he pitted and it was clear that I should do one more lap."

Nico Hulkenberg

"I lost ground off the start, but recovered two places in the first chicane, then seemed to fight the Red Bulls all race, even though I was struggling with the brakes."

Vitaly Petrov

"Although I picked up five places on lap 1, it wasn't enough to get near the points. It's very hard to pass, as the low downforce makes it tricky to catch a slipstream."

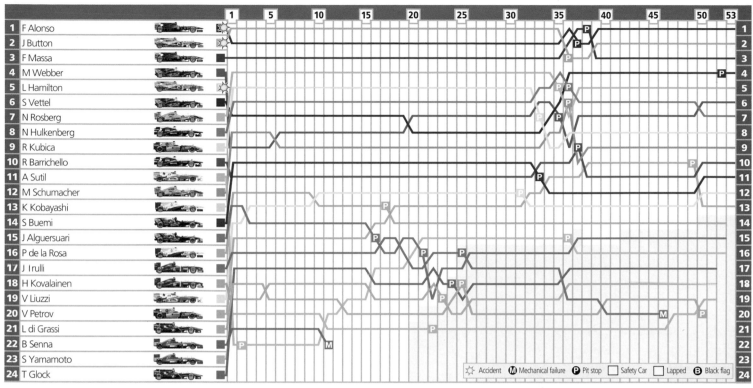

	Driver
1	F Alonso
2	J Button
3	F Massa
4	M Webber
5	L Hamilton
6	S Vettel
7	N Rosberg
8	N Hulkenberg
9	R Kubica
10	R Barrichello
11	A Sutil
12	M Schumacher
13	K Kobayashi
14	S Buemi
15	J Alguersuari
16	P de la Rosa
17	J Trulli
18	H Kovalainen
19	V Liuzzi
20	V Petrov
21	L di Grassi
22	B Senna
23	S Yamamoto
24	T Glock

Legend: ☼ Accident Ⓜ Mechanical failure Ⓟ Pit stop ☐ Safety Car ☐ Lapped Ⓑ Black flag

QUALIFYING 3

	Driver	Time
1	F Alonso	1m21.962s
2	J Button	1m22.084s
3	F Massa	1m22.293s
4	M Webber	1m22.433s
5	L Hamilton	1m22.623s
6	S Vettel	1m22.675s
7	N Rosberg	1m23.027s
8	N Hulkenberg	1m23.037s
9	R Kubica	1m23.039s
10	R Barrichello	1m23.328s

GRID

	Driver	Time
1	F Alonso	1m21.962s
2	J Button	1m22.084s
3	F Massa	1m22.293s
4	M Webber	1m22.433s
5	L Hamilton	1m22.623s
6	S Vettel	1m22.675s
7	N Rosberg	1m23.027s
8	N Hulkenberg	1m23.037s
9	R Kubica	1m23.039s
10	R Barrichello	1m23.328s
11	A Sutil	1m23.199s
12	M Schumacher	1m23.388s
13**	K Kobayashi	1m23.659s
14	S Buemi	1m23.681s
15	J Alguersuari	1m23.919s
16	P de la Rosa	1m24.044s
17	J Trulli	1m25.540s
18	H Kovalainen	1m25.742s
19	V Liuzzi	1m25.774s
20*	V Petrov	1m23.819s
21	L di Grassi	1m25.974s
22	B Senna	1m26.847s
23	S Yamamoto	1m27.020s
24^	T Glock	1m25.934s

** 5-place penalty for impeding Glock * Started from the pitlane
^ 5-place penalty for gearbox change

RACE

	Driver	Car	Laps	Time	Avg. mph	Fastest	Stops
1	F Alonso	Ferrari F10	53	1h16m24.572s	149.656	1m24.139s	1
2	J Button	McLaren-Mercedes MP4-25	53	1h16m27.510s	149.561	1m24.598s	1
3	F Massa	Ferrari F10	53	1h16m28.795s	149.518	1m24.575s	1
4	S Vettel	Red Bull-Renault RB6	53	1h16m52.768s	148.742	1m24.493s	1
5	N Rosberg	Mercedes MGP W01	53	1h16m54.514s	148.685	1m24.491s	1
6	M Webber	Red Bull-Renault RB6	53	1h16m55.848s	148.642	1m24.278s	1
7	N Hulkenberg	Williams-Cosworth FW32	53	1h16m57.384s	148.793	1m24.576s	1
8	R Kubica	Renault R30	53	1h16m58.600s	148.554	1m24.560s	1
9	M Schumacher	Mercedes MGP W01	53	1h17m09.520s	148.204	1m24.947s	1
10	R Barrichello	Williams-Cosworth FW32	53	1h17m28.785s	147.589	1m25.239s	1
11	S Buemi	Toro Rosso-Ferrari STR5	53	1h17m29.628s	147.562	1m25.224s	1
12	V Liuzzi	Force India-Mercedes VJM03	53	1h17m30.678s	147.529	1m25.102s	1
13	V Petrov	Renault R30	53	1h17m43.491s	147.124	1m24.644s	1
14	P de la Rosa	BMW Sauber-Ferrari C29	52	1h16m34.616s	146.509	1m26.325s	1
15	J Alguersuari	Toro Rosso-Ferrari STR5	52	1h16m41.580s	146.287	1m25.472s	2
16	A Sutil	Force India-Mercedes VJM03	52	1h16m41.994s	146.274	1m24.937s	2
17	T Glock	Virgin-Cosworth VR-01	51	1h16m48.751s	143.248	1m27.765s	1
18	H Kovalainen	Lotus-Cosworth T127	51	1h16m51.146s	143.174	1m27.822s	1
19	S Yamamoto	HRT-Cosworth F110	51	1h17m46.321s	141.605	1m28.875s	1
20	L di Grassi	Virgin-Cosworth VR-01	50	Suspension	-	1m28.171s	1
R	J Trulli	Lotus-Cosworth T127	46	Gearbox	-	1m29.017s	1
R	B Senna	HRT-Cosworth F110	11	Hydraulics	-	1m30.880s	0
R	L Hamilton	McLaren-Mercedes MP4-25	0	Collision	-	-	0
R	K Kobayashi	BMW Sauber-Ferrari C29	0	Gearbox	-	-	0

CHAMPIONSHIP

	Driver	Pts
1	M Webber	187
2	L Hamilton	182
3	F Alonso	166
4	J Button	165
5	S Vettel	163
6	F Massa	124
7	N Rosberg	112
8	R Kubica	108
9	M Schumacher	46
10	A Sutil	45
11	R Barrichello	31
12	K Kobayashi	21
13	V Petrov	19
14	N Hulkenberg	16
15	V Liuzzi	13
16	S Buemi	7
17	P de la Rosa	6
18	J Alguersuari	3

	Constructor	Pts
1	Red Bull-Renault	350
2	McLaren-Mercedes	347
3	Ferrari	290
4	Mercedes	158
5	Renault	127
6	Force India-Mercedes	58
7	Williams-Cosworth	47
8	BMW Sauber-Ferrari	27
9	Toro Rosso-Ferrari	10

Fastest lap
F Alonso 1m24.139s
(154.013mph) on lap 52

Fastest speed trap
S Buemi 215.429mph
Slowest speed trap
S Yamamoto 201.324mph

Fastest pit stop
1 S Vettel 21.558s
2 M Webber 22.078s
3 F Alonso 22.154s

 Adrian Sutil
"I was pushed wide into the gravel in one of the early corners on lap 1 and lost a lot of places. So we decided to change to the harder tyres as a strategic move."

 Jaime Alguersuari
"I lost time around my stop. Maybe we did it early, and I came out behind Barrichello, partly due to the Lotus and Virgin I caught before the stop not moving over."

 Jarno Trulli
"It was a very good race until I lost second gear. Then the gearbox gave up. But the race had been satisfying until then, as I was pulling away from Timo."

Sakon Yamamoto
"I was very worried about the incident in the pitlane. I asked if he was OK and was told that he wasn't badly injured. Apart from that, I had good pace."

 Pedro de la Rosa
"I had a good start and overtook Alguersuari. Then I tried to keep contact with the guys in front. But I lost that contact to Rubens and then had quite a tough race."

Timo Glock
"I nearly got past both Lotuses into Turn 1, but Jarno was better placed for Turn 2 and was able to stay in front. I pressured him, but suffered with my rear brakes."

 Vitantonio Liuzzi
"It was a nice race to drive, but from 19th it was always going to be hard to score, particularly as there weren't any safety cars. At least I had some good fights."

Jaime Alguersuari
"I'm pleased with my drive, but really don't understand why I got the drive-through penalty. Although I did cut the chicane, I didn't gain any advantage."

Heikki Kovalainen
"I lost places at the start, managed to pass Lucas, but was stuck behind Timo. I didn't have the straightline speed to pass him so wasn't able to make a move."

Bruno Senna
"It was a bit of a shame to have a mechanical failure in the car, because I had a strong race. But now we just have to keep working as hard as always."

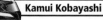 **Kamui Kobayashi**
"I realised on my installation lap that something was wrong, then I had problems shifting. I started from the pits, but soon had to stop because of the problem."

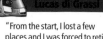 **Lucas di Grassi**
"From the start, I lost a few places and I was forced to retire from the race with a mechanical problem with just a lap to go. It was a race to put behind us."

2010 FORMULA 1 SINGTEL SINGAPORE GRAND PRIX
SINGAPORE

TWO ON THE TROT

Fernando Alonso had won in Singapore before, but this time there was no taint over his victory, just admiration for the way in which the Ferrari ace kept Red Bull's Sebastian Vettel behind him

We'd talked for months about the five-way battle for the championship, but as of Saturday evening qualifying, the Singapore GP was about two men.

Sebastian Vettel and Red Bull Racing seemed to have the upper hand through most of practice, but when it mattered in qualifying Fernando Alonso got the lap in. Just as at Monza, he set the pole time on the first run.

Vettel's first run was spoiled by being too close behind Michael Schumacher, and the second was scrappy, as he nearly brushed the wall. That left him hoping that he could get past the Ferrari at the start and, despite one of the best getaways made by an RB6 for some time, he didn't quite make it.

That's because Alonso slammed the door in his face at Turn 1. It was indicative of the fact that Alonso knew he had to take risks to close the gap to those ahead. Almost unnoticed behind, Lewis Hamilton did pretty much the same to Jenson Button, secure in the knowledge that his team-mate would have to back off.

After that, we were treated to 61 laps of a cat-and-mouse battle between Alonso and Vettel, reminiscent of what we saw between Alonso and Button in Italy, except that this time the Spaniard led all the way.

Alonso seemed to have the race under control, but

DAVID HUNT
TEAM LOTUS F1 BRAND OWNER

"How did my connection with Lotus come about? From 1990–94, I'd been consulting to the Peter Collins-led management and was asked to try and rescue the team from the administrator. Kenny Wapshot and I had set up Team Lotus Japan to bring in Japanese money. We were asked to represent a consortium who wanted to buy it but didn't want their names known.

I was asked to front it, but they didn't have the money ready, so Kenny and I were prevailed upon to put up the funds, which we did. We were told that if we bought it, certain things would happen and we'd be alright. We did, and we weren't. We were left holding a rather large, expensive baby.

There was no plan to own a team, and certainly not one in trouble. We woke up one day and realised we owned a team that had all its contracts breached, no sponsorship, no drivers and 96 staff, some of whom had been there 25 years plus, since 'Chunky' (Colin Chapman) himself.

The only option to keep the brand in F1 was a deal with Pacific GP, which we did. I had to make the entire staff redundant and when I did so I made a little speech saying that we'd bring Team Lotus back to F1, somehow.

We didn't try to exploit the brand in any arena outside F1. I was offered opportunities like the chance to brand bottles of water, but the aim was always to bring Team Lotus back into F1 in proper order. Clearly, Tony Fernandes is here for the long haul and wants to make it competitive.

We have endured legal challenges from Group Lotus since Proton's ownership. The route they took each time was to say that we hadn't been using our registered trademarks and therefore they were void. Under trademark law, you have to be either using the trademark or making genuine efforts to do so, for the proper purpose. We have continually made genuine efforts to return the trademarks to their proper use, so Group Lotus has never succeeded. It's just that getting into F1 isn't the same as opening a corner shop...

I plan to help Team Lotus raise sponsorship and, having nurtured and protected the brand for as long as I have, I want to see it move up the grid, hopefully take its 80th win and more championships. You're never going to replace Colin Chapman, but in Mike Gascoyne you've got an experienced Norfolk-born maverick engineer, and Tony Fernandes is a maverick business tycoon."

in a radio conversation Vettel told his team that he was taking it easy, biding his time. He duly edged closer as the pit stops approached.

Some way back in third, Hamilton was the first of the leading pack to stop, and that opened a window for the two ahead to come in. Red Bull Racing reacted immediately to pit Vettel and Ferrari did the same for Alonso. Vettel could have been told to stay out, but the team stuck with its call. The two cars came into the pits together and left in the same formation. RBR's only hope was to push Ferrari into a fumble, but it was Vettel who cracked, losing a few tenths as he tried to leave in second gear. So, for the second race in succession, Ferrari outfoxed a rival at the crucial moment.

"The only way to pass Fernando was to get the undercut," said Christian Horner. "Which is the faster out-lap. As soon as Hamilton pitted, it created a space, so we went for that space. Unfortunately, Ferrari could probably see that, and covered us.

"Going longer, you would have dropped further behind. The out-lap on the new tyres is so powerful. They covered us, so we were always going to have to make the pass on the track."

After Kamui Kobayashi crashed on lap 31 and

brought out a safety car, Vettel showed just how fast he was on the harder tyre, sticking right with Alonso, harrying him relentlessly.

"It was a fantastic result," said Ferrari engineering head Chris Dyer. "He drove a perfect race, following an absolutely perfect lap in qualifying. We were a bit nervous about the strategy, as there was more tyre degradation here than normal, and it wasn't so clear what was going to happen around the stops. So it was nice to be able to build a few seconds at the start to make us a bit more comfortable when the stop came."

Red Bull Racing had certainly given McLaren a thumping, but there was no denying that with a car that was as fast if not faster than the Ferrari, Red Bull had been beaten fair and square.

"Qualifying dictated the finish," Horner admitted. "Unfortunately, we didn't get pole position, but Sebastian drove a fantastic race. He pushed Fernando every lap. It was fantastic driving from both of them going lap for lap, after two hours."

Conversely, it was a disastrous day for Hamilton. To the surprise of many, both McLarens dropped back quickly from the leaders in the first part of the race.

"I think the lap times of Fernando and Sebastian

OPPOSITE TOP Christian Klien stepped up at HRT when Sakon Yamamoto suffered food poisoning

OPPOSITE BOTTOM Fernando Alonso leads into Turn 1 from Sebastian Vettel, the McLaren duo of Lewis Hamilton and Jenson Button, then Mark Webber

ABOVE Michael Schumacher has his front wing replaced after clashing with Nick Heidfeld's BMW Sauber

TALKING POINT
THE LOTUS POSITION

On Friday in Singapore, a media posse was herded into a small room on the second floor of the Pan Pacific Hotel to witness Tony Fernandes, his shareholding Malaysians, the Lotus drivers and David Hunt sitting under a projection of the Team Lotus logo complete with its 'ACBC' (Anthony Colin Bruce Chapman) initials.

This took place a couple of days after Group Lotus has issued a statement revealing a link-up with the crack Nicolas Todt/Frederick Vasseur-owned ART team in GP2 and GP3 with the cars to be branded Lotuses in 2011. Therefore, this was nothing to do with Lotus Racing, whose boss, Fernandes, already has his own Air Asia GP2 team.

Throughout 2010, Lotus Racing competed in F1 under licence from Group Lotus, which was bought by Proton in 1996. Fernandes, however, had apparently fallen out with new Group Lotus CEO Dany Bahar (formerly of Red Bull Racing and Ferrari) and had been told that his licence would not be renewed. Hence he was looking at Fernandes Racing, unless he did a deal with David Hunt, who has owned the disputed rights

to the Team Lotus F1 brand since the team went under in 1994.

With Todt Jr, son of FIA President Jean, lodging and then withdrawing an ART F1 entry earlier in the year, and Group Lotus drawing attention to its racing activity in the IRL and sportscars, you could understand paranoia breaking out in the Fernandes/Lotus Racing camp. After all, Toyota's bespoke F1 facility was sitting there in Cologne waiting for someone to commission it...

In the background, Todt was telling Lotus Racing people that he wasn't spoiling for a fight over the Lotus brand, but that when someone brings lucrative sponsorship to his GP2/GP3 teams, he certainly isn't going to turn it down.

Lotus Racing looks well set to progress in 2011, after starting with

an empty factory and four people in September 2009. The team will use a Renault engine and Red Bull Racing drivetrain in 2011, and with a nucleus of the old Toyota F1 race team in place, will be aiming higher than the 10th place overall that was this year's target.

Hunt wasn't saying what Fernandes paid him, or would pay him, but he believed the brand was worth considerably more. Somehow, though, you got the feeling that the legal battle over the rights to race under the Lotus name was only just beginning and that, ultimately, the matter could well be dictated by high-level political sources in Malaysia. If not quite a case of 'my Daddy is bigger than your Daddy,' maybe it was 'my politician is bigger than your politician'...

were much quicker than anyone else," said Martin Whitmarsh. "With the option tyre, I think we were overheating them, and our pace fell away. On the prime, it was a bit better. We were probably giving too hard a time to the rears under traction, and so we fell away."

Button confirmed that was the issue: "At the start, I thought I'd take it easy, because we suffered on Friday with the rear end going away. And I think it helped me a bit towards the end of my stint. The last three laps before my pit stop I was pulling in Lewis, who I think was suffering with the rear tyres going away. The balance wasn't good and I didn't have a stable rear end, and I really don't like that."

Both McLarens became easy pickings for Mark Webber, as once again Red Bull Racing made an interesting call that paid off. In Hungary, Webber had stayed out in the lead when others pitted, and he then had enough pace to turn that into victory once Vettel was penalised for staying too far behind the safety car. At Monza, Red Bull kept Vettel out until the penultimate lap, when he came in for his mandatory stop.

In Singapore, the team did the opposite, ditching Webber's soft tyres when the safety car came out on lap 3 after Vitantonio Liuzzi stopped on track. The Australian had the least to lose of the top five, in that he could be pretty confident that whatever he did, fifth place was going to be the worst-case scenario. Yet, if it worked out, he could haul himself up the race order.

Webber showed that, despite being the World Championship leader, he was willing to fight. He overtook Glock, Kobayashi and Schumacher in short order, and he certainly couldn't be fully confident that the last-named would leave him any space.

His problem was that, initially at least, his new hard tyres weren't as good as the softs still used by the leaders. Webber also had to bear in mind that he'd have to run them for 58 laps, so he had to leave himself a margin.

When Webber got behind Rubens Barrichello's

Williams, he ran out of momentum. Eventually, the team gave him a hurry-up, but almost immediately a close call at the tight lefthander (Turn 18) where Kobayashi crashed later gave him food for thought.

Before long, Alonso and Vettel were way too far ahead to be vulnerable. However, the McLarens were running at a similar pace to Barrichello, and Webber was close enough to jump them both when they pitted, as Horner explained: "The pace we could see Rubens was doing was similar to Lewis's. Thirty-three seconds was the magic number we needed, and it was well within that. The gap to Hamilton stayed consistent, but the two guys at the front were going at warp speed!"

OPPOSITE Felipe Massa worked his way forward from the back of the grid to eighth place

ABOVE Lucas di Grassi raced to 15th place for Virgin Racing, as the only finisher from the new teams

BELOW The moment it all went wrong for Lewis Hamilton, as he attempts to turn in and take third place from Mark Webber, who wasn't prepared to cede the corner

the way he goes racing. When he got to the next corner, he was convinced he was ahead and swept across on what was pretty much the normal line.

The problem was that Webber was still there. With his left-side wheels over the kerbs, and scrabbling on the edge of adhesion on the tighter inside line, Webber nudged the McLaren out of the way, and into retirement with a broken wheel.

The stewards decided that it wasn't worth punishing either driver for the contact. Views were split on which of the pair, if anyone, was in the wrong. Webber had the option to back off a touch, while Hamilton was the man who could have made sure there was room. The teams defended their drivers.

"Lewis didn't give Mark enough space," said Horner. "Mark had the inside line and Lewis just closed him down too much, just a bit too deep on the way into the corner, and Mark couldn't avoid contact. It's one of those things, a racing accident. It would have been very, very unfair to have penalised Mark for that, so thank you to the stewards for making the right call."

"If you don't want to take the risks, stay in the garage," said Whitmarsh. "You don't overtake any driver without some risks. I think it wasn't a late brake or a dive, he got past on the straight, he was in the lead going into that corner. He left a bit of space. I think Mark was a bit aggressive going into that corner and I think Lewis was not in error in what he did."

That Webber was able to stay safely ahead of Button, while nursing a vibration from a tyre that had been pushed slightly off the rim by Hamilton's rear wheel, was impressive. Neither man was entirely happy afterwards but, unlike Hamilton, they both logged vital points by finishing in third and fourth places respectively.

Nico Rosberg had a great run to fifth for Mercedes, ahead of Barrichello, Robert Kubica and Felipe Massa, the last named charging through from the back of the grid in his Ferrari after a glitch in qualifying.

ABOVE Heikki Kovalainen led the new-team class until the final lap when his Lotus's Cosworth engine went up in flames

BELOW Robert Kubica had to work for his seventh place after having to pit to replace a punctured tyre, dropping him from sixth to 13th

Hamilton in particular must have been frustrated to not only have lost a place at the stops, but find himself 8s shy of Webber. However, Kobayashi's accident and the ensuing safety car gave him a chance to sit behind Webber as they awaited the restart. In front of Webber were the lapped Virgins of Timo Glock and Lucas di Grassi. Hamilton knew that if they got in the way, it could give him his only chance to surprise Webber.

Glock was soon dispatched, but di Grassi couldn't get out of the way until Turn 5. Trying to pass him, Webber got sideways and lost momentum heading onto the straight that followed. Hamilton's jerk to the right and attempt to pass was instinctive, inspired and so typical of

SNAPSHOT FROM
SINGAPORE

CLOCKWISE FROM RIGHT Regular life in Singapore carries on regardless of who is on track; Nick Heidfeld has a breather after colliding with Schumacher; the American winners of the F1 in Schools competition celebrate; Virgin third driver Jerome d'Ambrosio has a seat-fitting; tyres as art; Lewis Hamilton walks back to the pits; Jenson Button is kept cool in the pits; Bernie Ecclestone poses with the medical and safety cars; Michael Schumacher had a tough race; a warm welcome

RACE RESULTS
SINGAPORE MARINA BAY

Official Results © [2010]
Formula One Administration Limited,
6 Princes Gate, London, SW7 1QJ.
No reproduction without permission.
All copyright and database rights reserved.

RACE DATE September 26th
CIRCUIT LENGTH 3.148 miles
NO. OF LAPS 61
RACE DISTANCE 192.028 miles
WEATHER Humid but dry, 30°C
TRACK TEMP 31°C
ATTENDANCE 244,000
LAP RECORD Kimi Räikkönen,
1m45.599s, 107.358mph, 2008

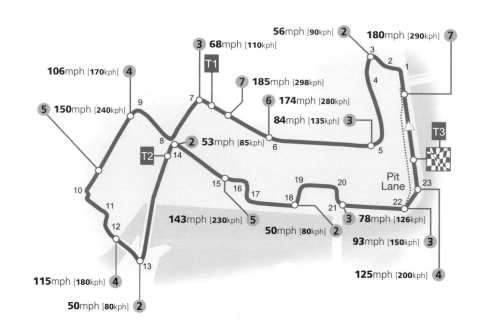

	PRACTICE 1		
	Driver	Time	Laps
1	M Webber	1m54.589s	10
2	M Schumacher	1m54.708s	24
3	A Sutil	1m54.827s	15
4	S Vettel	1m55.137s	12
5	J Alguersuari	1m55.160s	20
6	J Button	1m55.333s	12
7	V Liuzzi	1m55.510s	15
8	S Buemi	1m55.523s	15
9	R Kubica	1m55.672s	11
10	V Petrov	1m55.914s	20
11	F Alonso	1m56.090s	12
12	K Kobayashi	1m56.339s	22
13	N Heidfeld	1m56.458s	18
14	N Rosberg	1m56.598s	8
15	H Kovalainen	1m56.603s	12
16	R Barrichello	1m56.615s	17
17	N Hulkenberg	1m56.840s	14
18	L Hamilton	1m56.884s	9
19	F Massa	1m57.760s	22
20	T Glock	1m59.034s	19
21	J d'Ambrosio	1m59.275s	16
22	B Senna	1m59.783s	23
23	C Klien	2m03.424s	17
24	F Fauzy	2m05.694s	11

	PRACTICE 2		
	Driver	Time	Laps
1	S Vettel	1m46.660s	29
2	M Webber	1m47.287s	27
3	J Button	1m47.690s	28
4	F Alonso	1m47.718s	20
5	L Hamilton	1m47.818s	28
6	R Barrichello	1m48.302s	31
7	F Massa	1m48.341s	28
8	N Rosberg	1m48.679s	26
9	R Kubica	1m48.855s	15
10	M Schumacher	1m48.889s	31
11	N Hulkenberg	1m49.153s	32
12	K Kobayashi	1m49.438s	30
13	N Heidfeld	1m49.558s	26
14	V Petrov	1m49.608s	30
15	V Liuzzi	1m49.896s	28
16	A Sutil	1m49.984s	11
17	J Alguersuari	1m50.191s	31
18	S Buemi	1m50.896s	35
19	H Kovalainen	1m51.878s	30
20	T Glock	1m52.150s	22
21	L di Grassi	1m53.431s	25
22	J Trulli	1m53.526s	27
23	B Senna	1m54.725s	27
24	C Klien	1m55.542s	25

	PRACTICE 3		
	Driver	Time	Laps
1	S Vettel	1m48.028s	15
2	F Alonso	1m48.650s	16
3	L Hamilton	1m49.000s	12
4	F Massa	1m49.023s	18
5	N Rosberg	1m49.056s	17
6	M Webber	1m49.212s	13
7	N Hulkenberg	1m49.304s	17
8	R Kubica	1m49.520s	16
9	A Sutil	1m49.916s	15
10	S Buemi	1m49.949s	16
11	V Petrov	1m50.040s	15
12	R Barrichello	1m50.053s	16
13	J Button	1m50.060s	12
14	J Alguersuari	1m50.067s	15
15	M Schumacher	1m50.067s	14
16	V Liuzzi	1m50.868s	16
17	N Heidfeld	1m51.016s	15
18	K Kobayashi	1m51.027s	17
19	T Glock	1m52.340s	14
20	H Kovalainen	1m53.146s	15
21	L di Grassi	1m53.297s	15
22	J Trulli	1m53.681s	11
23	C Klien	1m54.826s	16
24	B Senna	1m55.367s	16

	QUALIFYING 1	
	Driver	Time
1	F Alonso	1m46.541s
2	S Vettel	1m46.960s
3	M Webber	1m47.088s
4	R Kubica	1m47.657s
5	N Hulkenberg	1m47.984s
6	J Button	1m48.032s
7	J Alguersuari	1m48.127s
8	R Barrichello	1m48.183s
9	L Hamilton	1m48.296s
10	M Schumacher	1m48.425s
11	A Sutil	1m48.496s
12	N Rosberg	1m48.554s
13	N Heidfeld	1m48.696s
14	V Petrov	1m48.906s
15	K Kobayashi	1m48.908s
16	V Liuzzi	1m48.988s
17	S Buemi	1m49.063s
18	T Glock	1m50.721s
19	H Kovalainen	1m50.915s
20	L di Grassi	1m51.107s
21	J Trulli	1m51.641s
22	C Klien	1m52.946s
23	B Senna	1m54.174s
24	F Massa	No time

	QUALIFYING 2	
	Driver	Time
1	S Vettel	1m45.561s
2	F Alonso	1m45.809s
3	M Webber	1m45.908s
4	L Hamilton	1m46.042s
5	J Button	1m46.490s
6	N Rosberg	1m46.783s
7	R Kubica	1m46.949s
8	R Barrichello	1m47.019s
9	M Schumacher	1m47.160s
10	K Kobayashi	1m47.599s
11	J Alguersuari	1m47.666s
12	N Hulkenberg	1m47.674s
13	V Petrov	1m48.165s
14	S Buemi	1m48.502s
15	N Heidfeld	1m48.557s
16	A Sutil	1m48.899s
17	V Liuzzi	1m48.961s

Best sectors – Practice	
Sec 1	F Alonso	28.957s
Sec 2	S Vettel	41.091s
Sec 3	S Vettel	36.192s

Speed trap – Practice		
1	R Kubica	180.259mph
2	N Heidfeld	179.576mph
3	A Sutil	179.079mph

Best sectors – Qualifying	
Sec 1	S Vettel	28.382s
Sec 2	S Vettel	40.897s
Sec 3	F Alonso	35.688s

Speed trap – Qualifying		
1	R Kubica	180.446mph
2	R Barrichello	179.762mph
3	A Sutil	179.576mph

 Jenson Button

"On the prime, I had an issue with rear-end stability, so not being able to challenge a Red Bull car that had 30 extra laps on its tyres showed us their speed."

Michael Schumacher

"I had two racing incidents with other cars that meant that I had to make my stops at times which weren't ideal, and consequently my race was compromised."

Sebastian Vettel

"I came in on the same lap as Ferrari and I made a mistake. That's the story of the race. I tried to push Fernando into a mistake, but he didn't make a major one."

Felipe Massa

"It was a very difficult race after qualifying. We chose a strategy hoping for some help from a safety car that unfortunately came out on track too early."

 **Rubens Barrichello**

"While my brakes were hot, the lap times were good and I was catching Kubica, but with the interruptions of the safety cars I kept losing brake performance."

Robert Kubica

"I had a right-rear puncture and that dropped me from sixth to 13th. I had fresher tyres in those laps, but it's not easy to pass here, so it was fun picking them off."

 Lewis Hamilton

"I got clipped, my tyre was blown, and that was it. There are four races to go. I'm 20 points behind Mark, but that's not insurmountable. I'll keep fighting."

Nico Rosberg

"Our aim is to finish as the best behind the top three teams and I was able to profit as two of them had issues with Felipe in qualifying and Lewis in the race."

 Mark Webber

"I passed a few guys, then couldn't pass Rubens. We had another restart and I got caught behind a Virgin, and Lewis got a run on me and we made contact."

Fernando Alonso

"This win is very significant. We wanted to confirm our success in Monza at a different type of track and we succeeded at the end of a very hard and stressful race."

 Nico Hulkenberg

"If someone had offered me eighth, I'd have grabbed it! I needed huge concentration for a long race with a car close in front and another close behind."

 Vitaly Petrov

"We stopped under the first safety car and I was the first runner on primes behind Webber, but Hulkenberg pushed me out in Turn 7. It cost me three places."

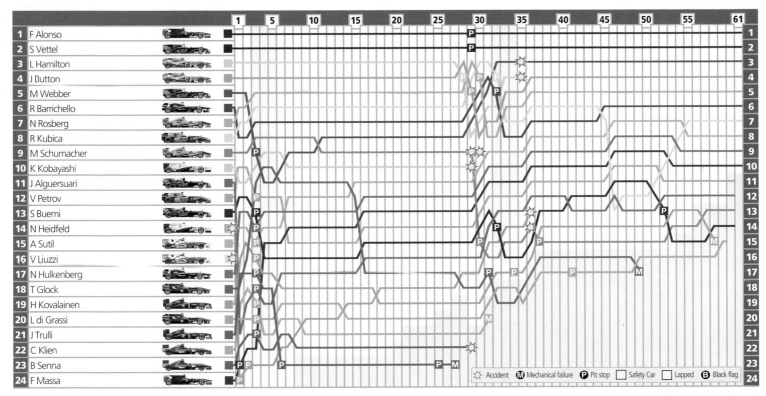

	Driver		1	5	10	15	20	25	30	35	40	45	50	55	61	
1	F Alonso															1
2	S Vettel															2
3	L Hamilton															3
4	J Button															4
5	M Webber															5
6	R Barrichello															6
7	N Rosberg															7
8	R Kubica															8
9	M Schumacher															9
10	K Kobayashi															10
11	J Alguersuari															11
12	V Petrov															12
13	S Buemi															13
14	N Heidfeld															14
15	A Sutil															15
16	V Liuzzi															16
17	N Hulkenberg															17
18	T Glock															18
19	H Kovalainen															19
20	L di Grassi															20
21	J Trulli															21
22	C Klien															22
23	B Senna															23
24	F Massa															24

☼ Accident Ⓜ Mechanical failure Ⓟ Pit stop ☐ Safety Car ☐ Lapped Ⓑ Black flag

QUALIFYING 3

	Driver	Time
1	F Alonso	1m45.390s
2	S Vettel	1m45.457s
3	L Hamilton	1m45.571s
4	J Button	1m45.944s
5	M Webber	1m45.977s
6	R Barrichello	1m46.236s
7	N Rosberg	1m46.443s
8	R Kubica	1m46.593s
9	M Schumacher	1m46.702s
10	K Kobayashi	1m47.884s

GRID

	Driver	Time
1	F Alonso	1m45.390s
2	S Vettel	1m45.457s
3	L Hamilton	1m45.571s
4	J Button	1m45.944s
5	M Webber	1m45.977s
6	R Barrichello	1m46.236s
7	N Rosberg	1m46.443s
8	R Kubica	1m46.593s
9	M Schumacher	1m46.702s
10	K Kobayashi	1m47.884s
11*	J Alguersuari	1m47.666s
12	V Petrov	1m48.165s
13	S Buemi	1m48.502s
14	N Heidfeld	1m48.557s
15	A Sutil	1m48.899s
16	V Liuzzi	1m48.961s
17^	N Hulkenberg	1m47.674s
18	T Glock	1m50.721s
19	H Kovalainen	1m50.915s
20	L di Grassi	1m51.107s
21	J Trulli	1m51.641s
22	C Klien	1m52.946s
23	B Senna	1m54.174s
24	F Massa	No time

* Started from the pitlane
^ 5-place grid penalty for gearbox change

RACE

	Driver	Car	Laps	Time	Avg. mph	Fastest	Stops
1	F Alonso	Ferrari F10	61	1h57m53.579s	97.817	1m47.976s	1
2	S Vettel	Red Bull-Renault RB6	61	1h57m53.872s	97.813	1m48.141s	1
3	M Webber	Red Bull-Renault RB6	61	1h58m22.720s	97.416	1m49.706s	1
4	J Button	McLaren-Mercedes MP4-25	61	1h58m23.963s	97.399	1m49.711s	1
5	N Rosberg	Mercedes MGP W01	61	1h58m42.973s	97.139	1m50.125s	1
6	R Barrichello	Williams-Cosworth FW32	61	1h58m49.680s	97.047	1m50.334s	1
7	R Kubica	Renault R30	61	1h59m20.138s	96.635	1m49.255s	2
8	F Massa	Ferrari F10	61	1h59m46.876s	96.275	1m52.079s	1
9	A Sutil	Force India-Mercedes VJM03	61	2h00m05.995s*	96.020	1m52.473s	0
10	N Hulkenberg	Williams-Cosworth FW32	61	2h00m06.370s*	96.015	1m52.213s	0
11	V Petrov	Renault R30	61	1h57m57.619s	96.158	1m51.903s	0
12	J Alguersuari	Toro Rosso-Ferrari STR5	60	1h57m59.746s	96.129	1m52.333s	1
13	M Schumacher	Mercedes MGP W01	60	1h58m06.513s	96.037	1m49.680s	2
14	S Buemi	Toro Rosso-Ferrari STR5	60	1h58m11.029s	95.976	1m49.710s	1
15	L di Grassi	Virgin-Cosworth VR-01	59	1h59m32.061s	93.309	1m52.513s	2
16	H Kovalainen	Lotus-Cosworth T127	58	Fire	-	1m53.051s	1
R	T Glock	Virgin-Cosworth VR-01	49	Hydraulics	-	1m53.559s	1
R	N Heidfeld	BMW Sauber-Ferrari C29	36	Collision	-	1m52.475s	2
R	L Hamilton	McLaren-Mercedes MP4-25	35	Collision	-	1m50.750s	1
R	C Klien	HRT-Cosworth F110	32	Hydraulics	-	1m57.766s	1
R	K Kobayashi	BMW Sauber-Ferrari C29	30	Spun off	-	1m53.957s	0
R	B Senna	HRT-Cosworth F110	29	Collision	-	1m57.962s	1
R	J Trulli	Lotus-Cosworth T127	27	Hydraulics	-	1m56.386s	3
R	V Liuzzi	Force India-Mercedes VJM03	1	Collision	-	-	0

* 20s penalty for corner-cutting

CHAMPIONSHIP

	Driver	Pts
1	M Webber	202
2	F Alonso	191
3	L Hamilton	182
4	S Vettel	181
5	J Button	177
6	F Massa	128
7	N Rosberg	122
8	R Kubica	114
9	A Sutil	47
10	M Schumacher	46
11	R Barrichello	39
12	K Kobayashi	21
13	V Petrov	19
14	N Hulkenberg	17
15	V Liuzzi	13
16	S Buemi	7
17	P de la Rosa	6
18	J Alguersuari	3

	Constructor	Pts
1	Red Bull-Renault	383
2	McLaren-Mercedes	359
3	Ferrari	319
4	Mercedes	168
5	Renault	133
6	Force India-Mercedes	60
7	Williams-Cosworth	56
8	BMW Sauber-Ferrari	27
9	Toro Rosso-Ferrari	10

Fastest lap
F Alonso 1m47.976s
(105.097mph) on lap 58

Fastest speed trap
R Kubica 181.751mph
Slowest speed trap
H Kovalainen 171.871mph

Fastest pit stop
1	F Alonso	30.236s
2	R Barrichello	30.293s
3	N Rosberg	30.380s

Adrian Sutil
"It was a hard race, in the heat and humidity and having to race the whole way. I always had a car close behind! Starting 15th, this was the most I could have done."

"I clashed with Kobayashi on lap 1. We decided to change the front wing and tyres. I came out behind Petrov. Later, I had to pit again to pressurise the hydraulic system."

Jarno Trulli
"I had a good start and was running with Heikki, but had a puncture after the first safety car, then the hydraulic problems that have affected me a few times before."

Christian Klien
"I enjoyed being back in F1, even though a comeback in Singapore might be one of the most difficult. I got a good start, was able to gain some positions before retiring."

Nick Heidfeld
"Michael knocked me out of the race. My race was compromised, as Liuzzi tried to pass from way on the outside in Turn 4. Then he braked early and I hit him."

Timo Glock
"Both Lotuses passed me, but I retook Trulli. At the first safety car, I stayed out and 10th. A few laps from the end, I had a hydraulics problem and my race was over."

 Vitantonio Liuzzi
"I was trying to pass Heidfeld into 7, but was squeezed into the wall, damaging the front wing. It must have cracked the suspension, as the lap after it broke."

"It went wrong before the start with a coolant leak, which meant I started from pitlane. Then it was the most boring race of my career as I was stuck in a train of cars."

Heikki Kovalainen
"I was going and the car had felt good, but I clashed with Buemi. I think I cracked the fuel tank pressure release valve and it looks as if that caused an airbox fire."

Bruno Senna
"As soon as I got into the braking area, the flags came out, but it was too late. There was no way to avoid the accident. I didn't have any notice of what was going on."

Kamui Kobayashi
"After I passed Michael, I had to push to score a point, but the tyres were gone. I misjudged this in Turn 18 and hit the barrier. Then Senna crashed into my car."

Lucas di Grassi
"We opted to pit in the first safety-car period but were unlucky with the second, which made us lose a lot of time. After that, I focused on reaching the end of the race."

2010 FORMULA 1
JAPANESE GRAND PRIX
SUZUKA

RED BULL DOMINATES

Red Bull Racing was tipped for glory at Suzuka, a track tailor-made for the strengths of its RB6s, and Sebastian Vettel duly controlled the race, with Mark Webber right behind

We'd known well in advance that Suzuka was tailor-made for the Red Bull RB6, so it was no surprise that Sebastian Vettel duly scored his second successive victory in the Japanese GP, with team-mate Mark Webber in his wheel tracks.

Vettel hadn't won a race since Valencia in June and, since then, little had gone right for the German. This win came at the perfect time. Having slipped up on occasions when doing the chasing, he demonstrated once again that if he gets into the first corner in front, he can drive a race with metronomic precision. Behind at the first corner, Webber knew there was nothing he could do, but he was happy to accept the points for second.

Meanwhile, Fernando Alonso kept his title challenge alive with third, as McLaren fell off the pace a little – at least in terms of the championship – with Lewis Hamilton again enduring a tough weekend.

Torrential rain on Saturday meant that there was no meaningful running in the morning, and forced the postponement of qualifying until Sunday morning. That certainly created a stressful schedule for the drivers and the teams, but it all went pretty smoothly. The only real benefit was that the engineers had just a few hours to fuss about the race.

Having dominated Friday practice, Vettel did the same in qualifying, topping all three sessions. However, in the one that counted, Webber very nearly usurped him, the Australian getting to within 0.1s.

Hamilton had a far-from-straightforward two days. He crashed heavily at Degner on Friday morning – a silly mistake resulting from pushing too hard too soon – and after repairs he only managed a few laps right at the end of P2. So, more than anyone else, he lost out through the lack of any dry running in P3.

Then, after a Saturday afternoon spent hanging around waiting for something to happen, he had to face up to a five-place grid penalty after the team found some gearbox issues that forced a change.

Despite his restricted mileage and lack of fine-tuned knowledge of the package – a new rear wing was dropped before Sunday morning qualifying – Hamilton still qualified third. The Red Bulls were always going to be untouchable over one lap, so it was as good as it could get, at least before those five penalty places were added.

Hamilton's demotion promoted Robert Kubica to third, ahead of Alonso and Jenson Button. The World Champion took a gamble and qualified on the prime

tyre, which ensured that he'd be on a different race strategy to those around him. Meanwhile, Felipe Massa was a frustrated 12th for Ferrari, having simply failed to get a decent lap in during Q2.

The race started with high drama, as two separate accidents triggered an immediate safety-car period. Vitaly Petrov clipped the nose of Nico Hulkenberg's slow-starting Williams as they accelerated away from the grid, and the Renault turned sharp left into the barrier. Seconds later, Massa found himself on the grass on the inside of Turn 1 after being squeezed by Nico Rosberg. The Brazilian lost control and collided hard with an innocent Vitantonio Liuzzi.

Meanwhile, Kubica had made a great start to get up to second place behind Vettel. Then, while the field was running behind the safety car, there was more drama when his Renault lost a rear wheel and had to stop. The others were also loose, the team simply having failed to tighten the wheel nuts sufficiently. What a way to throw away a podium...

The green flag finally flew after six laps, and over the first stint Vettel had no problem staying ahead, as he and Webber edged away from their pursuers, led by Alonso, Button and Hamilton. Hamilton had

INSIDE LINE
SEBASTIAN VETTEL
RED BULL RACING DRIVER

"It was an incredible day, with qualifying and the pole position in the morning and then the afternoon continuing the same way.

Most of the guys didn't sleep from Thursday until Saturday, so it was good there was no qualifying and they didn't have to touch the car... They deserved the 1–2.

This track is like it was drawn especially for us. With all its high-speed corners it's always a pleasure and, with the car getting lighter and lighter as the race goes on, it's just more and more fun.

I got a good start from the clean side of the grid, which was the key, and I could see that Robert Kubica had a bit of momentum on me, but the run to Turn 1 was too short for him. Then the safety car stayed out quite long and Robert had his wheel problem, so after that we were able to pull away from the field.

I had a little bit of a rest behind Jenson, who ran long on the primes. We couldn't really go through him, so we had to wait until he pitted.

Mark was obviously pushing, but I knew that passing isn't so easy and I just went as fast as I had to. I was given the pace Fernando was doing for the majority of the race.

It's been a tough season with a lot of ups and downs and not so trouble-free, but still I think we're in a very good position. I'm really happy to be back here and to have won. It's about time, too! I love this circuit. It's always special to come to Suzuka. The fans love it and I think the atmosphere for all of us is special.

It was a very good day for Red Bull Racing all round. Obviously, it was a special experience with qualifying and the race in one day. It wasn't easy in terms of focus to be ready straightaway this morning and this afternoon, but I think the team did a very good job, and the pit stops were spot on.

It's the first time I've won a grand prix for a second time, and ultimately you have to fall in love with this track. Someone pointed out that the only other drivers to have won back-to-back races at Suzuka are Mika Häkkinen and Michael Schumacher, and that they went on to win the championship. So maybe that's a good omen. I wouldn't mind!"

McLAREN'S SACRIFICIAL LAMB?

"We were a bit concerned by Jenson Button's race strategy," said Red Bull's Christian Horner on Sunday evening. "We knew we would come out behind Jenson after the pit stops, and then he started to back everybody up towards Hamilton. But then Lewis developed a problem and they aborted that strategy. It looked a little bit like Jenson was being used as a sacrificial lamb..."

The Red Bulls were half-a-second a lap quicker than anything through Suzuka's flat-out uphill sector-one sweepers, and McLaren had little to lose by adopting a different approach.

Hamilton's five-place grid penalty for a gearbox change limited what they could do with him, so it was Button who gambled on starting the grand prix with the prime tyre.

The intention, then, would not have been to use Button as a 'blocker.' The thinking would have been that with all the rain the track surface would be very 'green' and therefore the rest of the top 10, option-shod, would probably have to pit early.

Some estimated that the options would last only 10–12 laps. There was a chance even the Red Bull pace might not be enough to clear some of those who started further back on the grid on primes. Button, therefore, could lead the race and run uninterrupted in clean air.

Things looked good when he qualified within 0.02s of Alonso, despite using the harder tyre for a three-lap qualifying run. However, track temperature had risen, which allowed the surface to rubber in more quickly, meaning that the frontrunners on their options weren't in trouble. Hamilton, who was the first of the leading group to pit, went 22 laps into the 53-lap race.

At this stage, Button's strategy clearly wasn't going to work. The best thing would have been for McLaren to pit him, maybe even a lap before Hamilton, and put him on the option tyres which, with the track rubbered in, would have been capable of a 30-lap stint. Instead, they left him out for another 16 laps, until lap 38. For the next 15 laps, Button was around 1s a lap slower than Hamilton. If McLaren wasn't using Button to back everyone into Hamilton, what were they doing?

Unfortunately, the scenario didn't play out. On lap 38, Hamilton lost the use of third gear, his times dropped off by 2s and McLaren called Button in. Had that not happened, we may have seen Button, Vettel, Webber, Alonso and Hamilton running in a five-car train, which could have become uncomfortable for Red Bull. Also, it would have been team strategy, not team orders…

gained three places after the early chaos, but he had to sit behind team-mate Button, who didn't quite have the expected pace on his prime tyres.

Vettel looked secure in front, and Webber's only real chance to do anything about his team-mate was at the pit stops. The German came in at the end of lap 24, and Webber followed a lap later, but he was too far behind to make the extra lap pay.

Thereafter, the Red Bulls ran in close formation to the flag, their only concern coming when they had to sit patiently a little way behind Button, who stayed out for a late stop and thus held the lead for a while.

"I made a good start, which was the key, from the clean side," said Vettel. "I could see Robert got a bit of momentum, but the way down to Turn 1 was too short for him. Then we had the safety car, which stayed out for a long time with the incident with Kubica. After that, both Mark and I were able to pull away, and we controlled the pace until the end."

Meanwhile, Alonso had a relatively lonely race in third place. It was his fifth podium in six races – the only exception being Spa, where he crashed. Significantly, Ferrari had lately been fastest or very close to the front-running pace at every kind of track.

"I was more or less alone the whole race, no pressure from behind and impossible to catch Red Bull in the first part of the race," said Alonso. "In the second part, they managed the gap to Button a little bit. They were playing a little bit with that gap and I was able to run close to them but never close enough to put pressure on.

"Anyway, we knew that before coming here, third place was maybe our maximum position. However, we're convinced that this was the worst track for us for the remaining circuits of the championship, so it was a good weekend."

Conversely, Massa's position in the team was further weakened after his first corner contretemps.

There was a bit more excitement behind the

top three. Button and Hamilton ran together until Hamilton stopped, but on the harder tyres Button stayed out a lot longer, and as noted earlier he held the lead ahead of the Red Bulls when he did so.

When he finally came in, he dropped back to fifth place behind his team-mate. However, Hamilton then began struggling after losing third gear, a problem unrelated to the one suffered with the gearbox he'd abandoned before qualifying. Inevitably, his pace slowed and he dropped back to fifth place behind Button, but fortunately no further.

"In the end, we asked him to stay in fourth gear and above, which was costing him a second and a half a lap," said McLaren engineering head Paddy Lowe. "That's why Jenson overtook him in the hairpin, as he was doing the rest of the race with fourth to seventh.

"The thing that was quite nerve-wracking was when Rosberg had his shunt because, if they'd called a safety car at that point, the field would have bunched up, and he would have fallen prey to the cars behind. As it was, he had a 20 second gap…"

Having adjusted his driving, Hamilton made it safely to the end. Despite this extraordinary accumulation of problems in one weekend, including

OPPOSITE TOP It's over and out for Robert Kubica as his Renault sheds a wheel behind the safety car

OPPOSITE BELOW Fernando Alonso was the best of the rest, finishing third behind the Red Bulls

TOP Mercedes team-mates Nico Rosberg and Michael Schumacher enjoyed an entertaining scrap

ABOVE The crowds in the grandstands brought rainwear with them on race day, just in case…

ABOVE Jaime Alguersuari was able to resist Kamui Kobayashi, but only for a short while

BELOW Red Bull Racing Chief Technical Officer Adrian Newey gets a blast of Champagne from the team's race winner, Sebastian Vettel

two gearbox issues, the 2008 World Champion still earned 10 points for fifth.

"We had high hopes that we'd come away with more points than we did," said Lowe. "It was encouraging in the race, the pace was good actually. We just let ourselves down with two gearbox problems on Lewis's car.

"The prime-tyre strategy with Jenson didn't work out, as the option didn't degrade the way that it might have done, and at the same time he wasn't getting the pace he needed on the prime tyre, as it didn't seem to be working well. So that could have gone better.

"However, the pace of the car was good. Lewis was very quick at various stages in the race, and he could have challenged Alonso at the end, if not for his gearbox problem."

Michael Schumacher had one of his best races of the season to claim sixth place. His Mercedes team-mate Rosberg made his tyre change behind the safety car after the first-corner dramas, and was thus able to run to the end of the race. Schumacher sat behind the title contenders for the first part of the race, but Rosberg got ahead when the seven-time World Champion stopped. Schumacher then made some fairly aggressive overtaking attempts, but he couldn't find a way by. Then Rosberg had a spectacular spin into a gravel trap when his Mercedes shed a rear wheel, which like Kubica's, had simply worked loose.

The star of the race was Sauber's Kamui Kobayashi, who was racing in front of his home crowd for the first time as an F1 driver. After a disappointing qualifying session left him 14th, he made a good start and put in a charging performance. Helped towards the end by a late pit stop that left him on fresher rubber than his rivals, he made a string of aggressive passing manoeuvres at the hairpin. In the course of the race, he twice passed and banged wheels with Jaime Alguersuari. Kobayashi also outfoxed Sauber team-mate Nick Heidfeld, the German still managing to score his first 2010 points with eighth place, ahead of Williams' Rubens Barrichello and Toro Rosso's Sebastien Buemi.

Further back, the high rate of attrition helped Heikki Kovalainen and Jarno Trulli finish 12th and 13th for Lotus. Not only did this put Lotus at the top of the new teams again, but this excellent result went some way to securing the team a valuable 10th place in the constructors' table.

SNAPSHOT FROM
JAPAN

CLOCKWISE FROM RIGHT The hairpin looks great in the sunshine; Lewis Hamilton was 'treated' to a meagre parade-lap ride; conditions on Saturday were... wet; when rain stopped play, Timo Glock took on Virgin Racing team-mate Lucas di Grassi in a game of poker; two hats for Heikki Kovalainen after his firefighting in Singapore; the fans were as passionate as ever, but not all of their wishes would come true; meeting 'Robert Kubica' was clearly a thrill for this fan; Bruno Senna inspects some merchandise; the marshals get their message across and Kamui Kobayashi clearly took heed; the safety car went out on a number of exploratory laps before qualifying was cancelled on Saturday

RACE RESULTS

JAPAN SUZUKA

RACE DATE October 10th
CIRCUIT LENGTH 3.608 miles
NO. OF LAPS 53
RACE DISTANCE 191.126 miles
WEATHER Dry & bright, 26°C
TRACK TEMP 33°C
ATTENDANCE 190,000
LAP RECORD Kimi Räikkönen, 1m31.540s, 141.904mph, 2005

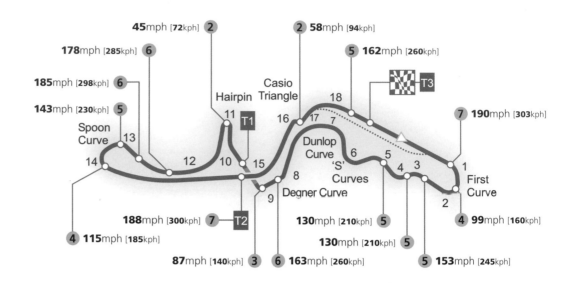

#	PRACTICE 1 Driver	Time	Laps
1	S Vettel	1m32.585s	23
2	M Webber	1m32.633s	23
3	R Kubica	1m33.129s	23
4	A Sutil	1m33.639s	13
5	L Hamilton	1m33.643s	9
6	R Barrichello	1m33.677s	21
7	N Hulkenberg	1m33.707s	24
8	M Schumacher	1m33.739s	20
9	N Heidfeld	1m33.791s	23
10	N Rosberg	1m33.831s	9
11	F Massa	1m33.929s	25
12	J Button	1m34.042s	19
13	F Alonso	1m34.169s	23
14	K Kobayashi	1m34.271s	19
15	V Petrov	1m34.373s	24
16	V Liuzzi	1m34.379s	21
17	S Buemi	1m34.991s	26
18	J Alguersuari	1m35.684s	22
19	H Kovalainen	1m36.949s	25
20	T Glock	1m37.329s	17
21	J Trulli	1m37.388s	23
22	J d'Ambrosio	1m37.778s	23
23	B Senna	1m38.814s	28
24	C Klien	1m39.443s	26

#	PRACTICE 2 Driver	Time	Laps
1	S Vettel	1m31.465s	32
2	M Webber	1m31.860s	29
3	R Kubica	1m32.200s	32
4	F Alonso	1m32.362s	34
5	F Massa	1m32.519s	35
6	J Button	1m32.533s	28
7	V Petrov	1m32.703s	32
8	M Schumacher	1m32.831s	27
9	A Sutil	1m32.842s	26
10	N Hulkenberg	1m32.851s	26
11	N Rosberg	1m32.880s	26
12	K Kobayashi	1m33.471s	31
13	L Hamilton	1m33.481s	8
14	R Barrichello	1m33.564s	16
15	N Heidfeld	1m33.697s	33
16	S Buemi	1m34.055s	32
17	J Alguersuari	1m34.055s	37
18	V Liuzzi	1m34.310s	33
19	H Kovalainen	1m36.095s	37
20	J Trulli	1m36.333s	33
21	L di Grassi	1m36.630s	28
22	T Glock	1m36.834s	28
23	B Senna	1m37.352s	33
24	S Yamamoto	1m37.831s	34

#	PRACTICE 3 Driver	Time	Laps
1	J Alguersuari	1m55.902s	9
2	T Glock	2m07.497s	6
3	S Buemi	No time	4
4	J Button	No time	3
5	L Hamilton	No time	3
6	N Hulkenberg	No time	2
7	R Kubica	No time	2
8	M Schumacher	No time	1
9	N Rosberg	No time	1
10	S Vettel	No time	1
11	M Webber	No time	1
12	F Massa	No time	1
13	F Alonso	No time	1
14	R Barrichello	No time	1
15	V Petrov	No time	1
16	A Sutil	No time	1
17	V Liuzzi	No time	1
18	J Trulli	No time	1
19	H Kovalainen	No time	1
20	S Yamamoto	No time	1
21	B Senna	No time	1
22	N Heidfeld	No time	1
23	K Kobayashi	No time	1
24	L di Grassi	No time	1

#	QUALIFYING 1 Driver	Time
1	S Vettel	1m32.035s
2	N Hulkenberg	1m32.211s
3	N Rosberg	1m32.238s
4	R Barrichello	1m32.361s
5	M Webber	1m32.476s
6	M Schumacher	1m32.513s
7	F Alonso	1m32.555s
8	J Button	1m32.636s
9	F Massa	1m32.721s
10	K Kobayashi	1m32.783s
11	R Kubica	1m32.808s
12	L Hamilton	1m32.809s
13	V Petrov	1m32.849s
14	N Heidfeld	1m33.011s
15	A Sutil	1m33.186s
16	V Liuzzi	1m33.216s
17	J Alguersuari	1m33.471s
18	S Buemi	1m33.568s
19	J Trulli	1m35.346s
20	H Kovalainen	1m35.464s
21	L di Grassi	1m36.265s
22	T Glock	1m36.332s
23	B Senna	1m37.270s
24	S Yamamoto	1m37.365s

#	QUALIFYING 2 Driver	Time
1	S Vettel	1m31.184s
2	M Webber	1m31.241s
3	L Hamilton	1m31.523s
4	J Button	1m31.763s
5	F Alonso	1m31.819s
6	R Barrichello	1m31.874s
7	N Rosberg	1m31.886s
8	N Hulkenberg	1m31.926s
9	R Kubica	1m32.042s
10	M Schumacher	1m32.073s
11	N Heidfeld	1m32.187s
12	F Massa	1m32.321s
13	V Petrov	1m32.422s
14	K Kobayashi	1m32.427s
15	A Sutil	1m32.659s
16	J Alguersuari	1m33.071s
17	V Liuzzi	1m33.154s

Best sectors – Practice
Sec 1	S Vettel	32.407s
Sec 2	S Vettel	41.110s
Sec 3	R Kubica	17.721s

Speed trap – Practice
1	S Buemi	191.693mph
2	R Kubica	190.885mph
3	V Petrov	190.761mph

Best sectors – Qualifying
Sec 1	S Vettel	31.670s
Sec 2	F Alonso	41.220s
Sec 3	L Hamilton	17.746s

Speed trap – Qualifying
1	J Button	192.811mph
2	R Kubica	192.500mph
3	M Schumacher	192.003mph

Jenson Button
"The drivers ahead weren't struggling on the option as much as we'd hoped. We were compromised and stayed out too long. It was fun once we'd fitted options."

Michael Schumacher
"The car felt really good, and the opportunity to make up places was just what I hoped for. It was fun to be racing Nico, so it's a shame what happened to him."

Sebastian Vettel
"This circuit is very special: the fans are incredible and to get my second win here is fantastic. To have qualifying and the race in one day is a unique experience."

Felipe Massa
"Rosberg got away poorly and I moved to the left, but Sutil was coming. Then I moved right, but found myself on the grass. At that point the car took off on its own."

Rubens Barrichello
"My car was skating all over the track. I also had a lot of vibration. I managed to salvage some points, but I really thought that I was going to finish higher up."

Robert Kubica
"I was warming the tyres behind the safety car and nearly lost it. It became so difficult to follow the safety car that I moved to the side, then lost the wheel."

Lewis Hamilton
"I made a mistake on Friday, then we changed the gearbox and got a grid penalty. Then I had gearbox problems in the race. That's an unfortunate amount of bad luck."

Nico Rosberg
"My start was poor, but our strategy was good to change tyres under the safety car on lap 1. I was able to keep Michael behind, then something broke at the rear."

Mark Webber
"Sebastian had an extra half-tenth in qualifying, and pole is a nice thing to have for this race. Ultimately qualifying was vital, but I'm happy with how I drove."

Fernando Alonso
"I started defensively, trying to keep the McLarens at a distance, especially Jenson, who was on a very different strategy. Then we realised they were not a threat."

Nico Hulkenberg
"I didn't get off the line at all. I then saw Petrov coming behind me. He touched my front-right wheel and that was it. You never want to finish a race that early."

Vitaly Petrov
"I passed Massa and was passing Hulkenberg with Heidfeld on my right when he started to go left and I had to move left to avoid him, but I hit Hulkenberg."

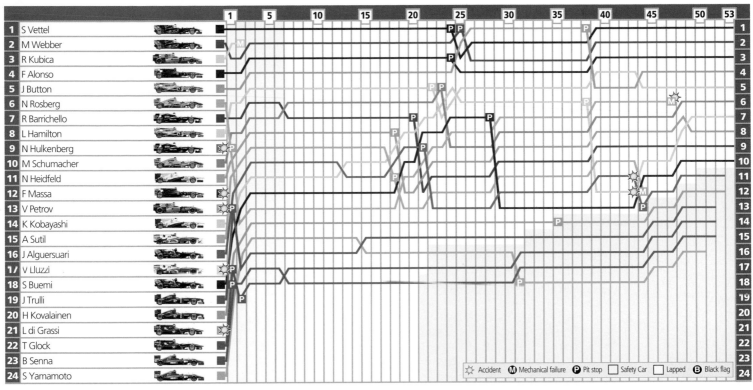

| | | Accident | M Mechanical failure | P Pit stop | Safety Car | Lapped | B Black flag |

QUALIFYING 3

	Driver	Time
1	S Vettel	1m30.785s
2	M Webber	1m30.853s
3	L Hamilton	1m31.169s
4	R Kubica	1m31.231s
5	F Alonso	1m31.352s
6	J Button	1m31.378s
7	N Rosberg	1m31.494s
8	R Barrichello	1m31.535s
9	N Hulkenberg	1m31.559s
10	M Schumacher	1m31.846s

GRID

	Driver	Time
1	S Vettel	1m30.785s
2	M Webber	1m30.853s
3	R Kubica	1m31.231s
4	F Alonso	1m31.352s
5	J Button	1m31.378s
6	N Rosberg	1m31.494s
7	R Barrichello	1m31.535s
8*	L Hamilton	1m31.169s
9	N Hulkenberg	1m31.559s
10	M Schumacher	1m31.846s
11	N Heidfeld	1m32.187s
12	F Massa	1m32.321s
13	V Petrov	1m32.422s
14	K Kobayashi	1m32.427s
15	A Sutil	1m32.659s
16	J Alguersuari	1m33.071s
17	V Liuzzi	1m33.154s
18	S Buemi	1m33.568s
19	J Trulli	1m35.346s
20	H Kovalainen	1m35.464s
21	L di Grassi	1m36.265s
22	T Glock	1m36.332s
23	B Senna	1m37.270s
24	S Yamamoto	1m37.365s

*5-place grid penalty for gearbox change

RACE

	Driver	Car	Laps	Time	Avg. mph	Fastest	Stops
1	S Vettel	Red Bull-Renault RB6	53	1h30m27.323s	126.727	1m33.653s	1
2	M Webber	Red Bull-Renault RB6	53	1h30m28.228s	126.706	1m33.474s	1
3	F Alonso	Ferrari F10	53	1h30m30.044s	126.664	1m33.823s	1
4	J Button	McLaren-Mercedes MP4-25	53	1h30m40.845s	126.412	1m33.529s	1
5	L Hamilton	McLaren-Mercedes MP4-25	53	1h31m06.918s	125.809	1m35.182s	1
6	M Schumacher	Mercedes MGP W01	53	1h31m27.256s	125.343	1m34.853s	1
7	K Kobayashi	BMW Sauber-Ferrari C29	53	1h31m31.361s	125.250	1m34.486s	1
8	N Heidfeld	BMW Sauber-Ferrari C29	53	1h31m36.971s	125.122	1m35.521s	1
9	R Barrichello	Williams-Cosworth FW32	53	1h31m38.169s	125.094	1m35.597s	1
10	S Buemi	Toro Rosso-Ferrari STR5	53	1h31m40.129s	125.050	1m35.116s	1
11	J Alguersuari	Toro Rosso-Ferrari STR5	52	1h30m33.120s	124.201	1m34.365s	2
12	H Kovalainen	Lotus-Cosworth T127	52	1h32m07.726s	122.076	1m37.620s	1
13	J Trulli	Lotus-Cosworth T127	51	1h31m30.576s	120.536	1m39.710s	1
14	T Glock	Virgin-Cosworth VR-01	51	1h32m00.772s	119.877	1m39.813s	2
15	B Senna	HRT-Cosworth F110	51	1h32m02.330s	119.842	1m40.329s	1
16	S Yamamoto	HRT-Cosworth F110	50	1h31m10.190s	118.610	1m39.806s	1
17	N Rosberg	Mercedes MGP W01	47	Accident	-	1m36.108s	1
R	A Sutil	Force India-Mercedes VJM03	44	Engine	-	1m36.319s	1
R	R Kubica	Renault R30	2	Lost wheel	-	2m41.378s	0
R	N Hulkenberg	Williams-Cosworth FW32	0	Accident	-	-	0
R	F Massa	Ferrari F10	0	Accident	-	-	0
R	V Petrov	Renault R30	0	Accident	-	-	0
R	V Liuzzi	Force India-Mercedes VJM03	0	Accident	-	-	0
NS	L di Grassi	Virgin-Cosworth VR-01	-	Accident	-	-	-

CHAMPIONSHIP

	Driver	Pts
1	M Webber	220
2	F Alonso	206
3	S Vettel	206
4	L Hamilton	192
5	J Button	189
6	F Massa	128
7	N Rosberg	122
8	R Kubica	114
9	M Schumacher	54
10	A Sutil	47
11	R Barrichello	41
12	K Kobayashi	27
13	V Petrov	19
14	N Hulkenberg	17
15	V Liuzzi	13
16	S Buemi	8
17	P de la Rosa	6
18	N Heidfeld	4
19	J Alguersuari	3

	Constructor	Pts
1	Red Bull-Renault	426
2	McLaren-Mercedes	381
3	Ferrari	334
4	Mercedes	176
5	Renault	133
6	Force India-Mercedes	60
7	Williams-Cosworth	58
8	BMW Sauber-Ferrari	37
9	Toro Rosso-Ferrari	11

Fastest lap
M Webber 1m33.474s
(138.968mph) on lap 53

Fastest speed trap
J Button   163.980mph
Slowest speed trap
S Yamamoto   156.523mph

Fastest pit stop
1	J Button	21.252s
2	M Schumacher	21.261s
3	K Kobayashi	21.427s

Adrian Sutil
"I came in early so I could push when everyone else pitted. Near the end, I went into 130R and the tyres started to slide and smoke came out the back of the car."

Jarno Trulli
"I'm happy to have got a point, but it was frustrating as I was catching Barrichello by 1s per lap and maybe if I'd switched to the option earlier I'd have got past."

"I had a good start and came in under the safety car to switch to primes. I came out behind Yamamoto and got past pretty quick, then went after Heikki."

"It was a tough race and I had fuel pressure drops. But it was a special feeling to race at Suzuka again and to help the team take its sixth double-car finish."

Nick Heidfeld
"I could've finished one place higher, but was on a different tyre strategy to Kamui, and he was faster with his fresh option tyres, whereas I started on the options."

"When the safety car came out, we decided to do two stops in a row to get the option tyre out of the way. I came out behind Yamamoto and just couldn't get past."

Vitantonio Liuzzi
"I passed five or six cars before the first corner, but when I went into Turn 1 I saw Felipe coming up on the inside. I don't think he was in control of the car at the time."

"In the later part, Kobayashi was faster, but that isn't a reason to let him past, so I fought as hard as I could and we touched and I had to pit for a new nose."

Heikki Kovalainen
"I stayed out during the safety car. The target was to build enough of a gap to allow me to pit without losing places, and we did that, though it was close with Jarno."

"I'm really happy, as I was able to achieve my best result yet. After an exciting start, it was a good decision to pit early, and I was able to fight for positions."

Kamui Kobayashi
"It was a tough race. I saw the accidents in front of me at the start, and was lucky not to be hit. Later, it wasn't easy to overtake and I suffered damage in contact."

"I was confident there was more to come out of the car, so I'm disappointed that I wasn't able to take part, as I had a big crash in 130R while going to the grid."

2010 FORMULA 1
KOREAN GRAND PRIX
YEONGAM

ALONSO GOES TOP

The first miracle was that the track was completed. The second was that foul weather failed to prevent the race happening. The third, for Fernando Alonso, was taking the points lead

The inaugural Korean GP began behind a safety car and, after an early red flag, the teams faced the prospect that the result might be called based on those three slow laps. However, the race ended more than two hours later, in near darkness with the drivers struggling to see much beyond the bright lights on their steering wheel displays.

The driver who ultimately came out on top at Yeongam was Fernando Alonso, the Spaniard seizing the World Championship lead heading to the penultimate race in Brazil.

That the race happened at all was a miracle. After months of uncertainty, the track surface was laid less than a fortnight beforehand, and the FIA's Charlie Whiting passed the venue fit for purpose just 10 days before first practice. Early arrivals could scarcely believe that the event would happen, as work was going on all around. Practice went ahead on schedule on Friday, although as late as Saturday there were still army recruits screwing together grandstand seats.

The Hermann Tilke-designed layout proved to be a hit, thanks to its unusual triple identity. The first sector comprised long straights and big stops, the second fast sweeping turns, and the third was a wall-lined

YUNG CHO CHUNG

YEONGAM RACE PROMOTER

"We worked really hard in the past few months, because we were behind schedule building the circuit due to the weather. In July and August, we had 38 days non-stop rain. I had to change the plan, but even with the deadline approaching we never thought about cancelling it.

Bernie [Ecclestone] never said it would be postponed, he was just worried about the schedule. The main FIA concern is safety, so they don't worry about the grandstands and the other facilities. Bernie worries about those things, but I gave a detailed plan, even minute-by-minute, and sent it to him. He trusted me to get it done, which is why it happened.

There was just one time he was worried and sent me one line: 'Don't let me down, please!' In the motorsport industry, he's like a father to me. He taught me a lot, so when I promised it would be ready I couldn't let him down.

The emotion of meeting the deadline was huge, and I was almost crying when the first car was running. This was 13 years after I conceived the idea.

We have 4.5 million square metres of land, and the first stage was to put the circuit here. We designed mixed use – with a permanent track for F1 and a shorter version, and we can develop and sell the other land. First, we had only approval from the government to build the circuit, and now we have approval to build other facilities.

The problem is, people only want to build hotels and marinas – they are not interested in schools and hospitals. So we'll have some commercial areas first and can develop more over the next seven years.

I want to make sure it looks a lot greener next year. You want people to enjoy the rest of the facilities. People say it's a nice circuit, better than they expected, but I feel terrible. I'm not 100 per cent satisfied.

When I listen to the complaints, one is that towels in the hotel rooms are too small. That's because Koreans shower and use just a small one. We have tried to educate the hotels to provide bigger ones. Also, with the beds, Koreans often sleep on the floor because of the under-floor heating systems. That may be why some rooms don't look so good...

I was so worried when we did the three laps and then they stopped it. I was worried the race would be cancelled. It was tough for me because new people came here after driving all the way from Seoul, and Pusan, but we definitely showed how strong F1 is, even with rain. It was a great show. People loved it. We had 42,000 people on Friday, 62,000 on Saturday and 100,000 for the race."

street circuit with tight corners and a challenging fast kink onto the pit straight.

There were some issues with kerbs, and on Friday night a poorly aligned wall had to be moved back, but otherwise the place got a thumbs-up. Not least from Red Bull Racing, who dominated qualifying as Sebastian Vettel edged out team-mate Mark Webber. Alonso looked comfortable in third, while Lewis Hamilton was disappointed to be fourth. Tyre graining was a major issue, and a dry race would have seen multiple pit stops, much like at Montréal.

However, rain had been predicted for Sunday. Steady drizzle fell on cue on Saturday evening and continued into the following morning, turning run-off areas to mud. The track was soaked for the start, and after a 10-minute delay the race kicked off behind the safety car. However, conditions proved impossible, and it was red-flagged after three slow laps. It wasn't a question of aquaplaning, but visibility. A combination of the waterlogged, muddy verges and fresh asphalt meant that the water wouldn't go away.

An hour passed with the cars on the grid, and there was the prospect that daylight would run out and the race would be called at three laps – with the top 10 being awarded half points.

Fortunately, the rain abated and, after a further 14 laps behind the safety car, the action finally got underway. Vettel hung onto the lead, but Webber ran wide and spun into the wall on the second racing lap. Alonso nipped by into second, but the damaged RB6 rebounded into the path of Nico Rosberg, who was running fourth after passing Hamilton on the first lap. It was only Webber's second retirement of the year after his Valencia crash, and it cost him his championship lead.

The safety car was called for and, at the restart, Vettel continued to run strongly in the lead. After a few laps, the track dried enough to make

intermediates an option, although those who switched too soon struggled initially to find performance.

However, just as the crossover point approached there was another safety-car period, triggered after Scuderia Toro Rosso's Sebastien Buemi ran into the side of Timo Glock's Virgin.

Vettel and Alonso didn't have time to pit straight away, but everyone behind came rushing in. The leaders came in at the end of the next lap. Alonso's crew struggled with one wheel and, when the Spaniard dashed out of the pits, Hamilton had relieved him of second place.

That looked as if it would be a crucial gain for the McLaren driver in the championship battle, but when the green flag was waved he ran wide at Turn 1, handing the position back to Alonso.

Vettel looked likely to save the day for Red Bull Racing, staying clear of Alonso. However, with eight laps to go, his title hopes took a blow when he suffered a spectacular engine failure. To lose a surefire win through no fault of his own was a bitter pill for the German driver and his team.

What was impressive was the calm way he dealt with this late retirement. It wasn't just the loss of his

OPPOSITE TOP After three laps behind the safety car, and with conditions too treacherous to race, the red flag was flown. The cars waited on the grid for an hour before they tried again

OPPOSITE BOTTOM The race resumed behind the safety car, with Sebastian Vettel splashing around ahead of Mark Webber for another 14 laps before they were let go

TOP Jenson Button and Michael Schumacher tussled over fifth before Button's afternoon unravelled

ABOVE Sebastien Buemi assaulted Timo Glock and was hit with a grid penalty for the Brazilian GP

TALKING POINT
WEBBER'S ACCIDENT

Coming to Korea, Mark Webber had an 11-point championship lead and had failed to finish just the once, which was a consequence of his dramatic accident when trying to fight back after a poor opening lap in Valencia and an early pit stop.

While his major title rivals made things tough for themselves – Vettel at Spa, Hamilton at Monza and Singapore – Webber protected that most tenuous of leads, with Fernando Alonso and Ferrari coming on stronger all the time.

It has been nip and tuck with Vettel more or less everywhere, an average of just over a tenth of a second separating them in qualifying throughout the season. At Suzuka, it had been seven hundredths and it was a similar margin here again. As Webber acknowledges, so much is about Q3 on Saturday afternoon and the first lap on Sunday.

At Yeongam, Webber had not felt as confident as Vettel on the option tyre on his first Q3 run. For the second, therefore, he opted for a single two-lap run, while Vettel went for a one-lapper. Vettel got the pole and never looked anything less than 100% confident as he drove a fabulous race until disaster struck in the form of that blown engine.

Webber, normally so sure-footed in the wet, spun out of the grand prix early on when all he had to do was bring the car home somewhere at the top end of the points range. He dropped a wheel on the slippery Turn-12 exit and was gone.

"I thought I'd done enough to get it back, but it was gone," he grimaced after spinning into the wall on the right and then rebounding across the track, where he collected Nico Rosberg's Mercedes.

Rosberg, on *Twitter* later, wondered why Webber had not managed to brake before taking him out. It was a theme picked up by Gerhard Berger, who suggested to Austrian TV that Webber was trying to take out one of his championship rivals. Lewis Hamilton had been running behind Fernando Alonso's third-placed Ferrari, but had just been passed by Rosberg.

"He could have hit the brakes and stopped the car," Berger said. "He took out Rosberg, but it was the wrong one. I think in his mind he would have preferred Alonso or Hamilton."

Asked to clarify if he thought it was deliberate, Berger said: "He's gone off, he knows it's over and a million things go through your head. It's very obvious. You can see that his wheels are not locked up. Perhaps he had a brake problem but I don't think so."

Predictably enough, both Webber and Christian Horner rubbished the very notion.

25 points that counted, but also a swing of 32 in Alonso's favour.

"To be on top of the field all the time, controlling the race, looking after my tyres, I think there's nothing we could have done better," said Vettel. "Conditions were getting a bit trickier, it was getting a bit darker, but still I think I had something in hand. I was a bit unlucky with the lapped guys, both times I lost around a second, but I was maybe three-tenths of a second quicker per lap than Fernando if I wanted to be.

"I could have easily won, so I think there's no reason to lose motivation. We know we are the quickest, we have a very strong team and very strong car, so I can sleep tonight without any problems. Don't get me wrong, but I think I've done everything right today, so I feel a little bit like a winner."

Alonso was there to take advantage. He managed to keep his intermediate tyres alive in the closing stages as the track dried, and made it home safely at the head of the field, 15s clear of Hamilton.

It wasn't quite a faultless performance, in that there was a fumble in the pit stop. Other than that, neither team nor driver put a foot wrong. Between them, they more than made up for the Belgian GP, a race that ended with a bent Ferrari lying in the middle of the track. That was the only time he'd been off the podium since Silverstone.

"I think today was a great race because of the difficult conditions," said team principal Stefano Domenicali. "Difficult conditions with the rain, with the delay, to stay concentrated with all the things that were happening, and with the management of the tyres that he didn't know how they would last, as it was the first time in these conditions."

On balance, it was a good weekend for Hamilton, certainly in the light of recent disappointments. To finish second having qualified fourth was respectable. And yet, should he have won? When he ran wide

at the restart, he created a 14-point swing in the Spaniard's favour.

That had to be balanced against the fact that Vettel and Webber both retired in front of him, and Rosberg's departure in the Webber shunt also gifted him some points.

"That's a great result for Lewis," said McLaren engineering chief Paddy Lowe. "But he could have won it. He outbraked himself at Turn 1, didn't he? That's a shame, because he could have kept ahead, which would have ended up being the winning spot.

"Ferrari seemed a little bit quicker at that point, but I suspect he would have held him off. But, as

OPPOSITE Adrian Sutil creates a mist of spray ahead of the BMW Saubers of Kamui Kobayashi and Nick Heidfeld. Sutil would later clash with Kobayashi and earn a penalty

ABOVE The race was all but won for Sebastian Vettel, but then his Red Bull RB6's Renault engine failed

BELOW Vitaly Petrov needed a good finish to impress the Renault team, not a car-wrecking crash

you saw, he went off the circuit and was lucky to stay ahead of Massa, in that same incident."

It's to Hamilton's credit that he bounced back from that disappointment. He'd been criticised for his impatience in Italy and Singapore, but this time he brought the car home, recognising that he had to keep his tyres alive and that pushing to catch Alonso was ultimately a fruitless task.

"The life of the inters is always a concern," said Lowe. "We were trying to see where Ferrari were and trying to manage it. As it got to the end of the race, it was a question of were we going to run out of time, laps, tyres or light?

"It got to a point where I think Lewis realised that he wasn't going to make it to Alonso, so then he was into tyre-saving. Also, I think of all the drivers Lewis was the most uncomfortable with the light. He felt the light was gone, and we had that debate with the FIA. They'd have had to stop it a lap later, though, as it was actually dark."

It was a disastrous weekend for McLaren team-mate Jenson Button. The early change to intermediates looked like a clever roll of the dice, something that might propel him up the order and give him the sort of boost he enjoyed in the tricky races in Australia and China. In fact, it was a desperate effort to salvage something after he had struggled on full wets.

"I didn't have any wet tyres left," rued Button. "Along with not being fast, I was destroying tyres. I mean, the set-up we've got is slightly unusual, but not that unusual. I don't know where that went."

The change was a lap or two too early and, coming out in traffic, he struggled to get the tyres up to temperature. Even the best drivers can look like beginners if the tyres don't work and, coupled with a curious lack of confidence in his brakes, Button was really in trouble. Thereafter, he was just making up the numbers as he struggled home in 12th place.

Felipe Massa had a low-key run to third, earning useful points for Ferrari. Michael Schumacher secured the best result of his comeback season in fourth, ahead of Robert Kubica and Vitantonio Liuzzi. Those who made it to the end in one piece certainly deserved credit on a day that saw an unusual amount of contact as drivers slithered into each other. Indeed, Sebastien Buemi received a five-place grid penalty for the Brazilian Grand Prix for his assault on Timo Glock, while Adrian Sutil earned the same after hitting Kamui Kobayashi.

SNAPSHOT FROM
KOREA

CLOCKWISE FROM RIGHT South Jeolla province has big development plans; Fernando Alonso absorbs his win; a novel track parade; Christian Klien meets a local; she clearly works for the builders...; Christian Horner and Sebastian Vettel flank the world's fastest 80-year-old, Bernie; Lotus drivers Jarno Trulli and Heikki Kovalainen pray that the track will be ready; the fans were prepared for rain; the title protagonists: Hamilton, Alonso, Webber, Button and Vettel; the red flag led to a one-hour delay

RACE RESULTS
KOREA
YEONGAM

Official Results © [2010]
Formula One Administration Limited,
6 Princes Gate, London, SW7 1QJ.
No reproduction without permission.
All copyright and database rights reserved.

RACE DATE October 24th
CIRCUIT LENGTH 3.492 miles
NO. OF LAPS 55
RACE DISTANCE 192.108 miles
WEATHER Heavy rain, 19°C
TRACK TEMP 17°C
ATTENDANCE 170,000
LAP RECORD Fernando Alonso,
1m50.257s, 113.919mph, 2010

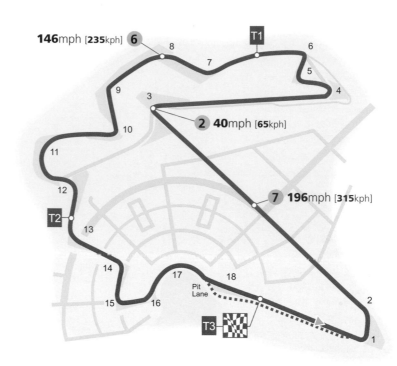

146mph [235kph] 6

40mph [65kph] 2

196mph [315kph] 7

PRACTICE 1			
	Driver	Time	Laps
1	L Hamilton	1m40.887s	15
2	R Kubica	1m40.968s	18
3	N Rosberg	1m41.152s	21
4	S Vettel	1m41.371s	18
5	J Button	1m41.940s	16
6	M Schumacher	1m42.022s	25
7	M Webber	1m42.202s	23
8	N Heidfeld	1m42.293s	18
9	N Hulkenberg	1m42.678s	21
10	R Barrichello	1m42.883s	23
11	V Petrov	1m42.896s	22
12	F Massa	1m43.054s	25
13	K Kobayashi	1m43.309s	20
14	A Sutil	1m43.602s	18
15	F Alonso	1m43.928s	21
16	S Buemi	1m43.940s	23
17	V Liuzzi	1m44.887s	21
18	J Alguersuari	1m45.141s	26
19	T Glock	1m45.588s	20
20	J d'Ambrosio	1m46.613s	17
21	H Kovalainen	1m47.115s	22
22	S Yamamoto	1m50.347s	29
23	B Senna	1m50.821s	15
24	J Trulli	1m51.701s	11

PRACTICE 2			
	Driver	Time	Laps
1	M Webber	1m37.942s	23
2	F Alonso	1m38.132s	30
3	L Hamilton	1m38.279s	29
4	R Kubica	1m38.718s	29
5	J Button	1m38.726s	19
6	F Massa	1m38.820s	32
7	S Vettel	1m39.204s	22
8	V Petrov	1m39.267s	28
9	N Rosberg	1m39.268s	29
10	K Kobayashi	1m39.564s	26
11	N Heidfeld	1m39.588s	25
12	M Schumacher	1m39.598s	26
13	R Barrichello	1m39.812s	35
14	V Liuzzi	1m39.881s	27
15	A Sutil	1m39.971s	22
16	N Hulkenberg	1m40.478s	30
17	J Alguersuari	1m40.578s	29
18	S Buemi	1m40.896s	32
19	H Kovalainen	1m42.773s	29
20	J Trulli	1m42.801s	19
21	T Glock	1m43.115s	26
22	L di Grassi	1m44.039s	29
23	S Yamamoto	1m45.166s	19
24	B Senna	1m46.649s	3

PRACTICE 3			
	Driver	Time	Laps
1	R Kubica	1m37.354s	15
2	L Hamilton	1m37.402s	16
3	F Alonso	1m37.426s	15
4	M Webber	1m37.441s	13
5	N Rosberg	1m37.629s	12
6	F Massa	1m37.955s	16
7	J Button	1m38.419s	15
8	N Hulkenberg	1m38.501s	17
9	M Schumacher	1m38.630s	12
10	A Sutil	1m38.632s	18
11	V Petrov	1m38.668s	14
12	R Barrichello	1m38.733s	16
13	S Buemi	1m39.058s	21
14	K Kobayashi	1m39.145s	26
15	J Alguersuari	1m39.159s	21
16	S Vettel	1m39.780s	9
17	N Heidfeld	1m40.289s	17
18	V Liuzzi	1m41.591s	15
19	J Trulli	1m41.623s	15
20	T Glock	1m41.853s	17
21	H Kovalainen	1m42.095s	19
22	L di Grassi	1m43.111s	19
23	B Senna	1m43.417s	19
24	S Yamamoto	1m43.880s	20

QUALIFYING 1		
	Driver	Time
1	L Hamilton	1m37.113s
2	S Vettel	1m37.123s
3	F Alonso	1m37.144s
4	M Webber	1m37.373s
5	F Massa	1m37.515s
6	R Kubica	1m37.703s
7	N Rosberg	1m37.708s
8	M Schumacher	1m37.980s
9	N Hulkenberg	1m38.115s
10	J Button	1m38.123s
11	N Heidfeld	1m38.171s
12	V Petrov	1m38.174s
13	R Barrichello	1m38.257s
14	K Kobayashi	1m38.429s
15	A Sutil	1m38.572s
16	J Alguersuari	1m38.583s
17	S Buemi	1m38.621s
18	V Liuzzi	1m38.955s
19	J Trulli	1m40.521s
20	T Glock	1m40.748s
21	H Kovalainen	1m41.768s
22	L di Grassi	1m42.235s
23	S Yamamoto	1m42.444s
24	B Senna	1m43.283s

QUALIFYING 2		
	Driver	Time
1	M Webber	1m36.069s
2	S Vettel	1m36.074s
3	F Massa	1m36.169s
4	L Hamilton	1m36.197s
5	F Alonso	1m36.287s
6	N Rosberg	1m36.791s
7	J Button	1m37.064s
8	M Schumacher	1m37.077s
9	R Kubica	1m37.179s
10	R Barrichello	1m37.511s
11	N Hulkenberg	1m37.620s
12	K Kobayashi	1m37.643s
13	N Heidfeld	1m37.715s
14	A Sutil	1m37.783s
15	V Petrov	1m37.799s
16	J Alguersuari	1m37.853s
17	S Buemi	1m38.594s

Best sectors – Practice		
Sec 1	L Hamilton	52.428s
Sec 2	R Kubica	24.485s
Sec 3	M Webber	20.095s

Speed trap – Practice		
1	V Liuzzi	197.782mph
2	A Sutil	197.223mph
3	M Schumacher	196.912mph

Best sectors – Qualifying		
Sec 1	F Alonso	51.973s
Sec 2	M Webber	23.783s
Sec 3	S Vettel	19.550s

Speed trap – Qualifying		
1	N Rosberg	198.838mph
2	J Button	198.776mph
3	A Sutil	198.341mph

 **Jenson Button**

"I didn't have enough grip. Also, I lost several places when Adrian drove me off the circuit. The race should have been stopped earlier, as it was way too dark to race."

 Michael Schumacher

"The FIA did well to start the race behind the safety car, as it wouldn't have been possible to have a racing start. The only shame was Nico was put out."

 **Sebastian Vettel**

"To be at the front of the field for the whole race, controlling it and looking after the tyres, I think there's really nothing more that we could have done."

Felipe Massa

"After two poor weekends, I'm happy to have reached the podium. By the end, it was almost dark and the intermediates were deteriorating, especially the rears."

Rubens Barrichello

"I was lucky with the timing of the safety car and was in a good position until the closing stages. Unluckily, I ran out of tyres in the last five laps, losing two places."

Robert Kubica

"The first part was tricky as I had problems warming the tyres. I then had to look after the inters to get the benefit in the final laps when I managed to gain places."

 Lewis Hamilton

"It was a big surprise to see both Red Bulls go out. Fernando drove really well, but I'm very happy to have scored some points after a couple of disappointing races."

 Nico Rosberg

"It was really difficult to judge which way Mark's car would go and I took the decision to go left, but he spun more that way and I just couldn't avoid him."

 Mark Webber

"It was my fault, I got on the kerb on the exit of Turn 12 and it was a very slow-motion moment off the back of that kerb – it was my mistake and it wasn't my day."

Fernando Alonso

"It was a very difficult victory, given the track conditions. The final stages were notably difficult, as half the track was almost dry and the tyres were soon ruined."

 Nico Hulkenberg

"We did everything right, but had some bad luck. I was sixth near the end, but my engineer told me I had a slow puncture and I had to pit, costing me a big result."

Vitaly Petrov

"I'd stopped for inters on lap 20, so they were quite worn after the second safety-car period. But I lost the car on the penultimate corner and had a big crash."

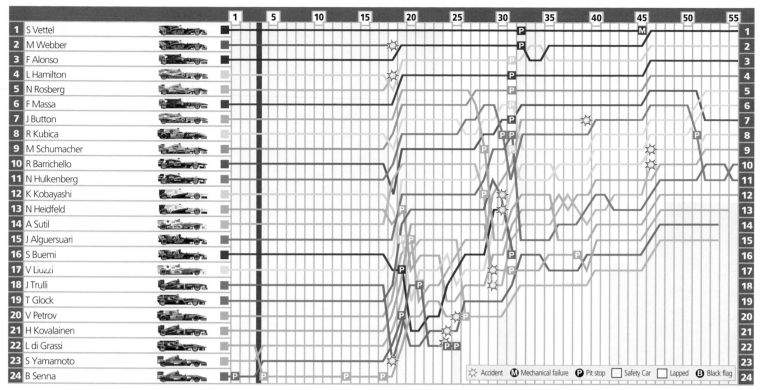

☆ Accident   Ⓜ Mechanical failure   Ⓟ Pit stop   ☐ Safety Car   ☐ Lapped   Ⓑ Black flag

	Driver
1	S Vettel
2	M Webber
3	F Alonso
4	L Hamilton
5	N Rosberg
6	F Massa
7	J Button
8	R Kubica
9	M Schumacher
10	R Barrichello
11	N Hulkenberg
12	K Kobayashi
13	N Heidfeld
14	A Sutil
15	J Alguersuari
16	S Buemi
17	V Liuzzi
18	J Trulli
19	T Glock
20	V Petrov
21	H Kovalainen
22	L di Grassi
23	S Yamamoto
24	B Senna

QUALIFYING 3

	Driver	Time
1	S Vettel	1m35.585s
2	M Webber	1m35.659s
3	F Alonso	1m35.766s
4	L Hamilton	1m36.062s
5	N Rosberg	1m36.535s
6	F Massa	1m36.571s
7	J Button	1m36.731s
8	R Kubica	1m36.824s
9	M Schumacher	1m36.950s
10	R Barrichello	1m36.998s

GRID

	Driver	Time
1	S Vettel	1m35.585s
2	M Webber	1m35.659s
3	F Alonso	1m35.766s
4	L Hamilton	1m36.062s
5	N Rosberg	1m36.535s
6	F Massa	1m36.571s
7	J Button	1m36.731s
8	R Kubica	1m36.824s
9	M Schumacher	1m36.950s
10	R Barrichello	1m36.998s
11	N Hulkenberg	1m37.620s
12	K Kobayashi	1m37.643s
13	N Heidfeld	1m37.715s
14	A Sutil	1m37.783s
15	J Alguersuari	1m37.853s
16	S Buemi	1m38.594s
17	V Liuzzi	1m38.955s
18	J Trulli	1m40.521s
19	T Glock	1m40.748s
20*	V Petrov	1m37.799s
21	H Kovalainen	1m41.768s
22	L di Grassi	1m42.235s
23	S Yamamoto	1m42.444s
24	B Senna	1m43.283s

* 5-place grid penalty due to avoidable accident in Japanese Grand Prix

RACE

	Driver	Car	Laps	Time	Avg. mph	Fastest	Stops
1	F Alonso	Ferrari F10	55	2h48m20.810s	68.349	1m50.257s	1
2	L Hamilton	McLaren Mercedes MP4-25	55	2h48m35.809s	68.248	1m50.430s	1
3	F Massa	Ferrari F10	55	2h48m51.678s	68.141	1m50.502s	1
4	M Schumacher	Mercedes MGP W01	55	2h49m00.498s	68.082	1m51.835s	1
5	R Kubica	Renault R30	55	2h49m08.544s	68.028	1m51.604s	1
6	V Liuzzi	Force India-Mercedes VJM03	55	2h49m14.381s	67.988	1m51.371s	1
7	R Barrichello	Williams-Cosworth FW32	55	2h49m30.067s	67.883	1m51.564s	1
8	K Kobayashi	BMW Sauber-Ferrari C29	55	2h49m38.699s	67.826	1m53.086s	1
9	N Heidfeld	BMW Sauber-Ferrari C29	55	2h49m40.917s	67.811	1m53.263s	1
10	N Hulkenberg	Williams-Cosworth FW32	55	2h49m41.661s	67.806	1m51.982s	2
11	J Alguersuari	Toro Rosso-Ferrari STR5	55	2h49m44.956s	67.772	1m51.962s	1
12	J Button	McLaren-Mercedes MP4-25	55	2h49m50.749s	67.746	1m52.193s	1
13	H Kovalainen	Lotus-Cosworth T127	54	2h49m27.567s	66.665	1m55.018s	1
14	B Senna	HRT-Cosworth F110	53	2h48m30.504s	65.799	1m59.290s	2
15	S Yamamoto	HRT-Cosworth F110	53	2h48m47.837s	65.686	1m58.313s	1
R	A Sutil	Force India-Mercedes VJM03	46	Crash damage	-	1m52.601s	1
R	S Vettel	Red Bull-Renault RB6	45	Engine	-	1m50.375s	1
R	V Petrov	Renault R30	39	Accident	-	1m53.031s	1
R	T Glock	Virgin-Cosworth VR-01	31	Crash damage	-	1m58.102s	0
R	S Buemi	Toro Rosso-Ferrari STR5	30	Accident	-	1m56.768s	1
R	L di Grassi	Virgin-Cosworth VR-01	25	Accident	-	2m02.635s	3
R	J Trulli	Lotus-Cosworth T127	25	Hydraulics	-	2m05.161s	2
R	M Webber	Red Bull-Renault RB6	18	Accident	-	2m00.025s	1
R	N Rosberg	Mercedes MGP W01	18	Accident	-	2m00.652s	0

CHAMPIONSHIP

	Driver	Pts
1	F Alonso	231
2	M Webber	220
3	L Hamilton	210
4	S Vettel	206
5	J Button	189
6	F Massa	143
7	R Kubica	124
8	N Rosberg	122
9	M Schumacher	66
10	R Barrichello	47
11	A Sutil	47
12	K Kobayashi	31
13	V Liuzzi	21
14	V Petrov	19
15	N Hulkenberg	18
16	S Buemi	8
17	P de la Rosa	6
18	N Heidfeld	6
19	J Alguersuari	3

	Constructor	Pts
1	Red Bull-Renault	426
2	McLaren-Mercedes	399
3	Ferrari	374
4	Mercedes	188
5	Renault	143
6	Force India-Mercedes	68
7	Williams-Cosworth	65
8	BMW Sauber-Ferrari	43
9	Toro Rosso-Ferrari	11

Fastest lap
F Alonso 1m50.257s
(113.919mph) on lap 42

Fastest speed trap
V Liuzzi   193.930mph
Slowest speed trap
N Rosberg   157.393mph

Fastest pit stop
1 N Hulkenberg   23.123s
2 N Hulkenberg   23.256s
3 N Heidfeld   23.423s

Adrian Sutil
"In the end, I tried to pass Kobayashi, but lost control of the car on a patch that was a bit more wet than I expected and went into the side of him."

Sébastien Buemi
"I lost the chance to score today. The accident? I braked late and locked the front wheels, so I could not turn and ended up going straight on and hitting Timo."

Jarno Trulli
"The power steering began to feel heavy behind the safety car. I struggled at the first corner and spun. Despite the team trying to get me back out, it was all over."

Sakon Yamamoto
"During the safety-car period, some changed onto inters, but we stayed on the wets. As the track dried sooner than expected, we also changed to inters."

Nick Heidfeld
"I changed to inters too early, as it wasn't easy to stay on the track. I couldn't defend my place against Adrian as, with the mirrors being so dirty, I just couldn't see him."

Timo Glock
"I was set for a good result as I had good pace and we were the quickest of the new teams. It's a huge shame we couldn't finish because of Buemi's mistake."

Vitantonio Liuzzi
"At the end, it was like a night race without lights and the steering-wheel lights were dazzling! Even though there was little grip, I was able to get into a rhythm."

Sakon Yamamoto
"I missed out on an opportunity to score, losing out during the pit stop, when a technical problem meant I went into the pits in ninth and came out 15th."

Heikki Kovalainen
"In tricky conditions, with people making mistakes, we could have seen our 10th position under threat, but we were there at the end and that's what counts."

Bruno Senna
"We opted to go very long on the same set of tyres. It was hard, as they were very used. Luckily, it all came together and I was able to achieve my best result so far."

Kamui Kobayashi
"When Sutil attacked, I stayed on the inside. I saw him in the mirror and thought that he wasn't going to be able to brake. We touched, but I was able to go on."

Lucas di Grassi
"We had made the right call by switching to intermediates early. On lap 15, I went out trying to avoid a crash with Yamamoto, who was ahead of me but slower."

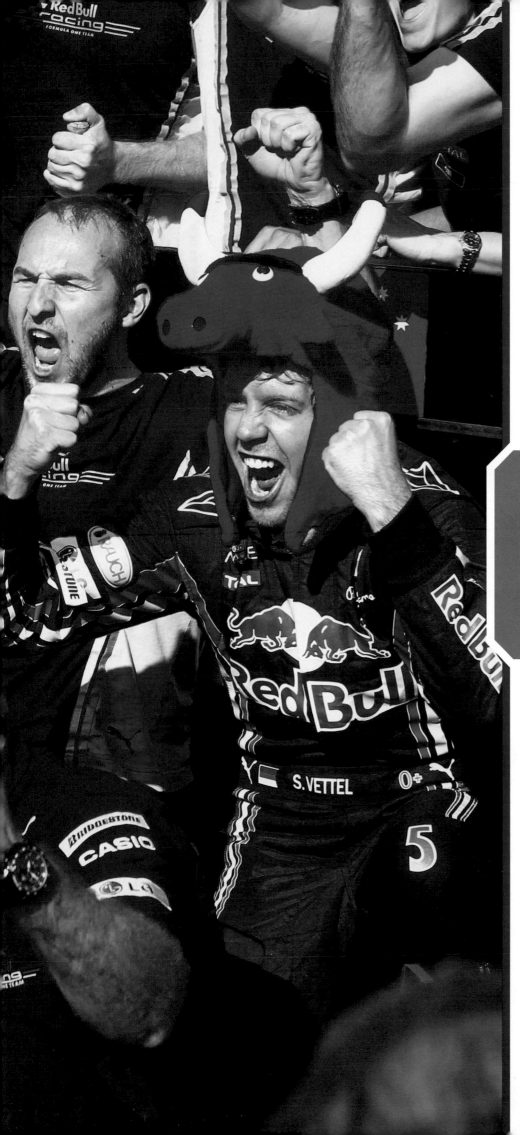

FORMULA 1 GRANDE PRÊMIO
PETROBRAS DO BRASIL 2010
SÃO PAULO

RED BULL'S CLINCHER

A 1–2 for Sebastian Vettel ahead of Mark Webber helped Red Bull Racing land its first constructors' title, but third place for Fernando Alonso kept him ahead with just one race to run

The Brazilian GP might not have been the most thrilling race of the year, but the result set up a four-way fight heading into Abu Dhabi, after Sebastian Vettel headed home Mark Webber and Fernando Alonso, while Lewis Hamilton just stayed in the hunt with fourth place.

Qualifying took place on a wet track, although right at the end of Q3 the line was dry enough for slicks. There was a mad rush into the pits, and then it was a question of getting in a lap and hoping that it was good enough. The big problem was to keep enough temperature in the tyres to keep them alive for the crucial final lap.

Against the odds, Nico Hulkenberg put in a superb performance, banging in three successive quick laps and claiming pole for Williams by over a second. This was no fluke, just a great performance by a talented rookie.

Behind him, it was business as usual as Vettel qualified second, just outpacing team-mate Webber. Hamilton was fourth, while Alonso was fifth, but relieved to be there given the lottery conditions. Rubens Barrichello underlined Williams's form by qualifying sixth fastest.

Felipe Massa was a disappointed ninth in the other Ferrari, while Jenson Button was frustrated not to make it out of Q2, the McLaren man starting 11th as he again struggled for grip. His slim championship hopes were effectively over.

As expected, race day proved to be sunny and dry, and Hulkenberg had a tough time, as Vettel got away well and dived down the inside to demote his compatriot's Williams to second.

"It worked as per plan," said Vettel. "I saw that Nico struggled a bit off the line and I used the momentum that I had. The grip was lower on the dirty side of the grid, but it didn't seem to be too bad. Then it was a close fight and he was trying to squeeze me down the inside. There was hardly any space left. I was just praying there was no debris, as it wasn't really the racing line I had to use."

Later in the lap, Hulkenberg went a little wide, allowing Webber through.

"Obviously, I was a bit more nervous than usual, but if you're nervous it's also good, it keeps you awake and sharp," the youngster explained. "I'm used to starting from the front in GP2 and F3, but this one was a bit special and different. My start was OK.

I lost one position to Sebastian, who had a very good start. And then it was a case of trying to keep in front of the big guns as much as I could. It was very difficult. I knew where to brake and what to do, but my car was sliding a bit more than theirs, so I was an easy target for Mark."

Alonso was quickly past Hamilton, the McLaren driver running wide and handing a place to his old rival for the second time in as many races. It was a crucial move for the Spaniard's title hopes.

However, as the Red Bulls made their escape, Alonso found himself stuck behind Hulkenberg. It took until lap 7 before he could find a way past,

and by then he'd lost touch with the Red Bulls.

Vettel soon edged a couple of seconds clear of Webber. The pit-stop sequence was triggered by Button, who was running 10th when he came in on lap 11. Massa was a couple of places ahead of him and he came in on the next lap, only to slow coming out of the pits. He had to stop again on the following lap due to a loose front wheel after a problem with the nut cross-threading, dropping the frustrated local hero towards the tail end of the field.

Meanwhile, other cars started pitting to change to primes. Hamilton had been stuck behind Hulkenberg for several laps before the German pitted, and had

OPPOSITE TOP A delighted Nico Hulkenberg acknowledges the applause of the Brazilian crowd after claiming his first pole for Williams

OPPOSITE BOTTOM Sebastian Vettel dives to the inside to take the lead from Nico Hulkenberg at Turn 1

ABOVE Fernando Alonso attacks Lewis Hamilton for fourth place at Turn 1 on lap 2 and fails, only to pass him further around the lap

INSIDE LINE
SEBASTIAN VETTEL
RED BULL RACING DRIVER

"It was a truly incredible day. It certainly wasn't an easy race to start with. We knew I was on the dirty side of the grid, but I had a good start. I then saw that Nico had a bit too much wheelspin and I used my momentum to squeeze down the inside.

Throughout the race, I was able to hold the gaps as I planned, so I could control the race from there. With the safety car, in the end it was the right choice not to try to pull away too much, to have some tyres left.

Lots of people talked us down at stages this year, sometimes right, sometimes not, so it's good to show them one race from the end what we are made of. It hasn't been that long since Red Bull entered F1. They can be proud of themselves. I'm not too worried about the guys in England – they know what to do – but for the race team, I think we are in the right country, with some good caipirinha to enjoy…

It was a busy race for lapped cars. You need to be extremely focused. You don't want to lose

a lot of time, but sometimes you don't know if they are giving way or just making a mistake. With some people, it's not always obvious but, all in all, I think all the drivers behaved and I managed to get through. It was nice to have the safety-car phase with two cars as a cushion, as I could push right away.

Mark was behind, so I was relatively safe. We were pulling away slightly, step-by-step from the Ferrari, so everything worked as expected. Winning the Constructors' Championship has been a mission.

When Red Bull entered F1, I was young and I remember my first trip. I had just got my driver's licence and I drove to England. It was in 2005, to Milton Keynes, and if I compare the place back then to

now, it's massive progress. I was just a little boy. Someone showed me around and I was fascinated, sparks in my eyes.

Now, to be part of the team and part of the driver line-up to give them their first championship is incredible. I don't really know how to put it into words. Big thanks to the guys in Milton Keynes, here at the track and also in Austria. It's not always just investing money: it's time, patience and a lot of passion."

TALKING POINT
THE WILLIAMS DILEMMA

It could just be that Williams' deal to supply HRT with transmissions for the 2011 season will safeguard the seats of Rubens Barrichello and Nico Hulkenberg next year.

With Williams chairman Adam Parr rumoured to be negotiating a deal to run GP2 Champion Pascal Maldonado with backing from PDVSA, the state oil company, Barrichello and Hulkenberg were feeling vulnerable.

The Williams technical team is keen to retain Barrichello and they also have a multi-year deal with 2009 GP2 Champion Hulkenberg, who took a sensational pole position at Interlagos. The Williams financial position is not helped by the expiry of sponsorship contracts with RBS, Philips and Air Asia at the end of the year, making Maldonado potentially attractive.

Technical Director Sam Michael tells *The Official Formula 1 Season Review*: "Our real turnaround was the Canadian GP. The car was more competitive there. We changed the aero package very significantly and that changed our direction. We changed how we developed the car and, in terms of philosophy, it was quite a big change to what we'd done for the past couple of years."

Barrichello is believed to have been key to that development and Michael confirmed this: "When you bring developments to the track with a driver like Rubens and have him tell you exactly and very quickly what it's doing, that's quite important. He's been exceptional for the team from that point of view."

In an era of reduced testing, such ability is considered particularly valuable. But Hulkenberg has also performed increasingly well and impressed Patrick Head with his maturity in Brazil.

On the subject of 2011, Head said: "Firstly, we're not making any statement on that until after the season, and secondly if we've got nasty things to tell people, I'll let Adam Parr do it…"

That seemed a fairly strong indication that he would like to see things remain as they are, in which case an HRT seat for Maldonado could be the best solution for all concerned. The deal could be structured in such a way that Maldonado does a learning year with HRT before being taken on by Williams. The funding could then potentially be split, giving HRT assistance at a difficult time too.

Geoff Willis, contracted to assist HRT throughout 2010, would be a likely candidate to oversee the build of a contracted-out chassis, which would likely be an improvement on the Dallara-built car that HRT raced throughout 2010. Barrichello and Hulkenberg looked like two men awaiting developments with interest....

lost ground to Alonso. Hamilton finally pitted on lap 20, emerging just in front of team-mate Button. Both the McLarens then had to work their way past Kamui Kobayashi, who was running a long first stint with his first set of prime tyres.

Alonso was the first of the top three to pit, on lap 24. Vettel came in a lap later, and Webber followed on lap 26. The stops made no difference to the order, and Vettel continued to run a couple of seconds ahead of Webber as the pair traded fastest laps.

The complexion of the race changed when Tonio Liuzzi crashed heavily at the second corner on lap 50, after an apparent front-suspension failure, bringing out a safety car. That should have made for an exciting restart, but there were two lapped cars in the queue between the Red Bulls, and many between Webber and third-placed Alonso.

Both McLaren drivers gave themselves a boost for the run to the flag by making an extra pit stop for new tyres. After climbing the order, Nico Rosberg also pitted. But, in the confusion, the Mercedes pit crew fitted primes instead of options. Fortunately, he was able to come back in and rectify that on the next lap without losing ground.

We thus looked set for an exciting restart, with the McLarens and Rosberg running in fourth, fifth and seventh positions on new tyres. Unfortunately, the lapped cars meant that Vettel was under no threat from Webber at the restart, and Webber was in turn safe from Alonso. The traffic made for some exciting passing moves, and there was considerable confusion among the drivers as they tried to work out who they were racing. Nick Heidfeld earned himself a drive-through penalty for holding up Rosberg, who was in fact a lap ahead.

None of this affected the order at the front, although Alonso kept Webber under pressure. For a while, Webber was under orders to take it easy, as there was an engine problem, so there was even less chance of him challenging Vettel.

"Normally, they don't ring us up unless there are issues," said Webber. "So the phone rang… it's never nice when they have to ask you to manage something. The safety car helped a bit, but it was back again the first lap after the safety car."

Nevertheless, the team safely completed the 1–2, which was enough to secure the Constructors' World Championship. As we'd seen so often before, Vettel is at his best when at the front.

"Mark was behind, so I was relatively safe," said Vettel. "I was always trying to keep two-and-a-half seconds gap. We were pulling away step-by-step from the Ferrari, so everything worked."

Alonso was delighted with third place and, while a better result could have won him the title, it left him in charge going to Abu Dhabi.

"At the beginning, with the time lost behind Nico, it was too much for us," he said. "The gap to Red Bull was around 14s, so we decided to control the gap to Hamilton, and try to be conservative with the engine settings. So, when the safety car came in, we pushed a little bit harder,

OPPOSITE If ever a driver was due a good result in Brazil, it's Rubens Barrichello, but a pit-stop problem and later a punctured tyre meant that he would score no points

BELOW Bruno Senna received rapturous support from the fans, but it didn't help his HRT go any faster

BOTTOM Jenson Button was the first to pit for new tyres, and it worked, as he started 11th and finished in fifth place

tried to see what was the real pace of the car and the real pace of Red Bull.

"We found ourselves with traffic, seven cars between Mark and me. So we spent five or six laps overtaking those cars and then the gap to Mark was 5s already so, even with fastest laps at the end, it was obviously not enough. It also seems that Mark was controlling engine problems, so we'll never know."

Hamilton finished fourth, which was just enough to keep him in the title hunt – 24 points behind, with 25 still on offer. Button dropped out of the title reckoning with his fifth place. Behind him, Rosberg was allowed past by team-mate Michael Schumacher to claim sixth, the latter realising that Nico's new tyres gave him a chance to push the McLarens.

The unfortunate Hulkenberg found himself back in eighth, although it was a crucial score, as it put Williams a point ahead of Force India in the constructors' battle: "I defended hard but fair. I drove the race without a mistake, kept Robert Kubica behind me all the time. If we had better pace, I could easily have finished fifth or sixth. We only got overtaken at the pit stops. Both Mercedes, Jenson, people who came from 14th were well ahead of us, which is quite unfortunate. With half-a-second better pace per lap, we could achieve a lot more."

Nevertheless, he'd done much to bolster his reputation, amid suggestions that there was no longer a seat for him at Williams in 2011. Meanwhile, Kubica took ninth place, while the final point went to BMW Sauber's Kamui Kobayashi.

After the race, there was frantic work in the paddock as the teams prepared for the dash to Abu Dhabi, where practice was due to kick off in just five days. The talk was of course all about the title permutations, and specifically what Vettel might do if swapping places with Webber would hand the title to the Australian driver.

"For me, it's pretty straightforward," he said. "I go to the Abu Dhabi GP, try to do my best, we have a strong car, I can rely on that and then we will see what happens. What do you want to hear? I can only tell you in that scenario you are describing, I can only tell you what you think. I think it's clear.

"It's one week away. As a kid, I never liked it when my parents teased me for something and didn't answer my question, so now I'm in a good position to tease you, so you will see...".

TOP LEFT Mark Webber could keep Red Bull team-mate Sebastian Vettel in sight, but was never in a position to challenge for the lead

BOTTOM LEFT Sebastian Vettel (right) congratulates Mark Webber on keeping Fernando Alonso at bay

SNAPSHOT FROM
BRAZIL

CLOCKWISE FROM RIGHT
Interlagos nestles in the suburbs of
São Paulo; Lewis Hamilton's McLaren
safely in *parc fermé* for the night;
the police were present, along with
their interpreters; the Red Bull Racing
team celebrate; Jenson Button
explains what happened on the way
back to the hotel; 16 years passed
between Uncle Ayrton's last outing
at Senna Interlagos and Bruno's
first; Emerson Fittipaldi was present
and demonstrated his 1972 Lotus;
Rubens Barrichello congratulates
Nico Hulkenberg on Williams's
first pole since 2005; Christian
Horner congraulates Adrian Newey
on Red Bull Racing clinching the
constructors' title; the Virgins plough
through the wet on Saturday

RACE
RESULTS
BRAZIL
INTERLAGOS

Official Results © [2010]
Formula One Administration Limited,
6 Princes Gate, London, SW7 1QJ.
No reproduction without permission.
All copyright and database rights reserved.

RACE DATE November 7th
CIRCUIT LENGTH 2.677 miles
NO. OF LAPS 71
RACE DISTANCE 190.067 miles
WEATHER Bright and dry, 24°C
TRACK TEMP 42°C
ATTENDANCE 157,582
LAP RECORD Juan Pablo Montoya,
1m11.473s, 134.837mph, 2004

PRACTICE 1			
	Driver	Time	Laps
1	S Vettel	1m12.328s	23
2	M Webber	1m12.810s	28
3	L Hamilton	1m12.845s	24
4	J Button	1m13.267s	24
5	R Kubica	1m13.370s	24
6	N Rosberg	1m13.516s	26
7	R Barrichello	1m13.546s	26
8	M Schumacher	1m13.643s	25
9	A Sutil	1m13.918s	26
10	N Heidfeld	1m14.000s	23
11	K Kobayashi	1m14.004s	23
12	N Hulkenberg	1m14.155s	29
13	F Alonso	1m14.246s	20
14	F Massa	1m14.267s	26
15	V Petrov	1m14.370s	23
16	V Liuzzi	1m14.487s	26
17	J Alguersuari	1m14.618s	30
18	S Buemi	1m14.734s	29
19	J Trulli	1m15.603s	25
20	T Glock	1m15.860s	20
21	H Kovalainen	1m16.057s	26
22	J d'Ambrosio	1m16.707s	28
23	C Klien	1m16.839s	18
24	B Senna	1m17.360s	30

PRACTICE 2			
	Driver	Time	Laps
1	S Vettel	1m11.968s	28
2	M Webber	1m12.072s	34
3	F Alonso	1m12.328s	36
4	L Hamilton	1m12.656s	33
5	F Massa	1m12.677s	19
6	R Kubica	1m12.802s	37
7	J Button	1m13.206s	33
8	N Heidfeld	1m13.222s	40
9	N Rosberg	1m13.333s	34
10	M Schumacher	1m13.346s	36
11	R Barrichello	1m13.520s	37
12	K Kobayashi	1m13.610s	41
13	N Hulkenberg	1m13.725s	39
14	A Sutil	1m13.741s	32
15	V Petrov	1m13.818s	26
16	V Liuzzi	1m14.045s	37
17	S Buemi	1m14.304s	33
18	J Alguersuari	1m14.578s	37
19	J Trulli	1m14.984s	47
20	H Kovalainen	1m15.101s	43
21	L di Grassi	1m15.433s	35
22	B Senna	1m16.070s	42
23	C Klien	1m16.082s	38
24	T Glock	1m16.150s	35

PRACTICE 3			
	Driver	Time	Laps
1	R Kubica	1m19.191s	16
2	S Vettel	1m19.500s	17
3	L Hamilton	1m19.536s	19
4	F Massa	1m19.735s	9
5	F Alonso	1m19.791s	9
6	V Petrov	1m19.887s	22
7	S Buemi	1m20.009s	24
8	N Rosberg	1m20.056s	13
9	J Button	1m20.164s	24
10	R Barrichello	1m20.320s	13
11	M Webber	1m20.337s	6
12	M Schumacher	1m20.421s	18
13	K Kobayashi	1m20.452s	22
14	N Hulkenberg	1m20.535s	12
15	J Alguersuari	1m20.541s	27
16	V Liuzzi	1m20.546s	20
17	A Sutil	1m20.613s	20
18	N Heidfeld	1m20.985s	25
19	J Trulli	1m22.326s	18
20	T Glock	1m22.449s	27
21	H Kovalainen	1m22.874s	20
22	L di Grassi	1m23.194s	22
23	B Senna	1m23.358s	20
24	C Klien	1m23.650s	19

QUALIFYING 1		
	Driver	Time
1	F Alonso	1m18.987s
2	M Webber	1m19.025s
3	S Vettel	1m19.160s
4	R Kubica	1m19.249s
5	K Kobayashi	1m19.741s
6	F Massa	1m19.778s
7	R Barrichello	1m19.799s
8	M Schumacher	1m19.879s
9	J Button	1m19.905s
10	L Hamilton	1m19.931s
11	N Hulkenberg	1m20.050s
12	S Buemi	1m20.096s
13	N Rosberg	1m20.153s
14	J Alguersuari	1m20.158s
15	N Heidfeld	1m20.174s
16	V Petrov	1m20.189s
17	V Liuzzi	1m20.592s
18	A Sutil	1m20.830s
19	T Glock	1m22.130s
20	J Trulli	1m22.250s
21	H Kovalainen	1m22.378s
22	L di Grassi	1m22.810s
23	C Klien	1m23.083s
24	B Senna	1m23.796s

QUALIFYING 2		
	Driver	Time
1	M Webber	1m18.516s
2	S Vettel	1m18.691s
3	R Kubica	1m18.877s
4	L Hamilton	1m18.921s
5	M Schumacher	1m18.923s
6	R Barrichello	1m18.925s
7	F Alonso	1m19.010s
8	N Hulkenberg	1m19.144s
9	V Petrov	1m19.153s
10	F Massa	1m19.200s
11	J Button	1m19.288s
12	K Kobayashi	1m19.385s
13	N Rosberg	1m19.486s
14	J Alguersuari	1m19.581s
15	S Buemi	1m19.847s
16	N Heidfeld	1m19.899s
17	V Liuzzi	1m20.357s

Best sectors – Practice			Speed trap – Practice			Best sectors – Qualifying			Speed trap – Qualifying		
Sec 1	S Vettel	18.529s	1	J Button	197.844mph	Sec 1	N Hulkenberg	18.452s	1	R Kubica	189.953mph
Sec 2	M Webber	36.334s	2	K Kobayashi	196.912mph	Sec 2	N Hulkenberg	37.549s	2	L Hamilton	189.766mph
Sec 3	S Vettel	17.044s	3	R Kubica	196.912mph	Sec 3	S Vettel	18.233s	3	S Vettel	189.766mph

Jenson Button
" We finally sorted the car for the race, I had decent race pace, I made some great passing moves, and the team made a couple of perfect calls on strategy."

Michael Schumacher
" I had a good start, gaining two places which I lost after my exit on the grass. With hindsight, my stop was maybe a little too early, leaving me stuck behind Adrian."

Sebastian Vettel
" We are the 2010 Constructors' Champions! Everyone matters in this team and I'm proud of them and of myself today – we had a straightforward race, no issues."

Felipe Massa
" When I went back out after the first stop I felt that something was strange with the right-front wheel and I had to come back to the pits to change tyres again."

Rubens Barrichello
" I was happy with my pace. Unluckily, after one of my overtaking attempts on Alguersuari, he ran over me and destroyed my front tyre so I had to pit again."

Robert Kubica
" I didn't have enough of an advantage over Hulkenberg to get past: I couldn't use our top-speed advantage, as I was stuck on the rev limiter on the straight."

Lewis Hamilton
" I was struggling to pass even the backmarkers in a straight line – Fernando shot past me at the start, too – and it almost felt like my F-duct wasn't working."

Nico Rosberg
" The team made a great call to get me on new rubber when the safety car came out. Annoyingly, Jenson did the same, so I couldn't make up any further positions."

Mark Webber
" Today is a sensational day for the team. Looking to the Drivers' Championship, I took a few points off Fernando today, so it's still all to play for in Abu Dhabi."

Fernando Alonso
" When the safety car came out, I thought it might be a chance to attack, but there were too many cars between me and Mark and it took too long to get past them."

Nico Hulkenberg
" The car wasn't easy to drive, but I kept Kubica behind me all the way. The team did a great pit stop and chose the right strategy; we just needed some more car pace."

Vitaly Petrov
" I tried to give everybody space, then at Turn 2 I had to take action to not hit Alguersuari. That put me on the kerb and I dropped to the back of the field by Turn 3."

	Driver		1	5	10	15	20	25	30	35	40	45	50	55	60	65	71	
1	N Hulkenberg																	1
2	S Vettel																	2
3	M Webber																	3
4	L Hamilton																	4
5	F Alonso																	5
6	R Barrichello																	6
7	R Kubica																	7
8	M Schumacher																	8
9	F Massa																	9
10	V Petrov																	10
11	J Button																	11
12	K Kobayashi																	12
13	N Rosberg																	13
14	J Alguersuari																	14
15	N Heidfeld																	15
16	V Liuzzi																	16
17	T Glock																	17
18	J Trulli																	18
19	S Buemi																	19
20	H Kovalainen																	20
21	L di Grassi																	21
22	A Sutil																	22
23	C Klien																	23
24	B Senna																	24

☆ Accident Ⓜ Mechanical failure Ⓟ Pit stop ☐ Safety Car ☐ Lapped Ⓑ Black flag

QUALIFYING 3

	Driver	Time
1	N Hulkenberg	1m14.470s
2	S Vettel	1m15.519s
3	M Webber	1m15.637s
4	L Hamilton	1m15.747s
5	F Alonso	1m15.989s
6	R Barrichello	1m16.203s
7	R Kubica	1m16.552s
8	M Schumacher	1m16.925s
9	F Massa	1m17.101s
10	V Petrov	1m17.656s

GRID

	Driver	Time
1	N Hulkenberg	1m14.470s
2	S Vettel	1m15.519s
3	M Webber	1m15.637s
4	L Hamilton	1m15.747s
5	F Alonso	1m15.989s
6	R Barrichello	1m16.203s
7	R Kubica	1m16.552s
8	M Schumacher	1m16.925s
9	F Massa	1m17.101s
10	V Petrov	1m17.656s
11	J Button	1m19.288s
12	K Kobayashi	1m19.385s
13	N Rosberg	1m19.486s
14	J Alguersuari	1m19.581s
15	N Heidfeld	1m19.899s
16	V Liuzzi	1m20.357s
17	T Glock	1m22.130s
18	J Trulli	1m22.250s
19*	S Buemi	1m19.847s
20	H Kovalainen	1m22.378s
21	L di Grassi	1m22.810s
22*	A Sutil	1m20.830s
23	C Klien	1m23.083s
24	B Senna	1m23.796s

* 5-place grid penalty for avoidable accident at Korean GP

RACE

	Driver	Car	Laps	Time	Avg. mph	Fastest	Stops
1	S Vettel	Red Bull-Renault RB6	71	1h33m11.803s	122.375	1m14.283s	1
2	M Webber	Red Bull-Renault RB6	71	1h33m16.046s	122.282	1m14.047s	1
3	F Alonso	Ferrari F10	71	1h33m18.610s	122.226	1m13.855s	1
4	L Hamilton	McLaren-Mercedes MP4-25	71	1h33m26.437s	122.055	1m13.851s	2
5	J Button	McLaren-Mercedes MP4-25	71	1h33m27.396s	122.035	1m13.932s	2
6	N Rosberg	Mercedes MGP W01	71	1h33m47.123s	121.606	1m14.184s	3
7	M Schumacher	Mercedes MGP W01	71	1h33m55.259s	121.431	1m15.219s	1
8	N Hulkenberg	Williams-Cosworth FW32	70	1h33m35.966s	120.132	1m14.985s	1
9	R Kubica	Renault R30	70	1h33m37.144s	120.106	1m15.161s	1
10	K Kobayashi	BMW Sauber-Ferrari C29	70	1h33m37.615s	120.097	1m14.748s	1
11	J Alguersuari	Toro Rosso-Ferrari STR5	70	1h33m44.982s	119.939	1m15.695s	1
12	A Sutil	Force India-Mercedes VJM03	70	1h33m45.492s	119.929	1m14.997s	1
13	S Buemi	Toro Rosso-Ferrari STR5	70	1h33m58.288s	119.657	1m15.935s	1
14	R Barrichello	Williams-Cosworth FW32	70	1h33m58.320s	119.655	1m15.227s	3
15	F Massa	Ferrari F10	70	1h33m59.032s	119.640	1m15.330s	3
16	V Petrov	Renault R30	70	1h33m59.733s	119.626	1m15.485s	2
17	N Heidfeld	BMW Sauber-Ferrari C29	70	1h34m00.983s	119.599	1m15.068s	1
18	H Kovalainen	Lotus-Cosworth T127	69	1h34m17.620s	117.544	1m17.161s	1
19	J Trulli	Lotus-Cosworth T127	69	1h34m18.462s	117.527	1m17.316s	1
20	T Glock	Virgin-Cosworth VR-01	69	1h34m24.680s	117.397	1m17.695s	1
21	B Senna	HRT-Cosworth F110	69	1h34m25.912s	117.372	1m17.731s	1
22	C Klien	HRT-Cosworth F110	65	1h34m26.440s	110.557	1m17.690s	2
NC	L di Grassi	Virgin-Cosworth VR-01	62	1h33m44.729s	106.236	1m16.767s	3
R	V Liuzzi	Force India-Mercedes VJM03	49	Accident	-	1m16.940s	1

CHAMPIONSHIP

	Driver	Pts
1	F Alonso	246
2	M Webber	238
3	S Vettel	231
4	L Hamilton	222
5	J Button	199
6	F Massa	143
7	N Rosberg	130
8	R Kubica	126
9	M Schumacher	72
10	R Barrichello	47
11	A Sutil	47
12	K Kobayashi	32
13	N Hulkenberg	22
14	V Liuzzi	21
15	V Petrov	19
16	S Buemi	8
17	P de la Rosa	6
18	N Heidfeld	6
19	J Alguersuari	3

	Constructor	Pts
1	Red Bull-Renault	469
2	McLaren-Mercedes	421
3	Ferrari	389
4	Mercedes	202
5	Renault	145
6	Williams-Cosworth	69
7	Force India-Mercedes	68
8	BMW Sauber-Ferrari	44
9	Toro Rosso-Ferrari	11

Fastest lap
L Hamilton 1m13.851s
(130.518mph) on lap 66

Fastest speed trap
K Kobayashi 195.110mph
Slowest speed trap
T Glock 184.305mph

Fastest pit stop
1 K Kobayashi 20.618s
2 N Rosberg 20.679s
3 M Webber 20.735s

Adrian Sutil
"After the safety car, I changed to the softs, but it was very hard to pass the Toro Rossos, as they were so quick on the straight. From P22 on the grid, P12 is positive."

Sebastian Buemi
"I made a super start and passed three cars. Then, on lap 2, I got by Kobayashi. I ran at a good pace and managed to fight off the guys coming up behind me."

Jarno Trulli
"I didn't have a great start, I had a lot of wheelspin, but pretty soon I was able to attack Timo and just as I was shaping up to pass him he pitted and I came out ahead."

Christian Klien
"The car stopped on the way to the grid due to fuel-pressure problems, but the mechanics fixed it. The race was a test for us to gain some race kilometres."

Nick Heidfeld
"I was just outside the points when the safety car came out, so the team decided to gamble and get me in for fresh tyres. However, with the penalty, the race was over."

Timo Glock
"Petrov had made a mistake in Turn 2, and I had to slow, which let Kovalainen pass me on the outside. Then I tried to follow him, but just didn't have the pace."

Vitantonio Liuzzi
"I'd been struggling with the brakes, and then going into Turn 2 something on the car let go and I couldn't turn in. The car just went straight on and into the barriers."

Lucas di Grassi
"I can be satisfied, as I really never expected to finish as high as 11th in the dry, as we lacked some topline speed. All the same, I enjoyed some good battles."

Heikki Kovalainen
"I made a good start and passed Timo. I then had a good battle with Jarno and Timo. As we neared the end, Jarno was close, so I had to make no mistakes."

Bruno Senna
"I had a strong race and finished just behind the other new teams. It was a good feeling before the race when the crowd was chanting and they gave energy."

Kamui Kobayashi
"When I was on the fresh tyres I could overtake both Toro Rossos, but it wasn't easy. You need good straightline speed to pass in Turn 1 and I didn't have enough of that."

Lucas di Grassi
"I loved the fantastic atmosphere, but the race didn't go as planned. We had a mechanical problem from early on and had to stop for the team to investigate."

2010 FORMULA 1 ETIHAD AIRWAYS ABU DHABI GRAND PRIX
YAS MARINA CIRCUIT

THIRD TO FIRST

Sebastian Vettel ranked third when he arrived in Abu Dhabi, but pole position and a masterful drive to victory made him World Champion, as Fernando Alonso and Mark Webber stumbled

In Abu Dhabi, all members of the Red Bull Racing team celebrated the constructors' title by wearing badges proclaiming 'Red Bull – Breakfast of Champions', which was a play on a slogan once popularised by James Hunt.

On Sunday evening, Sebastian Vettel matched a piece of history when he became the first man since Hunt in 1976 to win the World Championship by taking the lead for the first time all season at the final round. He did it because Ferrari messed up Fernando Alonso's race strategy in an extraordinary way, pitting the Spaniard when staying out was the logical move. Thanks to some brilliant driving by Renault's Vitaly Petrov, the move ultimately cost him the vital position that he needed to claim his third world title.

It was a popular success for Vettel, who also lowered Lewis Hamilton's record as the youngest ever champion, knocking 165 days off Lewis's 2008 standard as he was crowned at the age of 23 years and 134 days.

Vettel was ranked only third going into the Abu Dhabi GP weekend, and had to win, with Alonso fifth or lower. He put himself in the prime spot by taking his 10th pole of the season. At the end of a tense qualifying session, he held onto the top spot, despite a strong last lap from championship outsider Hamilton.

Alonso qualified third, and gave himself an excellent chance of holding onto his advantage if he could stay close enough to Vettel in the race. The Ferrari man was lucky to have enjoyed a clear run at the start of his last lap, as he'd come across team-mate Felipe Massa and Nico Rosberg, with his Brazilian team-mate moving out of the way, sacrificing his own chances.

Jenson Button qualified fourth fastest and gave McLaren considerable hope of retaining second place in the Constructors' Championship. This meant that Webber was squeezed down to fifth on the grid. The frustrated Australian tried something different from his team-mate, running a slow lap on the tyres before doing three fast ones consecutively, whereas Vettel had gone for it straight away.

Behind Massa, Rubens Barrichello did a good job to qualify seventh for Williams, ahead of Michael Schumacher, Nico Rosberg and an impressive Vitaly Petrov. One of the biggest surprises of the day was Petrov's team-mate Robert Kubica ending up 11th.

There was an extraordinary atmosphere in the build-up, as nobody could predict with any degree of confidence what might happen. A couple of tactless

BELOW Lewis Hamilton makes a bid for the lead at Turn 1, but poleman Sebastian Vettel holds on

OPPOSITE TOP Vitantonio Liuzzi was left with nowhere to go at Turn 6 and mounted Michael Schumacher's spun Mercedes

OPPOSITE BOTTOM Jarno Trulli blasts his Lotus through the early evening light, but it was a troubled race for the Italian veteran

INSIDE LINE
FERNANDO ALONSO
FERRARI DRIVER

"It's a sad feeling, as the race didn't go as we wanted. It's a shame to get to the end of the season and then lose the title at the final moment.

At the start, we were hoping that the McLarens would overtake Sebastian, but this time Jenson started very well, but not Lewis.

We were in a good position at that point, but then the safety car was brought out onto the circuit.

First, Vitaly made the decision to pit, which was a little bit unexpected, and then Mark stopped very early as well. We decided to cover Webber and we exited the pits in front of him.

It seemed to be the right thing to do at the time but, by the end of the race, that was maybe not the right thing. It's always easy to see the perfect strategy after the race.

I didn't have time to think. I saw that Webber stopped and Felipe stopped as well, and that Webber was gaining time, so for us it was a choice that we had to make. We either decide to pit and stay in front of Webber, or not stop and he gets in front of us.

For sure, we can see at the end of the race that maybe if we had stayed out like Button, it would have been enough. You never know if the soft tyres are going to degrade a lot more, then we could have overtaken more cars.

Our F-duct was working OK, but the Renault was very quick on the straights, and we knew from Saturday that they ran less rear wing than us. They were very quick in the second sector and not so quick in the last sector, but quick enough to protect their position.

It's been an interesting season, with ups and downs for everybody. It was a good first year of the relationship with Ferrari. For the past few years, I've been fighting to be in Q3 and now I've been fighting for the World Championship once

more. I've taken five wins this year, which puts me ahead of Niki Lauda and Juan Manuel Fangio, which is very special.

The best moment of the year was Monza, while the worst was Monaco, not being able to do qualifying. I will remember this year for a long time and, despite the final result, we've been fighting for the Drivers' Championship until the last race, with the third-quickest car, as we are third in the Constructors' Championship.

I'm very proud of that, and the job the team has done and our approach to the last part of the year. We were very limited with engines from race four onwards, and we managed to fight for the championship to the last lap of the last race, so I think we did our best."

German journalists dropped a banana skin on the grid in front of Alonso's car. It was hastily removed by the team's furious PR man...

Against the expectations of many, the first lap passed without incident for the key contenders. Vettel led Hamilton into Turn 1, but crucially Button had a good getaway and got in front of Alonso, claiming third and putting the latter 'on the bubble'. One more place lost would cost Alonso the title and, with Webber on his tail, he couldn't afford any mistakes.

Further around the first lap came the incident that would lead to a chain reaction that would prove so expensive for two of the title protagonists. Rosberg gave Schumacher a gentle tap, sending his Mercedes team-mate into a spin. Several cars darted by without trouble, but Tonio Liuzzi hit the silver car hard, landing on top of it and almost striking the German's helmet. A safety car was called for, and several drivers who'd started on option tyres took the chance to switch to primes, ensuring that they could run to the flag. Among them were Rosberg and Petrov.

Once the green flag flew, Vettel edged away from Hamilton, who in turn was clear of Button, Alonso and Webber, as the top five drifted apart. It seemed to

TALKING POINT
A WORTHY CHAMPION

After perhaps the best season in F1 history, there was no denying that Sebastian Vettel, at 23 years and 134 days the youngest World Champion in the sport's history, is fully deserving of the accolade.

The Red Bull racer certainly did not back into the championship, he went out and won it. There were 10 pole positions, five victoriess and three fastest lap, and those final grands prix in Japan, Brazil and Abu Dhabi, with the pressure on, were truly sublime.

Vettel crossed the finish line, punched the air and then had to wait another half-minute, as Lewis Hamilton, Jenson Button and Nico Rosberg crossed the line and confirmed that Fernando Alonso had not got home in the first four. It was then he heard it on the radio: "Sebastian Vettel – Weltmeister!"

In the car, around the rest of the slow-down lap, Vettel was almost overcome, and he battled hard to keep the emotions in check as he stood on the podium.

"Most of the time in the race it was head down, just trying to focus on myself," he said, "but I saw the screens and obviously I saw that Robert Kubica was a long time in second place. I saw the Renault ahead of Lewis and I thought, 'wow', as Lewis knows how to overtake people and McLaren have quite good speed, but on the other hand the Renault F-duct is amazing. They also usually have quite a long top gear.

"Then I also saw a red car behind a yellow one and assumed that it had to be Vitaly in front of Fernando. So directly or indirectly, thanks a lot to Renault...

"I was actually thinking about Kimi's situation in 2007 [when he hauled in and passed the McLaren duo of Alonso and Hamilton], as it was a little bit similar. Obviously, we were in a stronger position in terms of how many points were missing, but in the end, if you know Kimi, you know that one big advantage, in that moment especially, is that sometimes he doesn't give a damn, he just does his own thing.

"That was my target all weekend long. But who would have thought that Ferrari starting from third with good pace would finish seventh? I'm just happy to put my name on the list of champions with drivers like Senna and Michael. I mean, I don't know...

"After the Belgian GP, where I hit Jenson, I called him in the evening and apologised. I think this is how it should be. It makes this moment even more appreciated – being on the podium with two guys like Lewis and Jenson. We respect each other. Lewis came to me and said congratulations. It's good if you can look into someone's eyes and you feel that they mean it..."

be stalemate, as once again the circuit proved that it didn't provide any overtaking opportunities.

Webber wasn't happy with his tyres though and, with nothing to lose in terms of the title fight, he pitted on lap 11. He'd had Ferraris either side of him, Alonso in front, Massa behind, and naturally the Maranello crew paid close attention to what he was doing. Webber was a dual threat, as if he got in front of Alonso, he'd help Vettel win the title, while he still had a chance in his own right.

Two laps after Webber's stop, Massa pitted, and then two laps after that, Alonso followed suit. The Australian had been caught for a while behind Jaime Alguersuari's Toro Rosso – one of the cars that pitted on lap 1 – and he lost vital seconds. That may have encouraged Ferrari to bring Alonso in, on the basis that the team knew that the delay to the Red Bull meant that he'd be sure to come out in front.

It worked, and initially it looked as though the team had pulled off a good move, ensuring that Webber couldn't jump Alonso. But then reality hit home. Ahead of Alonso were not just the cars that had yet to pit, but Rosberg and Petrov, both of whom had pitted on the opening lap and could run all the way to the finish. Taking Vettel, Hamilton and Button into account, in real terms Alonso was sixth, and thus two positions off where he needed to be.

On another day, on another circuit, the Ferrari might have despatched Petrov, although Rosberg might not have been so easy. However, helped by his efficient F-duct, and driving to ensure his ride for 2011, Petrov put in an awesome performance. Try as he might, Alonso couldn't find a way past the Renault, and the gap to those up ahead and those who had yet to stop began to extend.

Alonso's frustration was visible and, as the situation grew more desperate, his engineer urged him to use "all his talent" to find a way by.

Up front, Vettel was driving a copybook race, making no mistakes and keeping Hamilton safely behind. His focus was totally on winning the race, as it had to be, and the team wasn't distracting him with news of Alonso. Hamilton pitted from second place on lap 23, and RBR responded by stopping Vettel a lap later. Hamilton came out behind Robert Kubica, who'd yet to stop. Just like team-mate Petrov, the Pole kept the potentially quicker car behind for lap after lap, which allowed Vettel to escape.

Those pit stops left Button in the lead, and McLaren decided to leave the outgoing World Champion there, on the basis that he was going to pit and resume third come what may. So he stayed out until lap 39.

With the race drawing to its conclusion, Alonso was stuck in eighth place, with Kubica and Adrian Sutil yet to stop. The Force India driver wasn't an issue, but the gap between Kubica and Alonso grew to the extent that it looked as though he could pit and come out in front of the Ferrari. And that's what happened on lap 46, finally leaving Hamilton in free air.

It was too late by then of course, and Vettel reeled off the remaining laps to the chequered flag. When the other cars had crossed the line and Alonso's race

OPPOSITE Fernando Alonso made only one pit stop, but it proved to be at the wrong time and cost him the chance to claim his third F1 title

BELOW Pitting at the end of lap 1 helped Nico Rosberg to jump up the order to finish an eventual fourth

BOTTOM As the sun set, the lights went down on Mark Webber's title battle, as eighth place wasn't enough

ABOVE Fernando Alonso was
truly sick of the rear view of Vitaly
Petrov's Renault by the end of the
race, as the Russian kept him at bay

BELOW The Red Bull cap was
brought out for the second race
in succession, as Sebastian Vettel
wrapped up the Drivers' World
Championship for Red Bull Racing

position was confirmed, Vettel was told that he was indeed the 2010 World Champion.

"I was tempted to watch the giant screens, but I didn't," said Vettel, "as for the last 10 laps my engineer kept telling me all sorts of things about the gaps and pace. Partly I asked for it, to know where I was, but also things I had to watch out for which is fine. Mind you, I think in none of these 19 races has he been so alive in the final 10 laps.

"I was already thinking 'what's going on?' and I was seeing sometimes on the giant screens Lewis behind the Renault and also I think it was Alonso and his Ferrari behind the Renault. But then I just tried to

forget and kept driving, focusing on myself."

Hamilton and Button circulated together at the end, their second and third places confirming second place in the World Championship for McLaren. Rosberg's first-lap gamble was repaid with a worthy fourth place, while Kubica's opposite strategy of a late stop earned him fifth, ahead of Petrov.

Down in seventh place, three places shy of his third world title, was Alonso. On the slowing-down lap he vented his frustration by making a silly gesture to the Russian, which was an act that won him no friends.

"Obviously there was a safety car, so Rosberg and Petrov made a decision to stop, that also was a little bit unexpected," said Alonso. "And then Webber stopped very early as well.

"It's always very easy to see the strategy after the race, when there's nothing we can do or we can change. Someone did a better job than us, as they have more points at the end of the championship, so we congratulate them and next year we try again."

A subdued Webber crossed the finish line in eighth position, half-a-second behind Alonso and not far ahead of the trio of Alguersuari, Massa and Heidfeld, with the drivers' title having slipped from his grasp over the final few races.

Webber may have been disappointed, but that was nothing compared to the scenes at Ferrari, where glum faces demonstrated that everyone knew that they had thrown the title away with a bad strategy call. Had Alonso stayed out and run to the flag behind Button to claim fourth place – and maybe even had a chance to jump him at the stops – the scene would have been so very different.

In the end, Ferrari cracked under pressure, and Red Bull Racing's strategy of having two drivers up there and fighting for the drivers' title paid off. It was a remarkable end to a truly great season. Will we get more of the same in 2011?

SNAPSHOT FROM
ABU DHABI

CLOCKWISE FROM RIGHT

The sun sets, as Sebastian Vettel laps during practice; Red Bull Racing owner Dietrich Mateschitz celebrates with Christian Horner and Adrian Newey; Virgin Racing promoted its cuddly side; the patch of cement dust at Turn 6 made visibility tricky; a marshal hoofs it with a camera-carrying kerb marker, one of two demolished by Lewis Hamilton's McLaren; Richard Branson and Tony Fernandes get measured up for their 'air stewardess challenge'; Renault's promo girls look cool in the shades; the support was cosmopolitan and good-natured; Ferrari chief Luca di Montezemolo had high hopes of the drivers' title; the Yas Marina circuit offers some amazing vantage points

RACE RESULTS
ABU DHABI
YAS MARINA

Official Results © [2010]
Formula One Administration Limited,
6 Princes Gate, London, SW7 1QJ.
No reproduction without permission.
All copyright and database rights reserved.

RACE DATE November 14th
CIRCUIT LENGTH 3.451 miles
NO. OF LAPS 55
RACE DISTANCE 189.747 miles
WEATHER Hot & very dry, 29°C
TRACK TEMP 33°C
ATTENDANCE (RACE DAY) 55,000
LAP RECORD Sebastian Vettel,
1m40.279s, 123.893mph, 2009

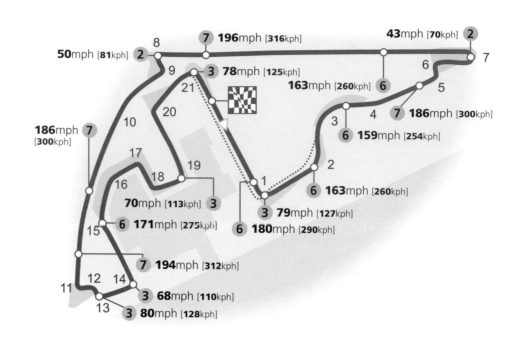

	PRACTICE 1		
	Driver	Time	Laps
1	S Vettel	1m42.760s	18
2	L Hamilton	1m43.369s	16
3	J Button	1m43.785s	19
4	M Webber	1m43.840s	19
5	R Kubica	1m44.080s	19
6	F Alonso	1m44.121s	17
7	M Schumacher	1m44.199s	19
8	K Kobayashi	1m44.604s	18
9	N Rosberg	1m44.718s	19
10	N Heidfeld	1m44.737s	19
11	F Massa	1m45.160s	18
12	V Petrov	1m45.445s	21
13	R Barrichello	1m45.474s	15
14	A Sutil	1m45.552s	20
15	V Liuzzi	1m45.585s	14
16	J Alguersuari	1m46.003s	20
17	N Hulkenberg	1m46.644s	19
18	S Buemi	1m47.105s	22
19	T Glock	1m48.450s	19
20	J Trulli	1m48.472s	17
21	L di Grassi	1m49.375s	13
22	B Senna	1m49.590s	18
23	C Klien	1m50.274s	17
24	F Fauzy	1m51.705s	18

	PRACTICE 2		
	Driver	Time	Laps
1	L Hamilton	1m40.888s	25
2	S Vettel	1m41.145s	28
3	F Alonso	1m41.314s	29
4	M Webber	1m41.315s	29
5	R Kubica	1m41.576s	31
6	F Massa	1m41.583s	21
7	V Petrov	1m42.096s	31
8	J Button	1m42.132s	28
9	V Liuzzi	1m42.203s	31
10	N Rosberg	1m42.222s	29
11	M Schumacher	1m42.246s	29
12	N Hulkenberg	1m42.449s	32
13	A Sutil	1m42.535s	21
14	K Kobayashi	1m42.768s	26
15	R Barrichello	1m42.914s	37
16	N Heidfeld	1m42.950s	34
17	J Alguersuari	1m43.128s	17
18	S Buemi	1m43.584s	33
19	H Kovalainen	1m45.180s	36
20	T Glock	1m45.259s	31
21	J Trulli	1m45.612s	35
22	L di Grassi	1m46.053s	29
23	C Klien	1m47.210s	32
24	B Senna	1m47.434s	28

	PRACTICE 3		
	Driver	Time	Laps
1	S Vettel	1m40.696s	18
2	M Webber	1m40.829s	15
3	L Hamilton	1m41.280s	13
4	F Alonso	1m41.490s	14
5	J Button	1m41.578s	17
6	V Petrov	1m41.685s	17
7	M Schumacher	1m41.690s	18
8	N Rosberg	1m41.729s	17
9	R Kubica	1m41.877s	18
10	N Heidfeld	1m41.893s	20
11	N Hulkenberg	1m41.934s	18
12	F Massa	1m41.978s	14
13	R Barrichello	1m42.316s	15
14	K Kobayashi	1m42.566s	16
15	A Sutil	1m42.587s	16
16	V Liuzzi	1m42.858s	14
17	J Alguersuari	1m42.993s	20
18	S Buemi	1m43.344s	18
19	H Kovalainen	1m44.876s	15
20	J Trulli	1m45.048s	23
21	T Glock	1m45.050s	20
22	B Senna	1m45.490s	16
23	L di Grassi	1m45.629s	22
24	C Klien	1m46.464s	17

	QUALIFYING 1	
	Driver	Time
1	F Alonso	1m40.170s
2	N Rosberg	1m40.231s
3	S Vettel	1m40.318s
4	L Hamilton	1m40.335s
5	M Webber	1m40.690s
6	J Button	1m40.877s
7	R Barrichello	1m40.904s
8	F Massa	1m40.942s
9	N Hulkenberg	1m41.015s
10	V Petrov	1m41.018s
11	K Kobayashi	1m41.045s
12	M Schumacher	1m41.222s
13	R Kubica	1m41.336s
14	N Heidfeld	1m41.409s
15	A Sutil	1m41.473s
16	V Liuzzi	1m41.681s
17	J Alguersuari	1m41.707s
18	S Buemi	1m41.824s
19	J Trulli	1m43.516s
20	H Kovalainen	1m43.712s
21	T Glock	1m44.095s
22	L di Grassi	1m44.510s
23	B Senna	1m45.085s
24	C Klien	1m45.296s

	QUALIFYING 2	
	Driver	Time
1	S Vettel	1m39.874s
2	J Button	1m40.014s
3	N Rosberg	1m40.060s
4	M Webber	1m40.074s
5	L Hamilton	1m40.119s
6	F Alonso	1m40.311s
7	F Massa	1m40.323s
8	M Schumacher	1m40.452s
9	R Barrichello	1m40.476s
10	V Petrov	1m40.658s
11	R Kubica	1m40.780s
12	K Kobayashi	1m40.783s
13	A Sutil	1m40.914s
14	N Heidfeld	1m41.113s
15	N Hulkenberg	1m41.418s
16	V Liuzzi	1m41.642s
17	J Alguersuari	1m41.738s

Best sectors – Practice		
Sec 1	S Vettel	17.593s
Sec 2	J Button	42.617s
Sec 3	L Hamilton	40.237s

Speed trap – Practice		
1	A Sutil	198.341mph
2	J Button	198.341mph
3	K Kobayashi	197.658mph

Best sectors – Qualifying		
Sec 1	S Vettel	17.397s
Sec 2	J Button	42.363s
Sec 3	S Vettel	39.399s

Speed trap – Qualifying		
1	J Alguersuari	197.347mph
2	S Buemi	197.223mph
3	V Petrov	196.477mph

Jenson Button
"It's been a really exciting year for F1. We've all had our ups and downs. Our main aim was to clinch second in the Constructors' Championship, and we did that."

Michael Schumacher
"I'm totally fine and wasn't hit by anything in the incident [with Liuzzi]. I went off the line, spun and because of the dirt there, the back of the car just came around."

Sebastian Vettel
"The start was very tight with Lewis, and I had some graining in the first stint, but then the car stabilised. I didn't know anything until I passed the chequered flag."

Felipe Massa
"We'd decided to pit early to try and stay ahead of Webber, but we didn't manage it and were then stuck in traffic almost all race, both myself and Fernando."

Rubens Barrichello
"I had a good battle with Sutil who ran long. He left his pit stop in front of me, but I dived past him on the outside of Turn 4. It was a huge, exhilarating move."

Robert Kubica
"When the safety car went in, I passed Sutil, which was crucial. I then got stuck behind Kamui for a while. Eventually, I got him and that was a key moment."

Lewis Hamilton
"I was able to match Sebastian's pace in the early part of the race. But, after my stop, I was stuck behind Robert and it was simply impossible to get past him."

Nico Rosberg
"I'm very pleased with fourth. It's the best that we could have hoped for from my grid position. Special thanks to Ross and James Vowles for a great strategy today."

Mark Webber
"Early in the race we knew we had to go for it with the strategy, but it left us exposed and Fernando covered us. I tried my hardest, but it wasn't enough."

Fernando Alonso
"It's a shame to lose the title at the final moment. Everything went wrong, from the start to strategy. With hindsight, it'd have been better not to pit so soon."

Nico Hulkenberg
"That was a tricky race. I started on the prime and did a long first stint and then a shorter one on the option, but car pace wasn't good so it didn't work out for us."

Vitaly Petrov
"I pitted under the safety car and then tried to push while looking after the tyres. I had a battle with Alonso, but had good top speed so could control the situation."

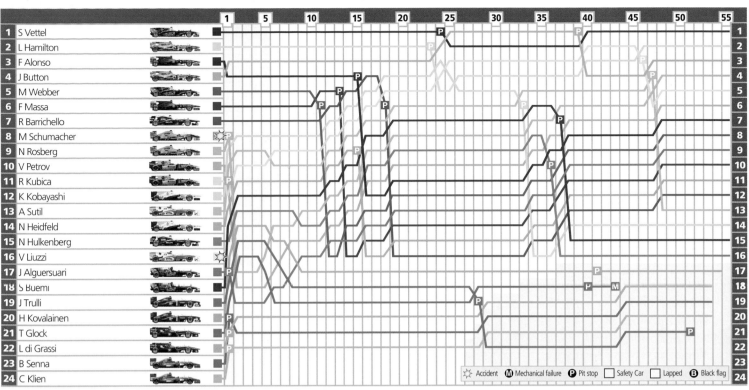

		1	5	10	15	20	25	30	35	40	45	50	55	
1	S Vettel													1
2	L Hamilton													2
3	F Alonso													3
4	J Button													4
5	M Webber													5
6	F Massa													6
7	R Barrichello													7
8	M Schumacher													8
9	N Rosberg													9
10	V Petrov													10
11	R Kubica													11
12	K Kobayashi													12
13	A Sutil													13
14	N Heidfeld													14
15	N Hulkenberg													15
16	V Liuzzi													16
17	J Alguersuari													17
18	S Buemi													18
19	J Trulli													19
20	H Kovalainen													20
21	T Glock													21
22	L di Grassi													22
23	B Senna													23
24	C Klien													24

☆ Accident Ⓜ Mechanical failure Ⓟ Pit stop ☐ Safety Car ☐ Lapped Ⓑ Black flag

QUALIFYING 3

	Driver	Time
1	S Vettel	1m39.394s
2	L Hamilton	1m39.425s
3	F Alonso	1m39.792s
4	J Button	1m39.823s
5	M Webber	1m39.925s
6	F Massa	1m40.202s
7	R Barrichello	1m40.203s
8	M Schumacher	1m40.516s
9	N Rosberg	1m40.589s
10	V Petrov	1m40.901s

GRID

	Driver	Time
1	S Vettel	1m39.394s
2	L Hamilton	1m39.425s
3	F Alonso	1m39.792s
4	J Button	1m39.823s
5	M Webber	1m39.925s
6	F Massa	1m40.202s
7	R Barrichello	1m40.203s
8	M Schumacher	1m40.516s
9	N Rosberg	1m40.589s
10	V Petrov	1m40.901s
11	R Kubica	1m40.780s
12	K Kobayashi	1m40.783s
13	A Sutil	1m40.914s
14	N Heidfeld	1m41.113s
15	N Hulkenberg	1m41.418s
16	V Liuzzi	1m41.642s
17	J Alguersuari	1m41.738s
18	S Buemi	1m41.824s
19	J Trulli	1m43.516s
20	H Kovalainen	1m43.712s
21	T Glock	1m44.095s
22	L di Grassi	1m44.510s
23	B Senna	1m45.085s
24	C Klien	1m45.296s

RACE

	Driver	Car	Laps	Time	Avg. mph	Fastest	Stops
1	S Vettel	Red Bull-Renault RB6	55	1h39m36.837s	114.284	1m41.739s	1
2	L Hamilton	McLaren-Mercedes MP4-25	55	1h39m46.999s	114.090	1m41.274s	1
3	J Button	McLaren-Mercedes MP4-25	55	1h39m47.884s	114.073	1m41.636s	1
4	N Rosberg	Mercedes MGP W01	55	1h40m07.584s	113.699	1m41.711s	1
5	R Kubica	Renault R30	55	1h40m15.863s	113.542	1m41.753s	1
6	V Petrov	Renault R30	55	1h40m20.357s	113.458	1m42.311s	1
7	F Alonso	Ferrari F10	55	1h40m20.634s	113.453	1m42.227s	1
8	M Webber	Red Bull-Renault RB6	55	1h40m21.080s	113.444	1m42.196s	1
9	J Alguersuari	Toro Rosso-Ferrari STR5	55	1h40m27.038s	113.332	1m42.727s	1
10	F Massa	Ferrari F10	55	1h40m27.705s	113.319	1m42.725s	1
11	N Heidfeld	BMW Sauber-Ferrari C29	55	1h40m28.388s	113.307	1m42.673s	1
12	R Barrichello	Williams-Cosworth FW32	55	1h40m34.523s	113.191	1m42.669s	1
13	A Sutil	Force India-Mercedes VJM03	55	1h40m35.162s	113.179	1m42.695s	1
14	K Kobayashi	BMW Sauber-Ferrari C29	55	1h40m36.395s	113.156	1m42.733s	1
15	S Buemi	Toro Rosso-Ferrari STR5	55	1h40m40.015s	113.089	1m42.573s	1
16	N Hulkenberg	Williams-Cosworth FW32	55	1h40m41.600s	113.059	1m42.397s	1
17	H Kovalainen	Lotus-Cosworth T127	54	1h41m18.182s	110.334	1m45.378s	1
18	L di Grassi	Virgin-Cosworth VR-01	53	1h39m54.475s	109.802	1m46.126s	1
19	B Senna	HRT-Cosworth F110	53	1h39m57.828s	109.741	1m46.255s	1
20	C Klien	HRT-Cosworth F110	53	1h40m11.300s	109.495	1m46.646s	1
21	J Trulli	Lotus-Cosworth T127	51	Rear wing	108.043	1m45.979s	1
R	T Glock	Virgin-Cosworth VR-01	43	Gearbox	-	1m46.837s	1
R	M Schumacher	Mercedes MGP W01	0	Accident	-	-	0
R	V Liuzzi	Force India-Mercedes VJM03	0	Accident	-	-	0

CHAMPIONSHIP

	Driver	Pts
1	S Vettel	256
2	F Alonso	252
3	M Webber	242
4	L Hamilton	240
5	J Button	214
6	F Massa	144
7	N Rosberg	142
8	R Kubica	136
9	M Schumacher	72
10	R Barrichello	47
11	A Sutil	47
12	K Kobayashi	32
13	V Petrov	27
14	N Hulkenberg	22
15	V Liuzzi	21
16	S Buemi	8
17	P de la Rosa	6
18	N Heidfeld	6
19	J Alguersuari	5

	Constructor	Pts
1	Red Bull-Renault	498
2	McLaren-Mercedes	454
3	Ferrari	396
4	Mercedes	214
5	Renault	163
6	Williams-Cosworth	69
7	Force India-Mercedes	48
8	BMW Sauber-Ferrari	44
9	Toro Rosso-Ferrari	13

Fastest lap
L Hamilton 1m41.274s
(122.676mph) on lap 47

Fastest speed trap
K Kobayashi 198.901mph
Slowest speed trap
L di Grassi 190.636mph

Fastest pit stop
1 M Webber 20.168s
2 R Kubica 20.188s
3 K Kobayashi 20.208s

Adrian Sutil

"Not such an exciting race, as I was driving alone and then had a late stop as we tried to make up positions. I came out side-by-side to Rubens and lost a position."

Sébastien Buemi

"I got a super start and passed five cars. The team brought Jaime in for a tyre change during the safety-car period and his strategy proved to be the better one."

Jarno Trulli

"My race was one of the ones I'll want to forget. I had a problem with the front wing to begin with, and then a rear-wing failure finished the race so I'm glad it's over."

Christian Klien

"It was a tough race and it was very hot inside the car. The car itself was difficult to handle with a lot of fuel, but the lap times got better with less fuel."

Nick Heidfeld

"Pitting for new tyres straight away was a very good move, as it put me three places further up. I was then able to close on Felipe, but had no chance to pass him."

Timo Glock

"I had good speed and could keep pace with Lotus. In the end, the gearbox got too hot and failed in the closing stages of the race, so it was disappointing."

Vitantonio Liuzzi

"I came around Turn 3 and saw a cloud of smoke. I couldn't move as there were cars around me. When the smoke cleared I saw Michael the wrong way round."

Jaime Alguersuari

"I was lucky not to be caught up in the Schumacher accident on lap 1, and after that it was a good choice to change tyres as soon as the safety car came out."

Heikki Kovalainen

"I made up places immediately and everything went to plan. The tyres weren't degrading and as the fuel burnt away I was able to pull away from those behind."

Bruno Senna

"Today was a good but very tough race. I tried to push and get close to our competitors in front, but then I was in traffic, so that didn't help us end further up."

Kamui Kobayashi

"I'm disappointed, as I wanted to score in the final race. I did what I could, but there was no way to overtake. My car was OK, but we had bad luck with our strategy."

Lucas di Grassi

"With a safety car on lap 1, we decided to go for the stop straight away to change to the primes. We then had to do more than 50 laps with the same set."

CHAMPIONSHIP RESULTS

DRIVER RESULTS

	Driver	Nationality	Car	ROUND 1 BAHRAIN GP March 14	ROUND 2 AUSTRALIAN GP March 28	ROUND 3 MALAYSIAN GP April 4	ROUND 4 CHINESE GP April 18	ROUND 5 SPANISH GP May 9	ROUND 6 MONACO GP May 16
1	Sebastian Vettel	German	Red Bull-Renault RB6	4P	RP	1	6P	3	2F
2	Fernando Alonso	Spanish	Ferrari F10	1F	4	13	4	2	6
3	Mark Webber	Australian	Red Bull-Renault RB6	8	9F	2PF	8	1P	1P
4	Lewis Hamilton	British	McLaren-Mercedes MP4-25	3	6	6	2F	14F	5
5	Jenson Button	British	McLaren-Mercedes MP4-25	7	1	8	1	5	R
6	Felipe Massa	Brazilian	Ferrari F10	2	3	7	9	6	4
7	Nico Rosberg	German	Mercedes MGP W01	5	5	3	3	13	7
8	Robert Kubica	Polish	Renault R30	11	2	4	5	8	3
9	Michael Schumacher	German	Mercedes MGP W01	6	10	R	10	4	12
10	Rubens Barrichello	Brazilian	Williams-Cosworth FW32	10	8	12	12	9	R
11	Adrian Sutil	German	Force India-Mercedes VJM03	12	R	5	11	7	8
12	Kamui Kobayashi	Japanese	BMW Sauber-Ferrari C29	R	R	R	R	12	R
13	Vitaly Petrov	Russian	Renault R30	R	R	R	7	11	13
14	Nico Hulkenberg	German	Williams-Cosworth FW32	14	R	10	15	16	R
15	Vitantonio Liuzzi	Italian	Force India-Mercedes VKM03	9	7	R	R	15	9
16	Sebastien Buemi	Swiss	Toro Rosso-Ferrari STR5	16	R	11	R	R	10
17	Pedro de la Rosa	Spanish	BMW Sauber-Ferrari C29	R	12	NS	R	R	R
18	Nick Heidfeld	German	BMW Sauber-Ferrari C29						
19	Jaime Alguersuari	Spanish	Toro Rosso-Ferrari STR5	13	11	9	13	10	11
20	Heikki Kovalainen	Finnish	Lotus-Cosworth T127	15	13	R	14	NS	R
21	Jarno Trulli	Italian	Lotus-Cosworth T127	17	R	17	R	17	15
22	Karun Chandhok	Indian	HRT-Cosworth F110	R	14	15	17	R	14
23	Bruno Senna	Brazilian	HRT-Cosworth F110	R	R	16	16	R	R
24	Lucas di Grassi	Brazilian	Virgin-Cosworth VR-01	R	R	14	R	19	R
25	Timo Glock	German	Virgin-Cosworth VR-01	R	R	R	NS	18	R
26	Sakon Yamamoto	Japanese	HRT-Cosworth F110						
27	Christian Klien	Austrian	HRT-Cosworth F110						

RACE SCORING

1st	25	POINTS
2nd	18	POINTS
3rd	15	POINTS
4th	12	POINTS
5th	10	POINTS
6th	8	POINTS
7th	6	POINTS
8th	4	POINTS
9th	2	POINTS
10th	1	POINT

DATA KEY

D	DISQUALIFIED
F	FASTEST LAP
NC	NON-CLASSIFIED
NS	NON-STARTER
P	POLE POSITION
R	RETIRED
W	WITHDRAWN

QUALIFYING HEAD-TO-HEAD

Red Bull-Renault
Vettel–Webber **12–7**

McLaren-Mercedes
Hamilton–Button **13–6**

Ferrari
Alonso–Massa **15–4**

Mercedes
Rosberg–Schumacher **15–4**

Renault
Kubica–Petrov **17–2**

Williams-Cosworth
Barrichello–Hulkenberg **13–6**

Force India-Mercedes
Sutil–Liuzzi **16–3**

BMW Sauber-Ferrari
de la Rosa–Kobayashi **7–7**
Kobayashi–Heidfeld **4–1**

Toro Rosso-Ferrari
Buemi–Alguersuari **11–8**

Lotus-Cosworth
Trulli–Kovalainen **11–8**

HRT-Cosworth
Senna–Chandhok **7–2**
Chandhok–Yamamoto **1–0**
Senna–Yamamoto **5–1**
Klien–Senna **2–1**

Virgin-Cosworth
Glock–di Grassi **16–3**

Race results for both drivers, ie, first and second listed as 1/2 with team's best result listed first.

CONSTRUCTOR RESULTS

1	Red Bull-Renault
2	McLaren-Mercedes
3	Ferrari
4	Mercedes
5	Renault
6	Williams-Cosworth
7	Force India-Mercedes
8	BMW Sauber-Ferrari
9	Toro Rosso-Ferrari
10	Lotus-Cosworth
11	HRT-Cosworth
12	Virgin-Cosworth

ROUND 7 May 30 TURKISH GP	ROUND 8 June 13 CANADIAN GP	ROUND 9 June 27 EUROPEAN GP	ROUND 10 July 11 BRITISH GP	ROUND 11 July 25 GERMAN GP	ROUND 12 August 1 HUNGARIAN GP	ROUND 13 August 29 BELGIAN GP	ROUND 14 September 12 ITALIAN GP	ROUND 15 September 26 SINGAPORE GP	ROUND 16 October 10 JAPANESE GP	ROUND 17 October 24 KOREAN GP	ROUND 18 November 7 BRAZILIAN GP	ROUND 19 November 14 ABU DHABI GP	TOTAL POINTS
R	4	1P	7P	3PF	3PF	15	4	2	1P	RP	1	1P	256
8	3	8	14F	1	2	R	1PF	1PF	3	1F	3	7	252
3P	5	R	1	6	1	2P	6	3	2F	R	2	8	242
1	1P	2	2	4	R	1F	R	R	5	2	4F	2F	240
2	2	3F	4	5	8	R	2	4	4	12	5	3	214
7	15	11	15	2	4	4	3	8	R	3	15	10	144
5	6	10	3	8	R	6	5	5	17	R	6	4	142
6	7F	5	R	7	R	3	8	7	R	5	9	5	136
4	11	15	9	9	11	7	9	13	6	4	7	R	72
14	14	4	5	12	10	R	10	6	9	7	14	12	47
9	10	6	8	17	R	5	16	9	R	R	12	13	47
10	R	7	6	11	9	8	R	R	7	8	10	14	32
15F	17	14	13	10	5	9	13	11	R	R	16	6	27
17	13	R	10	13	6	14	7	10	R	10	8P	16	22
13	9	16	11	16	13	10	12	R	R	6	R	R	21
16	8	9	12	R	12	12	11	14	10	R	13	15	8
11	R	12	R	14	7	11	14						6
							R	8	9	17	11		6
12	12	13	R	15	R	13	15	12	11	11	11	9	5
R	16	R	17	R	14	16	18	16	12	13	18	17	
R	R	21	16	R	15	19	R	R	13	R	19	21	
20	18	18	19										
R	R	20		19	17	R	R	R	15	14	21	19	
19	19	17	R	R	18	17	20	15	NS	R	NC	18	
18	R	19	18	18	16	18	17	R	14	R	20	R	
		20	R	19	20	19	R	16	15				
									R		22	20	

ROUND 1 March 14 BAHRAIN GP	ROUND 2 March 28 AUSTRALIAN GP	ROUND 3 April 4 MALAYSIAN GP	ROUND 4 April 18 CHINESE GP	ROUND 5 May 9 SPANISH GP	ROUND 6 May 16 MONACO GP	ROUND 7 May 30 TURKISH GP	ROUND 8 June 13 CANADIAN GP	ROUND 9 June 27 EUROPEAN GP	ROUND 10 July 11 BRITISH GP	ROUND 11 July 25 GERMAN GP	ROUND 12 August 1 HUNGARIAN GP	ROUND 13 August 29 BELGIAN GP	ROUND 14 September 12 ITALIAN GP	ROUND 15 September 26 SINGAPORE GP	ROUND 16 October 10 JAPANESE GP	ROUND 17 October 24 KOREAN GP	ROUND 18 November 7 BRAZILIAN GP	ROUND 19 November 14 ABU DHABI GP	TOTAL POINTS
4/8	9/R	1/2	6/8	1/3	1/2	3/R	4/5	1/R	1/7	3/6	1/3	2/15	4/6	2/3	1/2	R/R	1/2	1/8	498
3/7	1/6	6/8	1/2	5/14	5/R	1/2	1/2	2/3	2/4	4/5	8/R	1/R	2/R	4/R	4/5	2/12	4/5	2/3	454
1/2	3/4	7/13	4/9	2/6	4/6	7/8	3/15	8/11	14/15	1/2	2/4	4/R	1/3	1/8	3/R	1/3	3/15	7/10	396
5/6	5/10	3/R	3/10	4/13	7/12	4/5	6/11	10/15	3/9	8/9	11/R	6/7	5/9	5/13	6/17	4/R	6/7	4/R	214
11/R	2/R	4/R	5/7	8/11	3/13	6/15	7/17	5/14	13/R	7/10	5/R	3/9	8/13	7/11	R/R	5/R	9/16	5/6	163
10/14	8/R	10/12	12/15	9/16	R/R	14/17	13/14	4/R	5/10	12/13	6/10	14/R	7/10	6/10	9/R	7/10	8/14	12/16	69
9/12	7/R	5/R	11/R	7/15	8/9	9/13	9/10	6/16	8/11	16/17	13/R	5/10	12/16	9/R	R/R	6/R	12/R	13/R	68
R/R	12/R	R/R	R/R	12/R	R/R	10/11	R/R	7/12	6/R	11/14	7/9	8/11	14/R	R/R	7/8	8/9	10/17	11/14	44
13/16	11/R	9/11	13/R	10/R	10/11	12/16	8/12	9/13	12/R	15/R	12/R	12/13	11/15	12/14	10/11	11/R	11/13	9/15	13
15/17	13/R	17/R	14/R	17/R	15/R	R/R	16/R	21/R	16/17	R/R	14/15	16/19	18/R	16/R	12/13	13/R	18/19	17/21	
R/R	14/R	15/16	16/17	R/R	14/R	20/R	18/R	18/20	19/20	19/R	17/19	20/R	19/R	R/R	15/16	14/15	21/22	19/20	
R/R	R/R	14/R	R/NS	18/19	R/R	18/19	19/R	17/19	18/R	18/R	16/18	17/18	17/20	15/R	14/NS	R/R	20/NC	18/R